W9-BJI-868

Emergent Design

Emergent Design

The Evolutionary Nature of Professional Software Development

Scott L. Bain

Addison-Wesley

Upper Saddle River, NJ • Boston • Indianapolis • San Francisco
New York • Toronto • Montreal • London • Munich • Paris • Madrid
Capetown • Sydney • Tokyo • Singapore • Mexico City

Illustrations by Andrea Chartier Bain

The publisher offers excellent discounts on this book when ordered in quantity for bulk purchases or special sales, which may include electronic versions and/or custom covers and content particular to your business, training goals, marketing focus, and branding interests. For more information, please contact:

U.S. Corporate and Government Sales
(800) 382-3419
corpsales@pearsontechgroup.com

For sales outside the United States please contact:

International Sales
international@pearsoned.com

This Book Is Safari Enabled

The Safari® Enabled icon on the cover of your favorite technology book means the book is available through Safari Bookshelf. When you buy this book, you get free access to the online edition for 45 days.

Safari Bookshelf is an electronic reference library that lets you easily search thousands of technical books, find code samples, download chapters, and access technical information whenever and wherever you need it.

To gain 45-day Safari Enabled access to this book:

- Go to www.informit.com/onlineedition
- Complete the brief registration form
- Enter the coupon code 8SI6-DAYH-12FU-8VHW-REXK

If you have difficulty registering on Safari Bookshelf or accessing the online edition, please e-mail customer-service@safaribooksonline.com.

Visit us on the Web: informit.com/aw

Library of Congress Cataloging-in-Publication Data

Bain, Scott L.
Emergent design : the evolutionary nature of professional software development / Scott L. Bain.
p. cm.
Includes index.
ISBN 978-0-321-50936-9 (hardcover : alk. paper) 1. Computer software—Development. 2. Computer software—Development—Vocational guidance. I. Title.

QA76.76.D47B345 2008
005.1—dc22

2007050637

ISBN-13: 978-0-321-50936-9
ISBN-10: 0-321-50936-6
Text printed in the United States on recycled paper at Courier in Westford, Massachusetts.
First printing, March 2008

To Alan Shalloway and all instructors and staff at Net Objectives, whose collegial support and innovative ideas have contributed endlessly to my development as a technologist and educator.

And . . .

To Andrea and Griffin, who have enriched my entire life, and for whom I do pretty much everything I do.

Contents

Chapter 10
Paying Attention to Disciplines: Unit Testing 169

Chapter 11
Paying Attention to Disciplines: Refactoring 213

Series Foreword
The Net Objectives Product Development Series

Alan Shalloway, CEO, Net Objectives

If you are like me, you will just skim this series foreword and move on, figuring there is nothing of substance here. That would be a mistake. Unless you have read this foreword in another book in the series, please take a moment with me at the outset of this book. I want to consider with you a tale that most people know but don't often think about. That tale is about what is ailing this industry. And that tale sets the context for why we created the Net Objectives Product Development Series and this particular book.

I have been doing software development since 1970. To me, it is just as fresh today as it was almost four decades ago. It is a never-ending source of fascination to me to consider how to do something better and it is a never-ending source of humility to have to confront how limited my abilities truly are. I love it.

Throughout my career, I have also been interested in other industries, especially engineering and construction. Now, engineering and construction have suffered some spectacular failures: the Leaning Tower of Pisa, the Tacoma Narrows Bridge, the Hubble Telescope. In its infancy, engineering knew little about the forces at work. Mostly, engineers tried to improve practices and to learn what they could from failures. It took a long time—centuries—before they had a solid understanding about how to do things. Does that mean that we, software developers, have an excuse to take longer than we need before we understand how to do things? No!

No one would build a bridge without taking into account well-known practices of bridge building (stress, compression, and the like), but software developers get away with writing software every day based on "what they like" with little or no complaint from their peers. Why do we work this way?

However, this is only part of the story. Ironically, much of the rest is related to why we call this the "Net Objectives Product Development Series." The Net Objectives part is pretty obvious. All of the books in this series were written either by Net Objectives staff or by those whose views are consistent with ours. Why "Product Development"? Because when building software, it is always important to remember that software development is really *product development*.

Michael Kennedy, in his 2003 book, *Product Development for Lean Enterprise*, defines product development as "the collective activities, or system, that a company uses to convert its technology and ideas into a stream of products that meet the needs of customers and the strategic goals of the company."

Mary and Tom Poppendieck, in their excellent book, *Implementing Lean Software Development: From Concept to Cash* (2006), note:

> It is the product, the activity, the process in which software is embedded that is the real product under development. The software development is just a subset of the overall product development process. So in a very real sense, we can call software development a subset of product development. And thus, if we want to understand lean software development, we would do well to discover what constitutes excellent product development.

In other words, software—in itself—isn't important. It is the value that it contributes—to the business, to the consumer, to the user—that is important. When developing software, we must always remember to look at what *value* is being added by our work. At some level, we all know this. But so often organizational "silos" work against us, keeping us from working together, from focusing on efforts that create value.

The best—and perhaps only—way to achieve effective product development across the organization is a well-thought-out combination of lean principles to guide the enterprise, agile practices to manage teams, and technical skills (test-driven development, design patterns). That is the motivation for the Net Objectives Product Development Series.

For too long this industry has suffered from a seemingly endless swing of the pendulum from no process, to too much process, and then back to no process—from heavyweight methods focused on enterprise control to disciplined teams focused on the project at hand. The time has come for management and individuals to work together to maximize the production of business value across the enterprise. We believe lean principles will give us guidance in this.

Lean principles tell us to look at the systems in which our work takes place and then relentlessly improve them in order to improve our speed and quality (which will drive down cost). This requires

- Teams to own their systems and continuously improve them
- Management to train and support their teams to do this
- An appreciation for what constitutes quality work

It may feel like we are very far from achieving this in the software development industry, but the potential is definitely there. A lean approach helps with the first two principles, and an understanding of technical programming and design has matured far enough to help us with the third.

As we incorporate into existing coding and analysis approaches the discipline, mindset, skills, and focus on the value of lean, agile, patterns, and test-driven development, we will help software development move from being merely a craft to being a true profession. We have the knowledge required to do this; what we need is a new attitude.

The Net Objectives Product Development Series helps to develop this attitude. We aim to help integrate management and individuals in work efforts that "optimize the whole":

1. **The whole organization:** Integrating enterprise, team, and individuals to best work together.
2. **The whole product:** Not just its development, but also its maintenance and integration.
3. **The whole of time:** Not just now, but in the future. We want sustainable ROI from our effort.

Emergent Design: The Evolutionary Nature of Professional Software Development

This particular book addresses the technical dimensions of product development. It describes what we mean by software becoming a profession. At the same time, it discusses the necessity of building software in an evolutionary way. However, this evolution of a design is not ad hoc by any means. It is guided by well-defined and proven measures of quality. It is these measures that we must pay attention to when making decisions.

While hard-and-fast rules cannot be applied everywhere, principles can be. Ten years ago, the argument that we did not have a well-established set of rules may have carried water. That is no longer true.

Back in 1984, I began my own exploration of what quality software meant. I remember the year well, because of an incident that occurred and two questions that occurred to me as a result. The incident was the discovery of a bug, after which I asked myself, "What was I doing that I put a bug in my code?" My first reaction was to realize that I always talked about finding bugs, like I didn't put them in there. You don't walk out to your driveway in the morning and say, "Look what I found! My car!" (Okay, okay, I actually do this with my car keys, but that's a different story.) In other words, we talk about bugs as if they just show up—not as if we put them in the system. I assure you, gremlins are not coming into your programs in the middle of the night and inserting bugs into your code. The realization I had was to ask, "How could it take me 14 years to ask this question?" (This is how I remember it was 1984.)

It wasn't as if I had never wondered how to become a better programmer. It is just that it required more introspection and retrospection than I was used to: about what I did and how I could do it better. I needed to take an "outsider's view" to be able to study the system of programming. What can be done to improve it?

Many of us have embarked on this journey. It has given rise to the object-oriented languages, the elucidation of the proper use of design patterns,[1] and agile programming methods such as test-driven development. It is very clear that we know enough of the basics of what software developers must pay attention to, that merely appealing to what we like or don't like is not sufficient. We must be able to demonstrate that we have found a better way or we must follow what the industry has proven to be effective.

This is not an enforcement of standards from above. This is a matter of developers accepting the responsibility to build upon the shoulders of others. We must recognize that we cannot reinvent the wheel every time, and that just because we don't understand something doesn't mean it is not something of value. We must look to best practices when possible and adjust them as necessary.

1. See Shalloway and Trott, *Design Patterns Explained: A New Perspective on Object-Oriented Design, Second Edition*. Addison-Wesley, 2005.

The End of an Old Era, the Beginning of a New One

I believe the software industry is at a crisis point. The industry is continuously expanding and becoming a more important part of our lives every day. But software development groups are facing dire problems. Decaying code is becoming more problematic. There seems to be no end in sight to the burden on an overloaded workforce. While agile methods have brought great improvements to the many teams, more improvements are needed. By creating a true software profession, combined with the guidance of lean principles and incorporating agile practices, we believe we can help uncover the answers.

I hope you find this series to be a worthy guide. To assist you along the way, we have created a resources page at our Web site (http://www.netobjectives.com/resources), which Scott refers to in several places in this book. You should know that the site also contains much information outside the scope of this book. You will find resources on the other components of our lean-agile approach, including lean, agile, scrum, design patterns, and more. Please visit it and take advantage of what it offers.

Preface

Designing and creating software is hard.

I like that it's hard. I like a challenge. I like solving puzzles. That's probably what attracted me to computers and programming in the first place.

It's just that it's a little bit *too* hard. I don't want it to be easy; I'm not asking for that. I just want it to be a *little* easier, a little more predictable, and a little less chaotic.

I'd like to be able to tell someone, at the beginning of a project, what my software will generally be able to do when it's done, and feel confident that I'm right in what I'm saying. I'd like to be able to tell how long it will take to get the project done, and how much, generally, it will cost. And, I would like to be successful in these predictions and estimates—at least most of the time.

I'd like to feel like I know what I'm doing. Really *know*.

Anyone who has developed any complex software has surely had this experience: at about month 9 of a 12-month project, we're fine; we're on-track. At month 10, we're 4 months behind. How is that possible? Obviously, we were not fine at month 9—we just thought we were. Why didn't we know?

Or, perhaps we have a working system, one that seems just fine, and then the end users want some new function or capability. It is a reasonable request. Things change; we know that. The pace and scope of change in our world is on the rise.

But when we try to make the change the customer wants, things seem to fall apart in unpredictable ways. It makes us hesitant, knowing this can happen. It makes us resistant, even hostile at the prospect of accommodating such changes. The longer a person has been in development, the more likely he is to feel such resistance.

This is not our fault.

Software development has not been around for very long, in the grand scheme of things. Other, similarly complex endeavors (medicine, the law, architecture, and so on) have been around for hundreds, even thousands, of years, and in that time a whole set of standards, practices, and general wisdom has been captured and handed down from generation to generation. This has helped to increase the rate of predictable success for each new batch of doctors, lawyers, and builders, and in each case has led to the formation of an organism we call *the profession*.

Professions have their own lives, their own existence. For example, the profession of carpentry has been around for thousands of years, though no carpenter is that old. Professions provide a sort of safety net for those individuals in their practice.

The purpose of this book is to examine what we need, as software developers (or *programmers*, if you like), to get that kind of value from what we do, from each other, and from the practice itself. I'd like to take a step back, look at the *nature* of what we're doing, and derive a set of best-practices, general wisdom, and specific patterns of activity that will elevate our business into a true profession, or something akin to that, with all the benefits that such a thing provides.

However, it's not my intention to stay purely theoretical, as interesting as that might be. I want to talk about real things, about the aspects of software development that are too hard, that are too limiting, and to suggest better ways of going about this job. I want to focus on things that are truly valuable.

My contract with you is this: Everything I will investigate, suggest, present, demonstrate, and so on, will have as its core intent the goal of improving our lot as creators of software. No matter how interesting or compelling a thing might be, if there's nothing "in it for us," then I'm going to leave it out.

One thesis I'm going to start off with right now is this: Software development, by its very nature, is a process of evolution. We do not analyze, design, and build; we create something that works, is of high quality, and is valuable as it stands, and then we evolve it in stages toward the product that the world needs. I've got a long way to go to demonstrate this, and in order to get there I'm going to need a set of supportive concepts and techniques.

Here are the things I'll start off examining.

Qualities

How do we know when software is good? Because it works? We all know plenty of software that works but is not good. When presented with two or three ways of doing something, how do we determine which one is best? What does *best* mean? Following the general tenet of this book, *best* should have something to do with value to the developer, and a resulting increase in success, which yields value to the customer. The qualities we will focus on provide this kind of in-the-moment guidance that can help us make better decisions, more reliably: coupling, cohesion, eliminating redundancy, making things testable, and the granddaddy of them all: encapsulation. Included in this discussion will be those negative indicators (pathologies) that can help us to see when one or more of these qualities is not being adhered to.

Principles

What are the fundamental theories that define good software? In other words, what are the points of view we can take on a system that give us a better chance at achieving the qualities, after we know what those are? Principles say "this is better than that" or "this is more important than that." Principles promise better results in terms of the qualities we will emphasize, given that software needs to be able to change in order to meet the needs of a changing world.

Practices

Practices are things that you can do as part of your day-to-day coding activities, which will help you in significant ways. The practices I am most interested in are those that help you in multiple ways, and yet are not a burden. Lots of bang, little bucks. Also, since practices are truly valuable when they are shared and promoted to all the developers on a team (or in an organization or even, perhaps, to the profession), they should be things that are easy to teach others to do.

Disciplines

Similar to practices, disciplines are *things you should do*, but they are larger scale, take longer to learn, and are not without cost. However, the value they offer is so fundamental and profound as to make them worth the effort and time they require. Unit testing and refactoring are examples of disciplines, as is the notion of test-driven development. I'll cover them all.

Patterns

Patterns represent what we've done before that has worked. But I don't mean just a cookbook or a set of templates; software is more complicated than that. By a *pattern* I mean the set of interrelated points of wisdom that reflect what we, as a group, know about certain situations, those that we find ourselves in again and again. We've been there as a profession, even if some of us have not as individuals. Patterns are a way of sharing the wealth of experience, as a community of colleagues, and supporting one another toward greater success. Patterns are different from principles in that they are *contextual*. Principles apply generally; patterns apply differently in different situations. We'll examine these concepts in terms of each pattern's *forces*, and see how this view of patterns makes them much more useful to us than simply canned designs would be. There are lots of patterns, and lots of patterns books, so I provide an appendix that contains an overview of the patterns I use in the book to illustrate their role in an emergent design.

Processes

In general, how does software development work? How do we find out what we need to build? How do we know when we're done? How do we know when we're on track? And more importantly, how do we know when we're not on track? When we are off track, what do we do? I've tipped my hand already a bit in suggesting that creating software is an evolutionary process, but that's obviously just the seed of the idea.

I'm not alone in this pursuit, of course. In this book, I definitely draw upon the work of others including Alan Shalloway, Martin Fowler, Ward Cunningham, Kent Beck, Ron Jeffries, and Robert Martin, just to name a few. I've learned a great deal from these people and others like them, and I acknowledge their efforts in the Bibliography and point you to the resources they have provided our profession.

I've been accused of being developer-centric, as have some of the colleagues I just mentioned. In my case, this is true. I focus on the developer not just because I am one myself, but also because I believe if we want better software, we need to do a better job supporting development. To me this means a focus on the developer (e.g., an important part of quality health care is making good doctors). It does not mean that I value software if it does not get used: Unused software is worthless, in my opinion. Therefore, while I certainly focus on those things that help developers succeed, the goal is *better* software and the *right* software, which certainly will benefit all concerned.

There is other work to be done, certainly. I do not pretend to have solved the problem by bringing valuable ideas and practices to my fellow developers; but this is my part along the way.

I believe strongly that software development is on the brink of becoming a profession—in the true sense of the word—and that going that last mile, filling in the missing pieces, is one of the most important activities of our current era. In years to come, I think we will look back at this time and realize that this was the era when software development matured to the degree that it could reliably meet the needs of the modern world, and I'm very excited to be a part of it.

So, let's begin.

Acknowledgments

I worked as a software developer for many years at KFMB TV/AM/FM in San Diego, California. During that time, I learned a tremendous amount from the colleagues I had in the area and in that industry, but none more than my good friend, Sassan (Sean) Azhadi, who is now a senior vice president with the San Diego County Credit Union. Sean was my sounding board, investigatory partner, and dear friend through all those years. He's also the main reason I still have a full head of hair—more times than I can count, his generous and absurd sense of humor kept me from pulling it all out.

During those years I was also very fortunate to stay in touch with close friends in a Saturday-night gaming group. Most of my critical thinking skills I owe to my friendship and interaction with Dr. Francis (Brett) Drake, Dr. Frank (Todd) Tamburine, Doug Hansen, Brenner Roque, Chuck Comfort, and my brother, Christopher.

Like a lot of developers who've stayed in the game long-term, I experienced a time of personal burnout, mostly because I was trying to maintain software that was not designed to be maintainable (nobody to blame but myself, of course). Also, after leaving broadcasting, I had a bad experience with a dot-com blowout, which did nothing to improve the situation.

My "way back" was mostly through two individuals: Bruce Eckel, whose book, *Thinking in Java,* helped me to finally understand OO (and to accept its value), and Alan Shalloway, who helped me to see what patterns really are and how they can make a fundamental difference in the maintainability of software. Without the guidance I got from Bruce's book, I never would have approached Alan, and without Alan's patient tutelage and partnership . . . well, I suppose I'd be doing something else for a living and not having nearly as much fun.

It is also because of Alan that Net Objectives exists, and because it does I have had the privilege to work with, and learn from, many other smart people, including Rob Myers, Rod Claar, Dan Rawsthorne, Jeff McKenna, Ed Lance, Amir Kolsky, Jim Trott, and David Bernstein.

I also have benefited from the works of many other authors, and I have tried my best to give them due credit (in footnotes) wherever possible. Also, when one gets to the end of writing a book it's very difficult to have much perspective on it; you've spent too much time with it and are too close to it to really see it anymore. Because of this, a careful review by others who had not seen the book before is invaluable. I am indebted indeed to Donna Davis, Jeremy Miller, and Matt Heusser for their thoughtful and careful review of the manuscript and for their numerous helpful suggestions for improvement.

This was my first time through the experience of publishing a book, and I really did not know what to expect from the process. The folks I worked with at Addison-Wesley were amazingly helpful, patient, and professional. I owe countless thanks to Dr. Christopher Zahn, Raina Chrobak, and Christopher Guzikowski for everything they did to help me.

Finally, I am blessed indeed to have married someone who is as interested in technology as I am. Andrea is a software developer as well as a fine artist, and so not only have I been able to draw upon her talent in helping me to illustrate this book, but in addition, every chapter, article, PowerPoint slide set, and the like, that I have created over the years has always benefited from her careful review and her countless suggestions for improvement. Everything I do would be far weaker without her collaboration and support.

About the Author

Scott L. Bain is a thirty-year veteran in computer technology, with a background in development, engineering, and design. He has also designed, delivered, and managed training programs for certification and end-user skills, both in traditional classrooms and via distance learning. For the past eight years, Scott has been working for Net Objectives in Puget Sound, teaching courses and consulting on design patterns, refactoring, unit testing, and test-driven development. Along with Net Objectives CEO Alan Shalloway, Scott has contributed significantly to the integration of design patterns in agile environments. He is a frequent speaker at developer conferences such as JavaOne and SDWest.

CHAPTER 1

Software as a Profession

In this chapter, we will investigate what I hope is an interesting set of questions. Sometimes, the real value of a question is not so much in finding a specific answer, but in allowing the investigation of the question to lead you to other, perhaps more valuable questions. Also, sometimes discovering a question that is not being asked, or is not asked very often, can help us see opportunities that we are missing, which can also lead us to further, valuable discoveries.

I've been "in software" for a long time, but it occurs to me that we've reached a point in our industry when "stepping back" to see the nature of what we're doing might be a useful thing.

How Long Have Human Beings Been Making Software?

The answer to that question, like so many others, is "it depends."

What do we include in the notion of making software? Do we include the very early days when programming consisted of wire-wrapping PC boards and exchanging tubes? What about the Jacquard loom?

Maybe not. But should we include the days of data processing: punch cards and mainframes and waiting overnight to see if your program ran properly, input-by-punch card or tape, output-by-printout, no interaction, no VDTs?

For my purposes here, I think we should start in the mid-to-late 70s, when small desktop systems originally emerged, and we began to develop interactive software for people to use directly.

It is not that I consider data processing to be less important or interesting or complex; it is just that the differences are so great between what they[1] did then and what we now do that I don't see much wisdom carrying over. It is like riding a horse versus driving a car: They are both complex activities that require knowledge and skill, but knowing how to do one really does not help you to do the other well.

But wait! What about the emergence of object-oriented (OO) languages and techniques, as opposed to the procedural languages like C and Pascal that used to hold sway? Should the pre-OO, procedural era also be considered a separate kind of activity?

I don't think so. In fact, I think that much of what we now call object orientation grew out of the maturation of procedural programming—in essence, that the best practices we used to make procedural languages work well led to the concepts that got "built in" to object-oriented languages.

In fact, I think object orientation started as a way of programming before there was even an object-oriented language at all. For now, suffice it to say that I think the object-oriented paradigm shares a lot of wisdom with the procedural one.

Assuming we agree, I'll include the era of *structured programming* as part of our history. (For more on this discussion, see Chapter 4, "Evolution in Code: Stage 1.") So, I would say we have been making software in this sense for 30 to 35 years.

Okay, another question.

What Sort of Activity Is Software Development?

Is it a job, a craft, a profession, or what? Some would say it's an art or a science. Some would say it's engineering. Some would say a branch of deductive logic. I believe the value in asking this question is not so much finding the answer, but rather following it to other questions that may arise by asking it.

---

1. Well, "we," I guess. When I got my start, I keyed my punch cards on a keypunch machine that required you to file notches in a lead rod to change the tab stops. I don't miss those days at all.

We have lots of words for the things people do to make a living and allow them to contribute to the world around them: job, work, trade, craft, avocation, métier, pursuit, art, career, profession, and so forth. Different people use these words in different ways, but there are indicators, distinctions, expectations, and assumptions accompanying them that are fairly universal.

Take training, for instance. Most people would attach the concept of "extensive training required" to the notion of *profession* or *trade*, and less so to *work* or *job*.[2] This is not to say that all jobs are easy, but certainly there are rigors associated with entering a profession or trade that one does not expect to go through for a job.

Another distinction is licensing and oversight. Doctors, lawyers, accountants, contractors, and the like are licensed by the state to ensure that they are competent, that their skills and training meet a minimal standard. Generally, this is because of the extensive damage they can do if they are not competent. Of course, this also implies that there is an agreed-upon set of minimal standards that these professionals can be held to, and that they are the right standards.

Furthermore, because of the rigors and standards expected of them, professionals (and craftspersons) form supportive organizations—guilds and unions and professional organizations—to support them and promote their success. These organizations also provide a focused place for shared wisdom and accumulated knowledge to persist and to be handed down from one generation to the next.

When one is engaging in complex and sometimes life-critical activities, there is advantage to having this kind of support. It tells the professional if she is "up to snuff" on the critical aspects of her profession, and what to do if she is not. To those served by the professional, the advantage is also pretty clear: It is important to me that my doctor knows what he is doing, and that someone who can tell whether he does or not (better than I) is confirming this.

Also, professions tend to develop specific, highly specialized languages. Doctors, for instance, call removing your appendix an appendectomy,

---

2. I am making a distinction here in using the term *job*. Naturally, anything one does that involves work and produces value can be termed a job, even if your job is being a doctor. Here, my meaning is what most people would call a *job-job*, as in something you do because you need money, primarily, and really do not expect it to be a long-term thing. I just feel funny writing "job-job."

whereas removing your colon is a colostomy. Why is one an -ectomy and the other an -ostomy? I don't know, but doctors do, and I'll bet there is a lot to the distinction that is important to them. All we know is something of ours is leaving our bodies.

So, I'm going to somewhat arbitrarily settle on the word *profession* to indicate a vocation that requires extensive, lengthy training, has very specialized language to describe what the professionals do and to allow them to communicate with high fidelity to one another, and usually has a professional organization supporting them. Professions have extensive traditions behind them, well-defined communities of practice and support, and collected wisdom that is shared among all its members. A profession provides access to peer-review on activities and ideas, and a licensure or certification process, usually as part of an academic discipline or disciplines, to give confidence both to the professionals and those they serve.

Also, there is a clearly defined path to follow if you want to become a doctor, or a lawyer, or a master cabinetmaker. When society needs more of them, we know what process to take individuals through to increase their numbers, and we know how to tell young people to prepare for a given professional career.

So where does software development fit?

Software development is certainly complex and requires extensive training and experience to do it well. Not everyone can do it, not because it is fundamentally beyond some people, but because not everyone would *want* to do it, or would keep doing it for very long. It requires a certain temperament, a technical bent, and a fundamental love of problem-solving that does not exist in everyone.

Also, there are supportive organizations and groups that have formed over time, where software developers seek to share what we know and how we do things. The entire open-source movement is, among other things, an example of collegiality among software developers—as are Java User Groups and .Net Developer Study Groups. Developers almost always support these efforts on their own time, because they feel such groups are valuable.

Therefore, I would say that software development is, by nature, a professional activity. Whether or not we have been conducting it as a profession, we *should* be, in my opinion. I'm going to set aside the question of whether we should be regulated by the government, because my focus here is to discover those things that a software profession would provide that would be of direct benefit to developers and the quality of the software they produce.

If you'll allow me this, consider the following:

We have not been creating software for long. Most professions and crafts are hundreds or even thousands of years old and have had a long time to work out the fundamentals that underlie them.

For example, imagine what medicine was like when it was 35 years old. I imagine there was much attaching-of-leeches, shaking-of-rattles, and letting-of-blood. Interestingly, medicine in that form *did* enjoy a certain degree of success. It turns out that bleeding a person can reduce a fever, though it is not a very good way of doing so (sometimes you end up reducing it *all the way*). Even today, a fair percentage of the good a doctor can do for you has to do with your confidence in medicine, and your belief that the treatments you are being given will help to make you feel better.

So, witch doctors did have some success. Just not very often. Nor was the process terribly reliable, dependable, or predictable. Sound familiar?

Also, within this 35-year period that comprises our history, how much has changed, in terms of computing power, the relationship of business and daily life to software, and so forth? The human body is still pretty much what it was when medicine began, so doctors can lean heavily on their past traditions and discoveries while they learn new techniques and move their profession forward. We don't have that luxury. Computers are fundamentally different than they were just a few years ago.

For example, computers are orders of magnitude faster. Also, when I began writing software, critical resources like disk storage and memory were not only expensive, but also limited (there was no such thing as a 100-gigabyte hard drive, at any price). If you go back far enough (not that far, really), the only individuals who interacted with computers at all were trained, highly skilled operators. Yes, these are big, incremental changes, but change is the fundamental reality over the span of even one person's career.

So, what is the chance we are doing it completely right, this "making software" stuff? Pretty slim, I would say. In fact, I think it is rather amazing that we can do it at all, given that we are probably still at the leech-and-rattle stage, at least to some degree.

In other words, I am saying that I think software *should be* conducted as a professional activity, but that it *isn't yet.* Not quite.

What Is Missing?

Let's compare software development to what other professions typically have.

- *Specialized language.* In software development, the language has always tended toward implementation specifics. Words like loop, switch, break, and "exception" are specialized but very low level. A master carpenter does not talk in terms of angles and inches when describing how you make a mortise-and-tenon. The term itself captures all those specifics, and also communicates *why* you'd do it this way or that way, what you will likely run into in terms of *difficulties and opportunities,* and what you'll *gain or lose* as a result of choosing this path. Specialized language at this higher level helps professionals make decisions better, often together as colleagues.

  Part of my thesis here is that the Design Patterns movement is, among other things, an attempt to add this specific, high-level language to what we do, to promote our level of professionalism. This was not necessarily the intention behind the movement but turned out to be a significant, if unintended, contribution.

  I also think this, in part, explains the popularity of patterns and pattern books. I think a lot of us have had the feeling that something is missing in what we do, and how we think and talk about it. In listening to this instinct, we are maturing toward professionalism.

- *A clear path to entry.* If someone asks you what they should do to "become" a software developer, what do you tell them? Go to college? Read a given set of books? Get a vendor-supported certification? Just get a job and fake it 'till you make it?

  I can tell you, at least in general terms, what you should do if you want to become a successful civil lawyer. Go to college, law school, intern at a law firm, pass the bar, become an associate, and work toward becoming a partner. Want to become a criminal lawyer? There are similar but different steps to that goal, and they are well defined also.

  A colleague of mine, Adam Milligan, put it this way: "We have med school and law school...where is the dev school?" There isn't one. Hospitals hire residents to allow seasoned doctors to train them; they understand that medicine must work this way if they are to produce new doctors, at the level of quality that's essential for patient health and well-being. The software development business has not bought into this yet, and it needs to.

- *Peer-review.* Doctors and lawyers have peer-reviewed journals and other mechanisms for support among professionals. These mechanisms allow the professionals to move the profession forward and allow for a reality check on new practices and procedures.

  We have some of these things in software development, but they are very *ad-hoc,* and not well organized. You can Google a problem and scan Usenet for answers, but your results will be spotty. Many of the user and study groups I mentioned earlier are grassroots attempts to create peer-review in software. The same can be said about the extensive use of blogging to share ideas and wisdom among software; there is lots of great stuff out there, but it is very chaotic.

- *Standards and practices.* There are certain things a doctor simply knows to do, always; by doing so, she is guaranteeing a certain level of success or is at least avoiding a guarantee of failure. For instance, doctors know that *cleanliness* is very important. They sterilize instruments and wash their hands carefully before interacting with a patient.

  Doctors did not always know this, by the way. Up until the mid-to-late 1800s, surgeons did not bother to wash their hands or instruments before cutting into patients, and as a result their failure rate (dead patients) was much higher than it should have been. Hungarian-born doctor Ignaz Semmelweis, while working at a birth clinic in Vienna in 1860, suggested that there were tiny, invisible, microscopic things making people sick, and that doctors should wash them off of their hands and instruments before treating patients.

  At the time, he might as well have been blaming ghosts or evil spirits. He was laughed at, almost lost his license three times, and finally had to intentionally infect himself to make his point. Only after Dr. Semmelweis' death was the germ theory of disease developed, and he is now recognized as a pioneer of antiseptic policy and the prevention of infection.[3]

3. This is not an isolated incident of being considered insane because of a keen insight. Marconi was institutionalized for believing you could transmit magic waves through the air that could transmit information.

> *All* doctors know this now. They do not have to rediscover this basic truth of medical procedure. They wash their hands before they even meet informally with a new patient.

In software development, we have traditionally had a tendency to expect each developer to discover such things on his own, to make the same mistakes we have all made, re-solve the same problems, and build from the ground up. It is actually part of the culture of "the cowboy coder" that developers would rather outdo each other than support each other.[4] This problem is exacerbated by the tendency in many organizations to move senior developers into management roles, rather than keeping them available to the junior folks. It seems as if the value of "those who know" is seen as secondary.

It is not just what we know or don't know. It is the things we have learned to pay attention to that are relatively more important than other things: what you must pay attention to now and what you can safely ignore or worry about later.

A profession is like an organism. There has been "medicine" for thousands of years, but no particular doctor has been around that long. The doctors practicing today gain support from this organism, and therefore can continue to benefit from the hard work and sacrifices of those like Dr. Simmelweis, even though he is long gone.

Who Is Responsible?

Generally speaking, one does not visit the doctor and say, "Y'know Doc, I'm thinking I might like an appendectomy." You tell the doctor what's wrong, and the doctor recommends the appropriate treatment.

In software development, since we have not thought of ourselves as professionals, the people we develop software for have not been thinking of us this way either. The stakeholders in a project often set the timelines, impose the process, and track our progress.

If software development were a profession, this would be up to us, or at least heavily influenced by us. We would be responsible for these decisions, and would be able to tell our customers what to expect and when to expect it, with a high degree of reliability. The current process is like

4. Actually, it's worse than this. In our "profession," there is little agreement about what is right. So we each learn our own way and go our own way.

going to the doctor for your operation and telling the surgeon, "You have an hour. I've got to be on the golf course by 11:00."

This involves a shift, not only for us, but for them. This involves building trust, changing the basic nature of the relationship between clients and developers, and proving our value through an increased rate of success.

This is going to be *hard,* I think. But it has to happen.

I believe that software development is not only a practice that should be conducted as a profession, but could be considered the most important profession of all as we move into the twenty-first century.

Why?

All the other professions use software, after all, and are therefore vulnerable to its cost and quality. When you fly on an airplane, you are flying on software, more and more. When the doctor scans your abdomen for tumors and looks at the display from the ultrasound machine, she is relying on software to tell her how to help you. When your identity gets stolen, that's somebody's software, somewhere, exposing you to risk.

And this does tie back, at least to some degree, to the question of regulation and certification. I am still formulating my opinion on what is appropriate for our profession here, but I have a concern. Over the coming years, as software penetrates more and more of the daily lives of ordinary people, failures of that software will become more and more a part of the social consciousness. If we continue to expose people to identity theft, medical and transportation accidents, viruses, Y2K (or daylight savings) type bugs, and so on eventually the citizens are going to ask someone to do something about this.

They will turn to the government, of course. I don't want to hit this too hard or come off as an alarmist, but frankly if the U.S. House of Representatives sets the standard for what constitutes professional software development, I don't think we're in for a good result. At all.

We have to do it ourselves, and I think we'd better get going. There is a lot to do, and I do not claim to be doing it all here. (It should be a community-based, grassroots effort.) But I hope this book will contribute some specific clarity on the key issues and encourage more of the same.

Uniqueness

Let's be clear: I am not saying software development is like medicine or law or any other profession. Medicine is not like the law either. Doctors are not carpenters.

Professions are unique. They have derived their own unique processes that are highly appropriate to their nature. These processes come from a fundamental understanding of that nature, built incrementally over time by the communities themselves. Medicine is practiced the way it is because of the experiences of medical professionals over the history of the profession.

Part of the problem in the current practice of software development is that it is based, largely, on a fundamentally flawed principle: that it is very much like something else. That is what the next two chapters are all about.

CHAPTER 2

Out of the Closet, Off to the Moon

Different people learn in different ways. Even those with similar levels of intelligence may absorb material very differently. For example, I learn best from pictures and analogies. Some of my colleagues learn better from code examples or by listening to someone speak. Still others never seem to "get it" until they have done a thing themselves.

I am going to suggest that patterns in software represent, among other things, an opportunity to build a *professional language*, if they are understood correctly. Unfortunately, in my experience, they usually are not understood correctly. This is because patterns are easy to misunderstand, even with the best of intentions. Therefore, at least for some of you, looking at them from a perspective that lives outside of software (an analogy or two) will be helpful.

Analogies certainly were helpful for me. The first example comes from an experience I quite literally stumbled into that helped me to see how I was misunderstanding patterns and therefore was missing out on a large part of their value. The second example analogy came from an intentional analogous application of a hobby of mine, the space program, to patterns in software.

Patterns and Professionalism in Software Development

I am primarily a teacher, and my company offers courses on a variety of software development topics from languages to agility, test-driven development, patterns, and so forth. One thing I have noticed is that patterns are far and away the most popular topic we teach. Courses scheduled on patterns fill up quickly, and there is always a waiting list.

Of course, I would like to think that this is because we are such wonderful teachers. Honesty requires me to acknowledge that something else is also at work here, however. It is the patterns themselves that are attracting the students.

Net Objectives was primarily established by Alan Shalloway, teaching patterns courses and consulting on design, using patterns in a mentoring way. He brought me on to expand capacity, and voila! Net Objectives (the company I work for) was born.

Our initial focus was on design patterns, but as the company grew and expanded into lean-agile software development, testing, use cases, and other areas, so has our concepts of patterns.

All along, however, patterns have continued to be inherently attractive to developers, testers, designers, analysts, and their managers. Why?

I have an idea why, at least in many cases, developers seem to be gravitating toward patterns, even given the ever-growing popularity of eXtreme Programming (XP) and other "lightweight" development methodologies. I think it is an unconscious (or perhaps subconscious) realization by many that software development itself is maturing toward the point where it will eventually become an actual profession, as I mentioned in the previous chapter.

The purpose of this book is to examine the state of software development today, why and how it is moving toward establishing itself as a profession, what that will mean when we get there, and how patterns relate to this evolution.

Let me start by sharing two very different analogies.

Andrea's Closet

My wife, Andrea, is a very small person. However, she has a lot of clothes. In fact, my son Griffin and I are forced to keep all of *our* clothes in soggy cardboard boxes out in back of the house, as every square inch of closet space is taken by Andrea's things. No, that is not true. But she really does have a ton of stuff.

When we moved into our home, I admitted the obvious to myself and gave her the entire walk-in closet in the master bedroom. It was modern construction, and so they had put in some fairly inexpensive coated white-wire shelves and hangar rods, which Andrea's mountains of clothing instantly ripped from the wall. No joke; it was an avalanche.

I was faced with solving a problem in carpentry. Anyone who knows me is laughing hysterically now, because until recently the only tools I owned would fit in a pocket-protector (not even a hammer, had I). Nevertheless I felt . . . well . . . reasonably competent in these "male areas," so I presumed I could figure it out.

I needed to come up with an arrangement that would make the best use of the closet space and would not collapse under the weight of her clothing. There were closet organizer systems around, but they all looked far too wimpy for Andrea's wardrobe-for-the-cast-of-*Nicholas-Nickleby* amount of clothing.

Wood, I thought: big pieces of wood, and nails, and glue, and so forth. The scene from *The Matrix* where Neo asks for "guns, lots of guns" comes to mind: "wood, lots of wood." Off I went to The Home Depot. My first attempt (or the first one I'm willing to tell you about, anyway) was something like Figure 2.1.

Figure 2.1 My first attempt at a closet arrangement

The vertical pieces were heavy plywood, and the poles were wooden doweling, with brass fittings at each end. This seemed strong enough, but this plan did not meet all the requirements of the problem. The long coats, gowns, and dresses when hung on the upper pole "ran into" the lower pole and got wrinkled. Wrinkles, I found out by validating with my "customer," was definitely a failure of the user acceptance test, as shown in Figure 2.2.

Obviously, there needed to be more hanging space. I could get that by removing the lower rod, but then there would be a lot of wasted space, as shown in Figure 2.3.

I am not a carpenter but I could see the obvious. Clearly, I needed a divided space, with room for long coats and gowns on one side of the divide, and double rods on the other side, to make the best use of space when hanging short things like blouses and slacks, something like Figure 2.4.

I drew this out, we talked about it a bit, and then I built it. And then I rebuilt it (which is another long story).

This was successful initially (the customer signed off, and it "shipped"), but in practice it fell short of the mark. First, while Andrea has dresses and coats, she does not have so many as to fill half the entire closet space. I had just thought "divided" and mentally leapt to "half" from that word. In actuality, she needed less long space and more double-rod space.

Figure 2.2 The failed user acceptance test: wrinkled clothes

Figure 2.3 Waste

Figure 2.4 Creating a divided space is better

Also, the pole on the long side kept pulling free of the plywood. When I said she has a "ton" of clothing, you probably thought I was being facetious. By far, the heaviest stuff was the long coats and dresses, so regularly the entire right side would collapse on her, and I would have to rebuild that side of the closet.

I had a seriously unhappy end user, and not one I could escalate to the next level of customer service. Major bug remediation was required, in other words. Pull the product back in and fix it.

I tried a lot of things, most of them helping a little, none of them helping enough. I asked Andrea how likely her long-area-width needs were to change, and she said the coats, dresses, and gowns she had at the time represented the quantity she was ever likely to have. I asked this because I was considering an adjustable partition. This would have been both hard and expensive to make (assuming I knew how in the first place). So, we measured the width that would be needed, and I redesigned it that way, shown in Figure 2.5.

Then, because I was jockeying the space back and forth quite a bit, by accident, I made a good decision: For the top pole, which exists on both sides of the divide, I used a single long pole, drilled a hole in the partition, and fed it through (as opposed to using the two shorter poles with the brass fittings connecting them to the center partition).

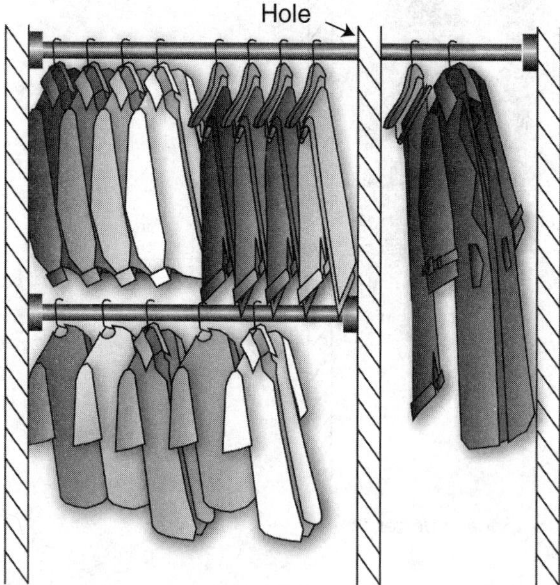

Figure 2.5 My next redesign

Why? Well, I saw this cool thing called a hole saw at the store and, the tool-geek that I was becoming, I wanted one. This justified the purchase. Also, I had more doweling than I had little brass fittings (I was running out of the latter), and when I discovered this I had already visited The Home Depot six times that day, and I was not about to go back. In other words, it was dumb luck.

As it turns out, I had stumbled onto the right way to do this project. Here is why: When the pole is a single piece, it's actually like a teeter-totter, with the center partition (the hole) the fulcrum. Clothes on one side help balance the clothes on the other, as shown in Figure 2.6. Even though it is not perfectly balanced, the amount of relief this provides on both sides means that the little brass fittings are more than strong enough to hold. After making this change, the thing never pulled free again. Also, if I *did* need to make the center partition adjustable, or even just move it once more, this makes it much easier to do so. The partition can slide back and forth along the top pole. The bottom pole is still a problem, and would need to be a telescoping version (or something), but the problem is certainly simplified.

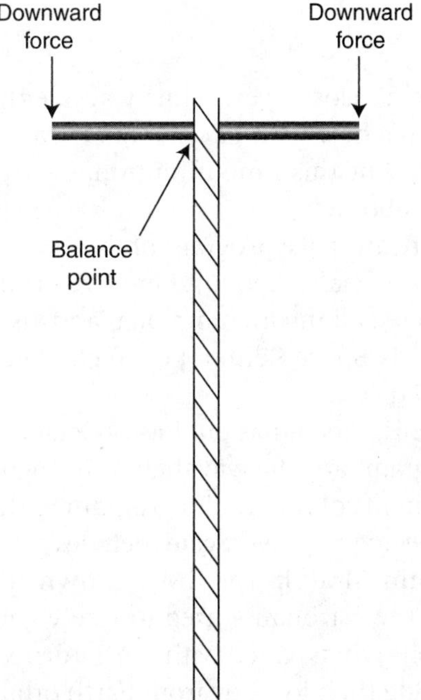

Figure 2.6 The right way to balance the load

What is my point? If I ever run into this problem again, there are some things I know now that I did not know before, and might never have known if I had not gotten absurdly lucky:

> *Analysis.* Make sure to ask how many of the clothes are long clothes so you can place the divider properly and efficiently. Alternately, consider an adjustable divider position if the extra cost and labor is warranted by a high probability of change in the number of long clothes.
>
> *Implementation.* Make the upper pole full length, running through a hole in the center partition. This will balance the weight, and relieve downward pressure on the fittings. This also makes an adjustable partition somewhat easier, if it is needed.
>
> *Testing.* Make sure the fittings are not bending after one week of use. If they are, replace them before they drop heavy wooden poles on your wife's head.

Write all this on a 3x5 card, and call it the Divided Closet pattern.

Off to the Moon

The insights I gained from building Andrea's closet were a lucky accident, but they led me to think about patterns in a new way. I decided to try and make this "aha" moment happen again, but this time intentionally, by investigating something I do know a lot about.

I have an abiding interest in the American space program of the 1960s and 70s (projects Mercury, Gemini, and especially Apollo). I have read all the books, watched all the movies, collected all the memorabilia, and visited both Cape Canaveral and the Kennedy Space Center. I even climbed inside a Mercury capsule (see Figure 2.7)!

As with any kind of obsessive hobby, this pursuit has put lots of detailed knowledge into my brain about these programs and the way they were engineered. Let's examine two of the components of the Apollo program with which you are probably familiar to some degree and investigate their designs.

First, there was the Apollo Command Module (or CM), shown in Figure 2.8. This was the spacecraft that the astronauts used to safely get from the surface of the Earth to Earth orbit (when paired with the Saturn V rocket). It then provided life support during their journey from Earth orbit to lunar orbit (when paired with the Service Module). Finally, it conveyed them back to the Earth's surface safely at the end of the mission.

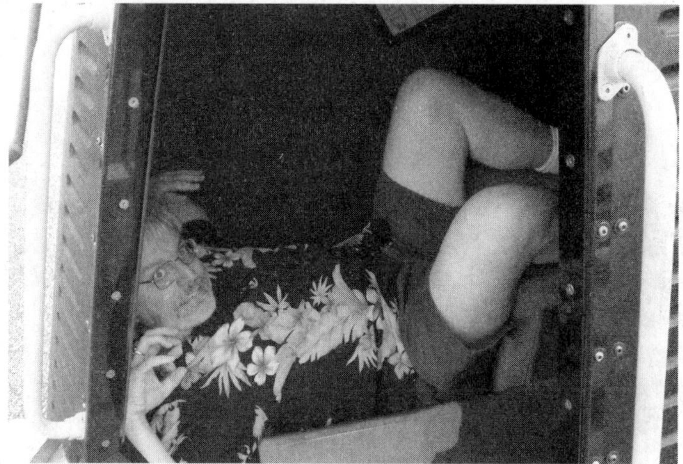

Figure 2.7 Me in a Mercury capsule. Gosh, those guys were tiny!

Figure 2.8 The Command Module

Another, similar component was the Apollo Lunar Module (or LM, pronounced "lem"), shown in Figure 2.9. This was also a spacecraft, and it had a role very similar to that of the CM. The LM was intended to convey astronauts from orbit around the moon to the surface of the moon, provide life support while they explored the surface, and finally convey them back from the surface and into lunar orbit, safely.

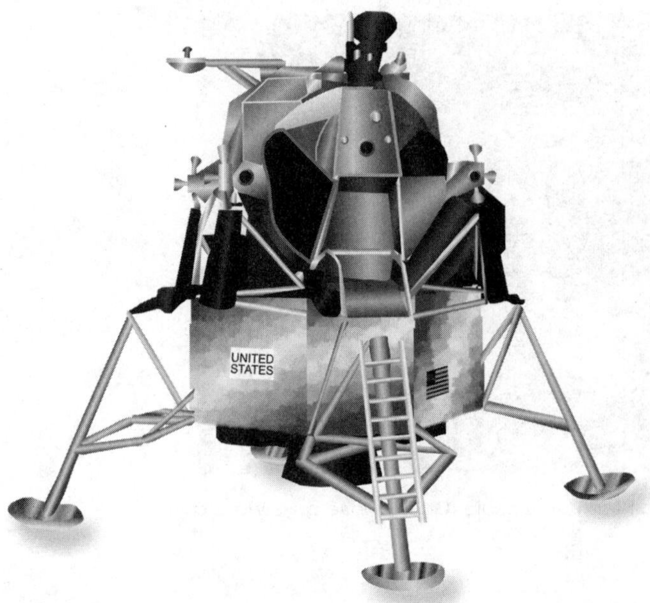

Figure 2.9 The Lunar Module

The two spacecraft had extremely similar jobs to do conceptually: ferry the astronauts between an orbital position and a ground position, safely, as shown in Figure 2.10, and also give them an environment in which to live for extended periods.

Even with the similarity in their jobs, Figure 2.11 shows just how differently these two spacecraft were designed. Their shapes were different, their sizes were different, their weights, materials, and components were different, and yet they were conceptually almost the same.

The reason they were differently designed is that they had a different *contextual force*, which drove the engineers to different solutions and, as we will see, different consequences. This varying contextual force was this: CM did its ferrying to and from the Earth, whereas the LM did it to and from the moon. The Earth is relatively larger than the moon, and due to these differences in mass they exert different amounts of gravity.

This difference alone might imply a difference in design: more gravity (Earth) could require a more robust design to stand up to the greater pressure. However, where it gets really interesting is when we investigate how the size variation, which results in the force of gravity variation, leads us to see further critical distinctions.

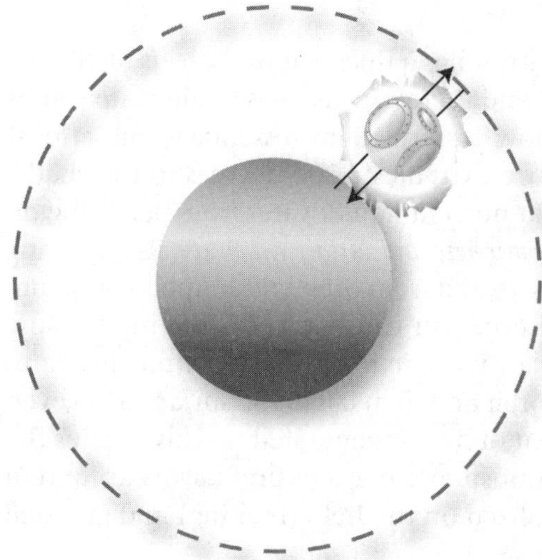

Figure 2.10 Ferrying the astronauts

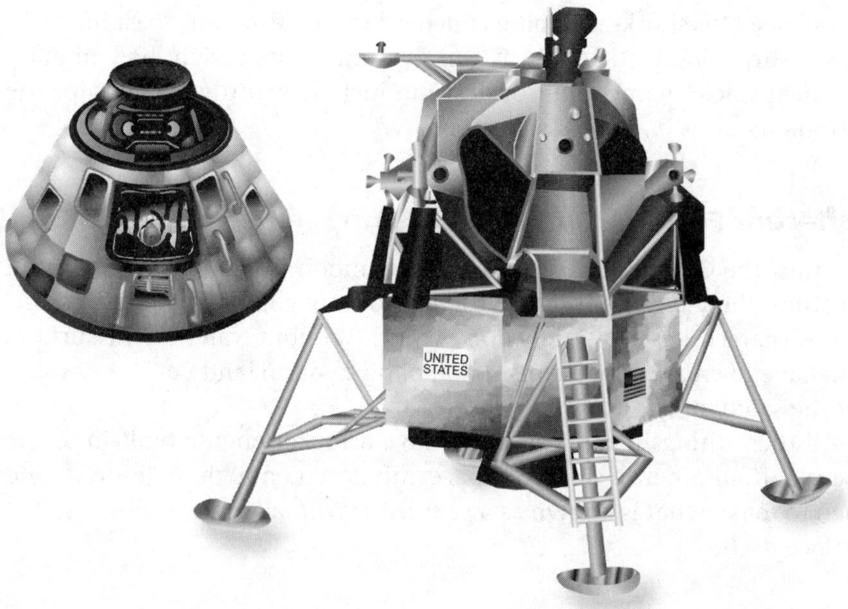

Figure 2.11 CM and LM, side-by-side

Forces Lead to Forces

Because the Earth has more gravity, it has a thick atmosphere, is blanketed and has moderate temperatures, and therefore also has liquid water on its surface. Because the moon has low gravity, it has (essentially) no atmosphere, which leads to temperature extremes (-200 degrees in the shade, +200 degrees in the sunlight) that prevent liquid water from persisting on its surface. Thus, *the presence of atmosphere and surface water* are also differing forces in the problem of transiting to and from orbit in the Apollo program.

When you have an atmosphere, you can use aero-braking to slow down—that is, the spacecraft can use friction with the atmosphere to decrease its speed enough to de-orbit and then fall to the surface. However, in doing so a tremendous amount of heat is generated, so this implies the need for heat protection. The atmosphere helps us and harms us, and in their design the engineers capitalized on the help (braking) and guarded against the harm (heat).

When you have an atmosphere and surface water, you can also use parachutes to further slow the spacecraft to a safe landing speed and can use the water to cushion the spacecraft when it impacts the surface (splashdown). In Earth gravity, this will be a fairly hard landing nonetheless, so there will be the need for shock-absorbing couches for the astronauts to sit in.

Not surprisingly, the CM was aerodynamic in its design, had an ablative heat shield, parachutes for descent, included sturdy couches for the astronauts to sit in, and was "seaworthy."

Different Forces, Different Design

Contrast the CM with the LM, where the moon was the target. Without an atmosphere, you cannot use friction to slow you down, and you cannot use parachutes at all (they don't work). Without water on the surface, you have to create a mechanism that allows you to land very, very softly for the safety of the astronauts.

All these things mean you must have a rocket engine built-in to the spacecraft, in order to slow the spacecraft down enough to de-orbit, and then to make what is known as a *powered descent*[1] all the way down to the surface itself.

1. This implies a rocket motor with a *throttle*. Up to this point, rockets had two states: on and off. Using a rocket to land, which had not been done before, required an entirely new kind of engine. We could make a similar analysis of different rocket engines and find similar forces in their designs.

The LM was not aerodynamic, because there was no reason for it to be, but it had its own rocket (and fuel) to allow for a soft landing. It had no heat shield, because the lack of an atmosphere on the moon also has an advantage: no friction and therefore no extreme heat applied to the spacecraft during descent.

Powered descent is a hard technical problem, which gets harder the heavier the spacecraft is, so the LM had to be lightweight. But, because the landing would be soft, the heavy couches were not needed for the astronauts (they stood up in the LM cabin), and therefore the LM could, in fact, be much lighter.

And There Are More Contextual Forces

Because the Earth has an atmosphere and water, it also has life and a civilization. This is good, because getting the astronauts, and the spacecraft, out of the deep gravity well of the Earth requires a really large, powerful rocket. The one they used (the Saturn V) required vast numbers of people and a huge infrastructure to launch it.

On the moon, the astronauts would obviously be alone (little green men being unlikely) and therefore would have to launch their way out of the lunar gravity well without any assistance from a ground crew. There could be no cranes, no fuel trucks, and no blockhouse. The LM could not be a single spacecraft. It had to have two parts: the ascent stage, which was mounted atop the descent stage. When it came time for the astronauts to leave, the lower half served as the launch platform for the upper half, as shown in Figure 2.12.

In essence, the LM was "prepackaged to launch" when it left the Earth, so the astronauts would not have very much to do in order to return to lunar orbit. The *ascent stage* used a very simple rocket motor that had very few ways to fail.

The different forces in the problems of landing on/leaving the Earth and landing on/leaving the moon, all of which stem from the differences in the masses of these bodies, led to completely different decisions in the design of the spacecrafts. In software patterns, we call these *contextual* forces and *implementation* forces.

These two kinds of spacecraft design can be thought of as patterns. Let's call them the *capsule pattern* and the *lander pattern*. They capture and communicate all the details listed in the preceding, as well as another set of forces: the *consequent* forces.

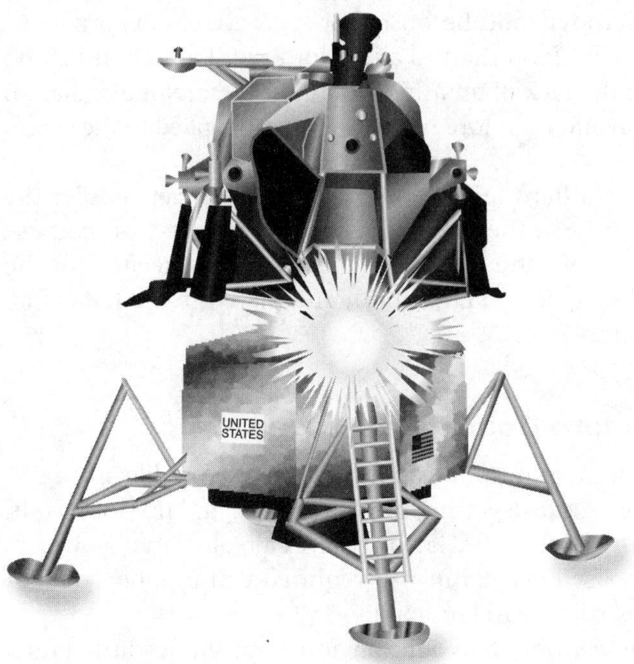

Figure 2.12 Lunar launchpad

The Costs and Benefits

Let us back up and consider the cost-benefit trade-offs that had to be made.

- The CM ended up being relatively small, the LM ended up quite large. The CM was small to minimize weight and to present a smaller profile to the heat of re-entry. The LM was larger because it was two spacecraft, each with its own engine, fuel, and control systems, and because its profile was unimportant.
- The CM turned out to be very tough. The LM was incredibly flimsy. The CM needed to be tough because it had to survive a fiery re-entry. The LM had to be very, very light (even though it was large) because a powered descent requires this, even in low gravity. Since the LM never had to endure the inferno of an Earth re-entry, and was used in one-sixth gravity, it could be built out of lightweight materials and had a very thin skin.

- The CM came home. All of the CMs used in Apollo are in museums today, but none of the LMs are. Half of each of those LMs is sitting on the moon, and the other half in each case was lost. Thus, the LM was a disposable spacecraft, whereas the CM could theoretically have been reused (though none were). As a consequence, anything that one wanted to be able to analyze, later, from the trip could not be left in/on the LM.

If you've ever seen the movie *Apollo 13,* you know that the LM was used as a lifeboat for the stranded astronauts when the CM's service module suffered an explosion. However, they could not "throw away" the CM, because they needed it for re-entry. This is a consequence of the designs of these two spacecraft.

These issues, or forces, drive design decisions, as shown in Table 2.1.

Table 2.1 Design decisions driven by three types of forces

	Capsule Pattern	Lander Pattern
Contextual Forces	Ferries to and from Earth, where there is strong gravity, an atmosphere, liquid water, and a supportive infrastructure for launch.	Ferries to and from the moon, where there is weak gravity, no atmosphere or liquid water, and where the launch must be conducted by the astronauts alone.
Implementation Forces	Titanium shell, ablative heat shield on a blunt-end, aerodynamic body. No rocket engine, so must be paired with the Saturn V for launch.	Thin-shelled, lightweight, capable of powered descent. Two-part design allows the lower half to serve as the launching platform for the upper half.
Consequent Forces	Spacecraft is tough, and will survive/persist after the voyage. It is also relatively small/cramped.	Spacecraft is flimsy, and is consumed and disposed of as part of the process. Spacecraft is larger than a capsule.

On to Mars

When we travel to Mars, we will definitely need a lander of some sort. But even though many of the forces in the problem are the same as when landing on the moon (the astronauts will have to land softly on a hard surface and take off by themselves when it's time to leave; a two-part spacecraft is a likely candidate design), the fact that Mars is larger than the moon means it also has enough gravity to retain an atmosphere, though it is much thinner than the Earth's.

Aero-braking will be possible, parachutes will work, and heat will be a problem.

These differences do not make the Apollo capsule and lander patterns useless to the engineers who will design the lander for Mars. On the contrary, the lessons learned, the forces identified, and the implementation possibilities we understand (with their various consequences) will make their jobs much easier, and drastically increase their probability of success.

The Value of Patterns

This is what patterns are. This is the value they bring. They help us to capture the best practices that have been discovered, sometimes at great cost, in the past. They bring value at every level of our process—note how the Divided Closet Pattern helps me in analysis, implementation, and testing as well, much as the lander and capsule patterns help aerospace engineers at every stage in their process.

You will also note that I have avoided the term *design patterns* scrupulously. It is a misnomer; they are just *patterns* or *software patterns*. Remember Andrea's closet? The Divided Closet Pattern applied to analysis, implementation, and testing, and had value for me in all these areas. I also use patterns in testing, deployment, refactoring, and as tools for collaboration.

Patterns can help us to avoid making old mistakes, and they can help us to more *reliably* see the opportunities for better design, even when these are not obvious.

They increase *our* reliability. In a way, isn't that what a profession does? Doesn't a profession *support* the professional, when he or she is not necessarily having the best day? When I am not sure I am on the right track, the patterns give me clues: "Hey, if it is *that* sort of problem, *this* tends to work out well. But watch out for *these* things, and consider if *this* is possible." In other words, the pattern does not really tell me what to do, but rather it tells me what to look out for, what to pay attention to.

Patterns are collections of wisdom from software development itself—and they give names to each "kind of thing" we do. If you and I are both "patterns people" and I say, "You know, I am thinking of using a Façade here," you not only know what I am planning to do, but what kind of problem I think I am facing, and also some caveats and opportunities that will come next.

If you disagree with my plan, you *know what you are disagreeing with*. In our ensuing conversation, we are much more likely to be on the same page, not having one of those "parallel arguments" that go nowhere for hours. "A set of three object adapters would solve the same problem, and be more cohesive," you might say. And then we would be having a highly communicative and much more focused discussion.

Professionals talk like this. Listen in to the paramedics who have come to resuscitate your wife after the closet collapsed on her for the third time, and you will hear all kinds of terms that seem foreign to you, but obviously speak volumes to these medical experts. Listen to the contractors working on your home remodeling project and realize that, there under the jargon, they are deciding what you really can afford to spend on this room extension.

As I have said, these professions are organisms in their own right. They carry with them what has been discovered, the various ideas and concepts that have proven valuable, and a zeitgeist that is unique to the community that practices each one.

I think this guidance is what we need, and we know it. Software projects are too unreliable, especially for the developers. Things can seem to be going along fine, and suddenly everything explodes and nobody knows what to do. We can fail when we do not expect to, succeed where we have not before, and can rarely predict for the people paying the bills when one thing will happen versus the other.

Why is this? A big part of the problem lies in how we look at software development itself, in what we think its nature is. And a lot of that comes from the way our history has played out so far.

Summary

Patterns are useful in that they allow us to build on the experience of others. As they become more widespread in use, a common set of clear concepts and reliable capabilities will also be more widespread and shared among all developers who study them. This will take us closer to becoming a true profession.

There is value for us in this pursuit. As we become more reliable, as our profession supports us more and more in our daily pursuit of predictable quality, so will our confidence increase. Most people who make software got into the business because they found it intellectually stimulating, energizing, and fun. The movement toward professionalism is a movement away from those things that tended to destroy our enthusiasm and energy for high-quality development.

CHAPTER 3

The Nature of Software Development

To do something well, it helps to understand it. I think we all want to do a good job as software developers, and I think we will have a better chance of doing a good job if we take a little time to investigate the nature of what we are doing.

Once upon a time, I was a Boy Scout. My troop was planning a white-water rafting trip down the Colorado River in the eastern part of California, just above the Imperial Dam. We were given safety training before the trip began, and one thing they emphasized was what to do if we fell out of the raft, which was a distinct possibility in some of the rougher sections.

They said, "If you become separated from the raft:

1. Keep your life vest on, and
2. Do not fight the current."

Keeping your life vest on means you will be less dense than the water (which is why you float), and not fighting the current means you will not run into the rocks. The current, after all, goes *around* the rocks, not through them, and as you will be less dense than the water, it will be able to take you around them too.

This can be uncomfortable. The water can go through narrow defiles that are not fun for a person to go through, but it will not slam you into a boulder that can injure you or kill you. So, do not fight it. Let the nature of the river take you.

This lesson has many implications in life, but here I am suggesting that software development has a nature, a way it "wants" to flow. If we follow this by coming to understand it and then align ourselves with it, then everything will get easier, less dangerous, and ultimately more successful.

I'll begin with the notion that software projects fail more frequently than they ought to, and examine why this might be. I'll examine some of the fundamental assumptions that underlie the traditional view of the nature of what we do, and then look for ways to change these assumptions in the light of what we now have come to understand about software and its role in the world. Finally, I'll show how this new understanding will impact the choices we make, the qualities we emphasize, and how design patterns can help us to accommodate change in systems.

We Fail Too Much

For most of my adult life and some of my teenage years, I have been writing programs. I started using Basic and Pascal and then moved on to C and other languages, including such esoteric and unusual examples as PL1 and Forth.

Moving from language to language, platform to platform, era to era, much has changed. But there are some fundamentals that seem to have held their ground. We have looked at some of them (side effects, for instance, always seem to be a concern).

One of these constants, perhaps the one that has stuck in my throat the sharpest, is the notion that the failure rate of software projects is way, way too high.

Of course, for the majority of my career I was never sure if this was just my own experience; maybe I was just not very good at this stuff. I would ask other people, friends, and colleagues who also "cut code" and they would tell me their war stories, projects they had been on that had gone disastrously wrong.

But, I also knew that people like to tell those kinds of stories. It is human nature; war stories are dramatic, exciting, and often lead others to try and "top" them in the sort of round-robin, coffee-klatch conversations that developers often get into.

So, was it just me, this low rate of success? What did I even mean by success, anyway?

I was pretty much responding to a feeling: I did not have the confidence that I would like to have; I did not feel like I had a "handle" on things a lot of the time.

Definitions of Success

What defines success in software development? In summary, a software development project is successful if it delivers the value expected for no more than the cost expected. This means

- The software is ready on time.
- Creating the software cost what it was supposed to cost.
- The software does what it needs to do.
- The software is not crippled by bugs.
- The software gets used, and does make a positive impact. It is *valuable*.

The first two, of course, are often related to each other. The time we spend to make software is a big part of the cost, because the largest cost is developer time in the vast majority of projects.

However, I have been on projects that delivered on time, but required the efforts of a lot more developers than was planned for, so the project ended up costing more. Either way, when we are late or over budget, we harm the business we are trying to help; it often has plans contingent on the release of the software, and having to change those plans can be expensive and sometimes harm its relative competitive position in the marketplace.

The third point, which could be called *functional completeness*, is of course a relative thing. Software could always "do more," but the real question is whether the software does the most critical things it was needed to do, and therefore has a potential for a positive impact that is commensurate with the cost and effort it took to make it.

No software is free of bugs but there is a clear difference between software that fundamentally works, with a bug here or there that will have to be remediated when found, and software that is so buggy as to be unusable.

Sometimes software that is delivered "on time, on budget" is not actually finished when it is shipped, which becomes clear when we find a lot of bugs, or find that a lot of crucial features are missing.

In the final analysis, the real critical issue is: Are they using it? How much value is it producing in the world? I think that sometimes we have taken the attitude that this is not in our scope, not our problem. We made it, it does what we promised, and it works, so if they do not use it, then that is their problem.

I do not feel that way anymore. I don't think we can.

First, if the software is not being used, why is that? Perhaps the problem it was intended to solve has disappeared, or changed so much that the software no longer addresses it well enough. Perhaps the customer was wrong when he asked for features x, y, and z, and found out too late for me to change what I was making. Perhaps the software works, but is too hard or unpleasant to use, and people shy away from it.

Whatever the reason, software that sits on the shelf, unused, has no value (see "Appendix C, The Principle of the Useful Illusion," for my thoughts on this). In a sense, software that exists only as little reflective dots on a CD-ROM and is never running, does not really exist at all in any useful way.

I do not want to spend my time on valueless things that do not really exist, do you? I think one of the attractive things about software development, at least to many of us, is the idea that we can *make things* and that these things actually work (and do something useful). That an idea, something that starts in my mind, can have a life outside of my personal domain is a little bit magical, and it is what got me hooked on computers and computing in the first place.

Also, I want to go on doing this. I want to have lots of opportunities, and to be able to choose from a wide variety of projects, choosing the one(s) that are most interesting to me. If software does not deliver sufficient value to the people who pay for it, I don't think this is likely to happen.

So, if we can agree that this checklist is right (or at least close to right), the question remains: How are we doing? Luckily, someone took on the task of answering this question for us.

The Standish Group

In 1994, a think tank known as The Standish Group[1] set out to answer this question. For more than 10 years, it studied a whopping 35,000 development projects and evaluated them in a number of ways. Its definition of *success* was nearly identical to the five-point checklist I outlined earlier.

The report Standish produced is long and detailed, but the overall, bottom-line numbers were shocking and, well, believable to anyone who has ever been involved in making software.

1. http://www.standishgroup.com

Projects that "hit all the marks" were called *successful*, of course. Those that were utter disasters, those that used up time, resources, and energy but were ultimately cancelled without producing anything were called *failed*. And, of course, there are many, many projects that end up with something, but are late, too expensive, very buggy, and so on; these were called *challenged*. Only 16% of the projects were classified as successful! The majority of projects, 64%, were classified as challenged, and 20% were considered failed.

Troubling.

First of all, as a teacher, I can tell you that very few developers, even today, know about these numbers. On the other hand, people who pay the bills for software development know them very well.

They know them and they sometimes think they can explain them. The interpretation I hear most often from project stakeholders when they quote these numbers is that software development is not conducted in a predictable way and that the processes that control it are too chaotic. Some even go so far as to say that software is not really developed in a professional manner, that software developers do not really focus on delivering business value; they just want to be involved with the cool tools and work around neat-o computers. I have even heard some business people express the opinion that developers actually *like* to deliver buggy code so that they can be paid to fix the bugs. Either way, the image that a lot of nontechnical business people have about software developers is basically that of the closeted nerd: unsocial, arrogant, and unconcerned with the needs of "normal" people.

The failure rate suggested by The Standish Group study would *seem* to fit this view.

I travel and teach all over the country and overseas as well. I have met more software developers in the last six months than you will likely meet in your whole life. The clear impression I get from meeting so many developers in so many parts of the world is that the notion that we, as a group, do not care about doing valuable work is *dead wrong*.

I admit that I used to know a few guys like that, back in the 70s and early 80s. There were developers who would overestimate their projects on purpose, and spend most of the time playing games or posting on bulletin boards. The image of the software developer as basically the comic book guy from *The Simpsons* was a part of the mythology of the time.

But those guys—if they ever did exist—are pretty much gone. Sadly, the image continues to live on. So, if you feel from time to time as though you are not trusted by the people who pay you to make their software, there might be some truth to that.

Besides the waste involved, there is another reason these numbers are so disturbing. I suspect that those projects called *challenged* and *failed* earlier, which in the Standish study amounted to 84% of all projects, are quite often those "death march" experiences that burn out developers.

We cannot afford the high turnover that has become commonplace in the software development industry, but it is unrealistic to think that your average adult developer will stay long in the business after he or she has gone through two, three, four, or five projects that required late nights, weekends, hostile and panicked managers, and an exhausting lifestyle that is hard to maintain.

Also, universities are seeing notable declines in enrollment in their computer science and computer engineering programs. It seems that the next generation does not view our business as all that attractive, and part of that might be the impression that the death march is the normal way software is made.

So, one way that this book could potentially be valuable to you would be if I could suggest a way to improve on these numbers. If we were more successful, this would have at least three positive effects.

- Software would be developed in a more effective/efficient manner.
- The people who control the purse strings of development would trust us more, would treat us more like professionals, and would tend to be less controlling.
- We would be able to sustain long-term development careers more reliably.

I am going to try to do that, but first we have to examine another troubling piece of data from that same study.

Doing the Wrong Things

Another rather stunning figure from The Standish Group study concerned the number of features in the average piece of software that actually end up getting used. Figure 3.1 summarizes the findings.

Yes, you are reading that correctly. It says that 45% of the features we, as an industry, put into software are *never* used by anyone. Never.

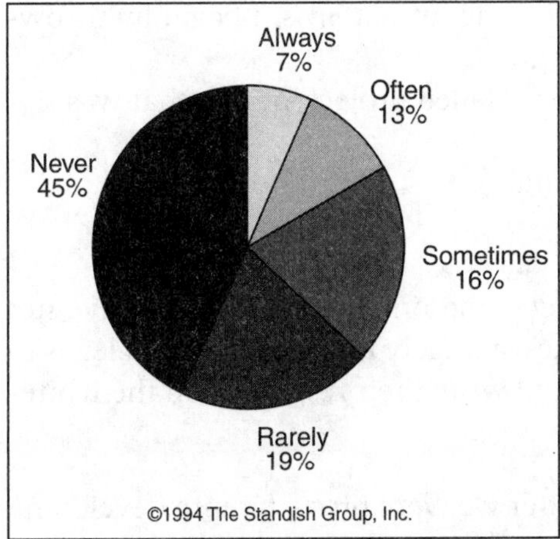

Figure 3.1 Breakdown of features by usage

If that does not bother you overly, think of it this way: That 45% represents our time—time to analyze, design, code, test, debug, redesign, re-code, re-test, and then finally deploy features that no one wants, no one needs, and no one will use. How much better could you do your job if you had 45% of your time back? Furthermore, this means that 45% of the code we are writing represents needless complexity. We are adding classes, tests, relationships, and so on that are never needed and are almost certainly in our way when we are maintaining the rest of the system.

Also, take note: The percentage of use is consistently smaller as features are used more often. Rarely is 19%, which is less than Sometimes, which is 16%, and so on down to Always, which is a mere 7%.

We get this wrong, not only at the extremes of Never and Always, but at *every point in between*.

Why? What is it about our process that drives us to make the wrong things, more often than not? If we could figure out a way to stop doing that, or even just a portion of that, this alone could improve our lot significantly.

Doing the Things Wrong

I teach quite a lot. This gives me access to lots of developers, day in and day out, and so I like to ask them questions about how things are going for them, and why they think things are the way they are.

In my most popular class, which is about patterns, I begin by throwing a question out to the entire class:

"How many of you have been on a failed project, or one that was significantly challenged?"

Naturally, they all raise their hands.[2]

Next, I ask:

"What happened?"

This is a question they do not expect, and one that likely they have not been asked much before. Sometimes, a largely unasked question leads to very valuable discussions. I listen and write their responses on the whiteboard. Here are some typical responses.

- The requirements changed after we were pretty far into developing the code.
- My project was dependant on another project, but we did not get what we expected from the other team, and so we had to change our stuff to match what they did.
- The customer changed their minds. A feature they were sure they did not need ended up being important, because the marketplace changed while we were developing the software.
- We did not realize the best way to get a key feature to work until we got well into the project.
- The technology we were using was unreliable, and so we had to change horses midstream.
- The stakeholders imposed an unreasonable schedule on us.
- We committed to a schedule we could not meet, as we later determined.

. . . and so on. I have gone through this process dozens of times, in large and small companies, with individual developers in public courses, here in the United States and abroad, and the answers are basically always the same.

2. I used to start by asking how many have been on a completely successful project. The fact that almost nobody ever raised their hands was too depressing, especially to them, so I stopped asking that one.

Looking for a through line, a common element that seems to underlie all or most of these causes of failure, consistently drives to the same conclusion. There is a thing that makes us fail, and that thing is *change*. Requirements change.

- Our customers do not know what they want; or
- They know what they want but they don't know how to explain it; or
- They know and can explain what they want, but we misunderstand them; or
- They know, can explain, and we get it, but we miss what is important; or
- All of this goes right, and the marketplace changes around us anyway; and so things have to change.

Technology changes. Fast. Faster all the time. I do not think there is much point in hoping that this is going to stop, that we're going to finally have a stable environment in which to develop our software.

Change has been, traditionally, our enemy, and I think we have known it for a long time.

Who would rather work on maintaining an old legacy system, as opposed to writing something new? I ask that question a lot too, and rare is the developer who would choose maintenance.

Maintenance is, of course, change. Change is a chance to fail. Nobody wants to be the one who broke the system. Nobody wants to be the one who's going to have to stay late, or come in this weekend, and fix the thing.

And so, we find ways to avoid making changes.

Sometimes, we put a contract or a control board between ourselves and our customers. Sign the contract, and they cannot change the spec unless they jump through a series of hurdles, which are designed to discourage them from making the change at all.

But even if that works, it does not work. Remember that fifth metric of software success? The software has to be used, it has to deliver value. If it does the wrong things, even if they were the things in the signed contract, then it will fail in this respect.

Another approach is to try to create a design that is set up to change in any possible, imaginable way.

But even if that works, it does not work. This is typically called *over-design* and it creates a whole other problem: systems that are bloated at best and incomprehensible at the worst. Plus, my experience is that the one thing that comes along to derail you later is the one thing you didn't think of in the over-design—Murphy's Law, as they say.

So, what do we do? How can we safely accommodate the changes our customers want, and likely need? What has made us so brittle?

Why did we ever try to develop software the way we did (and the way some people still do)? Examining this question can lead us to some interesting conclusions, and can perhaps give us some guidance that will help us to continue this upward trend, and perhaps even speed things up.

Time Goes By, Things Improve

The initial findings quoted in the preceding section are from the first Chaos Report, which was issued in 1994. Since then, Standish has updated these findings each year, basically taking on a year's worth of data and allowing the oldest data to fall out.

We are doing better; that's the good news. The failure rate, for instance, had dropped from 20% to 16% by 2004, and the rate of success had almost doubled, up to 34%. Taken together, failed and challenged projects still dominate, but the trend is definitely taking us in the right direction.

Jim Johnson, the chairman of the Standish Group, has said that a lot of this improvement has come from the trend toward developing software in smaller pieces and from a renovation in the ways projects are managed.[3] That makes sense to me. However, even in 2004, according to Standish, we still wasted over $50 billion in the United States alone. We're on the right track, but we have a lot farther to go.

One Reason: The Civil Engineering Analogy

Back in the day when microcomputers[4] first hit businesses, they arrived on the scene (in many cases) without a lot of planning. It was hard to

3. http://www.softwaremag.com/L.cfm?Doc=newsletter/2004-01-15/Standish
4. They were not even called PCs yet because they were relatively rare.

predict what impact small, interactive systems would have on business processes, productivity, the nature of the workday, and so on.

At the same time, a lot of software developers were ahead of the curve on this; very early micros (like the Apple II, the Heathkit, and the TRS-80) were sold more to hobbyists and experimenters than businesspeople. Naturally, these were often the people who were later called on to write the software for these new PCs that started showing up in the workplace.

That was how I started, in broadcast television and radio; making software was not my "job," but people had heard that I had built my own computer and knew how to "program," and would ask me to write things for them since, at that time, little software existed for the PC, especially the vertical-market software that would apply specifically to broadcasting. Many of my friends and colleagues were experiencing the same things in banking, insurance, education, and other industries.

In those days, software *seemed* to sort of "happen," but it was extremely difficult to predict when it would be ready, or what it would do, or what it would be like. This was probably annoying to stakeholders, but acceptable since software was only a fringe issue for most businesses.

All that changed in the 80s with the introduction of inexpensive clone computers.

In a remarkably short few years, PCs were everywhere, and the vast majority of business processes, including very critical ones, had moved to the PC and therefore to software. It was rather shocking how fast this happened, and most people did not realize it had until it was already a done deal.

Business people suddenly realized how very vulnerable they were to the software used to run their business. The software's quality, when new software would become available, what it did and did not do, and so forth, had a profound impact on a company's well-being.

In the mid 90s, the CBS Network hosted a new media conference in Chicago, where the primary topics included the impact of the Internet on broadcasting, and just exactly how the affiliate stations could get control over their exploding automation. Most of the people in attendance were station managers; I was one of the very few techies there, and as such was a popular person to have at your dinner table. These guys were pretty worried.

They knew, and I knew, that the development of software had to be brought under some form of management, that developers had to be accountable to and supported by some kind of process. The chaotic style of developing software was producing chaos in business, and this had to stop.

Business people also knew that they had *no idea* how software development worked, or how one could control it. They also did not consider the making of software to be a professional activity, so they didn't ask us (not that we would have known what to say if they had).

They looked around at the other industries they *did* understand to try and find an analog or metaphor that could guide them. A lot of different things were tried, but what was settled on was what came to be called *the waterfall.*

The idea was that software is essentially like building a large, one-off structure, like a bridge or a skyscraper. The project is complex, expensive, and will be used by many people. We never build the same thing twice, but there is a lot of repetition from one edifice to another.

We all know this process, or something like it:

1. Analyze the problem until you "know it," and then document this.
2. Give this analysis to designers who will figure out how to solve this problem, with the given constraints, using software, and then document this design.
3. Give the design to the development team, who will write the code.
4. Hand it off to testers to do the quality assurance.
5. Release the code.

This has been remarkably unsuccessful, but you can understand the thinking.

Before we build a bridge, we analyze the soils, find the bedrock, measure the high and low point of the river, figure out how many cars it will have to handle per hour at peak times, research local laws, see how the bridge will interact with existing roads and structures, measure if ships can clear it beneath, and so on. Then we get an architect to design a bridge that meets these requirements.

If he does the job correctly, the construction team's job is simply to follow this design as accurately and efficiently as possible. Many of the engineering disasters that have become famous in recent history can be traced back to changes, seemingly insignificant, that were made by the construction team to the plan prepared by the engineers. Because of this, the virtues of construction are considered to be *compliance* and *accuracy*, not invention.

The tester (the building inspector) comes last, to make sure the bridge is safe, work up a punch list for changes, and then finally approve it for use. Finally, the cars roll onto it.

The problem is that analysis for software development is not like analysis in engineering.

When we analyze, we are analyzing the requirements of a human business process, in which very few things are fixed. To communicate what we find, we do not have the highly precise languages of geology, law, hydrodynamics, and so forth to describe the situation; we have the relativistic language of business processes, which does not map well to technology. Thus, communication is *lossy*.

And even when we get it right, business processes and needs change, as do our perceptions as to what was needed in the first place. Bedrock *is* where it *is*, and will *still* be there tomorrow, but people change their minds about how they should run their businesses all the time.

They have to. The market changes around them. In fact, the realities, priorities, and constraints of business are changing at a faster rate every year. Also, the variations in software systems are generally much greater than the variations encountered when building the 247th overpass on Interstate 5.

Also, the analog to the construction step in civil engineering would seem to be the coding step in software development. I think that is a misunderstanding of what we really do when we code. If the virtue of construction is compliance and accuracy, I would equate that to the compile process, not the coding process. If so, where does the creation of code fit? Analysis? Design? Testing? This would seem to be a pretty important distinction to make, and yet we have traditionally left it in the construction position.

So, given our failure rate, why have we continued to develop software like this?

Giving Up Hope

Of course, one reason we have not changed the way we do things is because most of us have assumed the problem is not the process, but ourselves. In other words, we have believed that the reason the waterfall process does not succeed very often is that we are not doing it right.

Software developers have often been thought of as arrogant. I disagree; I think most are very self-questioning and tend to lack confidence. This can sometimes come off as arrogance, but in general, self-assured people don't have to brag.

Lacking any defined standards, software developers have traditionally had no way to determine, for themselves, if they were really *good* at their jobs. Without any notion of what makes a good developer, we live and die by our latest success or failure. This lack of a set of standards is part of what has kept us from becoming the profession we should be, in my opinion.

So, because we tend to worry that the failures in our projects stem from our own faults, we do not suspect that the problem might be the methodology itself.

Einstein said it: "Insanity is doing the same thing over and over again and expecting a different result."

I think we have been a little bit nuts. Well, maybe not nuts. Maybe just hopeful.

Think back to your high school mythology class and the story of Pandora's Box. Pandora, the myth goes, opened a box and unwittingly released all the evils of the world. The last thing that emerged from the box was hope.

When I was a kid, upon hearing this tale, I thought "Awwwwww. Well, at least we have hope!"

No, no. That is not the point. Instead, the point is that *hope is evil*.

As long as we hope that *this time* we will get the requirements right, and stable, then we will keep doing things the way we always have. If we hold out the hope that *this time* we will be able to write code without bugs, then we'll keep writing it as we always have. The hope that *this time* we will be on time, be on budget, just be *better* will keep us from changing what we do.

We give out T-shirts at our courses with cartoons and pithy phrases on them, and by far my favorite shirt says:

"I feel so much better since I gave up hope."

Ignoring Your Mother

Another reason that many of us probably stuck with the waterfall is that it seems to follow the advice our mothers gave us: "Never put off until tomorrow what you can do today."

Waiting is procrastinating, and procrastination is bad, right?

Well, not always. I did some work for a company that created security systems for AS400 computers in Java. When I started that project I did not know anything (at all) about AS400s, only a modicum about security, and only the aspects of Java that I had used before—certainly nothing about the nuances of Java on the AS400.

After I had been on the project for a few months, I knew a *lot* about AS400s, a *lot* about security, especially as it applies to that particular operating system (OS400), and a *lot* about Java as it is used in that environment.

Anyone who has coded anything significantly complex will tell you that midway though the coding she became *much* more knowledgeable about the business she was automating, whatever it was.

Spend six weeks writing code for an embroidery machine and I guarantee you will know more about embroidery afterward than you ever knew (or wanted to know) before. Why not capitalize on this fact, and let what we learn (later) influence and *improve* the design?

Mom said, "Do not put things off." She was right about that when it comes to some things, maybe most things, but not here. I should put off everything I can, because I will be smarter tomorrow than I am today, in just about every way.

Of course, the key to making that work lies in knowing what you *can* put off and what you *cannot.*

Bridges Are Hard, Software Is Soft

There are advantages to the "softness" of software that the waterfall-style approach to software development does not allow us to capitalize on.

After you have laid the foundation for a skyscraper and put up a dozen floors, it is pretty hard to move it one block to the north. That is the nature of physical construction, and that is why architectural plans are generally not made to be changed; the cost of change is usually too high, or even impossible.

In software, however, there are ways of designing that allow for change, even unforeseen change, without excessive costs. Those ways are a big part of what this book is about.

We Swim in an Ocean of Change

One crucial aspect of success for any endeavor is to understand and react to the environment around us. When life gives you lemons, you make lemonade. You can try to make iced tea, but you are always going to be struggling to make it taste right.

It may well be that a process like the waterfall was appropriate at some point in the history of computers. Those who worked in data processing, for example, did tend to follow a very similar process, with a reasonable degree of success.

But the pace of change, the nature of change, and the ubiquity of change has altered the forces driving our success. The pace of change in business is on the rise. The pace of change in technology is on the rise. People change jobs, teams, and organizations much more frequently than ever before. The Internet has driven commercial change to a much higher rate than ever before.

And there is more to come. Computers, technology, and therefore software are permeating every aspect of our lives, and as we move faster as a species as a result of technology, technology will have to move faster as well.

Accept Change

So, give up hope and ignore your mother.

The first step to making a positive change is realizing that what you are doing now does not work. Requirements, technologies, priorities, teams, companies, everything will change. (See Figure 3.2.) There are things you cannot know until you know them. Give up.

Figure 3.2 The futility of fighting change

Now, if we accept these things, we can ask ourselves this question: Given all that, what would a really powerful way to make software look like? That is a good question, the right question, and it is the question about which many of our colleagues today are concerning themselves.

I am not sure we know the answer yet, but I think we are getting close, and we are certainly a *lot* closer to answering it than we would be if we had never asked.

Change is inevitable. Our process must be a process, therefore, of change.

Embrace Change

What is being suggested now, first by the fellows who dreamed up eXtreme Programming (XP), and then later by the entire *agile* movement,[5] is that we work in relatively short cycles (two weeks, a month, etc . . .), and that in every cycle we do every step—analysis, design, testing, coding—and then let the customer look at what we have done and tell us if we are on track or not.

Each cycle allows us to adapt our design to what the customer has told us, and also capitalize on what we have learned about his domain by working on the system in detail.

Part of what makes this work is *time boxing*, the idea that we limit the length of time we will work on a system before we stop and get what we have done so far validated (again, read Appendix C for my views on this).

The value of this is manifold, but right off we can see that it will prevent us from trying to predict too much. If *validating* the software is part of *making* the software, we will not try to gaze into our crystal ball and predict what we'll be putting into the iteration two months down the line; we will wait until we see how *this* iteration went.

It is also an acknowledgment that these phases (analysis, design, code, test) are highly interrelated.

- Your design is a reflection of your problem domain—while determining the design, insights on the problem domain, and therefore requirements, arise.
- Coding gives you feedback on the practicality of your design, and also teaches you about the problem domain.

5. http://www.agilealliance.org/home

- Considering the testability of a design can help you evaluate its quality (more on this later).
- Often, we come up with questions while designing, coding, or especially testing, which inform our analysis of the domain.

In other words, working incrementally changes "I wish I had thought of this sooner" to "Now I get it; let's do it this way." It is a fundamentally stronger position to be in.

Capitalize on Change

Agile processes are, among other things, an acknowledgment of the realization that software development is like . . . software development. It is not fundamentally like any other activity.

We are in the midst of defining a process that is uniquely suited to the nature of our particular beast, which should go a long way toward making us more successful.

It is also, I submit, another aspect of software development evolving into a true profession. We do not make software the way anyone makes anything else. We have our own way, because what we do is unique, complex, and requires special knowledge and skills.

Maybe that is part of what makes something a profession. Doctors do not work like carpenters. Lawyers do not work like teachers. Complex, unique activities tend to find their own process, one that suits them uniquely.

That said, it can be tricky to code in an agile process, where change is not only allowed for, but expected (and happens more frequently). If we ask the customer every couple of weeks if we are on track, there will generally be things that are not quite right, and so the answer will rarely be "Yes, that is fine." Since we are asking for validation more frequently, we will be making changes more frequently.

Frankly, even if we *do* get it perfect, it is human nature for the person being asked to validate the software to find *something* wrong. After all, he needs to justify his existence.

Earlier, I wrote that "there are ways of designing that allow for change, even unforeseen change, without excessive costs." I wonder how many of you let me get away with that.

"There are ways" is pretty vague, which is an important issue if, again, we are going to allow the customer (and ourselves) to change things more frequently.

Fortunately, this book is also about how patterns promote professionalism, and the value they bring to an evolutionary process. Pick any pattern you like and whatever else it does, I guarantee that it makes your design easier to change. Here are a few examples that should be familiar to you if you have studied design patterns already. (If you have not yet studied them, I have included in Appendix B, "Overview of Patterns Used in the Examples," descriptions of all of the patterns I use in this book.)

- *Strategy.* The Strategy pattern enables the programmer to substitute an algorithm or business rule without affecting the code using the rule. This makes it easier to add new implementations of an algorithm after the design is in place.

  For example, if you are amortizing the value of fixed assets and the customer says, "Oh, by the way," in the final month of your project, telling you about some other method of amortization he will need, you can plug it in more easily if you used a Strategy to vary it in the first place.

- *Decorator.* The Decorator pattern is designed to enable you to add functionality in front of (or after) the main entity being used, without changing the entities that use it. This makes it easier to add new functions, in different combinations and with varying numbers of steps, after the design is in place.

  For example, if your customer has reports with headers and footers, and then suddenly remembers a special case where an additional header and two additional footers are needed, you can add the functionality without changing what you already created, if you used a Decorator to encapsulate the structure of the reports, and the number and order of the headers and footers in the first place.

- *Abstract Factory.* The Abstract Factory pattern controls the instantiation of sets of related objects used under particular circumstances. If you design your main code so that it can ignore the particular implementations present, it can let the Abstract Factory decide which particular objects to use. This makes it easier to accommodate an entire new case.

> For example, if you design the system to run on UNIX and NT, and the customer realizes that, in this one case he forgot about, it needs to be deployed on Solaris, an Abstract Factory would allow you to add an entire new set of device drivers, without changing anything else in the codebase.

Of course, if you are *not* already up to speed on these patterns, fear not. We will dig into them more fully later in the book.[6] Simply know that they are not just cool ideas or clever bits of code; they are part of the fabric of our profession.

Patterns were and are discovered, not invented. Something becomes a pattern because it worked, because it helped someone else achieve a better design at some point in the past, and because that person recorded this success and passed it on to you—just like carpenters, masons, and lawyers have been doing for centuries.

And, just like *their* patterns helped them create their own unique processes for *their* fundamental professional activities, so do ours.

- Patterns support agility, even though patterns were originally discovered before agility became a force in our industry. Agility, in turn, helps codify a unique process for software development, and this helps define a professional community.
- Patterns help us to communicate, and to define what we are doing within the unique and specific boundaries of the software development profession. Moreover, the communication that patterns enable is not merely implementation-speak, but captures nuance, wisdom, caveats, and opportunities.
- Patterns provide a clear path to entry for new developers, who are seeking the repository of knowledge from the profession they aspire to engage. Studying patterns is a clear way to strengthen your grasp of good design.

This is why, at Net Objectives, we teach patterns in this way. Not as reusable solutions but instead as professional best-practices. How a pattern is implemented depends on the specifics of the problem domain, the

---

6. Others have written good books on the subject (see the Bibliography at the end of the book). Also, we've created a pattern repository for collecting this information (see Appendix B, "Overview of Patterns Used in the Examples").

language, and framework being used, and so on but the value of the pattern is always constant. This turns the study of patterns into a much more valuable pursuit.

Once patterns are understood at this level, however, a new and more interesting way to think about them emerges. In Alan Shalloway and James Trott's book, *Design Patterns Explained: A New Perspective on Object-Oriented Design,* they discuss

- The principles exemplified by patterns
- The practices suggested by patterns
- A way to apply these principles and strategies in software development generally, even when a particular pattern is not present

This new way of thinking about patterns moves us even closer to becoming a profession as we identify universal principles that inform software development. As patterns become more prevalent, a greater sharing of terminology, thought processes, concerns, and approaches becomes more widespread.

A Better Analogy: Evolving Systems

What is the nature of software development? Once upon a time, someone said,

"All software systems decay over time to the point that, eventually, replacing them is less costly than maintaining them."

This was stated as an inevitability, and I think we have tended to accept it as the truth (see Figure 3.3). Well, I may be embracing change, but I am rejecting this "truth."

If change is inevitable, I would agree that decay is inevitable only if change must always be decay. I think it has tended to be like this because we, as an industry, have not focused ourselves on making code inherently changeable. Our tradition, even if you take it back just a few years, is based on the idea that

- There is relatively little software in the world.
- Computers are very slow, so performance is the main issue.
- Memory and storage are expensive, and the technology is limited.
- Computers are more expensive than developers.

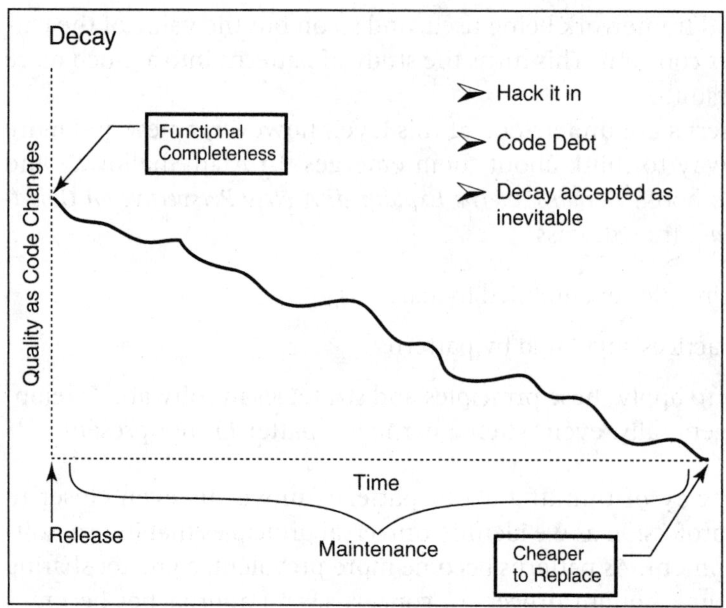

Figure 3.3 An inevitable truth?

If you make it faster, you are on the right track, right? Once upon a time, perhaps, when performance constraints were often make-or-break. But today?

- Computers are now a *lot* faster than they were then (orders of magnitude).
- Memory and storage are cheap and getting cheaper, vast and getting vaster.
- We have a *lot* more software to deal with.
- Developer time is a major expense in software development, maybe the main expense.

Computers are only going to get faster and more pervasive in our lives. And software is a *lot* more important today than ever in the past. Go get an MRI: Your doctor will be using software to find out what is wrong with you. Call 911 on your cell phone: Software sends the police to your aid. And tomorrow, who knows what software will be doing for us?

Look again at Figure 3.3. Do you want to fly in an aircraft that is primarily controlled by software that has decayed to the point where it is really bad, but not quite bad enough to throw away yet? No? Neither do I. That is why "hack it in," which was how we used to make changes, will not hold water any more.

Ward Cunningham of the XP Group says that when you make this kind of change you are incurring *code debt*. It is like putting something on a credit card because you cannot afford to pay for it right now.

Will it cost more or less later on? If it is hard to fix the problem properly now, will it be easier in a few weeks when the code is no longer fresh in your mind, and when the hack you put in today has caused three other, interdependent problems to emerge?

What if I did the right thing now? The argument against this, of course, is that it will cost more to do things right. I am not sure I buy that, but even if I did, I would say that the cost spent now is an investment, as opposed to a debt. Both things cost, but investments pay off in the future.

So I favor the approach shown in Figure 3.4.

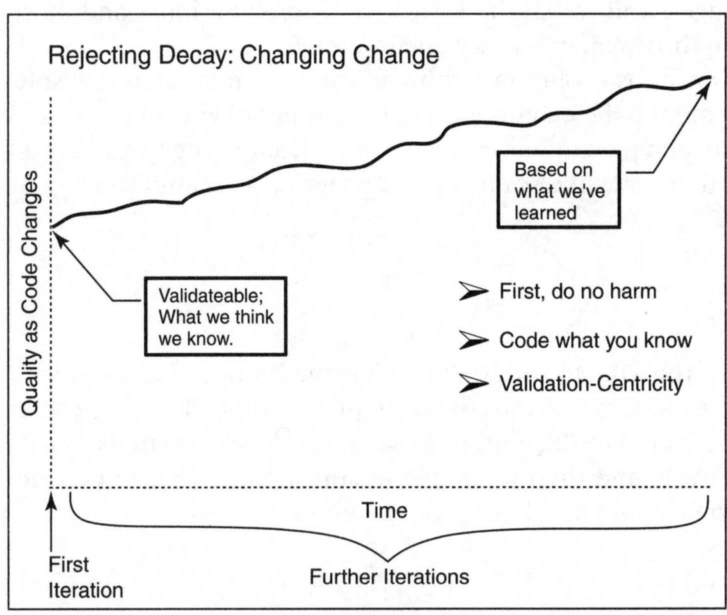

Figure 3.4 Rejecting decay: changing change

I say that decay is not inevitable if we refuse to accept it.

For this to be true, we must assert several things.

- We need something like the Hippocratic Oath: First, do no harm. I do not expect my software to be perfect (ever), but I think it is reasonable to hold myself to the basic standard that every time I touch it, I will take care not to make it any *worse*.
- We need to center ourselves on the notion that validating software (with those who will use it) is part of making the software.
- We need to code in a style that allows us to follow this do no harm oath.

So, what is that style? What is harm? What is the nature of maintainable code? How can we accommodate change if we are accepting that we don't know what/where it is when we start our project?

If we can answer these questions, we can be responsive. We can change our code in response to what we learn, when we learn it. We can keep the quality high, allow the customers to ask for new features when their business changes, and watch the system get more and more and more appropriate to the problem it is designed to solve.

My word for this is evolution. I think it is the essential nature of software development to be evolutionary, that this has always been so, and that the failure and pain in our industry comes from trying to make it all work some other way, like science or engineering or manufacturing or whatever.

Summary

I attempted in this chapter to establish that the nature of the software development is best characterized as one of evolution. The purpose of this book is to examine this notion of software development as evolutionary by nature, and then to enable it, support it, and give you the power that comes from developing in this way. If you agree, read on.

Evolution Versus Natural Selection

I know I am putting my head in the lion's mouth when I use a word like *evolution*. But I do not want to re-try the Scopes Monkey trial again. I am not talking about natural selection and the origin of the species here.

Evolution is a more general concept, and here I am talking about a conscious process of change, something we as humans do on purpose.

Therefore, I do ***not*** mean

- *Random mutation.* I do not mean we should just try any old thing until something arises as workable. We always do the best we can; we just give up hope on certainty.
- *Natural Selection.* I do not expect this just to happen on its own.
- *Millions of years.* Schedules tend to be a little tighter than this.

By evolution, I ***do*** mean

- Incremental, continuous change.
- The reason for the change is *pressure* from the domain.
- This pressure is a positive force. (We finally understand a requirement, or the requirements change in a way that will help solve the problem better, and so on.)
- That our response to the pressure is to change the system in a way that makes it more appropriate for the problem at hand.

This makes change a positive thing, because change means improvement, not decay. It means we have to be more than *willing* to change our code; we have to be *eager*. That is a big shift for most of us.

CHAPTER 4

Evolution in Code: Stage 1

One of the negative aspects of learning to do something in a more effective way is that it sometimes implies that something has been wrong with your approach up to now. This is particularly true when I, as a teacher, am asked to evangelize object-oriented techniques, test-driven development, and design patterns to people who are already experts at creating software in other ways.

Cobol and RPG programmers, for instance, will often arrive at my course thinking "I can do everything I need to do with what I already know. Why do I need to learn all this new stuff? Are you suggesting that my 20 years of experience are worthless now?"

I fully understand their point of view. When I first encountered a truly object-oriented design, I felt much the same. What I want to point out here, and what I try to point out to them, is that a lot of these "new" ideas are not so completely different from what they know now, but in many cases proceed from their best-practices. This has helped me in ways I did not expect.

There is a part of our mind that knows how to program algorithms. Most people learn their first programming language this way, by learning to functionally decompose a problem into procedural logic. Let's see how that ability can still help us, in a new way, when we turn to learning objects and patterns.

Procedural Logic Replaced with Object Structure

When adding new functionality to a mature system, what is the more difficult part of the job?

Writing the new code?

Or integrating the new code into the existing system?

I ask this question a lot, and the vast majority of developers say it is the integration that usually causes the most work.

Why is this? What is the difference between these two aspects of our job?

The first is about creating something. The second is about relating things that may be very different from one another, and that's usually more difficult and also less interesting. That is probably why so many of us would choose to re-write software rather than maintain it—it is easier and more fun.

This is not a new problem.

The Origins of Object Orientations and Patterns

When I first encountered object-oriented programming (Smalltalk and C++), it was a tough sell to me. I could not really see what the point of it was, and it did seem like a lot of extra work and complexity.

I had been doing procedural coding for quite a long time by then, and I thought, "I can make procedural programming do what I want; why change things?" In fact, I had seen other attempts to change the basic paradigm of creating software come and go: Forth, comes to mind. And Prolog.

I spent a reasonably large amount of time, effort, and passion on Forth, only to have it evaporate on me. In the case of Prolog, it was less so, because I had been burned by Forth. In any case, they had both promised to make everything better by making everything different, and at the end of the day, they offered me no value[1] at all. I cannot even remember how they worked anymore.

So, at least initially, I did not embrace object orientation. I thought it was just someone's pet idea, or his attempt at getting a Ph.D. In fact, given

1. I suppose you could say learning anything is valuable, but what I mean here is: I never delivered anything of value to any user in Forth or Prolog, nor did I ever make a dime using them. They were interesting, but did not deliver anything commensurate with the amount of effort it took to learn them.

how busy I was and how much energy the development community seemed to have on this object orientation stuff, I was rather annoyed by the whole thing. *Another flavor of the month that wants my time,* I thought. *Just leave me alone if you're not going to help me.*

I was wrong.

I was wrong because object orientation was not just some shiny new toy: Object orientation grew out of the very best-practices we procedural guys had been trying to follow for years, and then took them to the next level. It was not just someone's pet idea; it was actually the result of my own ideas, and the ideas of others like me, refined and built into a paradigm, and then a set of languages and frameworks.

For instance, long before object orientation was invented, many of us decided to reuse routines. When we created something useful, we would put it into a personal library of code, and reuse it in other projects. Once we knew something worked, once we had it figured out and debugged, tested, and solid, why redo it? This was an impulse toward *objects,* even if we did not realize it.

Like my colleagues, I had certainly noticed the pernicious nature of side effects. I would make a change over here, and gosh knows what happened elsewhere in the code. So, we tried to modularize code, making sure that the variables used by one section were not used elsewhere unless absolutely necessary, to reduce the headaches associated with making a change. We had lots of little rules and processes to promote this, but it was really a desire to *encapsulate,* even if I did not call it that.

I could go on, but the point is that object orientation is rooted in pragmatism, and thus is almost completely about helping the developer avoid certain traps. It was, I realized, full of things that were to my benefit; and once I saw that, I bought into it in a big way.

But if that is true, if it is really a codification/extension of what I knew to be good practice from the procedural paradigm, then it should also be possible to translate techniques from one to the other. In other words, how I used to do something in a procedural language should have an analog in object orientation, and if it is a very common thing, I would expect that to be a repeated *pattern.*

Yep.

So, if you are a procedural programmer making the transition to object orientation, one important thing to realize is that what you already know is valuable, and can "come along." The object-oriented approach suggests new ways of thinking about problems and new ways to accomplish tasks, but much of what made code good before is still true.

Not everything, of course. When computers were so slow and developer time was relatively unimportant, we used to do all sorts of things to "make it easy on the computer" at the expense of readable code. I don't think that translates into good objects, and I don't think it's an attitude based on reality anymore. I'm talking about the part of your mind that sees problems and thinks of algorithms, as many of us were taught to do in college.

Similarly, if object orientation is comfortable for you, but you are looking for the value that patterns can bring, one way to contextualize them is to understand how they relate to the code-logic solutions we still can use to solve problems within methods. There are certain forces in solving algorithms that lead us to use conditionals, switches, and so forth, and these same forces in an architectural perspective can lead us to object patterns that are analogous to these simple language elements.

An important distinction, however: As we will see, the patterns are not code. The patterns are something conceptually higher and far more significant than simple repeated solutions. But to understand them, to put them in the context of what you already know, it can be useful to consider the analogies between code logic and patterns.

An Example: Simple Conditionals and the Proxy Pattern

One of the most basic (no pun intended) procedural techniques is the simple conditional. We do something like Listing 4.1 (which is written in pseudo-code).

Listing 4.1 Simple Conditionals (Pseudo-Code)

```
Do some non-optional stuff
If (some condition is satisfied)
      Do some optional thing
Endif
Do some more non-optional stuff
```

In this case, the software will either do the optional thing, or it won't. The non-optional stuff (before and after) will always happen.

My friend Jeff McKenna (an associate of mine who has also worked with Ward Cunningham and Kent Beck) says something that I think makes an important point clear: An object-oriented approach tends to replace code logic with object structure. Put another way, when you do things in an object-oriented way, you usually end up with less code. Less code means less work, and less opportunity for introducing bugs during maintenance.

Let's say, for example, that you had some code that fetched all the titles that a given author had written from a flat data source of some kind (no SQL statements to lean on). The input to such a routine might be the author's name and the output could be an array of book titles. A fairly straightforward thing to do, I think you will agree.

But in addition, let's say, sometimes you needed to filter this list before returning it. Sometimes, depending on the needs of the entity asking for this function, you needed to return just the titles written in the current decade, rather everything the author wrote in his or her lifetime.

One could certainly handle this with a conditional, similar to the one previously. The first non-optional stuff would be the fetch of the information, the optional thing would be the stripping out of any titles that fell outside the current decade, and the second non-optional stuff would be the return of the list to the calling entity.

The object-oriented version of this would be to replace the conditional logic with an object structure, as shown in Figure 4.1.

Here, `TitleFetcher` is an abstract class or an interface; it's an idea, a concept. It defines how other objects "talk" to the actual objects that do the fetching. The `Client` object asking for this fetching behavior does not "know" this; from its point of view, `TitleFetcher` is the object that is doing the work. In actuality, `TitleFetcher` cannot even be instantiated.

The truth is that it will *either* be `BasicTitleFetcher`, which simply fetches all the titles and returns them (no matter what decade they were written in), *or* it will be `FilteringTitleFetcher`. Note the Uses arrow from `FilteringTitleFetcher` to `BasicTitleFetcher`.

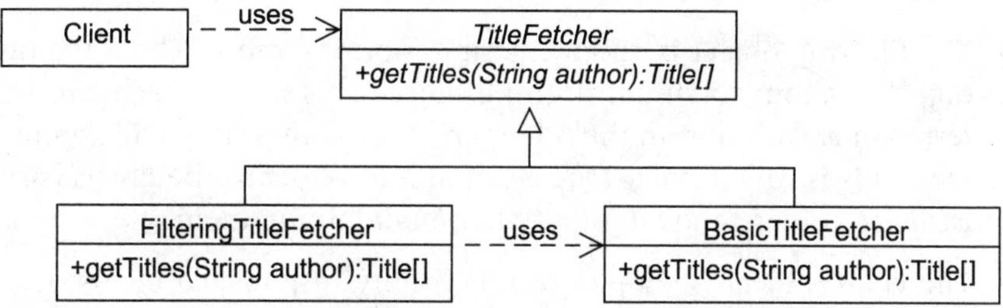

Figure 4.1 Replace the conditional logic with an object structure

The filtering version of the service (`FilteringTitleFetcher`) will use the basic version of the service (`BasicTitleFetcher`) to do the work, and then will strip out the titles that don't qualify (those not written in the current decade), and then return the smaller list back to the client.

Since the two objects appear to be identical from the `Client` object's perspective and therefore interchangeable to the `client`, we can change the `client`'s behavior by giving it either one version or the other, and so no conditional is needed in the `client`. We have replaced the if statement with this set of objects—at least from the `Client`'s view (the logic that actually instantiates the right `Fetcher` object may have an if in it, but as we will discuss later, that is likely a good tradeoff).

This is a design pattern called the Proxy pattern (see Appendix B, "Overview of Patterns Used in the Examples," for more on this pattern if you're not familiar with it). *Optional additional behavior* is a very common need for software systems, and so this particular way of handling the issue, using objects, is also pretty common. In one sense, design patterns represent common problems and their common solutions, in object orientation.

"Great," I hear you saying. "You have replaced a few lines of code with all this *stuff*. How is that better?" Good question.

Sometimes it is not. If you are coding up an algorithm, there are sometimes conditionals along the way that are just part of the way the algorithm itself works, and to break all those conditionals out into object structures would certainly create an awful lot of objects.

However, when the conditional has to do with the overall behavior of the system or service, in this case whether the resulting set of titles is filtered, there are advantages to doing it this way.

- The filtering code and the fetching code are in separate objects. This means that they are encapsulated from each other; the code in the filter cannot, even accidentally, mess around with the variables being used by the fetching routine. Every time I create a "wall" like this, I reduce the side effects that are possible when I change the code.

- The filtering object is about filtering, nothing more. The fetching object is about fetching, nothing more. This means each can be tested in isolation from the other, and therefore testing will be simpler. This is called *strong cohesion*, and it also means the objects are easier to understand later on, when maintaining them.

- The client object is simpler too. It is only responsible for its own issues, not the filter/don't filter and fetch issues. This improves its cohesion and testability as well.

Also, there really is no more work here, no more code to write; it is just written in different places. There is, in fact, probably less actual code (even if there are more classes).

To make it work, of course, something has to decide whether to give the `client` the filtering proxy to talk to, or just the basic object. How you do that depends on the nature of the application.

Let's say in this case that it is a setting in the Graphical User Interface (GUI) screen; the end user gets to decide whether to see all the titles, or just the titles from the current decade.

If we did this procedurally, the `client` would have to check the state of the `GUI` in the conditional logic, as shown in pseudo-code in Listing 4.2.

Listing 4.2 Checking the Client Procedurally (Pseudo-Code)

```
In Client:

get the list of titles
if(GUI filter box is checked)
    filter the list down to current decade
endif
return the list of titles
```

It is pretty clear that I have coupled the `client` to the `GUI`: the fact that there is a `GUI`, that it works a certain way, that you can get the state of the check box a certain way, all that. If the `GUI` changes in any significant way, I'll have to go back into this code and change it.

Now, imagine that there are many different objects that need this kind of behavior: If the `GUI` changed, I would have to remember to change them all.[2] This is the kind of thing that always got me into trouble in my procedural days, and made maintenance so difficult (and made me very resistant to changing my code; I always tried to find an excuse not to, to rewrite it instead).

The object-oriented answer to such a thing is almost always the same: Got a problem? Encapsulate it. How to do that is shown in Figure 4.2.

---

2. Alan Shalloway has a great way of stating the inevitability of such things, which he calls *Shalloway's Law*:

> For any system that has N things that now need changing, where N > 1, Shalloway will find at most N-1 of them to change.

I agree, though for me, it's often at most N-2.

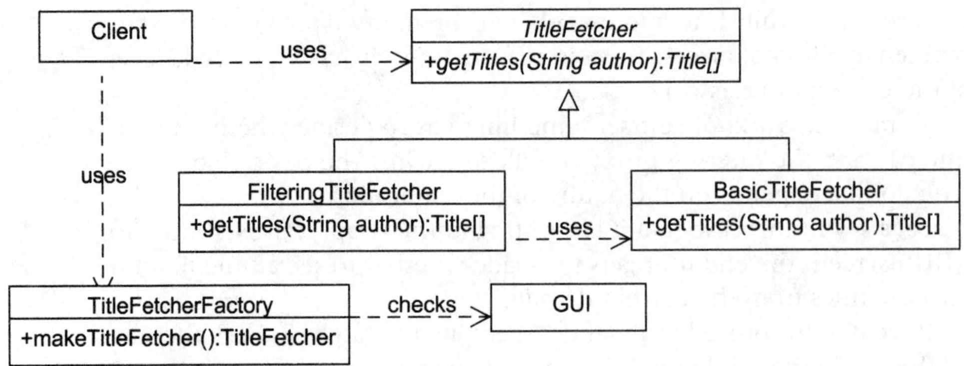

Figure 4.2 Encapsulating the problem

The only thing here that has any coupling to the `GUI` is this factory object. It checks the `GUI`, builds the appropriate object(s), and returns them to the `client`, which uses them.

"Oh great," I hear some of you saying. "Another object! More complexity!" I used to think that too, but I have come to realize that I was mistaking *unfamiliarity* with *complexity*.

I learned a long time ago that long, deeply nested functions were a problem for me to maintain. So, rather than putting everything about an algorithm in a single subroutine, function, method, or whatever, I would make a lot of smaller methods and call them, in sequence, from a "master" method.

Once I saw the value of this, I did not see adding more methods as making things more complex. Quite the opposite: I thought, "Oh good, another method," because I knew it would make things clearer for me in the future.

That is the shift here. Once I saw that using objects produced a benefit for me, and that using them properly was going to make my life significantly easier, I did not see them as added complexity but more as a safety net, as something "watching my back."

The Next Step: Either This or That

One step up in complexity from the simple conditional is the multi-path conditional, shown in pseudo-code in Listing 4.3.

Listing 4.3 Checking Multi-Path Conditional (Pseudo-Code)

```
do some non-optional stuff
if (some internal condition is satisfied)
     do option one
else
     do option two
endif
do some more non-optional stuff
```

The idea here, of course, is that there is some behavior that has two versions, and that we need to vary which version of the behavior occurs based on some internal condition in the system.

Sometimes, this is fine. Where it has gotten us into trouble before, as procedural programmers, is when

- "Some condition" is also influencing other behavior. That couples this behavior to the other behavior, even if this is not clear to me.
- It is likely that other options will emerge later. To accommodate this, I will have to add else if statements, which adds complexity and requires me to change the code.
- There is some code redundancy in the two options. Because each "leaf" here is a discrete block of code, I cannot reuse code from one block in another.
- This same decision must be made somewhere else. Then, the entire conditional and all its branches will be redundant.

Again, an object-oriented approach would help to solve these problems by replacing the code logic with objects and relationships. And again, since this is a very common sort of problem, the object-oriented solution is a well-known pattern called the Strategy pattern.

For an example of this pattern, let's say we have an entity in the system that is responsible for monitoring the health of a connection to another machine. On a regular basis, this monitor is polled by another entity in the system, and it then checks the connection to see if it is still up and running properly. Whether it is or not, it then sends a message elsewhere that indicates this status.

However, let's say where this status should be sent is a varying issue. Sometimes (during business hours, let's say), we want to send this information to a local display object; sometimes (after hours), we want to send this information to a pager, but in that case only if there is a failure. We do not want to wake the systems operator in the middle of the night to say that everything's fine!

The procedural approach is to create a slightly more complex conditional than we did in the `Title-Fetching` problem, shown in Listing 4.4.

Listing 4.4 More Complex Checking (Pseudo-Code)

```
get the status of the connection
if (it is between 8AM and 5PM)
    send the status to the local display
else
    if ()the connection failed) send the status to the pager
endif
do whatever cleanup is needed and return
```

The Strategy pattern replaces the if/else/endif with objects, and encapsulates the nested if (which is part of the after-hours algorithm) into one of them, as shown in Figure 4.3.

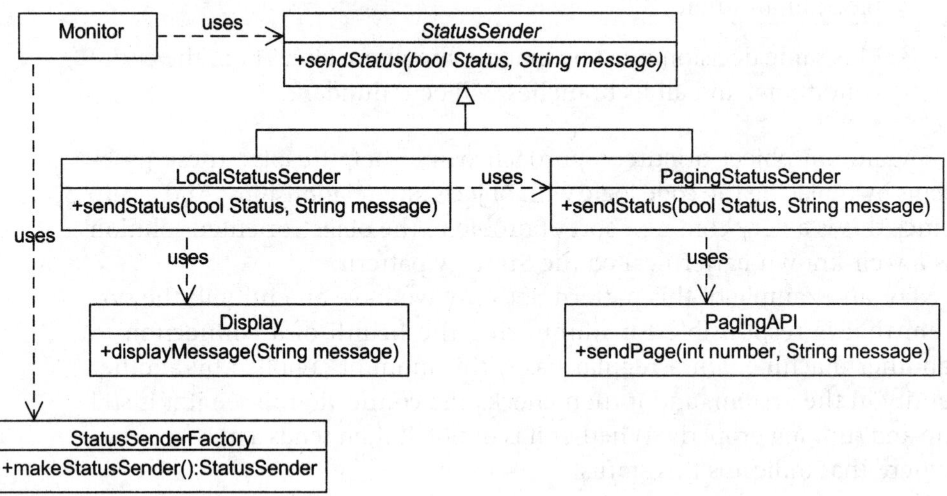

Figure 4.3 Strategy pattern

The `Monitor` is responsible for actually checking the connection and determining if it is currently working. It uses the `StatusSenderFactory` to get the right version of `StatusSender`, without any coupling to how that decision was made. Then, the Monitor sends the status via the `StatusSender` it is given, without knowing which one it is collaborating with.

The `StatusSenderFactory` checks the time of day and returns either the `LocalStatusSender` or `PagingStatusSender` accordingly. If these objects are stateless (which is likely), the factory only builds them once, and hands them out over and over, keeping performance high.

The `LocalStatusSender` displays the status message on whatever the local object is. Likely, it takes a reference to that object in its constructor, so the `StatusSenderFactory` must know about that, but that's okay; it is a *factory issue* in that case. Factories are usually involved with the constructors of the objects they instantiate, for obvious reasons.

The `PagingStatusSender` is responsible for checking whether the status is a failure, and sending a message to the pager if it is, doing nothing if it is not. Note that this guard conditional is part of the Sending to the Pager algorithm, so we would still likely accomplish that through normal code logic, an if/endif or something similar.

Why Bother?

Again, sometimes the answer is not to bother. But the advantages of this object-oriented approach over the procedural one are many.

- What if there are some things (state, function, whatever) that both the `LocalStatusSender` and `PagingStatusSender` have in common? Given the fact that they have a common base class, we can place those things in `StatusSender` and allow them to be inherited, nicely removing the redundancy.
- What if we get another variation of the status sending behavior? Let's say, on weekends, that the messages regarding the status of the connections should be written to a log file for someone to examine on Monday morning. With the object-oriented version, we could easily derive a new object from the `StatusSender` abstraction, without touching any of the existing objects except for the `StatusSenderFactory`. The more we can leave working code alone, the less likely we are to introduce bugs.

- What if something else starts to vary? Let's say that sometimes, regardless of whether we send the message to the display, log, or pager, we also might have to convert it to Spanish, depending on the preferred language of the person who will receive it. Adding this to the existing code logic in the Monitor increases its complexity, whereas simply pulling out another Strategy object does not. Remember, we're trying to hold ourselves to a new standard: Whatever you do, don't make things *worse*.
- What if, at a later date, we sometimes need to send the message to the display and the pager, or the pager and the log, or some other combination? As I will demonstrate later, object-oriented approaches are quite evolve-able, and here we could easily migrate this design to a Decorator pattern, if we adhere to a few simple practices. More on this later.

One Among Many

Another circumstance we often find ourselves in is the need to pick one behavior from a set of possibilities. Often, we base this decision on some external value or condition, and in the procedural tradition, would use a switch/case statement to organize the behavior, passing in the value or condition, and make the proper selection, as shown in Listing 4.5.

Listing 4.5 Incorporating a Switch/Case to Organize Behavior (Pseudo-Code)

```
do some non-optional stuff
switch (some external value or condition)
case 1:
     do option one
     break

case 2:
     do option two
     break

case 3:
     do option three
     break
endcase
do some more non-optional stuff
```

Sometimes, we could also end the stack of cases with a default case, one that "fires" if none of the other cases apply. Either way, the point of this structure is to select from a number of different possibilities, only one of which is appropriate at a given point in time.

If you are familiar with the Chain of Responsibility pattern, you can see that it is essentially an object-oriented way of solving this same problem, or resolving these same issues. See Appendix B for details on this pattern, if you are not familiar with it. The important thing to note is that the same essential forces that would lead you to the switch could lead you to the Chain. Therefore, the part of your mind that knows how to solve problems algorithmically can give you clues as to patterns you might want to consider, even if you decided they were overkill in a given case.

Summary

My point here is *not* to suggest that every place you used to put a simple conditional should now be accomplished using a Proxy, or that every switch statement should become a Chain of Responsibility.

Professionals know that there are always a number of ways of solving any given problem, and they make decisions based on the cost versus benefit, or return on investment, that each approach offers. We should do the same; if I decide to handle something procedurally, I want this to be a conscious decision, not something I did because I did not know about other options available to me.

Also, if I truly believe that the roots of object orientation (and therefore, the roots of patterns) lie in good practices that grew out of the procedural traditions of the past, then what I know about good procedural coding should still be valuable to me as I add to my collection of wisdom and technique, as I become more professional in my approach to software development.

So, whenever I am faced with a problem to solve, and I think, "I could use a series of simple conditionals here," I now know to at least *consider* the advantages of using a Decorator, and if I dismiss it as over-design, I at least want to know that I made that decision consciously.

Also, I want to emphasize the right qualities, adhere to important principles and follow good practices that will ensure I can easily switch to the object-oriented approach later on, if it turns out I was mistaken.

These things contribute to our professionalism too, and are the focus of Chapters 7, 8, and 9.

CHAPTER 5

Using and Discovering Patterns

I guess it's obvious by now that I think patterns are largely misunderstood.

People are interested in patterns, but even after studying them extensively, they tend to misuse them, then overuse them, and eventually stop using them. For a long time, I struggled with this myself. In fact, I was *teaching them* and still I could not point to any significant advantage they were giving me in actual practice.

Furthermore, when I had the occasional opportunity to meet a former student in my role as a consultant, I would practically never see that patterns were showing up in the code they had written since taking my class. "Great class!" they would say, and then proceed to show me designs they had settled on that clearly took no advantage of patterns.

One day, I had an experience that opened my eyes as to what patterns are, and are not, and how they could actually help me and my students. I want to share that experience with you here.

There are lots of books on patterns, and I am not going to duplicate their contents here. For descriptions of actual patterns, I am providing an appendix (see Appendix B, "Overview of Patterns Used in the Examples"), which contains a summary of all the patterns I will refer to in the book. Trying to learn all the patterns is pretty meaningless anyway; more are being discovered and recorded all the time, as I am about to demonstrate, in a conceptual way. What I hope to do here is to give you a point of view on patterns in general that will make them all easier to understand, apply, and get value from.

I also highly recommend *Design Patterns Explained: A New Perspective on Object-Oriented Design, 2nd Edition,* by Alan Shalloway and Jim Trott. It was the first edition of this book that really got me started on patterns, and is probably the best source for understanding them in detail. I also really like *Head First Design Patterns* by Elisabeth and Eric Freeman, Bert Bates, and Kathy Sierra. I recommend to my colleagues that they read both, and in that order.

Design from Context: More Carpentry from Scott

My family has a hexagonal backyard gazebo, which we built ourselves from a kit. The gazebo is very nice, and includes built-in benches along the interior surfaces of five of the six sides (all but the opening/entrance). As you can see in Figure 5.1, what was missing was a six-sided table in the center of the gazebo, which would allow us to take summertime meals out there.

All along, while landscaping our backyard, I had been thinking about Christopher Alexander and his book *The Timeless Way of Building*. This was the book that the original authors of the first Design Patterns book were working from, and I had gone back to read the original source in my desire to understand what they were getting at.

Figure 5.1 Gazebo from a kit

In that book, Alexander had described a pattern, The Courtyard pattern, as his way of introducing the reader to the overall concept of a pattern:

> . . . a courtyard which is properly formed, helps people come to life in it.
>
> Consider the forces at work in a courtyard. Most fundamental of all, people seek some kind of private outdoor space, where they can sit under the sky, see the stars, enjoy the sun, perhaps plant flowers. This is obvious. But there are more subtle forces too. For instance, when a courtyard is too tightly enclosed, has no view out, people feel uncomfortable, and tend to stay away . . . they need to see out into some larger and more distant space. Or again, people are creatures of habit. If they pass in and out of the courtyard, every day, in the course of their normal lives, the courtyard becomes familiar, a natural place to go . . . and it is used. But a courtyard with only one way in, a place you only go when you "want" to go there, is an unfamiliar place, tends to stay unused . . . people go more often to places which are familiar. Or again, there is a certain abruptness about suddenly stepping out, from the inside, directly to the outside . . . it is subtle, but enough to inhibit you. If there is a transitional space, a porch or a veranda, under cover, but open to the air, this is psychologically half way between indoors and outdoors, and makes it much easier, more simple, to take each of the smaller steps that brings you out into the courtyard.
>
> When a courtyard has a view out to a larger space, has crossing paths from different rooms, and has a veranda or a porch, these forces can resolve themselves. The view out makes it comfortable, the crossing paths help generate a sense of habit there, the porch makes it easier to go out more often . . . and gradually the courtyard becomes a pleasant customary place to be.

Our backyard is a sort of a courtyard, or at least I thought it was, so we created a set of crossing paths (see Figure 5.2), and we had left a gap in our back fence to allow a "view out."

Well, we built it, and were awfully happy with it. We'd gaze at it lovingly from the living room, and comment on how nice it was. However, it became pretty obvious that we were not actually using it.

Figure 5.2 Crossing paths

At first, we really did not know why. It was our son, Griffin, who suggested that something was missing, something that would be needed in order for us to put the gazebo to use for eating, working with our laptops, playing games, and so on

A table was a missing element; without it, we would not get into the habit of using the gazebo, because it was not "comfortable" to use it for any of the uses listed above. This fits very nicely with Alexander's notion of deriving design from the context of use; and I had missed it.

When it came time to add the table, I found that hexagonal tables are not that easy to find. I have never been much of a carpenter (remember Andrea's closet!), but the successful experience of building the gazebo had emboldened me to the point that I decided to design and build my own table, from scratch.

I tried to think of the *forces* in the table problem, and especially the context of its use. We planned on having backyard barbeques, parties, and also wanted to be able to work in the gazebo when the weather was warm and clear. The table needed to be flexible, and removable, as we thought we would likely use it outside the gazebo from time to time as well.

Although foldable or removable leaves, as shown in Figure 5.3, would make it possible to remove the table from the gazebo, it occurred to me that the six sections of the table could be made as stand-alone elements, sort of like TV trays, that could then be linked together to make a table when desired. This would also mean we could make half a table, or put five sections together but leave out the sixth, making serving easier.

Plus, if the sections could be used separately, then we could use them for buffets or similar parties where people do not sit together around a table.

The challenge, then, was to make the individual sections stable enough that they could stand on their own, and to make sure they would fit together into a table. This required that each component be robust, but also that the quality control on the measurements (and the resulting fit) was high enough that they would actually link up into an overall hexagon.

Lacking a radial arm saw or even a miter (and with the assurance from "management" that I would *not* be given a budget for them), I had to think creatively about my process. I knew the table would have to be made of cedar (to match the gazebo), and that wood tends to have irregularities and imperfections. Table 5.1 summarizes the situation.

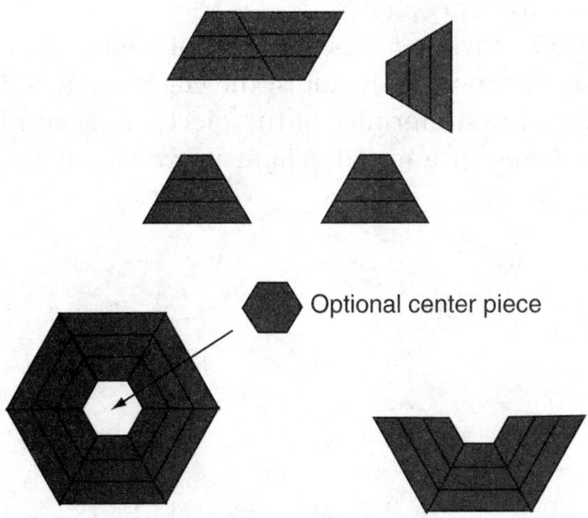

Figure 5.3 Flexible-use table idea

Table 5.1 The situation

Issue	Implications	Category
Table will be made of wood to match the gazebo	Wood is imperfect, so the design will have to allow for this	Constraint
No table saw or radial arm saw is available	All cutting will de done with a hand saw	Constraint
Table will be made of sections that come apart and can stand on their own	The sections must be designed to stand alone	Requirement
The sections should fit together cleanly	Need to check fit throughout construction	Quality Control

I decided to cut the pieces for the tabletop first, figuring that if I could get them to fit cleanly, I could add the planned leg structures afterward.

Right away, I found out that making the tabletop pieces fit well was much harder than I had expected. I was using 8-inch-wide boards and cutting them at a 60 degree angle, but the width of the boards was not totally consistent, and neither were my angles.

Getting the table pieces to fit together was a matter of trying, then sanding, then ultimately using a wood file to adjust the edges again and again and again. This affected the uniformity of the pieces, as seen in Figure 5.4, as each piece was being customized to fit in a particular place.

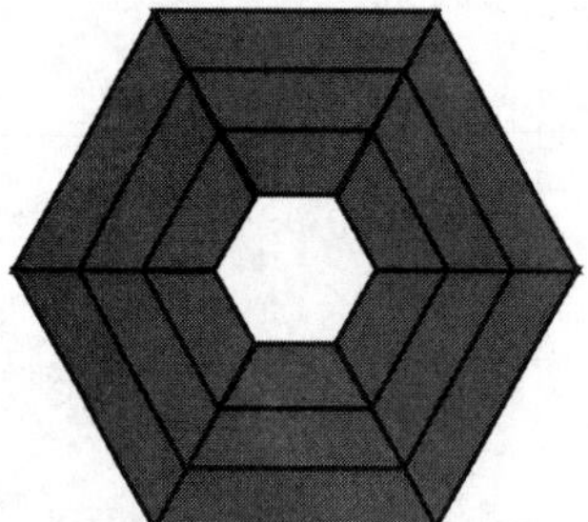

Figure 5.4 The table pieces were hard to make perfect.

My wife, Andrea, noticed my frustration, and pointed out that one particular configuration did, in fact, fit okay. I agreed, but pointed out that while the table would come together well in this one way, the resulting "wedges" would not be interchangeable; they would always have to be put together in this exact same order.

She pointed out that we had never *said* the pieces had to be interchangeable, and she was right. I had assumed a requirement that did not exist in the specification. Think about how often we do this in software.

By simply writing a letter on the underside of each section, I could record the way they went together, and ensure that they were always assembled in that order. This vastly simplified the fit-and-finish issue, but it was not until I was arranging the pieces in their context (relative to each other) that I realized that I had assumed a requirement not actually present in the problem. Rather, I had *derived a requirement* on my own. My process, which proceeded from this derived requirement, was making the implementation overly difficult and time-consuming.

Now it came time to build and attach the legs. In my initial thought about the table, I had assumed I would use a pedestal to hold it up, but now that I had decided to make these little table-ettes that could link together, that would no longer work. After all, each section had to stand on its own, and would have to hold up when people leaned on it, put food on it, and so on.

As I said, I was very much in a pattern frame of mind during this process, and so I thought to capitalize on patterns from the woodworking profession. After all, the guys who designed my gazebo kit seemed to know what they were doing; could I find some guidance there?

I had looked at the way the built-in benches worked, and decided to parrot this in the table design, since that would look nice (it would match) and I would be following the design pattern that a professional carpenter had picked. The benches were designed to stand alone, or mount inside the gazebo, and certainly had to hold up well with lots of downward pressure (we had to sit on them, after all).

I am not sure what the official term for this kind of leg is (see Figure 5.5), but I called them *box legs*.

I chose 2x2 cedar stock, and began cutting the pieces. My plan was to attach them to the table top (which was upside-down on the ground) and then flip the entire table over. Voila!

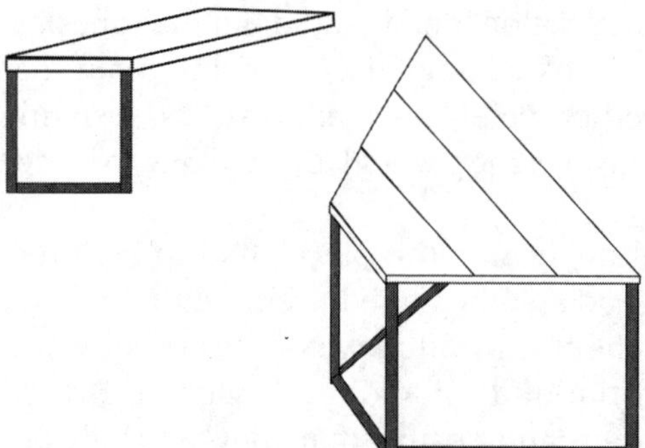

Figure 5.5 The box-leg pattern

But something in my head said, "Build one section completely and put it in the gazebo." Perhaps this was just my spider-sense tingling, but I do not think so. I think it was Alexander at my elbow telling me to design from context, to place the pattern (box legs) into the context of the overall solution (there in the gazebo) and then watch the interplay.

I did this and Andrea saw the problem immediately (see Figure 5.6).

The problem was that if all the table legs were like this, it would be next to impossible for people to "slide in" to the back section of the gazebo. There would be no room for their legs to slide past the table legs; essentially people would have to walk on the benches to get to the section of the table that was opposite the gazebo's opening, or do some weird kind of hip-limbo dance that I don't think we or our friends would be good at. It was wrong, and it would, once again, cause the gazebo to go unused.

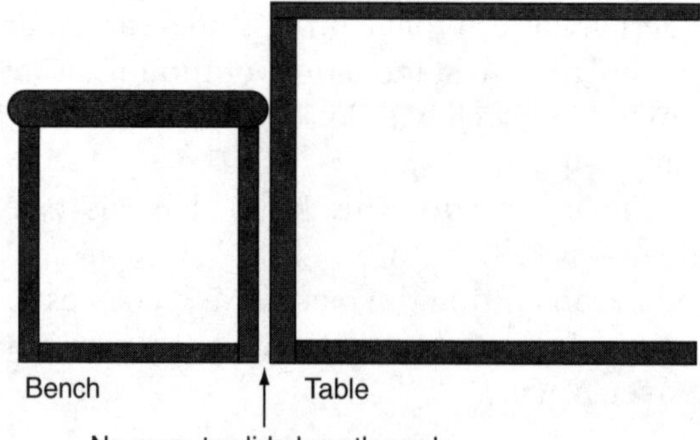

Figure 5.6 Side view of the leg problem

Why had I not seen this?

In tables I have used throughout my life, the typical pattern of use has been to pull the chair out, sit down, and scoot it back in. This experience, which was not applicable here in a gazebo with fixed benches, led me to misread the forces present, and how they would interplay.

Good thing I did not build all six sections before putting one of them in the gazebo, in the context where it would be used! (Hm, sounds like an early, even up-front unit test . . .)

And that is one of my points here. The context informed the solution, and even though the change I needed to make to "the canonical" box-leg pattern was trivial; it made a tremendous difference in terms of the usability of this table, and the resulting usability of my (rather expensive) gazebo.

Does this mean I cannot use the box-leg pattern? Yes, if I think of the pattern as a *pre-rendered solution* that has to be used precisely the same way in every context. If, instead, I think of it as an arrangement of implementation forces to solve a problem, then a slight modification to make it work in my current context should allow me to derive benefit from the smart guys who designed the benches.

Moving the legs back halfway, as shown in Figures 5.7 and 5.8, created enough room for people to easily get around them, and this made the table useable.

Guess what? It looked pretty nice, too. The natural solution is often the most satisfying, pleasing, and *facile* solution.

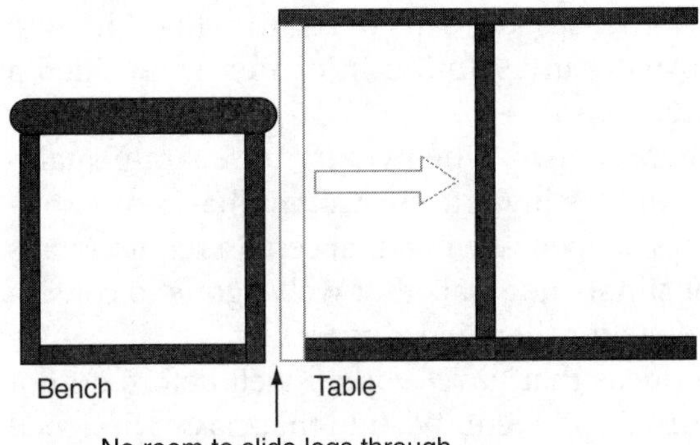

Figure 5.7 Solution to the leg problem

Figure 5.8 Photo of the final product

To summarize, I learned two key lessons. First, until I saw the table in context, I did not see the leg-position problem. Most tables use chairs that you can pull up and push back, and so normally the legs could be placed where I originally planned to place them, and this would cause no problem. The canonical form of this pattern would not, precisely, work given the context of the solution—fixed benches in an enclosed gazebo.

Second, if I had built the entire table outside the gazebo, I would have had to go back and change all the legs (six pairs of them) when I tried to integrate it afterward. By placing my solution in context, I avoided a tremendous amount of wasted effort.

This probably sounds rather familiar. When we try to separate analysis, design, implementation, and testing into their own phases of a software project, these same things happen. We find that certain requirements are missing, or erroneous, or simply not real, after we've gone to considerable time and effort to implement them in software.

We find that some design ideas that have worked well before do not work in the context of the current problem. We find that classes designed without considering testing issues are very hard to test meaningfully.

We find that much of this gets discovered late in the process, sometimes after a lot of work has been done, and has to be thrown out. We find ourselves scrambling at the end to fix all this, and this results in expense overages, missed schedules, unhappy customers, and (over time) burned-out developers.

Patterns Lead to Another Cognitive Perspective

The box-leg pattern I identified when I examined the bench seats from my gazebo kit was not without value; it had tremendous value conceptually, though my particular implementation had to be different. If I had never seen the box legs, I probably would have tried to build a pedestal table, or make traditional table legs, and likely the sections would never have been strong enough to stand on their own.

Patterns lead me to think about my problem differently, and that is their real value. If I use them for conceptual guidance, rather than trying to see them as canned solutions, they help me enormously.

Patterns Help Give Us a Language for Discussing Design

Choreography is an immensely complex thing—recording the way people move in a complex dance routine is almost as complicated as measuring weather patterns. It is even more difficult for one artist in a team that is producing something for the stage to communicate the various moves, steps, interplay, rhythms, and so forth that make up a dance.

To help address this, choreographers have created a language of dance, a set of codified movement patterns that help them to discuss various options for the dancers, to evaluate their appropriateness and beauty in a given situation, without have to use long, drawn-out descriptions of the moves.

Patterns in the software sense help us in the same way. If I can simply say, "We could use a decorator here" in a design or review session, and if everyone present knows what I mean, then we have saved a good half-hour and can quickly decide to explore or reject my suggestion. Together.

This language is all the more powerful if everyone in the team knows that "a decorator" can be many things, not just the one shown in the books. Choreographers know that a given step, a plie, or a jete is never actually performed the same way twice, but they understand its general nature, and how it will contribute to the dance. Decorators can be created using inheritance, delegates, arrays, linked lists; they can be highly dynamic, or essentially fixed; and so on.

Patterns in This Book

One of the values of patterns is that they help us to recognize an emerging design, as it is emerging, and this helps us to identify key elements and decision points more quickly.

In the case study chapter on evolution that comes later in the book, many common patterns will emerge, and integrate relatively easily because we will be following some basic practices, being guided by some fundamental principles, and paying attention to key qualities as we go.

There are decisions to make when you implement a pattern, and these are forces, too. For instance, in my box-leg pattern, I now know that one force is horizontal placement of the vertical supports. The next time I see a place where the box-leg pattern might help me, I will immediately know to consider this key force.

There are similar forces in all patterns. There are different ways to instantiate the objects, various levels of runtime dynamism, implications of relatively broad or narrow interfaces, and so on. I will cover these in the appendix on patterns. For now, the point I am making is that these forces, these decisions, are part of the patterns too, far more so than the class diagrams and code snippets that are often thought of as "the patterns."

Once I understand the following about patterns, their value to me in emergent design begins to become clear.

- Patterns are really best-practice techniques that help me to create a design that is appropriate given a set of forces in my problem.
- Patterns will be found in analysis, design, and implementation, not simply as part of an up-front formal design phase.

Emergent design is all about capitalizing on the evolving nature of the coding process, embracing change, and responding to the ever-growing competence I feel regarding the problem domain as I work and rework my solution, and thus gain experience. But I know that others have gone before me and solved similar problems in clever and interesting ways, and knowing the patterns helps me to capitalize on their experience wherever I can, whenever I find it appropriate to the problem before me.

I will assume throughout our investigations here that you know the specific patterns I refer to. If that is not true, fear not; I have explained all the patterns used in this book in Appendix B. Even if you *do* know the patterns I mention, it might be a good idea to pay a visit to the appendix, just to make sure that what *you* mean by, let's say, a Decorator pattern, is the same thing that I mean. I also think you will find the treatment there to be interesting and enjoyable.

By placing this information in an appendix, however, I leave the choice of when and how to use the information in your hands. Also, if you visit the Bibliography, you will find some recommendations for other books on patterns that I have found useful, and hope you will too.

Summary

Understanding what patterns are *not* is almost as important as understanding what they *are*, because misunderstanding their essential nature tends to cause them to be misused, overused, and finally abandoned by those who become frustrated with them.

In building my backyard table, I came to understand that the patterns are meant to provide you with wisdom, and to support your design process—not replace it. That's good news to me, because I don't really want my thinking to be replaced; I just want to make better decisions and to have a way to share what I learn with other developers. Used this way, patterns are more flexible, less constraining, and enable us to communicate rich ideas without limiting our thinking needlessly.

Next, we'll put patterns into the context of evolution, and to show how they both promote and are supported by good principles, practices, and qualities.

Chapter 6

Building a Pyramid

By this point, I hope I have established some goals for the rest of the book. As a teacher, I've noticed that it is very useful to put ideas into a context, to see how and why we are approaching them in the order we are, how one idea (like test-driven development) pertains to another idea (like patterns), and so forth.

It's time to start that process, and so I'm introducing the visual concept of "building a pyramid" to help you to absorb the rest of the book in just such a context.

Elements of the Profession

Disciplines, practices, principles, patterns, wisdom, and guidance accompany any defined profession. They are the essential elements that allow members of the profession to increase their efficiency and their rate of success. For the profession to grow, mature, and succeed, it is necessary to find the right elements and to ensure that they are understood in the right way.

There is a fundamental synergy between these elements.

- Understanding the qualities of code that make it maintainable leads us to make low-level decisions that end up being consistent with wise advice about design.
- Trying to make a design testable drives the code into higher quality.

- Following a simple practice like programming by intention helps us to see certain well-known patterns in our code, and to improve the cohesion of methods.
- Patterns are examples of following advice, adhering to practice, capitalizing on wisdom, and seeking high-quality code, from the past.

Sometimes, it is easier to understand, absorb, and retain these elements when they are placed into a context. For people who are linear thinkers, this book will help. It is laid out in a linear fashion, showing a progression of thought. If you are like me, more of a visual thinker, it might be helpful to see this context through a diagram. Figure 6.1 illustrates the essential elements of software development.

- *Emergent design* is the process of evolving systems in response to changing requirements, better understanding of existing requirements, and in response to new opportunities that arise from new technology, better ideas, and a changing world. To create efficiencies and minimize risk, it depends up the disciplines of test-driven development and pattern-oriented development.
- *Test-driven development (TDD)*, which provides coverage for refactoring and drives toward high-quality design when a particular pattern is not clear, or perhaps does not apply, and:
- *Pattern-oriented development (POD)*, which teaches us to use patterns as a way of aggregating best-practices, wisdom, and well-known variations of general solutions to problems in a context. Both TDD and POD depend upon key knowledge sets and skills including unit testing, refactoring, and patterns.
- Developers do the *testing*. Developers test in a different way and for different reasons than Quality Assurance experts do. Every developer should know how to write unit tests, even if he never actually writes one.
- Evolution requires change and *refactoring* is a disciplined way of making change, while exposing the project to significantly less risk. It allows us to introduce design at a later period, especially through the concept of *refactoring to open-closed*. Knowing you can do this reduces the design to over-design.

- Knowing *patterns* is a way of increasing your general understanding of good object-oriented design. Not every good design is a pattern, but every pattern is a good design, and the more patterns you know, the broader your understanding of what makes a design strong. Patterns are established through an underlying foundation comprised of wisdom, principles, practices, and pathologies.

- There is *wisdom* to build on. The gray hairs that came before us have wisdom to share. The Gang of Four (Erich Gamma, Richard Helm, Ralph Johnson, JohnVlissides), Martin Fowler, Bob Martin, Ivar Jacobsen, and so on have been down roads similar to those that face us today, and have learned lessons (sometimes at great cost) that we can now benefit from, if we pay attention to them.

- *Principles* are like distilled wisdom. If we distill the wisdom that comes from experience, we can discover certain universal concepts that can guide us, in a general way, in everything we do.

- Every profession has its *practices*. There are simple things that every profession discovers as universally beneficial. When we discover these things, and if we can determine that they are, in fact, universal, we strengthen ourselves fundamentally. This is all the more true if we can agree, as a community, on what these practices are.

- Knowing when you are on a wrong track is as important as knowing what the right track is. Defining well-known *pathologies* is a way of determining the wrongness of a design decision as early as possible, when its effect is as small as possible. Like patterns, they also give us a way to discuss these issues with other developers with high confidence that we are communicating well. Of course, everything in the preceding reflects and depends upon a good understanding of the following essential element.

- *Quality* is in the code. At the end of the road, there is always the code. The code is the pointy end of the sword, and no system will survive much evolution when the code is wrong.

A Visual Representation

Given these synergies and interrelationships, Figure 6.1 might help you to keep this more clearly in your mind.

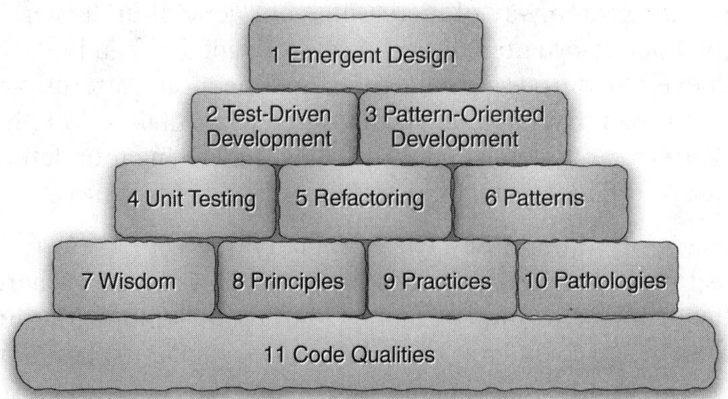

Figure 6.1 Disciplines, practices, principles, patterns, wisdom, guidance

Whether this diagram helps to clarify these interrelationships or whether the text that preceded it makes more sense to you, I hope you can see how an investigation of each of these topics will inform your understanding of those that are below, above, and beside them.

In addition, this gives another view of contextual design. There are essentially two kinds of context that we must focus on when creating software: domain context and universal context. Domain context comes from the problem you are solving and is different every time. Universal context is the collection of things that we know are always true, regardless of the problem. Our pyramid is populated by those things that I am suggesting are always important to focus on.

The next few chapters are all about these individual topics, presented as the key things I suggest we should pay attention to in order to promote the professionalism I believe we are looking for, and to enable us to design emergently.

Summary

I believe that building software is a process of evolution, not a process of "plan, do, review." I also think the process of building a capability in oneself is incremental. Reading a book or taking a course can never be enough but is always a starting point. Separating our key concepts into individual chapters will allow you to tackle each thing one at a time.

Also, some of this you know. In fact, you might know something very well (perhaps you're an expert on unit testing, mock objects, and the like), whereas something else might be new to you (very few people consider patterns as collections of forces, in my experience).

My recommendation is that you take the book in the order I present it, but when you get to a new idea, allow yourself to slow down, try one thing at a time, and move on only when you feel comfortable.

Just like our software, we simply want to be on an upward path with our own development. So long as we're not decaying, we'll get there.

CHAPTER 7

Paying Attention to Qualities and Pathologies

Historically, code has been more fun to write than to read. Writing code feels creative, progressive, and allows the author to express ideas and explore them. Reading code is tedious, sometimes confusing, and can sap one's confidence when puzzling out the intent of a piece of code.

Developers have often said that languages like C and APL are write-only languages, a sobriquet that is fairly applied to any code that is cheaper to rewrite than to figure out, when it comes time to make a change. But to say that something is cheaper to rewrite than to fix is to say that it is unmaintainable, and maintainability is one of the goals I am espousing in this book.

What would it take to write maintainable code? I suggest that it takes, at minimum, the following.

- The code must be clear. You should be able to tell, quickly and after a cursory read, what the code is intended to do, what the individual parts are for, and how they interact. Ideally, class names, method names, and method signatures should tell the bulk of the story.
- You should be able to change the code in one part of the system without adversely (or unknowingly) affecting some other part of the system. There should be no ripple effects. You should not have to wince when you make a change.
- When you need to change something, it should be obvious where the change goes, and that should be only one place in the system. In other words, once you find it, you should be able to, with confidence, stop looking elsewhere for it.

- When you make a change, you should be able to validate that you made the change you intended, that you did not change anything else, and that this validation is quick and relatively low-cost to achieve.

In this chapter, I am going to examine the qualities that describe code that is in this state. Then, as another way of considering these key concepts, I will examine the pathologies (indicators of illness) that help us to see when we are *not* writing code with these qualities.

Once I understand what I am looking for in quality code, I will have a much easier time evaluating a given piece of code and making changes to it that bring it in line with these qualities.

The Concept of the First Principle

A *first principle* is a basic principle from which other principles follow. First principles are powerful because they allow you to encapsulate a large amount of wisdom into a single point. An example of a first principle is the golden rule: Do unto others as you would have them do unto you. If you have kids, you have probably realized at one point or another that if you could get your children to follow this rule, you would be 90% of the way toward making them into good citizens. This is because most of the other rules we want our kids to follow actually are extensions of this one basic rule. That makes it a first principle.

In object orientation, we have several first principles that help to guide us at every phase of a project. A few are

- What you hide you can change (encapsulation).
- A thing should do what it says it does, and nothing else (cohesion).

Throughout this book, I will be looking for first principles, and pointing them out whenever I find them. A good first principle should be easy to remember and easy to understand, and it should be clear why it is important and what benefits we will gain by following it.

I am going to look for

- Encapsulation
- Cohesion
- Coupling
- Redundancy
- Readability
- Testability

Encapsulation

Maintainability is the goal—the ability to change the code without fear, without hesitation, and without feeling resistance. To work in an evolutionary style, we must see change not as an enemy, but as an ally, as a good thing, as something we are actually eager to do.

That is a tall order indeed.

One of our most important allies in this quest is encapsulation.

Encapsulation is a fancy word for hiding. We hide one part of the system from another part of the system, and in so doing we prevent one possible place where we might do unforeseen harm.

If a system is fundamentally encapsulated, we are fundamentally free to change it. If a system largely lacks encapsulation, we are not free, and thus the system cannot evolve.

Although the things that follow—coupling, cohesion, and redundancy—are, in fact, the key qualities that define good (changeable) code, encapsulation is a first principle, because it guides us toward them.

First, we will examine each of these qualities, and then discuss how each relates to encapsulation.

Cohesion

Cohesion is an often misunderstood term. I think it may be due to the fact that it sounds a lot like adhesion, and so people think it means "how well things are stuck together." I have heard people describing a team of developers as a "good, cohesive team," meaning that they get along well together and work closely without conflict.

As nice as this may be for the team, it has nothing to do with cohesion.

Cohesion refers to how much (or how little) the internal parts of something are working on the same issue, and how well they relate to each other. It is the quality of single-mindedness or singleness of purpose, and it makes entities (classes, methods) easier to name and understand.

For example, a team is strongly cohesive if it has established an identity and all of its members are working toward the same goal, in a consistent manner, regardless of their personal feelings for each other. One clear sign of cohesion is how easy it is to put a name to something. If you can call a team "the GUI team," then likely everyone in it is working on the Graphical User Interface, which may indicate or help to bring about strong cohesion. If you have to refer to them as "the team that does the GUI, the database proxies, and some of the business logic," then the team is going to have a tougher time being cohesive.[1] Even if the members of the team are best buddies.

Cohesion in our code is much like this. One can consider cohesion at the method level, the class level, or even at higher levels like package, application, system, solution. For my purposes, method- and class-cohesion is all I will need.

Method Cohesion

Consider the following code.

```
public class Application {
  public void process(String[] words) {
    // Loop through the array of Strings
    for(int i=0; i<words.length; i++) {
      String argument = "";
      // Reverse the characters in each String
      for(int j=words[i].length(); j>0; j--){
        argument += words[i].substring(j-1,j);
      }
      System.out.println(argument);
    }
    // Test for two particular Strings
    if(words.length == 2){
      if(words[0].toLowerCase().equals("mighty") &&
```

1. A team of human beings, of course, can be quite effective but lack cohesion. A cross-functional team, for example, can be a good thing. I just want to make it clear what this word means, and to suggest that software entities (which are not intelligent) should be cohesive.

```
            words[1].toLowerCase().equals("mouse"))
            System.out.println("...here he comes to save the day.");
        }
    }

    public static void main(String[] args){
        Application myApp = new Application();
        myApp.process(args);
    }
}
```

This is a simple little application that takes any parameters passed on the command line, reverses the characters, tests for the name of a remarkable fellow, and then makes an appropriate comment.

But it has weak cohesion.

Why?

A clue lies in the generic quality of the method name `process()`. It does not tell us what the method does because to name the method properly it would have to be something like

```
reverseCharactersAndTestForMightyMouse()
```

Difficult-to-name methods are a good sign that you have weak method cohesion.

In essence, the method `process()` is doing too much, and it is doing things that are not related to each other. Reversing the order of characters in each `String` parameter and testing them all together for a particular name are activities that have nothing to do with one another.

We could fix this by putting these different steps into their own methods, then calling those methods from `process()`, such as in the following code.

```
public class Application {

    public void process(String[] words) {
        for(int i=0; i<words.length; i++) {
            reverseCharacters(words[i]);
            System.out.println(words[i]);
        }
        if(isMightyMouse(words)) {
            System.out.println("...here he comes to save the day.");
        }
    }
```

```
  private String reverseCharacters(String forward){
    String reverse = "";
      for(int j=forward.length(); j>0; j--){
        reverse += forward.substring(j-1,j);
      }
      return reverse;
  }

  private boolean isMightyMouse(String[] names){
    boolean rval = false;
    if(names.length == 2){
      if(names[0].toLowerCase().equals("mighty") &&
         names[1].toLowerCase().equals("mouse"))
         rval = true;
    }
    return rval;
  }

  public static void main(String[] args){
    Application myApp = new Application();
    myApp.process(args);
  }
}
```

When I read the `process()` method, I am reading a series of steps, each step accomplished by another method. `process()` has become an organizing method, a scaffold that creates the general shape of the behavior, but then delegates the actual steps to other methods.

The methods `reverseCharacters()` and `isMightyMouse()` are easy to name because they each do a single, identifiable thing. It also helps with debugging. If the characters are not reversing properly, I know exactly where to look to find the bug, because the responsibility for doing this is clearly assigned to the properly named method, and only that method.

Cohesion of Perspective Level

Another aspect of cohesion you should be aware of is the level of perspective at which a method operates. Put simply, methods tend to accomplish their functionality by either of the following.

- Code logic directly in the method
- Calling other methods

The preceding `process()` method has a little bit of logic in it, but it is purely for sequencing the other methods and organizing the results of their actions. Mostly, `process()` calls `reverseCharacters()` and `isMightyMouse()`, where the actual work is done. This *aggregation of behavior* that `process()` does is at a level of perspective we call *specification*.

Levels of Perspective

In *UML Distilled,* Martin Fowler refers to the levels of perspective that Steve Cook and John Daniels identified in their book *Designing Object Systems.*

The three types of perspective are *conceptual, specification,* and *implementation.*

- The *conceptual* perspective deals with the system objects, which ideally represent entities in the problem domain I am writing for. If I am designing an application for a bank, these might be account, transaction, statement, customer, and the like.
- *Specification* means the public methods that form the interface of each object, but also the private methods to which they are delegated (see the example code on this page). So, `process()`, being the only public method of Application, is decidedly a specification-level issue, but from the point of view of `process()`, so are `reverseCharacters()` and `isMightyMouse()`. This is because `process()` is concerned with what they do (how they are called, what they return), but not how they do it.
- *Implementation* is concerned with the code that does the actual work. Nice that we still have that, eh?

The `reverseCharacters()` and `isMightyMouse()` methods are implementation-level methods; they have the code that does the dirty work.

It would be overstating things to suggest that I always write methods that are purely at one level of perspective or another—even here, `process()` has a little bit of logic in it, not just a series of method calls.

But my goal is to be as cohesive as possible in terms of levels of perspective, mostly because it makes the code easier to read and understand.

It would not be overstating things to suggest that I always strive to write methods that are cohesive in the general sense, that they contain code that is all about the same issue or purpose. When I find poorly cohesive methods, I am going to change them, every time, because I know that method cohesion is a principle that will help me create maintainable code, and that is something I want for myself, let alone my team and my customer.

Class Cohesion

Classes themselves also need to be cohesive. The readability, maintenance, and clarity issues that, in part, drive the need for method cohesion also motivate class cohesion.

In addition, we know we want our classes to define objects that are responsible for themselves, that are well-understood entities in the problem domain. A typical mistake that developers who are new to object orientation make is to define their classes in terms of the software itself, rather than in terms of the problem being solved. For instance, consider the following code.

```
public class BankingSystem {
  // No "method guts" are provided; this is just a
  // conceptual example
  public void addCustomer(String cName, String cAddress,
                          String accountNumber,
                          double balance) {}
  public void removeCustomer(String accountNumber) {}
  public double creditAccount(String accountNumber,
                              double creditAmount) {}
  public double debitAccount(String accountNumber,
                             double debitAmount) {}
  public boolean checkSufficientFunds(String accountNumber,
                                      double checkAmount) {}
  public void sendStatement(String accountNumber) {}
  public boolean qualifiesForFreeToaster(String accountNumber){}
  public boolean transferFunds(String fromAccount,
                               String toAccount,
                               double transferAmount) {}
}
```

It is easy to imagine the thought process that leads to code like this: "I am writing a banking system, and so I will name the class for what it is, a `BankingSystem`. What does a banking system do? Well, I need to be able to add and remove customers, manage their accounts by adding to them and withdrawing from them," and so on.

It is an assignment of responsibilities, but in the software sense. This comes from the procedural days, from what we called functional decomposition, and it essentially robs us of most of the power of object orientation. Object orientation allows us to model systems by discovering the entities that exist in the problem domain itself, and then assign them responsibilities that make sense for the way the business runs or the game plays, and so on.

What are the entities in the problem domain "banking"? Account, Customer, Statement—these are a few of them, and each of these should be its *own* class. There may be a `BankingSystem` class, but it will use these other classes to accomplish the responsibilities that they rightly have assigned to them.

Why is this important?

- One of the powerful concepts of object orientation is that software should model the problem directly, so that its structure and behavior are logical in terms of the issues being solved. Just as you would not organize a physical bank by having one big drawer in a file cabinet marked "Stuff", you should not model the problem in software this way either.

- Breaking the problem into classes with responsibilities makes the system easier to test, debug, and therefore maintain. If the statements are not printing properly, I know to look at the Statement class, or one of the classes it collaborates with, to find the problem. Mentally, I can focus myself in a very narrow way on the issue, rather than wade through a lot of unrelated material that will distract and confuse me.

- If I have to add something later, a new kind of customer or a new kind of account, then having discreet classes that deal with these issues gives me a place to make the changes and additions without affecting the rest of the system; we will actually see how this works later when we *refactor to the open-closed,* but without breaking the problem down into entities with responsibilities, this would be much harder or even impossible to do.

How Cohesive Is Cohesive Enough?

Assuming that class cohesion is important and that it will benefit me in terms of easy maintenance and extensibility in my project, how do I determine if my classes are cohesive?

First, simply being aware that this is important is half the battle. If I look at my classes with the "is this cohesive?" question firmly in my mind, I can probably make a pretty good determination. That said, there are some good metrics to use as well.

- A strongly cohesive class will have methods that access the same data members of the class frequently. If you count up the number of methods that access a key data member of the class, and then divide that by the total number of methods the class has, you have a metric that will allow you to compare one class to another, in terms of cohesion.
- A strongly cohesive class is difficult to break up into multiple classes. Ask yourself how hard it would be to break up a class, how much of each component class would have to be exposed through public methods to the other component classes; if the number is high, then likely the class is cohesive to begin with.
- As with methods, a strongly cohesive class should be easy to name, and the name should accurately and completely describe what the class is. Vague, generic, or lengthy class names can be an indication that the class is weakly cohesive and should be broken up.
- If your unit test is significantly larger than the class, or can fail in the same way for multiple reasons, this can be an indicator of weak cohesion. When a class contains multiple, unrelated issues, the test must test them all, and all their possible combinations. This is because once you are "inside" a class, you lose much of your opportunity to encapsulate.

This last point is, perhaps, my best answer today. When someone asks me "how small should my objects be," "when should I stop pulling things out of an object," or any of a dozen questions that are similar to these, I find the answer is nearly always "once you can write a good unit test for it, you've probably gone far enough."

Coupling

Coupling is a general term that describes the situation where one part of a system affects another part of the system in some way. Often, in object orientation, we are talking about two classes—one class is coupled to the other, if a change in the second class will cause a change (or a need for a change) in the first. Coupling is usually spoken of in terms of it being a problem, but in fact coupling is not bad in all cases.

In fact, some coupling is absolutely necessary, since a system with no coupling would not be a system at all. Coupling, in the good sense, is how individual objects are combined to create the overall system.

We do not want coupling that

- We did not intend
- We did intend, but we do not actually need

Intentional Coupling Versus Accidental Coupling

Bad coupling is usually termed *tight* coupling. Logical, necessary, helpful coupling is called *loose* coupling. Loose coupling is ideal; tight coupling is to be avoided.

I am not wild about these terms, frankly. For one thing, they do not stick in my mind, and I always forget whether loose or tight is the bad one. They both sound bad, in a way—loose things fall apart and tight things are hard to take apart and change.

My point is that part of what we are doing in promoting software development as a profession is getting terms like this more clearly defined, and to make sure they inform what we do.

To me, good coupling is coupling I (or you) put into the system on purpose, to achieve an end or solve a problem. The coupling that seems to "get me" is the coupling that I did not realize I had because it crept into the system without any intent on my part.

So, I use the terms *intentional* for good coupling and *accidental* for bad. It is not difficult to remember that accidental is bad—just think of a car wreck.

Coupling can occur at any level, from the code within a method to the architecture of the system overall. It can even occur in your driveway (see the following sidebar).

Driveway Coupling

I bought a new car a few years ago.

The next morning I went out to my car, got in, and started it. Once it was running, I tried to put it into reverse gear, but it would not go. The lever that selects from Park, Neutral, Drive, and Reverse would not move from Park to Reverse.

I was disappointed, and I called the dealer to explain the problem I was having. "Ah, yes, that always happens," he said. This was not what I wanted to hear. I had selected a car model that routinely broke its transmission?

That was not what he meant. "People are always confused about this model . . . and we always forget to tell them for some reason. To put that car into gear, you need to put your foot on the brake."

Okay. So it would not have gone into Drive or Neutral either, since my foot was not depressing the brake pedal. I did not know that because I was not trying to go into anything but Reverse (this is one reason beta testing is so difficult to get right). I was on a cell phone, so I tried it while the dealer was still on, and it worked.

"We sometimes just put our foot on the brake naturally when we start the car, so sometimes people do not run into this for a few days," he went on, "but invariably someone will call, within the first week, and report a failed transmission."

"Why did they engineer it this way?" I asked. The designer in me was curious.

"It is to make sure your foot is not on the gas. People use their same foot for the gas and the brake, so if the foot is on the brake, it is not on the gas." he explained. That seemed to make sense.

But later I began to think. Why didn't they just hook up a sensor up to the gas pedal? I may or may not put my foot on the brake when I go into gear, but I certainly will not be accelerating at that point. In fact, that was the concern—that I not put the car into gear while revving the engine. I reasoned that they did it because there was already a sensor on the brake pedal, for the brake light, and since there is no accelerate light, they would have had to add something to sense that the gas pedal was depressed.

This is bad coupling. The brake system and the transmission do not, logically, interconnect. My expectation did not include this as a possibility, and the reason the dealer forgets to tell people about this is that it is no more logical to him that it is to me. He does not remember.

I routinely forget to tell people about this rule when they are going to drive my car. It is not a rule that is explicitly part of braking or getting into gear. It was a kluge that was designed this way for the manufacturer's convenience. I imagine that someday, if my transmission needs to be fixed, the repairman will forget to hook up the line from the transmission to the brake pedal, and he too will think the thing is broken. He will forget to hook it up because it is not expected, not intuitive, not logical that he should have to—even the dealer forgot, after all.

And this poor repairman will chase his tail for hours, trying to figure out why the car will not go into gear any more. And I will sympathize.

I have had to maintain code.

Types of Coupling

For emergent design, class coupling is going to be our primary concern. It can be broken down into four types.

- *Identity coupling.* This is when one entity knows about the existence of another entity. It does not know how to use the other entity (does not access its public members), but simply knows that the entity, the type, exists. If a class A is designed to hold a collection of instances of class B, and needs to type check them when they are added to make sure they are indeed instances of B, then we have identity coupling from class A to class B.
- *Representational coupling.* This is when one entity calls public methods or accesses public data members on another entity to fulfill part of its own responsibility. This is also coupling because if the public interface of the second entity changes, then the first entity needs to change too.

- *Subclass coupling.* When a base type (usually class) has a number of derived types that extend it, other types should ideally only know about the base type. If all the subtypes share the same public interface (the public members inherited from the base type, overwritten for different behavior in each subclass), then outside "client" types can treat them all the same, as if they were the base class. If this is not so, if a client type knows specifics about the subtypes that exist, then this is subclass coupling to the polymorphic structure in question.
- *Inheritance coupling.* A subclass is inherently coupled to its superclass, because changes in the superclass will cause changes to the subclass due to inheritance. This is usually a good and powerful kind of coupling, because it helps to eliminate redundancy in the subclasses. However, it needs to be kept under conscious control, and can certainly be overused.

Avoiding subclass coupling and making proper use of inheritance coupling is the subject of many of the design patterns we are going to explore a bit later, so we will leave that discussion for those chapters. However, identity and representational coupling are easy to illustrate. See the following code.

```
import java.util.*;
public class WidgetContainer {
  ArrayList myWidgetList = new ArrayList();

  public void addWidget(Widget aWidget) {
    myWidgetList.add(aWidget);
  }

  public Iterator getWidgets() {
    return myWidgetList.iterator();
  }

}

public class Widget {
  public void widgetyBehavior() {
    System.out.println("Just being a Widget...");
  }
```

```
  public void storeSelf(WidgetContainer wc) {
    wc.addWidget(this);
  }
}

public class WidgetClient{
  public static void main(String[] args) {
    WidgetContainer myWidgetContainer = new WidgetContainer();
    for(int i=0; i<10; i++) {
      // Make a new widget, and have it store itself in the
      // container
      new Widget().storeSelf(myWidgetContainer);
    }
  }
}
```

Here we have `WidgetClient` creating 10 shiny new widgets, and then telling them to store themselves in a `WidgetContainer`.

`WidgetContainer` has identity coupling to `Widget`. You can see this because of the method

```
public void addWidget(Widget aWidget)
```

. . . which references the type `Widget`. The parameter `aWidget` is declared to be of type `Widget`. But none of the methods on any `aWidget` are ever called, so there is no representational coupling here. Change `Widget` all you want, and `WidgetContainer` does not mind, but remove `Widget` entirely and `WidgetContainer` breaks. This is why it is called identity coupling, because `WidgetContainer` is coupled to the existence of `Widget`. It comes to us from the mathematical principle of identity (a = a). This coupling is good, logical, explicit; I like to call it *intentional,* because it makes perfect sense for a type-safe container of something to know that the something exists, and what its type is.

`WidgetClient` has identity coupling to both `WidgetContainer` and `Widget`, which also makes sense since it's using one to contain the other. It creates a single `WidgetContainer`, and then creates a series of widgets and calls the `storeSelf()` method on each.

But then we see some oddities. Let's make a table of all the coupling we find here (see Table 7.1).

Table 7.1 Coupling found in the code

Class	Coupled to	Type of Coupling
`Widget`	`WidgetContainer`	Identity and Representational
`WidgetContainer`	`Widget`	Identity
`WidgetClient`	`Widget`	Identity and Representational
`WidgetClient`	`WidgetContainer`	Identity

`Widget` has identity and representational coupling to `WidgetContainer`. That is unexpected, since there is really no reason for the contained to know about the container.

Widget not only knows that `WidgetContainer` exists, but if you examine the code you will see that in Widget's `storeSelf()` method it calls the `addWidget()` method on the `WidgetContainer` that was passed in to the method, so there is coupling to that interface as well (which is representational coupling, coupling to the public face of another object, the way it represents itself to the outside world).

Furthermore, `WidgetClient` does not have representational coupling to `WidgetContainer` (it just makes one), but does have representational coupling to Widget (it calls the `storeSelf()` method on `Widget`). That is odd, because logically, if `WidgetClient` is using a `WidgetContainer` to store a Widget, we would expect `WidgetClient` to have representational coupling to the thing it is using, namely `WidgetContainer`.

Remember that we want our system to be as logical and as sensible as possible because we may have to figure out how it works six months from now, when much of our current understanding has been forgotten.

Finally, we have a bidirectional couple here: `WidgetContainer` and `Widget` have identity coupling to each other. In general, any time I see a bidirectional coupling like this, I start to get suspicious about the design, and wonder if it could be decoupled. Bidirectional coupling is especially bad because neither of the classes can be changed (or in this case, eliminated) without affecting the other.

The following code illustrates a better way.

```
import java.util.*;
public class WidgetContainer {
  ArrayList myWidgetList = new ArrayList();
```

```
  public void addWidget(Widget aWidget) {
    myWidgetList.add(aWidget);
  }

  public Iterator getWidgets() {
    return myWidgetList.iterator();
  }

}

public class Widget {
  public void widgetyBehavior() {
    System.out.println("Just being a Widget...");
  }
}

public class WidgetClient{
  public static void main(String[] args) {
    WidgetContainer myWidgetContainer = new WidgetContainer();
    for(int i=0; i<10; i++) {
      myWidgetContainer.addWidget(new Widget());
    }
  }
}
```

The coupling now is explicit, logical, expected. Let's see who is coupled to whom and how. Take a look at Table 7.2.

`Widget` is coupled to nothing at all. You can change anything you like in this system, and `Widget` will not break.

There is no bidirectional coupling here.

Table 7.2 Coupling after redesign

Class	Coupled to	Type of Coupling
`Widget`	Nothing	None
`WidgetContainer`	`Widget`	Identity
`WidgetClient`	`Widget`	Identity
`WidgetClient`	`WidgetContainer`	Identity and Representational

The only representational coupling that exists is in `WidgetClient`, which has representational coupling to `WidgetContainer`. Because we said all along that it uses the container to store its widgets, we would expect it to have representational coupling, and it does. This is not hard to remember, or to reconstruct in the future, because it makes sense that it works this way.

`Widget` now only fulfills its `widgetyBehavior()`.

Making objects responsible for themselves can be a misleading prescription, because it can lead to methods like `storeSelf()` in the first version of `Widget`. The problem lies in determining who is responsible for what.

Storing is not part of the widget-ish behavior, so it is not part of `Widget`'s responsibility. If `Widget` does not know about the `WidgetContainer`, we can use `Widgets` in scenarios where they are stored, not stored, stored in different ways, whatever, without changing `Widget`.

Try compiling the first version of `Widget` without a `WidgetContainer` in your project, and it does not compile. The second one does, because it is not coupled to the identity of `WidgetContainer`. In the first version of `Widget`, you would never be able to put `Widget` into a project without `WidgetContainer`, even if you were not using the container for anything. That alone should illustrate why it is bad or accidental coupling.

Redundancy

We all saw an example of redundancy rearing its nasty head just a few years ago.

The Y2K remediation effort cost countless billions of dollars, scared the heck out of entire countries, and in general disrupted progress in the technology sector. Many companies basically stopped doing any kind of new projects in the latter part of 1999, because they were putting their resources into fixing the Y2K bug.

What made Y2K hard to fix? Was it a complex problem? No! Not at all. Systems all over the world had stored the year portion of the date in innumerable records as a two-digit number, rather than a four-digit number. Not a complex problem at all.

Except that it appeared in billions of places, all of which had to be found and changed.

We can criticize the Cobol, RPG, etc. . . . programmers who wrote the original code this way, but the fact is I find redundancies in my own code and the code of colleagues all the time. It is easy to do; it tends to creep in on you, especially when you are creating an extension to a new system. Also, some aspects of the languages we use can promote redundancy. Consider the following code.

```
public interface Weapon{
  public void load(int rounds);
  public int fire();
  public void setSafety(boolean on);
}

public class Pistol implements Weapon{
  private int myBullets;
  private boolean safety = true;

  public void load(int bullets){
    if(bullets<=6){
       myBullets = bullets;
    } else {
      System.out.println("Pistol only holds 6 bullets");
    }
  }

  public int fire(){
    int rval = 0;
    if(safety){
       System.out.println("The Safety is on");
    } else {
       if(myBullets > 0) {
          System.out.println("Bang!");
          myBullets = myBullets - 1;
          rval = 10;
       } else System.out.println("Click!");
    }
    return rval;
  }

  public void setSafety(boolean aSetting){
    safety = aSetting;
  }
}
```

```
public class TommyGun implements Weapon{
  private int myBullets;
  private boolean safety = true;

  public void load(int bullets){
    if(bullets<=50){
        myBullets = bullets;
    } else {
      System.out.println("TommyGun only holds 50 bullets");
    }
  }

  public int fire(){
    int rval = 0;
    if(safety){
        System.out.println("The Safety is on");
    } else {
        if(myBullets > 9) {
           System.out.println("Budda Budda Budda!");
           myBullets = myBullets - 10;
           rval = 100;
        } else System.out.println("Click!");
    }
    return rval;
  }

  public void setSafety(boolean aSetting){
    safety = aSetting;
  }
}
```

There are lots of redundancies here—the way `setSafety()` is completely identical in both `Pistol` and `TommyGun`, for example. If I want to change the way this works—make the state persistent by writing it to the disk every time, for instance—then I must remember to change it in both places.

The Java and .Net interface type leads me to this inherently; it tends to create redundancies among the implementing classes. This is because the interface cannot have any actual implementation, so I cannot put common implementation into it, and allow the implementing classes to inherit.

What if I used an abstract class instead? Look at the following code.

```
public abstract class Weapon{
  protected int myBullets;
  protected boolean safety = true;
```

```
  public abstract void load(int rounds);
  public abstract int fire();

  public void setSafety(boolean aSetting){
   safety = aSetting;
  }

}

public class Pistol extends Weapon{

  public void load(int bullets){
    if(bullets<=6){
       myBullets = bullets;
    } else {
      System.out.println("Pistol only holds 6 bullets");
    }
  }

  public int fire(){
    int rval = 0;
    if(safety){
      System.out.println("The Safety is on");
    } else {
      if(myBullets > 0) {
         System.out.println("Bang!");
         myBullets = myBullets - 1;
         rval = 10;
      } else System.out.println("Click!");
    }
    return rval;
  }
}

public class TommyGun extends Weapon{

  public void load(int bullets){
    if(bullets<=50){
       myBullets = bullets;
    } else {
      System.out.println("TommyGun only holds 50 bullets");
    }
  }

  public int fire(){
    int rval = 0;
    if(safety){
```

```
            System.out.println("The Safety is on");
        } else {
            if(myBullets > 9) {
                System.out.println("Budda Budda Budda!");
                myBullets = myBullets - 10;
                rval = 100;
            } else System.out.println("Click!");
        }
        return rval;
    }
}
```

I have eliminated some of the redundancy already: The `setSaftey()` method is now in one place, inherited by both `Pistol` and `TommyGun`. Also, the data members `myBullets` and safety were common, so I put them in the superclass too and made them protected so the subclasses could still access them directly.

There's more I could do, of course. The weapons both operate in a conceptually similar way, only the details vary. If I am lucky enough to know the Template Method pattern, I could pretty easily get rid of all the other bits of redundancy here, without sacrificing any of the uniqueness of these two weapons.

Do you know that pattern? If not, look it up in Appendix B, "Overview of Patterns Used in the Examples," and see if the contextual forces of that pattern seem to lead you to it, given this problem.

Redundancy and Coupling

But haven't I introduced coupling in order to deal with the redundancy problem? The abstract superclass puts one rule in one place, but it also means that a change in the superclass (`Weapon`) will have an effect on the subclasses (`Pistol` and `TommyGun`). This is inheritance coupling, certainly, so have I traded one problem for another?

No, not really. Remember, accidental coupling is coupling that arises unintentionally, or for a misguided, unnecessary reason. Intentional coupling is coupling I intend, and which helps my project. I am generally not stupid, and neither are you. What we do on purpose is usually better than what happens beneath our notice.

Here, I am introducing inheritance coupling in order to solve the redundancy problem. I want changes in `Weapon` to propagate down to `Pistol` and `TommyGun`. It is my intent that this happen; it is no accident, and I am not liable to forget that it is going to happen. I am going to depend on it, in fact.

Protected Data Members

In my gun toting example, I used protected members `myBullets` and safety in the abstract class `Weapon`, so that I could access them via inheritance in the same way that I had been accessing them when they were local, private members of `Pistol` and `TommyGun`.

My next step is to change this. I would make `myBullets` and safety private, and then declare protected or public methods to `get()` them and `set()` them. Why?

We said that inheritance creates coupling. That can be a good thing, as it in the case of eliminating the redundancies we have dealt with. But a bad kind of inheritance coupling can emerge with protected data members.

With protected data members, subclasses are coupled to the existence of those members. If I later want to store the bullets outside the `Weapon` object, maybe in a `Clip` or `Magazine` object, I will now have to change `Pistol`, `TommyGun`, and whatever other subclasses I have created to now call methods to get the bullet amount rather than accessing `myBullets` directly. If I make a `getBullets()` method in `Weapon`, then make `Pistol`, `TommyGun`, and so on call it to get the bullet amount, then I can change the way it is stored and retrieved in that one place, `getBullets()`.

Also, with `get()` and `set()` methods, I can create read-only data members (just do not provide a `set()` method), or write-only, or I can put validating code into the `set()`, and so on.

This is such an important thing that it has lead to the creation of an entirely new language feature in .Net: the property.

Generally, protected data members are a bad idea. Public data members are even worse.

With that said, design at this level is often a balancing act between coupling and redundancy. The key is to have a considered reason behind your decision to keep things in the subclasses (at the cost of redundancy) or to put them in the superclass (at the cost of coupling them). If you have a sensible motivation that drives this decision, that sensibility will likely mean that the approach is clear and explicit, and will not cause maintenance problems.

Furthermore, the decisions you make are not set in stone. Remember, you are embarking on an evolutionary process here. You can expect to change things as you learn more about the project, as the requirements expand and change, and as you have new, better ideas. Refactoring, and adherence to your coding principles, will give you the confidence to make changes when this occurs, and your understanding of design (from your knowledge of patterns and commonality-variability analysis, which I'll cover a bit later on) will allow you to see the opportunities that arise for improved design that may result from the change process.

In other words, an emergent design.

Testability

One thing I have learned in recent years is that unit testing actually has great value in terms of evaluating code against these principles (see Chapter 10, "Paying Attention to Disciplines: Unit Testing").

As a consultant, I am usually called in when things are not going well. Companies rarely call in for extra help when everything is fine, after all. Consultants add a lot of expense.

In order to come up to speed on the team's activities, goals, and current situation, I need something to work with. Asking for design and requirements documentation is usually a forlorn hope. If the team is really in trouble, how up-to-date do you suppose these documents are?

However, I have noticed that reading unit tests can be very revealing. In a way, they are a record of the expectation of the developer or tester who wrote them, and therefore can reveal a lot about what a class is supposed to do.

Usually, one of the first questions I ask a customer's development team is whether it is unit testing. Generally, the answer is no.

Furthermore, when I suggest that unit testing might be a good idea, I generally encounter a lot of resistance, with the excuses that unit testing is "too hard," "too time-consuming," "frustrating,"and that it does not bring enough value for the trouble. At first, I would argue with them, until I tried to add tests to their projects, finding that it was all those things and more. This puzzled me, because tests that I wrote simultaneously with the coding were so were much easier, and were clearly worth the time and effort it took to create them. It turns out that code is hard to test when it is not designed to be testable in the first place, and so adding unit tests to an existing code base is awfully difficult.

But why? What is it about bad code that makes it hard to test?

Examining this question over and over again with different customer teams has been incredibly revealing. Some of the most common reasons are

- The class I want to test cannot be tested by itself. It has lots of dependencies that must be up-and-running for it to be able to perform its behavior. Also, this makes the tests slow to run, and therefore we can't run them very often. This makes the whole thing seem "not worth it."
- The class has so many permutations of its behavior that the test, in order to be comprehensive, must be enormous. This is usually the case when a class has multiple responsibilities, each of which can give various results; and so, there are many combinations that must be tested. A valid test must test all possible combinations because there is no way to ensure that there are no side effects inside a class.
- The issue to be tested is actually repeated in many places in the system, and so the tests will be very redundant and hard to maintain.

All of these represent design problems anyway! In the first case, I would suggest that there is too much coupling in the system if units cannot be tested in isolation (or with only a few other units in play). In the second case, I would argue that a class with multiple responsibilities is weakly cohesive in the first place, and will therefore be overly complex and poorly encapsulated. In the third case, if an issue is repeated in the system, there is a redundancy, and I know I do not want that.

In other words, considering the testability of the code I have written (or better yet, am about to write) is a great way to evaluate its quality, even if I cannot quite see how it stacks up in terms of coupling, cohesion, redundancy, and so on. If I cannot see a way to test it, maybe I should rethink what I am planning on doing.

It is like a first principle of first principles. It is one thing I can consider, which will cause me to consider other good things automatically.

Readability

Cohesion, coupling, and redundancy are like the three legs of a stool; you need to address them all if you want reliable stability. For a while, in my courses and when consulting or mentoring, these three were the focus of my attention when it came to coding principles.

However, I have added a fourth concern recently, after having worked with teams that did not address it well, and seeing the results.

Code needs to be readable.

Software developers tend to be intellectually minded people who pride themselves on the complexity of their thoughts, on being able to understand subtle, intricate, even arcane writings and discussions. It is a stimulating mental challenge to them to see how much they can do with a single line of code, or how cleverly they can accomplish a mundane task. Readability is for wimps, right? I have actually heard developers say things like, "If you can't read my code, you should not be messing with it," or "I can read my code, and that is all that matters."

The economics of software development say otherwise.

First of all, you may not be the only person who has to read your code. It is quite likely that another developer will have to maintain it in the future after you have been promoted, moved on to another project, or retired to your island in the Caribbean.

Secondly, you may have to read the code in a few months, or even in a few years, when other projects and other clever code have taken over your active memory, and at that point it can seem like reading something written by someone other than yourself.

Also, often good software is a reflection of good teamwork; your ideas may not always be the only ones, or the best ones for the part of the project you are working on. If other people cannot understand your code, how can they contribute their ideas to it? The synergy that comes from allowing multiple minds to address the same problem can be very powerful, and can lead to efficiencies that a single developer alone cannot achieve.

So, what makes for readable code? That is probably the subject of an entire book of its own, but we will address some of the more important aspects in Chapter 9, "Paying Attention to Practices."

Pathologies

It is important to know the qualities you want your code to have, but it is also important to empower yourself with a set of indicators that tell you that you are heading in the wrong direction. Ideally, I would like to know I am doing something I should not do before I have done very much of it. Also, we often are called upon to evaluate other people's code, or to revisit our own code from the recent or distant past.

Pathologies help us here. In truth, code, design, and system pathologies could be the subject of an entire book, but there are a few really high-leverage indicators that we can use as a basic set. Not surprisingly, they tie into the qualities that I listed earlier: coupling, cohesion, and eliminating redundancy.

Indicators of Weak Cohesion

Here are some indicators of weak cohesion.

- *Difficulty naming.* I would like the names of classes, methods, and other entities (delegates, packages, and so on) to reveal their intentions in their names. I would also like my names to be relatively brief, and yet still tell the whole story.

  When a class or method has a long name, or a vague name, the reason often is that a really informative name is very difficult to create, due to the fact that the class or method does a number of different things. This, of course, is weak cohesion, and causes lots of other problems anyway. When I cannot name things the way I want to, I suspect that my entities do too much.

- *Large tests.* When a class has multiple responsibilities, it can create large tests, because the test must cover all the possible combinations of these responsibilities. When I get to the chapter on test-driven development, I will examine this a bit closer, and will also show how the testing point of view can help with the other qualities as well.

- *Large classes and methods.* When a class or a method gets big and requires lots of scrolling in your IDE, or when it is hard to see well, I usually suspect weak cohesion. This is not an absolute; algorithms themselves can get large and yet still be about one responsibility, but it is, at least, something to investigate when I see it.

A student once told me a story that is pretty illustrative and also kind of funny. He was given a class to refactor. Someone had written the class in C#, but clearly did not know much about object orientation. The class worked fine (the author had been, obviously, a skilled programmer), but nobody could or would touch it. It was, essentially, one huge method.

He started by doing what I would probably do; he just scanned through the code without really reading it thoroughly, just to determine how tough this job was going to be. He was, of course, being asked how long this was going to take.

As he scanned along, hitting Page Down over and over, suddenly all the code disappeared from the screen. A few more page downs revealed blank screen after blank screen, and then suddenly the code was back again.

This happened several times. As he paged down through the code, sometimes for pages at a time, there would be nothing but a blank page, and then for pages at a time he would see code again.

He had been working all day, so he suspected that he may have corrupted the memory buffer of his Integrated Development Environment (Visual Studio, in this case). He restarted it. The same problem happened again, so he rebooted. Then he cold started. He checked out a fresh copy of the code from source-control. Same problem.

Now, he really hit the old "wall of voodoo." He figured it must be something strange, like a problem in the operating system or the installation of the IDE. He was, in fact, very close to taking a pretty drastic step and reinstalling either or both of these things.

Then he noticed how small the horizontal scroll button was at the bottom of his IDE.

The problem was actually very simple: the code was so complex, and had to do so much procedurally, that the nesting from the accumulating tabs in the code often pushed all the code off screen to the right, sometimes for pages at a time, until the conditional branching, looping, try/catches, and so forth all closed and the code drifted back to the right.

It was not good news (lots of work to do), but at least he knew it was not his machine. It was a problem with the code, and it was obviously very weakly cohesive.

Indicators of Accidental or Illogical Coupling

Here are some examples of accidental or illogical coupling.

- *Unexpected side effects.* The very thing we hope to avoid by paying attention to coupling is also a key indicator that we have not. When a change in one part of the system changes something in another part of the system, and this is surprising, unexpected, and illogical to you, then most likely there is coupling in the system that was not intended or does not make sense.

- *Hesitancy.* When you find yourself hesitant or resistant to making a change to the system, sometimes this is simply your subconscious telling you that you know the system has coupling in it that is going to "get you" when you try to change it. Of course, ultimately, we are trying to eliminate this hesitancy because we want to be able to evolve systems as we go, but when we feel it, we should pay attention to our own reactions.
- *Comments.* I have a love-hate relationship with comments. Too many comments are not a good thing, because they can get in your way (they make the code longer) and because they often do not get updated when the system changes. However, some comments can really help to make a system more readable and understandable.

  I have come to draw a distinction here. Some comments are about *what the code is doing* and often refer to other parts of the code in their explanation. This is an indicator of a problem. Why is the code simply not readable in the first place? Often, this is because it cannot be, as there are excessive dependencies with other parts of the system. This, of course, is a coupling problem.

  However, other comments are about *why the code is doing what it's doing,* which could reflect business or regulatory rules, and these can be difficult to make clear in the code. I like comments like these: the "why" comments as opposed to the "what" comments.
- *Large test fixtures.* When we examine unit testing, this will make more sense; in short, a unit test needs to create an instance of the class it is designed to test. Sometimes, it has to create other instances too, because the class it is testing needs them to operate. The collection of instances created in a unit test is called *the fixture* for the test by some people (yours truly included). A good overall view of the coupling in a system can be obtained by looking at the suite of unit tests that test it, and taking an average of the number of instances in the fixtures.

  This only works, of course, if the system has tests. Unfortunately, many of the systems that have serious coupling problems do not have tests, because the testing is too difficult.

Indicators of Redundancy

Here are some indicators of redundancy.

- *Redundant changes.* When you find yourself making the same change in multiple places, clearly the thing you are changing is redundant. However, because people tend to think of redundancy only in terms of code and state, they can miss this indicator.

  Here is a very common example: Imagine that the code `new Widget()` appears in several places in your code, because you instantiate that class in many places. Now imagine that the constructor of `Widget` changes. Or, that `Widget` becomes an abstract class, with multiple subclasses that represent different forms of the `Widget`. You will have to make the change(s) in every place where the code `new Widget()` appears. Does that mean you had a redundancy?

  Of course. You are probably thinking, "But wait! I do that all the time!" If you are thinking that, you are not alone, and it is a fairly common source of maintenance headaches. Luckily, I have an easy way out for you, and I will illustrate that in Chapter 9.

- *Inheriting from the Clipboard.* That phrase comes from a student of mine named Boon. She always said that if you copy code from one place and paste it into another, you are obviously creating redundant code. She calls it "inheriting from the Clipboard," which I think it pretty clever and memorable. When you copy code, ask yourself why you are doing it—and if the same operation is needed in two places, doesn't this indicate that you need a service in your system?

My boss and mentor Alan Shalloway puts it this way: There are three numbers in software: 0, 1, and infinity. 0 represents the things we do not do in a system (we do those for free). 1 represents the things we do once and only once. But at the moment we do something twice, we should treat it as infinitely many and create cohesive services that allow it to be reused.

It is helpful to be surrounded by smart people like Boon and Alan, and it is also an advantage of being part of a profession. Other professionals are your resources, and you are theirs.

Summary

I teach different things: design patterns, systems architecture, unit testing, test-driven development, and so forth. I've noticed that no matter what the topic is, so long as it is part of software development, I have to start by making sure that everyone understands the qualities in this chapter.

Of course, many do. However, it's very common to find that two people are using a word like cohesion very differently; or that one person thinks of coupling very simply (it's coupled or it isn't), whereas another has more depth (the different types of coupling).

I don't expect to have taught you anything new or earthshaking here (but if I have, so much the better!). The purpose here was to make sure you're emphasizing the same things I am, and that we're using these terms in the same way, and with the same depth.

Now, we have a foundation to build on.

Chapter 8

Paying Attention to Principles and Wisdom

Another value that a profession provides to its members is to define the overall principles that can guide them to success, with a relatively high degree of reliability.

A *quality* (see the previous chapter) is something in the nature of the code itself, and shows up in the choices we make when creating classes, methods, and relationships. A *principle* is a bit of wisdom about *all* designs, about those things that our profession tells us will make them more successful overall.

A quality tells you what to pay attention to. A principle tells you what to shoot for, which way to lean, where your best bets are.

I am not going to claim to have found *the* set of principles that define the professional practice of software development, rather I am going to offer up a few that I have found useful.[1] These, along with the *practices* that follow in the next chapter, are a starting point, one that I hope we will all build upon together.

The principles I will focus on here are separating use from creation, the open-closed principle, and the dependency inversion principle. Also, I will look at the general wisdom offered by the Gang of Four (GoF) to help us see how we can more reliably achieve designs that follow these principles.

---

1. Nor do I claim to have invented all this. Much of it comes from Bob Martin and his company Object Mentor (www.objectmentor.com), with the possible exception of separating use from creation, which is something I have been working on for a while now.

Separating Use from Creation

A well-crafted system tends to separate concerns from one another. Focusing on cohesion does this, as it tells us to make sure that each entity has a single concern (or responsibility in the system).

Other concerns can be separated as well. Let's begin with one that I find is fairly often missed, the separation of the instantiation of entities (creation) from their actual use.

Fowler's Perspectives

In his wonderful book *UML Distilled, Second Edition,* Martin Fowler codifies three levels of perspective from which one can consider an object-oriented design: conceptual, specification, and implementation.

- *Conceptual.* Conceptually, objects are entities with responsibilities, usually realized as abstract classes and interfaces (in Java or C#), which relate to each other in various ways to accomplish the goals of the application.

  If I were an object, the conceptual perspective would be concerned with "what I am responsible for."

- *Specification.* At the specification level, objects are entities that fulfill contracts that are specified in their public methods; they promise services they can deliver in a specified way.

  If I were an object, the specification perspective would be concerned with "how I am used by others."

- *Implementation.* The implementation perspective is the code level or the actual programmatic solutions that objects use to fulfill these aforementioned contracts, which therefore allows them to satisfy the responsibilities for which they were designed.

  If I were an object, the implementation perspective would be concerned with "how I accomplish my responsibilities."

Limiting the level of perspective at which any entity[2] in your system functions to one of these three has several advantages.

---

2. This could be a class or a method; some languages have other idioms such as delegates, and so on.

Similarly, limiting yourself to one of these perspectives during the mental process of designing any entity of your system is also advantageous. Here are the advantages.

- It tends to reduce *coupling* in the system. If relationships between objects are kept at the abstract level, the actual implementing subclasses are less likely to be coupled to one another. This is part and parcel of the advice given to us by the Gang of Four (The authors of the original *Design Patterns* book), which states that we should "design to interfaces."
- It tends to promote *cohesion* and clarity in the system, because we allow the details of the coded solutions to flow from the responsibilities that objects are intended to fulfill, and not the other way around. An object with a clearly defined, limited responsibility is not likely to contain lots of extraneous methods and state that have nothing to do with the issue at hand.
- It tends to give us opportunities to eliminate *redundancy* in systems, because the conceptual level entities we create (often abstract base classes) also give us a place to "push up" behavior and state that would otherwise be duplicated in implementation entities.
- It encourages *clarity* in our cognitive processes in general. Most people have a hard time keeping things straight when they attempt to think on multiple levels at the same time, and about the same issues.

Another Kind of Perspective

My purpose here, however, is to suggest another, similar distinction we can use in design to help us achieve the kind of flexibility and robustness that we are seeking in object-oriented solutions: the perspective of creation versus the perspective of use.

Consider the following bit of code, in which I'm intentionally making a mistake.

```
public class SignalProcessor {

    private ByteFilter myFilter;

    public SignalProcessor() {
        myFilter = new HiPassFilter();
    }
```

```
    public byte[] process(byte[] signal) {
        // Do preparatory steps

        myFilter.filter(signal);

        // Do other steps

        return signal;
    }
}
```

Here, a `SignalProcessor` instance is designed to use a `ByteFilter` implementation (`HiPassFilter`) to do a portion of its work.

This delegation is generally a good idea; to promote good object cohesion, each class should be about one thing, and collaborate with other classes to accomplish subordinate tasks. Also, this will accommodate different kinds of `ByteFilter` implementations without altering the `SignalProcessor`'s design. This is a pluggable design, and allows for an easier path to extension.[3] Not surprisingly, it also creates an opportunity for cleaner and more useful testing.

Conceptually, `SignalProcessor` is responsible for processing the signal contained in a byte array. In terms of specification, `SignalProcessor` presents a `process()` method that takes and returns the byte array.

The way `SignalProcessor` is implemented is another matter, however, and there we see the delegation to the `ByteFilter` instance when the "filtering stuff" is needed. In designing `ByteFilter`, we need only consider its specification (the `filter()` method), and we can hold off considering its implementation until we are through here.

Good, clean, clear.

The problem, however, is that the relationship between `SignalProcessor` and `ByteFilter` operates at two different perspectives. `SignalProcessor` is "in charge" of *creating* the needed instance of `HiPassFilter`, and is *also* the entity that then *uses* the instance to do work.

This would seem trivial, and is in fact quite commonplace in routine designs. But let's consider these two responsibilities—*using* objects versus

---

3. This is an example of following the open-closed principle, which we will look at shortly. For more information, see http://www.objectmentor.com/resources/articles/ocp.pdf.

making objects—as separate cohesive concerns, and examine them in terms of the coupling they create. As with Fowler's perspectives, we'll find that keeping these roles separate in systems will help us keep quality high, and ease the way for the evolutionary path that the system will follow.

The Perspective of Use

In order for one object to *use* another, it must have access to the public methods it exports. If the second object was held simply as "object", then only the methods common to all objects will be available to the using object, `toString()`, `Hashcode()`, and so forth. So, to make any meaningful use of the object being used, the using object must usually know one of three things:

- The actual type of the object being used
- An interface the object being used implements
- A base class the object being used is derived from

To keep things as decoupled as possible, we prefer one of the latter two options, so that the actual object being used could be changed in the future (so long as it implemented the same interface or was derived from the same base class) without changing the code in the using object.

The using object (client), in other words, should ideally be coupled only to an abstraction, not to the actual concrete classes that exist, so that we are free to add more such classes in the future without having to maintain the client object. This is especially important if there are many different types of clients that use this same service; but it is always, a good idea.

Put another way, we prefer that clients have abstract coupling to services.

A Separate Perspective: Creation

Naturally, if we exempt the client from "knowing" about the actual `ByteFilters` implementations that exist and how they are constructed, that implies that something, somewhere will have to know these things.

I am suggesting that this is another distinction of *perspective*: use versus creation. In the same way that the users of an instance should not be involved with its construction, similarly the builders of an instance should not be involved with its use. Therefore, we typically call such a "constructing object" a *factory*.[4] Figure 8.1 describes a design along these lines.

It is critical to consider the nature of the coupling from the two perspectives of use and creation, and therefore what will have to be maintained when different things change.

If you consider the `ByteFilter` abstraction and its two concrete implementations to be a polymorphic service (that is, that `ByteFilter` is a service with two versions, and this variation is handled through polymorphism), then `SignalProcessor` relates to this service from the use perspective, whereas `ByteFilterFactory` relates to it from the creation perspective.

The coupling from `SignalProcessor` to the `ByteFilter` polymorphic service is to the identity of the abstract type `ByteFilter` (simply that this abstraction exists at all) and the public methods in its interface. There is no coupling of any kind between `SignalProcessor` and the implementing subclasses `HiPassFilter` and `LoPassFilter`, assuming we have been good object-oriented programmers and not added any methods to the interfaces of these subclasses.

The coupling from `ByteFilterFactory` to the `ByteFilter` polymorphic service is quite different. The factory is coupled to the subclasses, since it must build instances of them with the new keyword. Therefore, it also is coupled to the nature of their constructors. It is also coupled to the `ByteFilter` type (it casts all references it builds to that type before

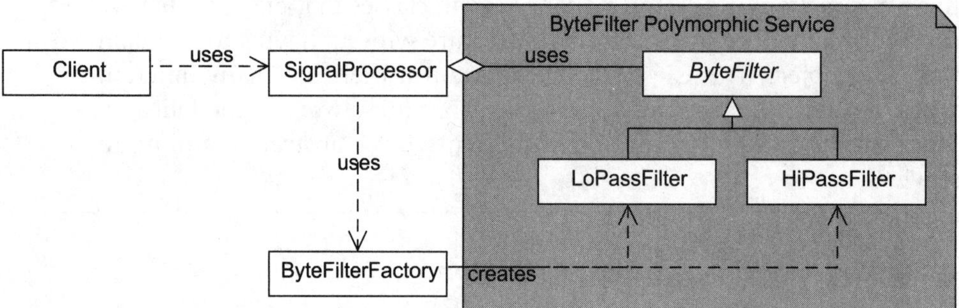

Figure 8.1 Use versus creation

4. In the terminology I am promoting here, a factory is anything that produces an instance. It may build the instance on demand, give out an instance built beforehand, or hand out an instance obtained from another source; from the perspective of the object using the factory, the details are irrelevant, and therefore the user does not couple to them.

returning them to the `SignalProcessor`), but not the public methods in the interface, *if we have limited the factory to the construction perspective only.* The factory never calls methods on the objects it builds.[5]

The upshot of all this is to limit the maintenance we must endure when something changes to *either* the users of this service *or* the creator of the specific instances.

If the subclasses change—if we add or remove different implementations of `ByteFilter`, or if the rules regarding when one implementation should be used versus another happen to change—then `ByteFilterFactory` will have to be maintained, but *not* `SignalProcessor`.

If the interface of `ByteFilter` changes—if we add, remove, or change the public methods in the interface—then `SignalProcessor` will have to be maintained, but *not* `ByteFilterFactory`.

It is interesting to note that there is one element of the design that both users and creators are vulnerable to: the abstraction `ByteFilter` itself. Not its interface, but its existence. This realization points up a fact long understood by high-level designers: that finding the right abstractions is among the most crucial issues in object-oriented design. Even if we get the interfaces wrong, it is not as bad as missing an entire abstract concept.

If we consider systems as evolving, emerging entities, as opposed to fixed and planned entities, we know we'll want to limit the impact of change overall. This principle helps us, because it tends to place the concrete coupling in a single entity: an object factory.

The Meaning of Clean Separation

Clean separation means that the relationship between any entity A and any other entity B in a system should be limited so that A makes B or A uses B, but never both.

Considering Construction Details Last

The notion that entities in a design have perspectives at which they operate implies a kind of cohesion. Cohesion, as I have said, is considered a virtue because strongly cohesive entities tend to be easier to understand,

5. For our purposes here, we do not consider the constructor to be part of the interface of an object.

less tightly coupled to other entities, and allow for more fine-grained testing of the system.

If we strive to limit the perspective at which any entity operates, we improve its cohesion, and the benefits are similar to those gained by cohesion of state, function, and responsibility.

The perspective of use versus the perspective of creation is one powerful way to separate entities for stronger cohesion. It also implies that construction will be handled by a cohesive entity, a factory of some kind, and that we should not have to worry about how that will be accomplished while we are determining the use relationships in our design.

In fact, leaning on this principle means that we can allow the *nature* of the use relationships in our design to determine the *sorts* of factories that will be the best choice to build the instances concerned (there are many well-defined creational patterns).

In their book, *Design Patterns Explained: A New Perspective on Object-Oriented Design*, Alan Shalloway and James Trott illustrate the notion of "design by context," wherein they show that some aspects of a design can provide the context by which one can determine/understand other aspects. The notion is a big one, implying much about the role of patterns in design, analysis, and implementation, but a key part of their thesis is this:

> During one of my projects, I was reflecting on my design approaches. I noticed something that I did consistently, almost unconsciously: I never worried about how I was going to instantiate my objects until I knew what I wanted my objects to be. My chief concern was with relationships between objects as if they already existed. I assumed that I would be able to construct the objects that fit in these relationships when the time comes to do so.

They then synthesized a powerful, universal context for proper design, as follows:

> Rule: Consider what you need to have in your system before you concern yourself with how to create it.

I had a hard time with this at first. Before I was an object-oriented developer, I was a procedural programmer, and in those days one's program tended to load all at once and then run—a very straightforward process. The idea that parts of my program, called objects, would be loading and running at various times throughout the runtime session seemed like a huge problem, and the first issue to resolve. The idea that it was actually the *last* issue to resolve took quite a leap of faith on my part, but I must say it has always proven to be the right path. This is an example of how a profession can provide you with wisdom that is hidden from the uninitiated, or even counter-intuitive from the relative neophyte's point of view.

At any rate, the separation of use and construction empowers you to follow this rule, and therefore to derive the benefits that flow from following it. Your system will have stronger cohesion, will be more extensible and flexible, and the task of maintenance will be significantly simplified.

The Real World

The seeming implication is that every class should have a factory that instantiates it. Am I really suggesting this? In fact, if you follow the logical implications of this book, it might lead you to believe that for every object in our design, you should have the following:

- An interface or abstract class that hides it
- A factory that builds it
- A unit test that explains it
- A mock object or set of mock objects that decouple it (Chapter 10)

For *every class*? No. What I want is the *value* of having done this, without doing it until it is actually necessary. I am greedy, you see. I want all the benefits of this approach, but I do not want to pay anything to get them, until I actually need them. I want the juice without the orange. I want to have my cake and eat it too. Don't you?

To satisfy my greed, I will want to lean on some key practices, the subject of the next chapter.

The Open-Closed Principle

We draw upon the wisdom that comes from the traditions of our profession. Some of this is relatively new; some is not.

Many years ago, Ivar Jacobson said, "All systems change during their life cycles. This must be borne in mind when developing systems expected to last longer than the first version."

I think I can feel fairly safe in saying that the modern economy expects pretty much all software to last longer than its first version. Hm. Well, maybe if our software is burned onto a chip, and sent to Jupiter on a probe, then we can assume we will not have to maintain it. But for everything else . . .

Somewhat later, Bertrand Meyer put it another way, "Software entities (classes, modules, functions, etc.) should be open for extension, but closed for modification."

This has come to be known as the open-closed principle.

The overall idea is this: As much as possible, we would like to set things up in our architecture in such a way that when things change, as we know they will, we will be able to accommodate each change by writing new code and cleanly plugging it into the existing system, rather than having to go back and modify the code that already exists.

Again, in the courses I teach, a question I often ask is (by a show of hands) how many of the students would rather work on older code, in maintenance mode, as opposed to starting a brand new project. I rarely get a hand raised.

Why is this? I think we can learn a little about the nature of software by paying attention to our own natural reactions. We would rather work on new software rather than change old code for a variety of reasons, including

- Writing new stuff tends to be more interesting. We like to be creative, and when we design something new it feels more stimulating in this way.
- It is a chance to get things right. Before we gave up hope, we worked under the belief that maybe *this time* we will get everything right and never have to change it. That hope, as misguided as it is, feels good.
- Maintenance is a chance to fail. It is a chance to be the person who broke the system, and naturally be the one expected to fix it.

I think this third reason is a very strong motivating force in software development.

Open-closed is a quality of your design. A design can be a little open-closed, somewhat open-closed, or very open-closed. I bear no illusions that any code can be *completely* open-closed, but it is a good goal to apply it everywhere you can.

Put another way, if you have two ways of solving a problem, all other things being equal, you should choose the one that is relatively more open-closed. It will make your life easier in the future. One major value of studying patterns is that they all, whatever else is true about them, tend to be more open-closed than the alternatives.

At the time Meyer coined the term, he almost certainly was referring to the use of inheritance to extend classes,[6] rather than change them. As we'll see when we investigate what the Gang of Four suggested as an alternative, this principle can be adhered to in many ways, and does not necessarily lead to the overuse of inheritance.

Open-Closed at the Class Level

If you look back at the previous section in this chapter, the ideal design for polymorphic service called `ByteFilter` was extremely open-closed, as shown in Figure 8.2.

If we get a new requirement that says, "we have to accommodate a square wave filter now," we can make the needed change by writing a *new* derived class of the `ByteFilter` abstraction, and the only code that has to change is in the `ByteFilterFactory` class. The `SignalProcessor` class is only coupled to the `ByteFilter` abstraction, so the code within it does not have to be touched at all. The class might not even have to be recompiled. This is also true of the client, and any future users of this `ByteFilter` polymorphic server.

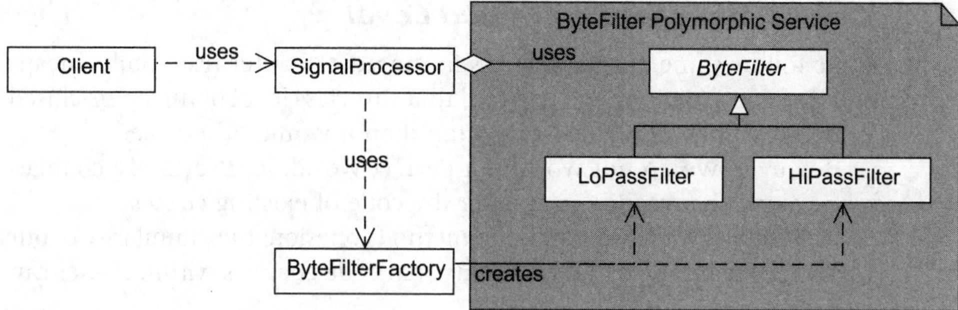

Figure 8.2 The `ByteFilter` polymorphic service

6. http://en.wikipedia.org/wiki/Bertrand_Meyer

This is an example of using delegation, rather than inheritance, to extend a system's flexibility. You'll note that `SignalProcesser` does not change.

My experience in designs that use factories (pretty much all of my designs use factories) is that while there tends to be *many* consumers of a service,[7] there is usually only a *single* factory to build the proper instances. So, although I may fail to be open-closed where the factory is concerned, at least I am very open-closed everywhere else in the system, at least regarding this service.

Therefore, factories promote the open-closed principle. They help us focus whatever code changes that will be needed in a single place.

Why bother? When we can achieve this kind of class-level adherence to the Open-Closed Principle, we lean heavily on encapsulation. The new thing we will have to create to accommodate the square wave requirement is its own class, encapsulated from all other entities in the system. The fact that we do not touch any of the other classes (except for the factory) means that they are protected also.

Remember that one of the main negative forces in traditional development has always been the unexpected side effects that can come from change. Here, what we have done is change what change is, from altering code to adding code.

We have changed the rules of the game: we do what we *like* to do (write new code) more often than what we would rather *not* do (maintain old code).

Open-Closed at the Method Level

If we follow some of the practices in the next chapter (especially encapsulating construction), we will find that this class level of the open-closed principle will be available more often than it would otherwise.

However, we do not work in a perfect world, and certainly changes come along that require us to alter the code of existing classes.

That said, if we pay attention to method cohesion, the granularity of our methods will increase the probability that code changes within classes can

---

7. In fact, one could argue that the more clients a service develops over time, the more successful and valuable the service has proven to be. We *hope* we'll get a lot of use out of any given service, which tends to mean many clients as the service persists.

The Kobayashi Maru

I'm a bit of a nerd, I'll admit. I've seen all things *Star Trek,* and I can recite lines from most of the episodes and films.

In *Star Trek II: The Wrath of Khan,* the filmmakers began with a trick played on the audience: the Enterprise encounters an ambush, and is destroyed, killing everyone. It turns out that this is a simulation, the final exam for starship captains at Starfleet, called the Kobayashi Maru, and is an unwinnable scenario by design.

Why they'd want to send a captain off on a failure was puzzling to me, but so be it. However, we learn later in the film that one graduate did, in fact, win the unwinnable scenario. Captain Kirk, of course.

How did he win? He's reluctant to say, but finally admits that he won by cheating. He reprogrammed the simulation so it could be won.

I think of the open-closed principle as sort of the Kobayashi Maru of OO design. I'd rather write new software than monkey around with old software, so I set myself up to win by changing the game. When something is open-closed, changing it *is* writing new software.

It's okay to cheat if it helps you.

be limited to adding methods, or if a method does have to be changed, to changing the code in a single method that is, at least in terms of its temporary method variables, relatively encapsulated from the rest of the class.

I am trying to avoid changing code that is entwined with other code; I want to get away, as much as possible, from "wading in" to a mass of spaghetti that I only partly understand.

I will go over this in detail in the next chapter when I discuss programming by intention, so I will leave this for now, except to say that this is another example of how following professional practices can be a safety net that protects you from having to make dangerous change.

The Dependency Inversion Principle

Another key decision that we have to make in design has to do with the public interfaces of our classes, and the signatures of our methods.

When you design the public interface (public methods) of a class, or the public interface (signature) of a method, there are two possible ways to make this decision:

- Code up the functionality in question, and then decide what sort of interface to provide to the rest of the system so that the functionality can be used
- Determine how the rest of the system would "prefer" to use this functionality (an ideal interface from the outside perspective), and then determine how to satisfy this need by implementing accordingly

In other words, you can decide how a thing will work and then how it will be used, or you can determine how a thing will be used and then how it will work.

Traditionally, we have started by writing the implementing code.

This seems logical. Once we know how the class or method works, we can decide how to expose its services to others. It turns out, however, that the opposite view is the stronger one.

We call this *dependency inversion*[8] because of this relationship, shown in Figure 8.3.

We can, quite accurately, state that Client here has a dependency to Service. It uses Service to get some work done, and so it depends on Service (and if you change Service's interface, you will have to change the way Client uses it, certainly).

However, we are stating that the way we determine what the interface of Service should be *in the first place* is by determining what would be most convenient for Client, before we even create Service's actual implementing code.

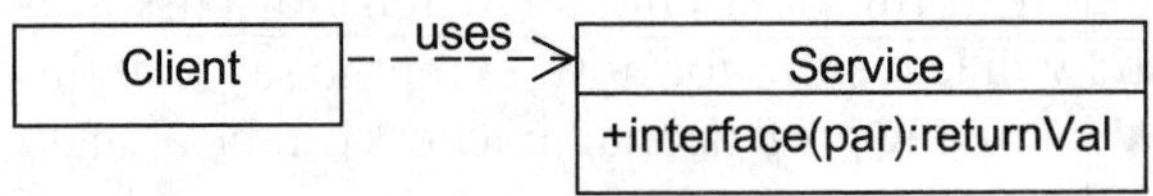

Figure 8.3 Dependency inversion

8. "We" being Alan, David, Amir, Rob, Rod, and I. Bob Martin, who coined the term, may have a different idea of what it means. Visit http://www.objectmentor.com/resources/articles/dip.pdf for his take on the DIP.

So, Client *depends* on Service, but the interface of Service *depends* on what Client wants it to be.

Why do it this way?

Because the way a particular piece of functionality is accomplished is very likely to change, but the needs of the client objects will tend to be more stable. Therefore, paying attention to the needs of the client object first tends to produce more stable interfaces, which leads to less, simpler maintenance.

There is a practice called programming by intention, covered in the next chapter, which helps to produce this inversion pretty much automatically, at the method level. Similarly, test-driven development, a discipline I will cover a few chapters on, forces you to do this at the class level.

Practices and disciplines do these things for us, which is why I am focusing on them in this book. However, understanding the principles behind a better design is also important; no set of rote practices will, by themselves, make you a professional.

Advice from the Gang of Four

The first two chapters of the Gang of Four's book is actually a treatise on object-oriented design. The wisdom they share there is fundamental to the patterns—that is, the various patterns are contextual applications of these key concepts.

In a way, the actual patterns themselves are not what is important about patterns. They are useful to know because they give us a leg-up on good design, help us to communicate at a higher level with others in our profession, and give us a way to capture what we know about particular, repeated situations in development.

However, what makes them important is that each pattern is an example of following the general advice that was presented in the initial chapters of the book, which itself is a particularly clear-eyed and wise view of what good object-orientation is in the first place.

Here is what they said, and what I think it means:

Gang of Four: Design to Interfaces

My first reaction to this: "Sure. What choice do I have?"

In my view at the time, the interface of an object is the collection of public methods that represent it to the rest of the system, and in a language like Java or C#, the public methods are all I have access to. If by "design to" they mean "create relationships between," the interface is all I could possibly choose.

Obviously, this is not what they mean.

Design is more than this. It is the structure of the classes, where the responsibilities are, how information is held and flows from one place to another, how behavior will be varied under different circumstances, and so on.

So, by "design to interfaces," the Gang of Four is really talking about two things:

- The assignment of responsibilities between client and service objects
- The use of abstractions to hide specific "implementing" classes

Designing to the Interface of a Method

For an example of this first idea, I got clear on this when my friend Jeff McKenna conducted a very interesting exercise in a class we were co-teaching.

He went to a student in the front row and said, "Tell me your driver's license number."

The student, after blinking for a moment or two, reached into his back pocket, pulled out his wallet, opened it, removed his driver's license, and read the number to Jeff.

Jeff asked the next student the same question. He did precisely the same thing.

Jeff then picked another student, a young lady, who was seated nearby. He said to her, "Tell me your driver's license number."

She picked up her purse from the floor, opened it, took out a snap-purse from inside, opened that, took out her wallet, opened that, and read the license number from the license without removing it from its glassine envelope inside the wallet.

He went from student to student, asking the same question in the same way. One of the students actually could recite his driver's license number from memory (perhaps he got pulled over a lot by the police). And then there was the guy who refused to tell Jeff his driver's license number—apparently, he threw an exception.

At any rate Jeff's point was that he took *no different action* with each student in order to obtain what he wanted, even though the actual steps each student went through to satisfy his request were different from student to student.

Jeff's design, his plan of action, what he said, and what he expected as a return, was to the interface of the student.

As a counter-example, imagine if Jeff had gone to the first student and said, "Reach into your back pocket, pull out your wallet, open it, remove your driver's license, and read the number to me." This would work with the majority of the male students in the class, but as soon as he got to the young lady with the purse, or the guy who had the number memorized, this request would no longer work.

Therefore, Jeff would either have to limit himself to wallet-on-the-hip students or would have to know a lot of different ways of asking for a license number, and know when to use each one. He would also, in each case, have to know which sort of student he was dealing with, and would have to add more complexity to his design when new students arrived who stored their driver's license number in yet different ways.

If he had been implementation specific in his design, Jeff would have severely limited his flexibility, because the responsibility of *how* to satisfy his request would be placed in the wrong spot. It would also

- Weaken Jeff's *cohesion*. He would have to know non-Jeff stuff (how each student stored their driver's license number) as well as his own issues (of which Jeff, believe me, has many!).
- Create accidental *coupling* between Jeff and this particular group of students. Later, if the first student started carrying his license in his shirt pocket, Jeff would have to change the way he interacted with him.

By placing the specifics of implementation in each student, and keeping the interface generic, this means Jeff stays simple (well, simpl*er*). It also means that we can, in the future, have a student come along who stores her driver's license in some way we never thought of (in her shoe or tucked in her hatband), and Jeff could take the same action as before.

There is a practice in the next chapter that helps us get this right most of the time, without even trying. It is called programming by intention. I will leave that for now, except to say that this practice helps us to follow the design to interfaces advice at the *method level*.

Designing to the Interface of a Class

Another way to consider this piece of advice has to do with class relationships. The Gang of Four suggests that when you have abstractions in a design, as shown in Figure 8.4, you should, whenever possible, try to create the relationship between these abstractions at the highest level possible, as shown in Figure 8.5, between AbstractionA and AbstractionB.

I sometimes paraphrase the Gang of Four here and call this design to abstractions. There are several advantages to this.

- There will be, quite simply, fewer relationships. If I create relationships among the implementation classes, in the preceding, I potentially end up with six of them. With the relationship "high up" at the abstract level, there is one-to-one, or perhaps one-to-many, rather than n-to-m.
- The derived, implementing classes will not be coupled to one another. If both Jeff and I talk to the students in the same way, the students would not be coupled to which teacher was asking for the license, any more than the teacher would be coupled to the particular student being asked. The relationship would be from Teacher to Student, which are the abstractions in this example.
- It is open-closed. We can add a derivation to either or both sides of the relationship without requiring a change in the code.

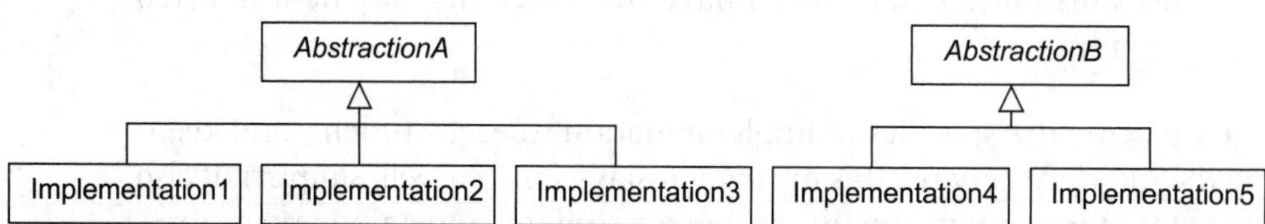

Figure 8.4 Abstractions in a design

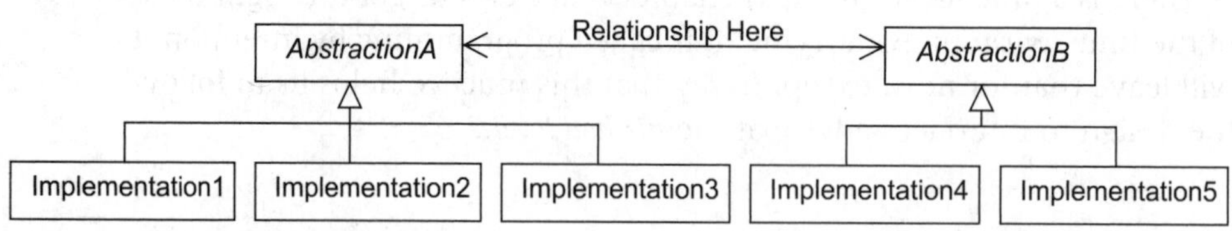

Figure 8.5 Relationship between abstractions

Designing to interfaces is a kind of limitation we impose on ourselves, and the benefits it yields are many. It is an example of how a profession can "learn things" that benefit all the members of the profession, rather than expecting each member to learn hard lessons on his own.

GoF: Favor Object Aggregation[9] Over Class Inheritance

The Gang of Four also says that we should favor an aggregation approach over the use of inheritance to vary behavior. The first time I read this I said, "Okay, I get that. Delegate. Do not inherit." Then I proceeded to read the individual patterns in the book, and inheritance was used everywhere.

I thought, "If I am not supposed to use inheritance, how come they are doing it every time I turn around?" Obviously, again, I was misunderstanding their meaning.

First, they are saying *favor* aggregation over inheritance. They did not say, "Never use inheritance, always delegate."

Secondly, the gang really intends that we use inheritance for something other than what we traditionally have used it for, which is to specialize existing concrete objects with new behavior. This was, in fact, the original meaning of open-closed. The Gang of Four suggests we use inheritance in a different, more powerful way.

Going back to the signal processor example, an older (perhaps more recognizable) approach to varying its filter mechanism would be to do the approach shown in Figure 8.6.

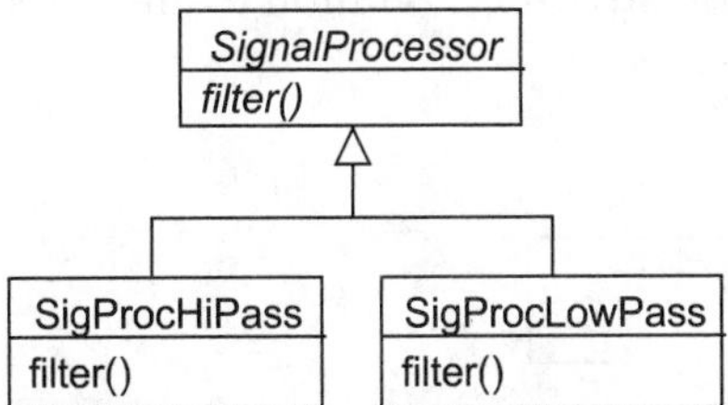

Figure 8.6 A different signal processor approach

9. The GoF actually used the term composition. In the days of unmanaged code, composition and aggregation implied different styles of memory management and cleanup when objects were no longer needed. I think this is a distraction for us here, and when you consider that the OMT and UML use these terms with precisely opposite meanings, I think it is best to stick with the more general notion of aggregation, or if you prefer, delegation. In C++, this may actually be composition, depending on which entity is responsible for cleaning up the memory of the service object(s).

The base class, `SignalProcessor`, implements all the behaviors, except (perhaps) `filter()`. The `filter()` method is either abstract in the base class, or the base class implements it with default behavior.

Either way, the derived classes override `filter()` with the specific filtering behavior desired.

Of course, this works and is a very common way of accomplishing and containing a variation in traditional object orientation. The Gang of Four says not to do this unless you have a very compelling reason to do so. A better way, which they suggest you should favor, is shown in Figure 8.7.

The first design uses inheritance to *specialize* a real thing, `SignalProcessor`. The second design uses inheritance to *categorize* the `HiPassFilter` and `LowPassFilter` as *conceptually the same thing* and therefore the base class is a concept, `ByteFilter`, not a concrete thing.

The advantages are several and, of course, tie back to the qualities I emphasized in the last chapter.

- Both `SignalProcessor` and the various filters are more *cohesive* because each is about fewer issues internally.
- The filters can be tested outside the context of the specific usage of `SignalProcessor`, and therefore are more *testable*.
- The coupling between `SignalProcessor` and the various filters is kept to the abstract level, and therefore the *coupling* is kept to a minimum, and only where it is most logical.
- There are fewer *redundancies*, because anything common to all filters can be placed in the `filter` base class.

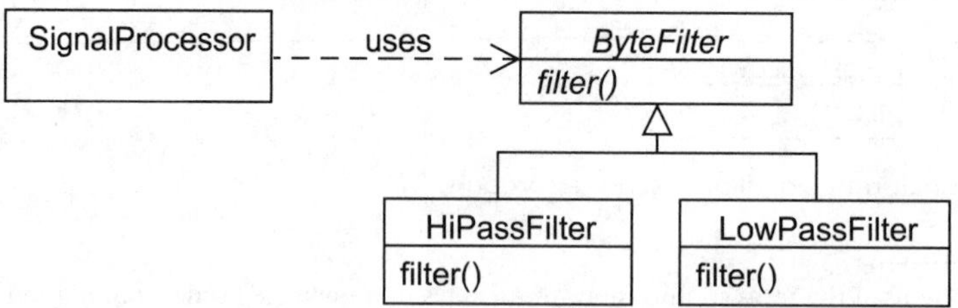

Figure 8.7 A better way is to use inheritance to categorize

Also, consider the runtime flexibility. In the first design, imagine that we had instantiated the `SignalProcessorHP` class, and it was up and running. Now imagine that, in the same runtime session, we had to switch to the low-pass filter; the only way to do this in the first design is to make a new instance of `SignalProcessorLP`, somehow transfer the state from the previous instance to the new one, and then kill `SignalProcessorHP`.

The real problem with this, apart from potential performance problems, is the "somehow transfer the state" step. We would have to do one of the following:

- Break encapsulation on the state of the SignalProcessor.
- Make each version of SignalProcessor able to clone itself into the other versions, which would, of course, couple them to each other.

Neither option seems very good.

Of course, the design using delegation renders this issue moot, because we can simply provide a mechanism (a `setFilter()` method) on the `SignalProcessor`, which allows us to give it a different `ByteFilter` subclass any time we want to switch the filtering algorithm, without breaking encapsulation on `SignalProcessor`'s state, or creating any unneeded and undesirable coupling between the various versions of the filter.

Even if we start out without this `setFilter()` method, perhaps because this dynamic aspect is unneeded or even undesirable, we can later make it dynamic by adding the method, without needing to touch any of the existing code in the service. Adding a new method, and leaving existing methods alone, is also open-closed.

Also, what if something else starts to vary? This seems to be so common that it is expected: something else, unforeseen in the original design, now starts to vary. Imagine in the `SignalProcessor`, there is a `prepare()` step, which was initially fixed and now has two versions: `LossyPreparation` and `PrecisePreparation`.

In the inheritance-heavy approach, we would simply inherit again (see Figure 8.8).

Note that the cohesion, testability, and dynamism problems are getting worse and worse here. It is also harder and harder to name these classes in such a way that they will fit nicely in my pages.

On the other hand, using delegation, as shown in Figure 8.9, scales more readily.

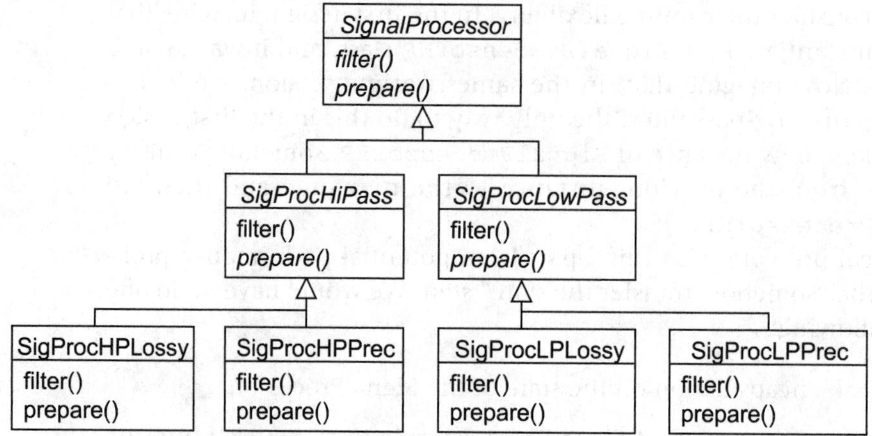

Figure 8.8 The inheritance-heavy approach

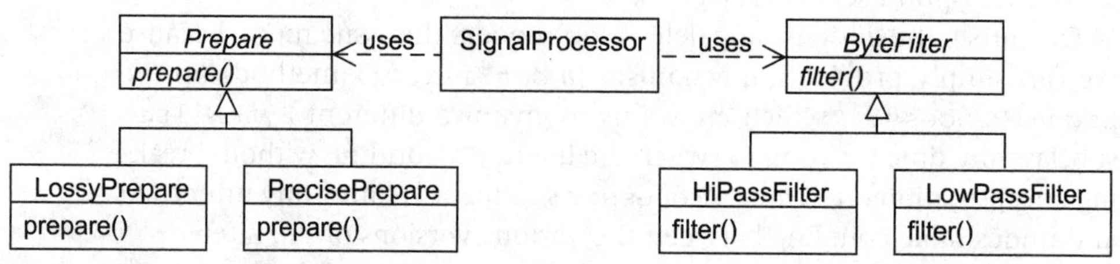

Figure 8.9 Using delegation

Not only is the cohesion of `SignalProcessor` not getting any worse, it is actually getting better each time we "pull an issue out," and more cohesion leads to easier and more useful tests.

And notice: We are focusing on larger issues than simply asking if it works. Both approaches will work.

As professionals, we are asking additional questions:

- How well will each of these stand up over time?
- What kind of return on investment will each provide for my customer?
- Which represents my desire to build things that will last, and continue to be valuable?

GoF: Consider What Should Be Variable in Your Design and Encapsulate the Concept That Varies

I must admit that this statement really blew my mind when I first read it. It literally stopped me cold, and made me wonder if I should even keep reading the book.

"Encapsulate the concept?" I thought. "How do you encapsulate a concept?" I knew how to encapsulate *data*, which was the point of objects in the first place (I thought), and I know how to encapsulate *function*, which was the advantage of methods and functions over old-style subroutines—you supply the inputs and receive an output, but you have no other coupling to a method or function. But . . . encapsulate a *concept*?

I was envisioning code like `private Beauty` or some such. It just did not make sense to me. What did concepts have to do with code?

Of course, the reason it did not make sense was my limited idea of what encapsulation is in the first place.

I thought of encapsulation as the hiding of data or, as I gained some sophistication with object orientation, the hiding of implementation. In truth, that is just the tip of the iceberg. Encapsulation is the hiding of anything at all.

This realization takes us in many fruitful directions, but here, in examining the general design advice of the Gang of Four, we can focus ourselves on the specific idea that *variation can be encapsulated conceptually*.

Let's go back to the delegation approach with the signal processor, shown in Figure 8.10.

If you think of encapsulation as the hiding of *anything*, then you can say that the abstract class `ByteFilter` *encapsulates* the derived classes `HiPassFilter` and `LowPassFilter`, because `SignalProcessor` cannot see them, does not know they exist, nor which one is actually being used during any given runtime session.

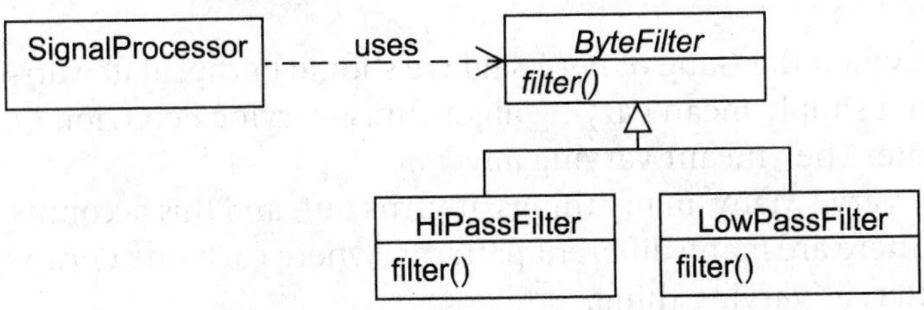

Figure 8.10 The delegation approach with the signal processor

Of course, ByteFilter is a conceptual class. It represents the idea of filtering bytes, and how another entity would interact with such a filter (the interface), without specifying any particular filtering algorithm.

This was what the GoF was suggesting: that we look for things we can encapsulate, and encapsulate them conceptually wherever we can. The benefits are many.

- We are free to change (add, remove, modify) any of the implementations of ByteFilter without changing SignalProcessor at all. We have achieved a high degree of open-closed-ness.
- The coupling between SignalProcessor and the ByteFilter service is purely to the interface.
- We get the dynamism mentioned in the preceding, in that we can change ByteFilters without remaking the SignalProcessor.
- Each class in the relationship is easier to test, individually, because it is more cohesive.

But wait. Did we not get all these benefits by following those first two pieces of advice: design to interfaces and favor aggregation over inheritance?

Yes, and in a sense, this third point is the point-of-all-points for the Gang of Four. But in the chaos of software development, our situational awareness varies greatly, and so having multiple ways to think of a problem increases the chance that we will not miss a critical issue.

Testing relates to cohesion. Cohesion relates to encapsulation. Encapsulation relates to redundancy. Redundancy relates to testing. Our goal is to find the truth, to find a design that reflects the true nature of the problem, and there are many ways to find the truth.

The main reason I have been focusing on the idea of building a true profession is that I believe the qualities, principles, practices, disciplines, and overall guidance we'll get from such a thing will greatly empower us to find these highly appropriate designs, and thus increase our success tremendously.

Furthermore, when the Gang of Four said we should encapsulate variation, they did not simply mean varying algorithms, varying behavior, or even varying state. They meant varying *anything*.

What else can vary? Many, many things, it turns out, and this accounts for the fact that there are many different patterns, where each one encapsulates some different varying thing.

For example, let us say we have a Client object that delegates to a single service object. Then, in a different situation, it delegates to two service objects. To handle this variation in code, we'd do something like this:

```
if (someConditional) {
    Service1.doOperation();
} else {
    Service1.doOperation();
    Service2.doOperation();
}
```

. . . or something similar. This is not open-closed, because if we add a case where three services are needed, we'll have to change this code. However, the Gang of Four would also tell us that this variation (1, 2, or more) is not encapsulated. It's an issue of *cardinality,* and if possible we should encapsulate that too.

Can we? Yes, if we know the Decorator pattern (see Appendix B, "Overview of Patterns Used in the Examples").

Or, perhaps the client always delegates to both services, but sometimes it does it in one sequence, sometimes in another:

```
if (someConditional) {
    Service1.doOperation();
    Service2.doOperation();
} else {
    Service2.doOperation();
    Service1.doOperation();
}
```

Again, this is a variation—one of order, or sequence—and it is not encapsulated. Could it be? Yes, the Decorator pattern sometimes hides this too. Unencapsulated, imagine what will happen if we get a third service, and then a fourth? How would this code look if it supported all the possible sequences then? What if both the number *and* the sequence needed to vary?

The point is, many, many things can vary, and we should encapsulate them as much as we can, because every time we do we get to win the Kobayashi Maru, the unwinnable scenario.

Software that decays sets us up to fail. Let's all take a page from Captain Kirk, and set ourselves up to win.

He always got the green-skinned alien dancing girls, after all.

Summary

Principles and wisdom help us in general ways. Adhering to a principle is a good thing, but there is really no end to it. A system could always be more open or closed to more things. There is always another level of abstraction, and therefore more encapsulation to add to systems.

How far do you go?

The concept of the practice, which is where we'll go next, is very different. Practices are eminently practical, simple, and doable. You follow them, or you don't. They are also easy to share with others, to promote them generally across a team. Like principles and wisdom, they are based on experience (often, the experience of others) and so are very well-grounded.

Practices help you to follow principles; principles give you a reason to follow practices. Now that we've discussed the reasons, we'll look at the actions that promote them.

Chapter 9

Paying Attention to Practices

One of the values of a profession (or a craft, for that matter) is that it defines a set of practices that you can follow, practices that will reliably increase your success rate.

To be most valuable, a professional practice should

- Be something you can *always* do, rather than having to *decide* whether to do it. Practices that you have to consider before you do them can be valuable too, but that is not our focus here.
- Be significant. A practice that does little for you is better left out of the recommended set, as a large number of practices will dilute the impact of any particular one.
- Require little or no extra work. We want to be greedy here; we want all of the good stuff without any of the bad, and without having to pay a lot for it. Naturally, there will be *some* cost to any truly valuable practice, but we would like it to be *essentially* free—a cost so low that you can treat it as free.

Doctors know to sterilize their hands, instruments, and even the part of the patient they are working on. Carpenters know to measure twice, and cut once. Lawyers know to save all legal documents, even if they seem trivial. They do not think about these things; they have them in their muscle memory, as it were. This frees up their conscious, decision-making capability to focus on more complex, situation-specific forces, and also gives them some certainty about what they can expect other doctors, carpenters, and lawyers will do, at a minimum.

I am by no means suggesting that I can or should offer a comprehensive set of practices in this book. Part of the evolution of our trade into a profession will be, I think, the pursuit and discovery of such practices, if we agree to share and promote them among our colleagues. Such things are best unearthed by the community itself, rather than imposed from "above."

The development practices covered in this chapter are

- Consistent coding style
- Programming by intention
- Encapsulating the constructor
- Performing commonality-variability analysis

Consistent Coding Style

Little things, repeated frequently over time and over long projects, can make a big difference. For example, some people write a class definition or statement block like this:

```
public class Transaction
{
    // Class definition here
}
```

Others would do it this way:

```
public class Transaction {
    // Class definition here
}
```

Which is correct? Should the opening and closing curly braces be at the same point of indentation, or should the statement that creates the block line up with the closing brace? I suppose one could argue back and forth about that for quite a while, and intelligent people can disagree. What is important is that you pick a style and be *consistent* in following it.

One project I worked on was in a very small company, with only two developers who were coding a particular system. During code reviews, I noticed that one of them would do this:

```
for(int i=0; i<array.length; i++ {
    array[i] = 100;
} // end for
```

whereas the other would omit the `end for` comment that accompanied the closing curly brace. When I would switch between code written by one of them to code written by the other, I would always have to adjust, and sometimes I would miss things.

When I asked why they did not both follow the same convention, it started a lengthy argument about the need for such comments, and it turned out that the developer who did not include the comments was using a sophisticated editor, one that color-coded the blocks based on level of nesting, whereas the commenting developer was using a simple plain-text editor. So, an inconsistency in the tools used to produce the code was resulting in an inconsistent view of what was needed to keep things clear, which in turn resulted in an inconsistent practice.

And this was on a team with only two developers!

Nowadays, when I begin to work with a new team, my first priority is to develop a set of coding standards that everyone can agree to follow, and then achieve a consensus on adherence to those standards. Most people code the way they do simply out of habit anyway, so it is often just a question of getting used to something new. It also helps if everyone is using the same tools to create the code in the first place.

What's my favorite coding standard? Pretty much any reasonable one, so long as it is followed by everyone on the team. A mediocre standard that everyone follows will trump a lovely, elegant one that is used by some and not by others.

Comments

Modern object-oriented languages are often thought to be *self documenting* because of the domain-specific modeling of classes and methods (entities called `Employee` and `calculatePay()` are more inherently understandable than `EmProc` and `IEsys101`).

Because of this, it is not an uncommon point of view to suggest that comments, especially excessive comments, should really be unnecessary if the code is truly readable. Put another way, if you need a lot of comments to make your code clear, one might rightly ask why the code is not clearer in the first place.

Also, comments are ignored by compilers, and so they can be ignored by developers when maintaining the code as well. As a result, a comment that is very old may contain out-of-date information, which can be worse than no information at all.

However, although a developer may strive for highly readable code that expresses *what* he has done, especially if a consistent coding standard has been maintained, it is often not so clear *why* he did it that way.

Human beings understand things better if they know why something is a certain way. The motivation behind a decision makes the decision easier to understand, and also easier to remember. Comments in your code are a good way to capture the intention that is in your mind at the moment you write it.

For others, or even for your own recollection later, comments can vastly improve your comprehension of the code.

```
// Get the rule based on the current ID
// ruleVector stores rules as Objects, so we need to cast the
// reference back to Rule
Rule firstRule = (Rule)(ruleVector.getRule(ID));

// If the rule is already active, or has a transaction stored,
// make it urgent priority
// We do this because the regulators require it
// (see pp 131, graf 5, of Functional Specification B)
if(firstRule.isActive() | (firstRule.getTransaction() !=
    null)) firstRule.setPriority(Rule.URGENT);
```

The first comment is not needed. The method name `getRule(ID)` tells you to "get the rule based on the ID," and the (Rule) cast tells you about the casting. The code is clear by itself, so the comment is just something else you need to keep up-to-date if the code ever changes.[1]

However, without the second comment, you would be able to understand the logic of the code (what it would do) but not the reason for doing it. To determine that would require several readings, and a reconnaissance of the code in the context of the system overall, which would take time and energy. These comments, easy to write (especially if I write them as I code), save me all that time and energy.

The distinctions here are

- Comments that tell you *what* the code is doing are an indication that the code is not clear enough: the methods are too weakly cohesive, and/or are not named expressively (named to reveal their intent).
- Comments that tell you *why* the code is doing what it is doing are helpful, because they express what the code cannot: arbitrary business rules.

1. . . . and you will not keep the comments up-to-date. Comments that describe code are notorious for being out-of-date. As the code changes, the comments are often left unchanged. Bob Martin (of Object Mentor) says something I like to repeat: Comments of this kind have another name. We call them lies.☺

Naming Classes, Methods, and Variables

In the section on cohesion in Chapter 7, I noted that one indicator that a class or a method is weakly cohesive is that it is difficult to name. Of course, you only notice that if you are attempting to create a descriptive name in the first place.

Descriptive class, method, and variable names are essential to readable code. Compare these two code fragments; here is fragment 1:

```
//fragment 1

if (e1.gact() < td.gc()) {
     p_sys.rem(e1);
} else {
     p_sys.rst(e1);
}
```

And here is fragment 2:

```
//fragment 2

if (employee1.getActiveDate() < TodaysDate.getCurrent()) {
     payrollSystem.removeEmployee(employee1);
} else {
     payrollSystem.resetActiveDate(employee1);
}
```

The second is much more readable, and the only difference is the way things are named, not what they are or how they are used. The logic is the same, but the naming changes the apparent or perceived complexity of the code. Languages like C++ are compiled into native code, and Java and C# are compiled into intermediate bytecode, anyway, so the length/verbosity of your method, class, and variable names does not affect the runtime performance of the system.

But it will affect your ability to maintain it. Even better:

```
// Company policy states that an employee whose active date is
// allowed to lapse must be removed from the payroll system
if (employee1.getActiveDate() < TodaysDate.getCurrent()) {
     payrollSystem.removeEmployee(employee1);
} else {
     // don't check again until tomorrow
     payrollSystem.resetActiveDate(employee1);
}
```

With well-named members and a comment that documents my intentions, I now have a code block that anyone can read and understand.

Virtues of Coding Standards

Eighty percent of the time, code is maintained or extended by those other than the original writer. This alone makes the economic advantage of coding standards pretty clear from the outset.

However, there is a subtler force here as well, which I alluded to at the beginning of this chapter. Software developers are key resources in your organization, and it is wise to use them in as efficient and sustainable a way as possible. Shops that burn developers out at a high rate have to replace them frequently, pay more to retain them, and in general tend to get less than their best effort as the burn-out proceeds.

Unmaintainable code burns developers out faster than anything I know.

Having to deal with changing requirements is irritating but it is much easier to do when the code is readable and clear, when decoupling makes extension easier to accomplish, when cohesion makes it easy to determine which part of the system must change, and when non-redundant code means you only have to make the change in one place.

In truth, we have to embrace change; we have to recast it from "the thing we dread" to a true ally in the development process. This may be the single most critical aspect of designing emergently, that we find a way to make change not only palatable, but desirable.

This is a fundamental shift for most of us—from change-as-enemy to change-as-helpful-tool.

Bugs can drive you nuts, but they are easier to locate in readable code. And they are easier to fix with confidence when *decoupling* means the bug affects a definable part of the system, when *cohesion* gives you a logical trail to follow to find the bug in the first place, and when *non-redundant* code means the fix can be put into a single place.

This book is about emergent design. What we will see is that emergent design works by refactoring and enhancing code, due to the changes, bugs, and extensions that we have to accommodate, while paying close attention to these principles of coding.

An old concept that I used to accept—code must inevitably decay over time—fades away in favor of something more hopeful—code can evolve over time, getting better and better every time I touch it.

Programming by Intention

Programming by intention is a new application of an old idea. Back when we all worked in purely procedural languages, many developers used a technique called *top-down programming*. In top-down, you would "stub out" functions that had not been written yet, perhaps having them return a message indicating their "coming soon" status, and then calling them from the main body of the code. Thus, your code always ran, and as you fleshed out the functions, it became more and more "done."

We often did this because compile and link times could be extremely long, and yet we wanted to get an "all up" version working of the system quickly. Also, some languages (like certain versions of Smalltalk) simply required this: the way to create a function was to call it from somewhere.

In object orientation, we can do the same thing with methods. If I am writing a class that sends messages, I might start by doing this:

```
public class Transmitter{
    String myDestination;
    public Transmitter(String aDestination){
        myDestination = aDestination;
    }

    public void transmit(String aMessage){
        openConnection();
        sendMessage(aMessage);
        closeConnection();
    }
}
```

If I tried to compile this, the compiler would complain because `openConnection()`, `sendMessage()`, and `closeConnection()` do not exist. That is okay. I don't mind the compiler giving me errors like that; in fact, I might use the compiler to remind me which methods I have not yet written. Why not? It is an automated to-do list.

What I *have* done is expressed my *intention* here. I have shown how I am breaking up the function, that the transmitter knows the destination (an IP address, perhaps, or some such), and that the message to send will vary.

I have also, just by programming in this style, created greater cohesion in two senses.

First, the methods I am delegating to are highly cohesive because they each do a single, defined thing—in fact, the thing that I was thinking of when I expressed my intention that the method should exist. My mind is single-threaded, so letting my intentions drive my method creation tends to produce cohesion in this sense.

Second, my `transmit()` method is written mostly (or completely) at the specification level (see "Levels of Perspective" in Chapter 7, "Paying Attention to Qualities and Pathologies"), rather than at a mix of specification and implementation. The other methods (the methods it calls) are written mostly at the implementation level of perspective.

Cohesive code tends to be more readable. Code that is programmed by intention tends to convey that intention, which is in turn more readable still.

The methods "expressed" in the `transmit()` method (`openConnection()`, `sendMessage()`, `closeConnection()`) will most likely be private methods, since the fact that the class fulfills its responsibility in this way is really only its "business." Public methods get coupled to, so we only make them public when the coupling is something we intend. Here, it is not intended. Remember, the Gang of Four recommends that we design to interfaces. These methods are implementation, not interface.

Because all these subordinate methods tend to be private, I like to call the master, overall method (usually public) the Sergeant method. The Sergeant delegates to the Privates. It is a silly pun, but it gives me an easy way to refer to them, as opposed to "that method that mostly calls the other methods" and "the methods that get called by the method that mostly calls the other methods."

I also like puns.

Are They Really All Private?

Of course, you may want to test one or more of these behaviors separately, and if you make the subordinate methods private, it is difficult to do so. As a practical matter, I sometimes make them public, but *treat them as private*.

Also, there are tricks and techniques for getting around this problem. At times, I have made these methods protected, and then derived my unit test from the class being tested. Some frameworks allow you to access private methods using testing proxies or delegates, or allow you to use mechanisms like "friends" in C++.

However, if I find I am doing these things a lot, I begin to wonder about the cohesion of this object. Should a single object contain a lot of behaviors that I want to test separately? Maybe it should use the behaviors, but not implement them itself. This is a good example of how testing can help in design, which is a major insight in and of itself. More on this later.

This might lead me to pull the behavior I want to make testable into a separate, service class, and delegate to it from the subordinate, private method in the current class. That way, it is testable on its own, but I don't break the encapsulation of the implementation of the current class.

If I did that, however, that would mean the current class would need an instance of this new service class in order to delegate to it. How will it get one?

I would certainly want to follow the next practice.

Encapsulating the Constructor

In Chapter 8, "Paying Attention to Principles and Wisdom," I said: "The relationship between any entity A and any other entity B in a system should be limited such that A *makes* B or A *uses* B but never both."

Does this mean that for every class in your design there should be another class termed "the factory," which other classes must use to instantiate it? Even when there is no variation, just a simple, single class of an ordinary sort? That does seem like overkill.

The problem is that we never know when something is going to vary in the future. Our abilities to predict change along these lines have traditionally been dramatically poor.[2] Luckily, there is a middle ground, which is to encapsulate the constructor in single classes.

To do this, one simply makes the constructor of the object private (or protected), and then adds a static method to the class that uses the constructor to return an instance. Here is a code snippet to illustrate the trick:

```
public class Sender {

    private Sender() {
        // do any constructor behavior here
    }

    public static Sender getInstance() {
        return new Sender();
    }
```

2. Put another way: If you are, in fact, capable of predicting the future, I would suggest you write code for fun and become a stock broker. My stock broker.

```
    // the rest of the class follows
}

public class Client {
    private Sender mySender;

    public Client() {
      mySender = Sender.getInstance();
    }
}
```

The key difference between this encapsulated constructor[3] and a more familiar approach is the fact that Client *must* build its Sender instance this way

```
mySender = Sender.getInstance()
```

rather than the more traditional `mySender = new Sender()` due to the private constructor on `Sender`.

I do not want the `Client` object to use `new`, basically. Object factories can solve this problem; data-binding frameworks can do it; and there are a variety of ways of hiding or encapsulating the creation of an object. The static method that I show above is merely a "do this at least" sort of thing, hence we call it a practice.

At first, this might seem pointless. After all, we have accomplished nothing special that we could not have done with the more traditional coding approach. However, what we have done is taken control of `new`.

The `new` keyword in modern languages like Java and C# cannot be overloaded, and thus we cannot control what it returns; it always returns, literally, the class named directly after the keyword. Anything that contains `new` in it is coupled to the specific concrete class that follows the keyword.

However, a method like `getInstance()` can return *anything that qualifies* as the type indicated. Thus, any entity that calls `getInstance()` is not necessarily coupled to a specific class. The value of this is clear when `Sender` changes, later, from a simple class to a polymorphic service.

```
public abstract class Sender {
    public static Sender getInstance() {
      if (someDecisionLogic()) {
          return new SenderImpl1();
```

3. I cannot say who first suggested this, but I learned it from Joshua Bloch, who wrote about it in his particularly useful book, *Effective Java Programming Language Guide*.

```
        } else {
            return new SenderImpl2();
        }
    }
}

public class SenderImpl1 extends Sender {
    // one version of the Sender service
}

public class SenderImpl2 extends Sender {
    // another version of the Sender service
}

public class Client {
    private Sender mySender;

    public Client() {
      mySender = Sender.getInstance();
    }
}
```

The main point here is that `Client` does not need to change when this variation comes about. The `Client` was never really coupled to the `Sender` class after we encapsulated the construction of it, which has become obvious because it is now really interacting with `SenderImpl1` or `SenderImpl2` without changing what it's doing.

You'll also note that `Sender` started out as a simple concrete class, without an abstract class or interface hiding it. After we had a variation, it evolved into an abstract class; here again, we don't see any change in the `Client` object as a result. This means we don't have to "put interfaces in" until we need them.

It is common for there to be many clients for such a service, and so the limited change here could decidedly be beneficial in terms of maintenance.

As I mentioned before, if we want to create valuable services, are we not essentially hoping that eventually we will have multiple clients for them, even if we do not now? Can a purely internal service become a public API at some point in the future? Sure. Can others on my team use my objects in ways I am unaware of? Often. When will this happen? I have no idea. I always want to design for multiple clients even if I do not have them now, if I can do it without excessive burden or over-design.

But wait! Aren't we violating the overall concept of limiting perspectives? After all, `Sender` is now both a conceptual object (an abstract class) and also an implemented class (in that it is now implementing factory behavior). Yes, we are, in a limited way, because we must sometimes bow to pragmatism in order to allow for unanticipated change, like this one, without putting in anticipatory code for every *possible* change.

In this example, `getInstance()` in `Sender` is making a simple decision about which subclass to build, and so long as that decision stays simple, we can probably live with it. If it becomes complex at all, however, we will want a separate factory to build the `Sender` subclasses. Does that mean the client objects will have to change, to switch from calling a static method on `Sender` to calling some other method on a separate factory? Not necessary. We can simply delegate.

```
public abstract class Sender {
    private static SenderFactory myFactory =
      SenderFactory.getInstance();

    public static Sender getInstance() {
      return myFactory.getSender();
    }
}

public class Client {
    private Sender mySender;

    public Client() {
      mySender = Sender.getInstance();
    }
}
```

This is optional, of course.

If the number of clients is small, or if we have a lot of time to refactor, we could change the clients to call the factory directly. It is just not necessary, and most important, we have not painted ourselves into a corner. You will also note that the constructor of `SenderFactory` (not shown) is obviously encapsulated as well, since `Sender` is using a static `getInstance()` method to build one.

We never know when *factories* might become polymorphic services either, so we encapsulate their constructors as well.

In addition, it is not at all uncommon for factories to be Singletons (a design pattern that ensures that only one instance of a class will ever exist, and provides global access to it, see Appendix B, "Overview of Patterns Used in the Examples," if you are unfamiliar with it). The refactoring steps from an encapsulated constructor to the Singleton pattern are trivial, as we will see in Appendix A, "Evolutionary Paths."

One of the major benefits of encapsulating construction is that it isolates future problems to one place. This makes maintenance much easier. For example, although there may be many clients for a service, it is rare that there are many factories. By putting the new function in the factory, a function that is often problematic, there is only one place that will experience changes.

Principles Versus Practices

I want to make a clear distinction here. Separating use from construction, *somehow*, is the principle. Encapsulating the constructor, as shown here, is a practice.

If you have a reason to create a separate object factory in your initial design, do so and you've gained the separation. If you're using an object-relational tool that creates instances for you from data in a database, you gain the separation that way. One client of mine instantiates objects in one section of code, serializes them, and then deserializes in the code that "uses" them. Separation again.

But none of these can be done *all the time*. Therefore, encapsulating the constructor is a fallback, an "at least do this" practice, when these other techniques are not warranted.

When you encapsulate, you don't have to over-design.

Making the Decision

Assuming this notion of encapsulating construction seems useful and virtuous to you, the next question that might well occur is

How does the *factory* (whether it is the static `getInstance()` method described above, or a separate object) decide which subclass to build? If the client holds the state that is needed to make the decision, won't we have to pass that into the factory? Doesn't that mean that we will have maintenance on the client(s) anyway?

Perhaps yes; perhaps no. The decision as to *which* subclass to build in a polymorphic set falls into one of the following three categories:

- An *intrinsic* issue, from the client's perspective
- An *extrinsic* issue, from the client's perspective
- A *rule* that does not vary by client

In the case of an *intrinsic* issue, state that the client possesses, it is true that the `getInstance()` method in the service class (`Sender`) will "grow a parameter" when the service becomes polymorphic, because the client will have to pass that information in so the decision can be made. This creates a bit of maintenance when the service becomes polymorphic, but consider this:

The client will be coupled to the state upon which the decision is made. That is unavoidable if the state is something that the client is responsible for, and is in fact a good thing in that case.

However, the client should not be coupled to *what that means* in terms of the proper version of the service to instantiate. If the rule in question changes, the client will not have to. This is where we failed on the Y2K issue: It was not that the date calculation change was hard, it was just *everywhere* and so it was expensive to change.

For example, let's say the client held a customer code, which bound to different rules for scheduling meetings with the customer.

A customer code of A or B means we can schedule meetings any time, and thus should instantiate the `AnytimeScheduler`. A customer code of C or D means we can only schedule meetings on the weekdays, and thus should instantiate a `WeekdayScheduler`.

Whereas it may be a perfectly reasonable cohesive issue for the client to hold the customer code, it is not reasonable for the rule "A|B=`AnytimeScheduler`, C|D=`WeekdayScheduler`" to be visible to the client. The binding of that rule is not his business, and should definitely be in one place, in case it changes. The factory becomes that one place.

A common example of an *extrinsic* issue is a GUI. If there is a GUI switch, set by the end user at runtime, which determines which of a set of polymorphic services is the right one to use, then we *definitely* do not want the client object building it. This is because the client would have to become coupled to the GUI in order to check it, and this is not a good path to be on. You never know when the GUI might change, or even cease to exist. Also, coupling to the GUI can make testing trickier.

However, if we have encapsulated the issue in a factory (again, an actual factory object or the static `getInstance()` method), we have minimized the coupling to the GUI to this one place, which makes it much easier to manage.

Finally, if it is just an arbitrary *rule* of some kind (we use `SenderImpl1` during business hours, and `SenderImpl2` when the shop is closed), we certainly want to encapsulate this, since such things are prone to change. The factory makes obvious sense in this case.

We cannot, using any set of practices, principles, or patterns, make the development of software into a simple, straightforward thing. The goal is to give the developers as much control over the situation as possible.

Commonality-Variability Analysis

The practice of encapsulating construction is one example of a key virtue in object orientation: separating issues into encapsulated islands of responsibility, and then limiting the coupling between those islands.

Another place where this shows up is in the patterns. The Gang of Four[4] recommended that we design to interfaces, which is another way of saying that relationships between entities should be established at the abstract level, so that coupling is, likewise, abstract. You will notice that this is a strong tendency in the patterns themselves; the clients of these patterns very frequently limit their relationships to an abstract base type. Factories help us to keep that relationship clean.

What the Gang of Four does not tell us is how to find these abstractions in the first place. If we are using one of the patterns defined in their book, the abstractions are indicated for us. However, not every good design is a Gang of Four pattern, and the patterns themselves can be implemented in any number of ways.

How can we find good, strong abstractions to design to when we do not have a specific pattern to apply in a well-known way?

In James Coplien's Ph.D. thesis, "Multi-Paradigm Design" (which became the book *Multi-Paradigm Design in C++*), he suggested that *commonality analysis,* as he defines it, is a strong way to determine *how* a set of objects might abstractly be considered the same, and then went on to suggest that *variability analysis* could be performed within the context of a given abstraction to determine how they were different.

Another way of saying this is that generally in object orientation we want to separate what will be changeable from what will be stable, and to encapsulate the changeable aspects wherever and whenever possible.

At Net Objectives, we use Coplien's techniques (which we call commonality-variability analysis, or CVA) as a way of defining the abstractions in a given domain and then, following the general thrust of the patterns, to use those abstractions to hide the varying implementations that are needed to meet current requirements. Thus, we remain open-closed for

4. Erich Gamma, Richard Helm, Ralph Johnson, and John Vlissides, authors of *Design Patterns: Elements of Reusable Object-Oriented Software.*

further variation as new requirements emerge, or as existing requirements change.

One nice thing about CVA is that you essentially already know how to do it. You have been doing it since you were about 8 months old, and started to conceptualize the world around you.

For instance, if you look outside your window and see the three things shown in Figure 9.1, you would have no difficulty identifying that these three things are trees even though they are really quite different from each other. If I asked you how they varied within the context of the concept tree you could easily point out that the pine and Joshua trees have needles, whereas the oak tree has leaves, and that the shapes of the trees are very different (triangular, round, and twisty).

If I ask you for other ways that these three things are the same, you could probably come up with alternatives: They are all living things, all plants, all made of cellulose, all generate oxygen, and so on.

The correct distinction mostly would have to do with your intent, or what we in software design call the context of the domain. As a firefighter, you might think of the trees as fuel, and they would vary by how readily they burn, how densely they grow, and so on. As a lumberman, you would think of them as lumber and they would vary by how straight the trunks were, how thick (useable) the branches are, the relative value to the consumer of redwood versus pine and so forth.

In CVA, we draw upon this very powerful part of our cognition, to create an analysis technique to help us find the concepts in the problem domain, which become abstractions in the solution domain, and then use them to encapsulate variation.

Figure 9.1 Commonality-variability analysis is something we do naturally.

Let's look at a concrete example.

The customer wants a system to amortize (deduct from his taxes) a portion of the value of the fixed assets owned by his company. He has to report to the state and federal government, yearly at tax time, the amount to be amortized for each asset for the given year.

In the process of gathering requirements, the following pieces of information emerge from the conversation:

> He owns various parcels of real property (land), which is amortized using the Double Declining algorithm, spread out over 33 years. This is true for both state and federal taxes.
>
> He owns company cars, which are amortized over 6 years, using the ACRS algorithm. However, cars purchased for business cannot be valued at greater than $30,000.00 due to a law regarding luxury cars. Anything over this limit may not be written off. This is true for both state and federal taxes.
>
> He owns office Automation equipment (computers and so forth), which are amortized over 3 years, also using the ACRS algorithm for the state. However, the federal government requires these assets also be calculated with an alternate algorithm, called Alternative Minimum Tax.
>
> Finally, he owns furniture and fixtures, which are amortized over 5 years using an algorithm called Straight Line. Also, separate reports must be generated for the state in which they were purchased, the state in which they were owned, and the federal government.
>
> When assets are retired, if there is remaining value, this is dealt with in various ways depending on negotiations with the government auditors at the time of purchase. The remaining balance may be written off, or lost entirely, or there may be an appraisal to see what the real remaining value is, which is written off.

CVA is not design; we want to decouple these requirements as much as we can before we start to look for objects and relationships. The main reason for this is that customers usually think of their businesses in terms of how they operate today, and how they have historically operated, but not *conceptually*.

For example, when our customer here said he owns "cars, which are amortized over 6 years, using the ACRS algorithm," he is coupling cars to a 6-year term and a particular algorithm for the write-off.

Business people think of trends when they make decisions, which is probably the right thing to do in business. As software professionals, we have to look at these same issues differently; we want to look for opportunities to decouple, encapsulate, and promote open-closed-ness for the *future* value of the system. Business people certainly understand the value of Return on Investment (ROI), but it is up to us to maximize it in the way we model their business in software.

The result of considering these requirements purely in terms of what is common and how those commonalities vary might produce the following view. Commonalities will be shown in bold, underlined text, and the variations within each common context will be listed in bullet points below them.

Assets

- Real property
- Automobiles
- Office automation equipment
- Furniture and fixtures

Amortization

- Double-Declining
- Straight Line
- ACRS
- Alternative Minimum Tax

Agencies

- State
- Federal Government

Disposal Rules

- Write off remaining value
- Write off appraised value
- Lose remaining value

Value Limits

- Luxury car limit

Terms

- 5 years
- 33 years
- 6 years
- 3 years

Notes

There is only one Value Limit in the system right now, the one for luxury cars. Can we establish a concept for something that has only one variation? Certainly, if we want to be open to adding more value limits in the future. Also, should the limit be called luxury car limit, 30,000 dollar limit, or something else? I like to do CVA with the customer present, so these questions can emerge and lead to productive discussions.

The Terms commonality varies purely by a number of years. Would we create a Terms abstract class and then derive classes for each of these varying terms? Probably not, but remember, we are not doing design at this point; we are only looking for concepts that can encapsulate variation. We will probably store the term simply as state on a class, encapsulating it that way.

In CVA, we look for the architecturally significant "is-a" relationships in a domain, so that we can *then* proceed to design, where we will look for ways to drive relationships between these abstractions, and to encapsulate everything that varies.

CVA is not hard, and it does not have to take a lot of time. It is not the answer but rather is a starting point that sets us up for strong design. I think of it as a practice because it is relatively easy to do (once you get a little practice under your belt) and pays off in multiple ways for the small amount of effort it requires.

Practices and Freedom

Always is an incredibly important word. It is dangerous when over-applied. There are really very few things to which "always" applies, yet I hear the word a lot, especially in my chosen field.

That said, when a true always is discovered, it is a very powerful thing. After you can establish a practice that can be universally applied to your benefit, without a "gotcha," then you are free to turn your attention to other, more subtle issues in the problem you are solving.

Because of that, you will do a better job.

Practices are part of the definition of a profession, and allow us to share what we know to be universally true, universally beneficial, with each other and with new people who enter the field. They are most valuable when they are

- Low cost
- Easy to teach
- Highly beneficial

It's also dangerous to call anything a true practice without a great deal of confidence that it is, truly, universal. Once it's called a practice, I'm going to do it without stopping to make a decision. We should add practices slowly, and with much consideration.

We also have to revisit our set of practices regularly, because changes to technology can create new concerns and evaporate old ones.

For instance, two universal concerns that dictated many decisions when I started as a developer were performance and memory usage (footprint). I would not say that these things are never important now, but they certainly are not always the critical make-or-break issues that they once were. What was universal in 1979 is not necessarily universal now.

This really means that we have to be highly collaborative, have to develop mechanisms for investigating new principles, practices, and patterns, and have easy ways to come to agreement and then disseminate them to the community at large.

I think this is a largely unsolved problem, one that we need to address over the next few years. I hope that books like this one will help, but they are by nature static, and we work in a highly changeable business.

When you visit Appendix B, you'll note that I and my organization are trying to get something started in our own small way, by supporting a Web-based repository for this kind of collaboration. It's a start.

Summary

Practices are important but only deliver their full value when they are shared among all practitioners. One of the reasons I focus so much on those practices that are easy to do is that they are also easy to teach.

I think it is the responsibility of the professional to teach things to other professionals when they do not know them. We are increasingly dependant upon (and therefore vulnerable to) the work of others, so it is in our own best interest to help them.

But it goes farther than this, I think. Establishing a set of reliable practices ensures that, more and more, our software can serve the needs of a changing world. As I point out frequently, software is becoming more and more important and influences the quality of life we enjoy to a greater degree every day.

I'm proud of that, and proud to be a part of it. I just want to do a good job, and I'm sure you do too.

Finally, I don't profess to have a comprehensive list yet, of course. This is something we have to figure out together, as a community (all of these practices have come from the community in the first place).

So . . . have a good practice to share? My ears are open. . . .

CHAPTER 10

Paying Attention to Disciplines: Unit Testing

I'm an older guy, and the bulk of my career predates most of the ideas I am putting in this book. Testing definitely qualifies. It's not that I didn't believe in *testing* during those years, I just didn't think it was my job. I thought it was a different domain, the domain of Quality Assurance, and that the QA people were there to catch my code as I tossed it over the wall to them.

Of course, I also sort of dreaded doing that, because I knew they were unlikely to come back with news I was eager to hear. In fact, without meaning to, I came to think of QA as "the enemy" to a certain degree.

So, when people like Kent Beck, Ron Jeffries, Ward Cunningham, and others starting promoting the idea that testing had value for developers and should be part of the development process, I was dubious—skeptical, even.

I was wrong. The value of writing tests, as a developer, proved itself to me quickly once I started doing it. In fact, I cannot think of anything that proved itself as fast as testing did.

If you're dubious, I don't blame you. But if you have not tried the kind of testing I'm going to outline here, I suggest that you give it a try for a while. If you are already an advocate, I have some things to add that I think you'll find valuable too.

Economies of Testing

In the last chapter, I outlined some practices that I find to be helpful, high-yield, and essentially no-cost. The fact that they cost you little or nothing means you can follow them all the time without having to think about them, freeing up the inquisitive and evaluative parts of your mind to deal with more complex issues.

Some practices, however, do have cost. For such a practice to also become a do-it-all-the-time sort of thing, it must yield truly profound value to the development process. It must solve many problems and provide critical guidance, to justify the extra work it takes to put it into practice.

These higher-level practices are things I am going to call *disciplines*, and the first one I want to examine is unit testing.

Here is an interesting dialectic:

- Most software development professionals extol the virtues of testing, and most modern software development processes include testing as one of the required elements in a project.
- Many, if not most, software developers do not test their code beyond making sure it compiles and—"let's see if it runs"—manual, functional testing.

I suppose the main reason for this is that most people feel testing is a cost they cannot afford. "I am too busy to write tests." "If I write the tests, I will not have time to write the code." These and similar statements are all too common among software developers. Indeed, many project managers discourage formal testing because they are concerned about their developers getting bogged down and becoming unproductive.

Alternately, teams often operate within a process that asks them to write the tests last. Developers see this as useless (not surprisingly) because they are staring at working code. Why write tests to prove that working code works?

Also, adding tests to a code that was not written with "testing in mind" is usually a very painful and annoying task. Code that works is not always particularly testable, as it may hide lots of implementation detail from outside entities; for this reason, the tests tend to be very coarse-grained (testing only the final, resulting behavior, and not the steps that produced it) and therefore are not very useful.

If testing is a time-waste, why is it so highly touted in the literature? Does it increase or reduce efficiency, in actual practice? Does it take more time than it saves, or save more time than it takes? Is it, in other words, worth it?

In my experience, it is unquestionably worth it, and in evolving a design I rely heavily on testing at very a low level (known as *unit testing*), where the testing is automated through an easy-to-use tool.

What makes unit testing useful? Hopefully, by the end of this chapter, you will see that it is useful in at least three ways.

- Writing tests is an investigation of my understanding of what the class under test is supposed to do. Understanding what you are going to do before you try to do it adds significant clarity to any process.
- The tests provide a safety net for refactoring. Emergent design is an incremental process, which means lots of change (even more change than we are used to). If we want to be aggressive in the changes we make, we need tests to increase our confidence that we have not broken anything.
- Tests are a kind of documentation, not about how the class operates, but about what it is supposed to do, from the outside perspective. This is very useful information for any new developer that comes into the picture, and needs to get up to speed on what came before. It can also help me in six months when I have forgotten what I did. Therefore, tests are a kind of design artifact, but with an advantage over functional specifications, UML diagrams, and the like: They compile and run. It's much easier to determine whether they are up-to-date with the system as it currently stands.

There is more than one kind of testing, of course. There are customer-acceptance tests, integration tests, load tests, and so forth.

What I am going to focus on here, and what I suggest will be the most profitable investigation for you, is specifically unit testing, and more specifically, automated unit testing.

Unit Testing

A unit test is designed to test a single functional unit in a system. If, for instance, I have a system that tracks financial transactions, and I have modeled a `Transaction` as a type in my system, then I will create a corresponding `TransactionTest` to demonstrate that the `Transaction` class is operating as expected.

For every class in the system, I create corresponding tests that send messages to the class via its public interface and evaluate the return value, to make sure it is what I expected it to be.

This would seem to double my work! I am not only writing `Transaction`, but also `TransactionTest`. As it turns out, this process actually saves me time and energy, and makes the development process less frustrating.

Why?

- First, unit testing *reduces debugging time*. In *Code Complete*, Steve McConnell (at times, quoting Harlan Mills and Phillipe Kahn) notes that programmers who advocate fixing bugs afterward rather than avoiding them up front tend to spend at least half of their time on this issue. Even worse, when a bug becomes elusive, it can bring a project virtually to a halt. Unit testing is about finding the bug immediately, at the level of the individual class, rather than waiting for it to show itself as part of the integrated project, where it then must be found.

- Second, unit testing *makes the development process more predictable*. Writing good unit tests does take time, but it is a more predictable amount of time than bug-hunting tends to be because it involves expressing things I know and understand, rather than hunting for the unknown. Predictability allows me to plan and schedule resources more efficiently.

- Third, unit testing *helps me to see quickly whether my class design is strongly cohesive, properly coupled, and non-redundant*. Weakly cohesive classes are very difficult to test because a class that does many unrelated things must have a test that tries every possible combination of those things, and such a test is laborious to write. Similarly, classes that are tightly coupled usually have to be tested together, because of the dependencies they have upon each other for their proper operation. If I try always to unit test by individual class, I find out about that coupling before it gets established too firmly. This becomes even more apparent when I demonstrate the test-first technique.

- Finally, unit testing makes me *think about my code in more depth in the first place*, especially if I write the tests as part of the same activity as writing the code.

Getting Shot by Your Own Magic Bullet

Unit testing is decidedly a powerful tool, and it can give you an increased sense of confidence and energy when refactoring your code. Up-front testing does even more in terms of efficiency and clarity.

However, there is a dark side.

If you fail to write adequate tests, your sense of confidence will be unwarranted, and you will proceed to forcefully, confidently, and energetically stomp all over your project. Test-writing is a skill, and automating the testing process does not eliminate the need for intelligent, skilled, experienced developers. Approach test-writing with the same diligence and care that guides you when you are coding your production classes.

Beware of

- *Tests that do not test enough.* Make sure you are testing for all the behavior you need for the class to operate as expected, and remember to test for exception handling.
- *Tests that give false positives.* Make sure that a test that *should* fail, *does* fail. Up-front testing helps enormously here, but only if you run the test before you change the class. Often, developers feel silly running tests that they *know* will fail, but this is very important to do, because it verifies that the test can, in fact, fail. A test that could never fail is, arguably, worse than no test at all.

Up-Front Testing

Is it better to write a class and then write the test that can verify its proper behavior? Or is it better to write the test first and then write the class to satisfy it?

Instinctively, I choose to write the class first; after all, I do not have anything to test until I do.

I used to think this way because I thought of a test as verification rather than an expression of intent. Now, I think of my designs as test-driven. I do not write the test to verify the code's behavior; I write it to define what the behavior should be before I write it. To do that, I have to understand what that behavior should be, and this is a good test for me to determine if I have "got it."

When I write unit tests, I am actually creating a set of documented expectations about my code: For example, "If I pass the method `add()` two integers, say a 5 and a 3, then it should return an 8." In order to write this, I must understand this intent well enough to think of an example, or a set of examples, that would test the class that seeks to fulfill my expectation.

In Douglas Adam's book *Hitchhiker's Guide to the Galaxy,* a tale is told about a huge, ancient, super computer called Deep Thought that is asked to provide the ultimate answer to "Life, the Universe, and Everything." Such a daunting task is possible, Deep Thought says, but "the program will take a little while to run." Seven and a half million years, to be precise.

Once begun, the process cannot be stopped until it completes (it is a little like shutting down my laptop when it's time to board the plane), and so this ancient civilization waits for its answer over the millennia. When the day arrives for the ultimate answer to Life, the Universe, and Everything, it turns out to be, as Deep Thought intones, "Forty-two."

The problem, of course, is that the people who asked the question did not really understand what they were asking, and so the answer did not make any sense to them. When asked if it can explain the question to which forty-two is the answer, Deep Thought regrettably says no, but it can design a better computer that will be able to. This computer turns out to be the Earth, and the civilizations on it.

The question, in other words, can be trickier than the answer.

Writing tests first forces me to examine my understanding of the purpose of the class (the question) I am about to create. It requires exact, detailed understanding because I cannot write specific tests with anything less. It is also a kind of documentation; implementation code records syntax and structure, but tests capture the semantics—not what can happen, but what is meant to happen under various circumstances.

This test-first technique can also help me avoid writing code I do not need. After I have created the tests, I need only write the code needed to pass them, and if the tests were complete, so is the code. In the example I will show later, you will see how writing tests first helped me to avoid some redundant and wasteful code.

Testing also satisfies the part of my nature that wants to write code and not just think about it. Perhaps this is a silly point, but I think it does bring some value to developers (like me) who are apt to leap to implementation too quickly. I do that because I like to code, and delaying it annoys me. Unit tests are typically written in the same language as the production classes will be, so even if my development process says I should wait until I understand what I am doing before I get too far into coding it, unit tests are code I can always write.

Finally, as I alluded to earlier, the testability of a class is often a great weather-eye for me; if a class is hard to test, it is often because it is weakly cohesive, or badly coupled, or has other quality issues that I did not see until I started to consider it in terms of the test. Now, I can certainly consider the testabilility of my code whether I actually write the tests first or not, but I am sure to do this if I am writing the tests before the code.

Tests tend to express single intentions, and thus the code that is created to satisfy them also tends to be about "one thing," which promotes cohesion in my methods and classes. Also, if I am writing a test case per class, the class written to satisfy the case tends to be decoupled from other classes in the system, which is also desired. I have to watch my code to make sure I eliminate redundancies, and so refactoring is an important part of this process; but in the end, my code will tend to be cleaner and of higher quality.

JUnit Framework

Unit tests are also helpful because they allow me, ideally, to retest my code each time I make a change.

Emergent design is all about code evolution, how to achieve strong and appropriate designs by refactoring code as requirements change, as new requirements are added, and as I come to understand the problem domain more thoroughly. But such evolution is tricky and dangerous if I do not have some way to confirm that each change I make has done nothing to harm the rest of the system.

So, I should test frequently, after each individual change. The more frequently I test, the easier it is to know what caused a failure; it will always be the change I "just made."

This could be an incredible time waster, unless I have a way of automating the entire testing process. Ideally, each time I make a change, I would like to hit a button and have the entire system tested, confirming (hopefully) that what I just did didn't break anything in it.

This is precisely what JUnit does.

JUnit was created by Kent Beck (of eXtreme Programming fame) and Erich Gamma (one of the Gang of Four, the authors of *Design Patterns: Elements of Reusable Object-Oriented Software*). It is a testing framework; it provides classes for you to extend and interfaces for you to implement, as well as an automated test-runner that organizes the execution of the tests. The JUnit framework is a simple, easy-to-understand tool that you can get for free from www.junit.org.

Whole books are written on JUnit and unit testing, so I will focus on a particular way of using it, which is the way I use it in my own projects and can therefore confidently recommend it for yours. Be aware, however, that there is more to the framework than I can cover here; so if you have a need that I do not cover, that does not mean JUnit cannot address it.

Other Unit Testing Frameworks

There are frameworks of the JUnit ilk for just about every popular programming language and environment you can name. NUnit and Visual Studio Team System for .Net languages, CPPUnit and CxxTest for C++, HTTPUnit for Web scripting, and so on.

They all work very much the same, with the differences primarily centering on those things that make the languages themselves different. (NUnit leans on .Net attributes, for instance.)

I have chosen JUnit because I need to focus on something if I am going to show a working example, and Java/Eclipse are available for free. The concepts I outline here will translate easily into the other *x*Unit tools.

JUnit Basics

When you download JUnit,[1] it comes in a Zip file. Unzip this to a convenient location, and then add the `JUnit.jar` file to your classpath. On

1. Important note: As of this writing, JUnit has undergone a complete redesign. If you know JUnit and use it in an earlier form, this material may look unfamiliar to you, because the 4.0 release changed most of the mechanisms of the framework.

my system, I placed the JUnit files under my `Program Files` directory in a subdirectory called `JUnit4.1`, so the classpath addition I made was

```
C:\Program Files\junit4.1\junit-4.1.jar;.
```

However, you may choose to place it elsewhere. Also, many distributions of Eclipse (a free java IDE) have this framework included in them. Similarly, a testing tool is included with some versions of Visual Studio for .Net.

After you have added JUnit to your classpath, the `JUnit` classes are available for import into your own tests. When I create a test, my convention is to name the test class with the same name as the class it is designed to test, plus the word `Test`. So, if I am writing a test for `ReportHeader`, I call the testing class `ReportHeaderTest`.

This class will contain a series of methods that conform to a specific convention. Each method must

- Grant public access
- Have a void return type
- Take no parameters
- Be marked as a test, for the framework to run it

JUnit uses two aspects of Java 5.0, annotations and static includes. My test methods must carry the `Test` annotation so that the testing tool will know to run them. I also like to name them test*something*, to make the code more readable. Also, other unit testing frameworks (and previous versions of JUnit) require this naming convention, so it's something I am accustomed to, and is likely familiar to other developers.

Examples are as follows.

```
public void testConstruction()

public void testIncrement()

public void testPutObject()
```

Within each of these test methods will be calls to methods called assertions that are provided in a static class called `Assert`. Each assertion expresses an expectation of the class being tested, and will report failures to the test-runner program. To make this easy, in Java, you can do a static import of the `Assert` class, which makes all the various assertions available without prepending them with `Assert`.

A *test case*, then, is a class that contains one or more `test` methods, which in turn make assertions about the class being tested. You design the test methods, and in so doing create a set of recorded expectations. Let's look at some examples.

JUnit Examples

For my purposes, I am going to describe a sample problem, and then solve it two ways.

- By writing code, then writing a test
- By writing the test case first, then refactoring the code repeatedly while adding test methods to the test.

The problem is a simplified version of an actual project that I worked on with a client. I am going to simplify it here so I can focus on the testing issues without having to wade through a lot of unrelated code, and also to avoid disclosing my client's code (those pesky non-disclosure agreements!).

In this problem, I have a security system that grants or disallows access to various parts of a large computer system. These permissions are stored in the system as *rules*. Each rule has the following:

- *A unique ID*. This is a string of characters that identifies the user, group, resource, and so on that is requesting a particular access, and the resource, process, or database transaction it wants to perform. It's a little like an XPath string, if you're familiar. The ID for a rule is immutable (it cannot be changed) and unique in the system. It is not optional, because a rule is meaningless without it.
- *A SQL string*. Transactions in the system being secured are expressed using the Structured Query Language, and so a rule will generally hold a SQL string that defines the resource being accessed. This can be empty (some rules are not about database transactions), but it is also immutable after the rule is created.
- *A priority*. This is stored as an integer, and may be 0 (low priority), 1 (medium priority), or 2 (high priority).

(Again, this is a vast simplification, but it will suffice for this example).

In addition, we will have a rule container, a class that can

- Store a rule, type-checking to make sure it is a rule and not some other object, and using the rule's ID as the key.
- Report the number of rules it currently holds.
- Return a given rule by ID.
- Check to see if another rule with the same ID is already being stored, when the rule container attempts to store a given rule. If there is one, the rule container will replace the existing rule with the new one, and force the priority of the new rule to high, or 2. This will allow the new rule to defeat any caching in the system.

Rule.java: Code First, Then Test

Let's model the rule itself first, and then write an appropriate test. Consider the following:

```
public class Rule {
        public static final int LOW = 0;
        public static final int MEDIUM = 1;
        public static final int HIGH = 2;

        private String myID;
        private String mySQL;
        private int myPriority;

        public Rule (String anID, String aSQL, int aPriority){
                myID = anID;
                mySQL = aSQL;
                myPriority = aPriority;
        }

        public String getID() {
                return myID;
        }

        public String getSQL() {
                return mySQL;
        }

        public int getPriority() {
                return myPriority;
        }
```

```
        public void setPriority(int aPriority) {
                myPriority = aPriority;
        }
}
```

This is a pretty straightforward data class. Since `myID` and `mySQL` are immutable, they have `get()` methods but no `set()` methods. `myPriority` has both, allowing it to be changed as needed. I also created the constants `Rule.LOW`, `Rule.MEDIUM`, and `Rule.HIGH` to make for more readable code. (I do not have to remember that 0 is low and so forth.)

I have left a few things out for now. This class is not in a package (or rather, it is in the default package), and I did not put validation in the constructor (assuring that the ID is not empty and that the priority is 0, 1, or 2), nor am I guarding against the priority being set to an invalid value, but the main behavior I need is here.

Let's look at the test case:

```
import static org.junit.Assert.*;
import org.junit.*;
public class RuleTest {
      private Rule testRule;
      @Test
      public void testRuleConstruction(){
            testRule = new Rule("testID", "testSQL", Rule.HIGH);
            assertEquals("is Rule ID correct",
                              "testID",
                              testRule.getID());
            assertEquals("is Rule SQL correct",
                              "testSQL",
                              testRule.getSQL());
            assertEquals("is Rule priority HIGH",
                              Rule.HIGH,
                              testRule.getPriority());
      }

      @Test
      public void testSetPriority(){
            testRule = new Rule("testID", "testSQL", Rule.HIGH);
              testRule.setPriority(Rule.MEDIUM);
              assertEquals("is Rule priority set MEDIUM",
                     Rule.MEDIUM,
                     testRule.getPriority());
```

```
            testRule.setPriority(Rule.LOW);
            assertEquals("is Rule priority set LOW",
                    Rule.LOW,
                    testRule.getPriority());
        }
}
```

Yes, the test code is slightly longer than the code it tests! As Deep Thought explained, the question is often trickier than the answer. Tests are meant to express our intentions, and the combinations of inputs and outputs that are both allowable and not allowable, and this can often be a larger job to write than code that is intended to operate only in an expected way. The test is an important tool for me because it gives me a place to investigate the variances and potential problems that my code will have to deal with.

Let's examine this in detail.

```
import static org.junit.Assert.*;
import org.junit.*;
```

The static import of the `Assert` class allows the simple calls to `assertEquals()` below. Static imports should be used sparingly, but are helpful in this version of JUnit. The import of `org.junit.*` gets me all the annotations I need.

```
    private Rule testRule;
```

To test the functionality of `Rule`, I need one to test. When testing, I usually need objects instantiated, sometimes in complex arrangements. These objects, taken all together, are referred to as the test's *fixture*. Here my fixture is a single `Rule` instance.

Why don't I need instances of any other classes to test `Rule`? It can be tested on its own. Does that tell us anything about it? I'll leave that hanging for just a little while . . .

```
        @Test
        public void testRuleConstruction(){
                testRule = new Rule("testID", "testSQL", Rule.HIGH);
                assertEquals("is Rule ID correct",
                                "testID",
                                testRule.getID());
```

```
        assertEquals("is Rule SQL correct",
                     "testSQL",
                     testRule.getSQL());
        assertEquals("is Rule priority HIGH",
                     Rule.HIGH,
                     testRule.getPriority());
    }
```

The annotation `@Test` is a flag to let the test runner know that this method is a unit test. The IDE I am using (Eclipse, because it's free and really nice) has a built-in test runner that looks for this.

This method tests the construction of the `Rule`, to make sure the state (data members) of `Rule` is properly set at construction time. Note that the method name is very descriptive; this can help when the test fails and I need to trace the problem.

First, I need my fixture object to be instantiated. I do so, setting `ID`, `SQL`, and `priority` to values I can then test for.

Next, I have three assertion methods. `RuleTest` statically imports the `Assert` class, which gives it access to all of its `assertxxxx` methods (which I detail at the end of the chapter) and here I am using `assertEquals`. This method compares two objects or primitives by value, and checks to see if they are equal. Note that this is different from checking to see if two object references point to the same object—that would be `assertSame()`. `AssertEquals` is testing for value equality.

- The first parameter is a message to be displayed by the test runner program if the assertion fails. This is optional (every assertion method is overloaded with a version that does not take the message `String`), but I always use it. Clarity, documented intentions, always good things.
- The second parameter is the value I expect. The assertion methods are overloaded to allow them to accept any primitive as well as an object reference.
- The third parameter is a call to the method I want to test.

If all three `assertEquals()` methods pass their test, this method will execute without any effect apart from the green bar I'll see in my test runner. If any one of these assertions fails, the test runner will immediately stop executing this method and report the failure to me, and throw up a red bar.

```
    @Test
    public void testSetPriority(){
          testRule = new Rule("testID", "testSQL", Rule.HIGH);
            testRule.setPriority(Rule.MEDIUM);
            assertEquals("is Rule priority set MEDIUM",
                   Rule.MEDIUM,
                   testRule.getPriority());


            testRule.setPriority(Rule.LOW);
            assertEquals("is Rule priority set LOW",
                   Rule.LOW,
                   testRule.getPriority());
        }
}
```

This is my second and final test of `Rule`. It tests to see that the `setPriority()` method works properly. You might note that I created the fixture as before: Each of these methods must stand alone, without any dependencies on the other methods in the class.

I compile these two classes, and (in Eclipse) tell the IDE to run RuleTest *as* a unit test, `Rule.class` and `RuleTest.class` into (see Figure 10.1).

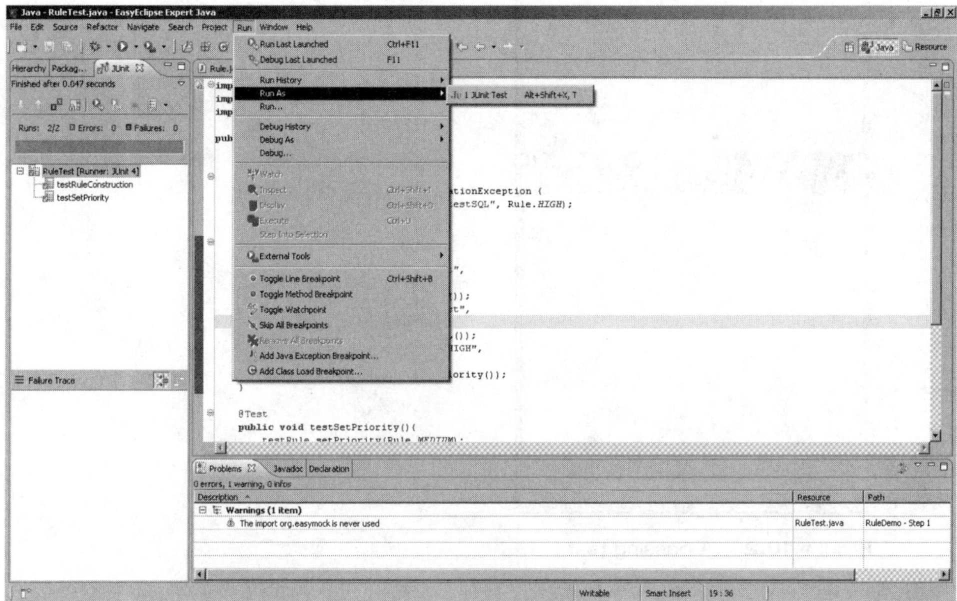

Figure 10.1 Eclipse selecting Run As on RuleTest

The tests should all pass, which is no fun for our first demonstration (try it anyway; see Figure 10.2). I usually pull the IDE's test runner out of the IDE (undocking it) and leave it running on my second monitor. Every time I make a change, I turn my head and run the test again.

This is rapid feedback, and it's a big part of what makes this kind of testing work. I test frequently, in small pieces; therefore, if anything is wrong I find out right away.

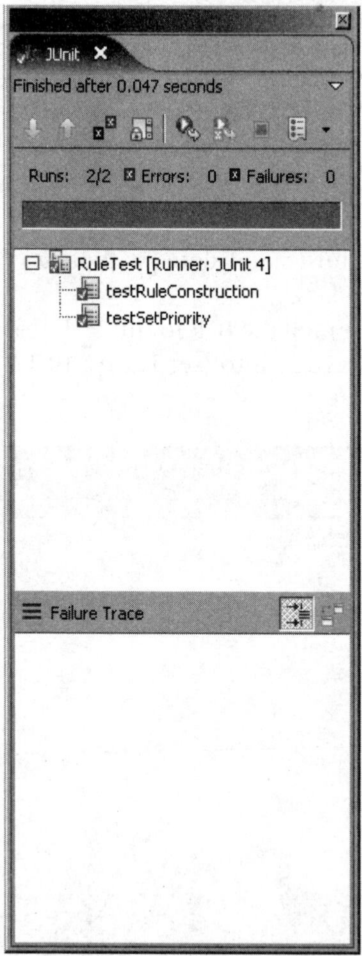

Figure 10.2 A passing test

So let's make a change: I will break the code on purpose, just so you can see how that gets reported.

```
public class Rule {
        public static final int LOW = 0;
        public static final int MEDIUM = 1;
        public static final int HIGH = 2;

        private String myID;
        private String mySQL;
        private int myPriority;

        public Rule (String anID, String aSQL, int aPriority){
                myID = anID;
                mySQL = aSQL;
                myPriority = aPriority;
        }

        public String getID() {
                return "BadID";
        }

        public String getSQL() {
                return mySQL;
        }

        public int getPriority() {
                return myPriority;
        }

        public void setPriority(int aPriority) {
                myPriority = aPriority;
        }
}
```

`getID()` will return "`BadID`" rather than the actual ID that was set by the constructor and store in `myID`, so the assert method that checks this will now fail (see Figure 10.3). Recompile `Rule` (no need to recompile `RuleTest`), and then run the test again.

Pretty straightforward message: We expected "`TestID`" and got "`BadID`". Go ahead and fix the code so it works again, and then recompile and rerun the test.

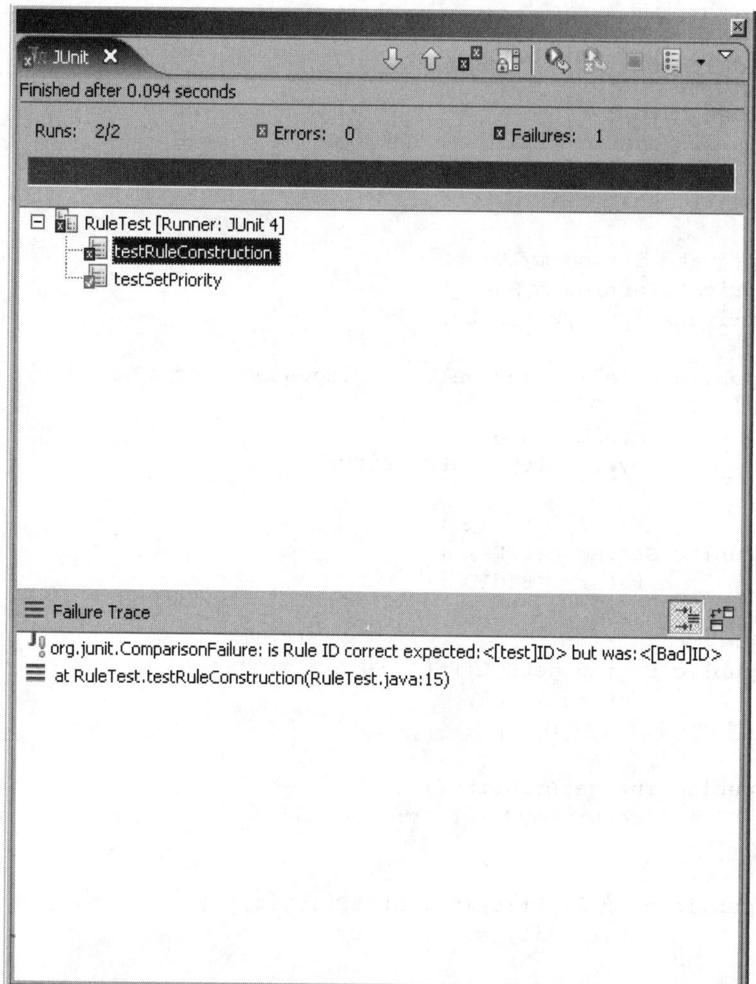

Figure 10.3 Rule failing the test

Rule is a very simple class, so you are probably thinking that in actual practice I would not bother writing tests for it, that for efficiency's sake I would only write tests for complex classes. In fact, I would write this test, and perhaps make it even more complete.

Why?

- When I come back in six months to change `Rule`, I want to be able to do so with impunity. If I can hit that Run button, I feel confident that I have broken nothing.
- Those other, more complex classes will likely use `Rule` a lot—it is a data class after all, and so it is meant to be used by other classes. That means that a change in `Rule` theoretically might break some other class. I need to know that, too.
- If I make my tests even more complete, I will express more about `Rule`. The test becomes a documentation of my intent, for other developers, or for myself in months to come.

RuleContainer.java: Test First, Then Code

Let's create our `RuleContainer`. However, this will be created opposite from the way I created `Rule`. I am going to

1. Create `RuleContainerTest`, with one test method that expresses a single intention (requirement)
2. Stub out `RuleContainer` (create methods, but no "guts")
3. Run my test, expecting it to fail
4. Change `RuleContainer` just enough to pass the test
5. Run my test again, expecting it to pass (fixing `RuleContainer` if it does not)
6. Return to 1, until there are no more intentions to express by tests

The requirements for the `RuleContainer` are as follows:

- Stores rules keyed by ID String
- Can report the number of rules it holds
- A duplicate ID String replaces an old rule with a new one
- When a rule replaces an old rule, it becomes high priority automatically
- Fetches rules by ID and returns them

The preceding items are the issues that become methods in my RuleContainer class. What to do with duplicates seems a further refinement on storing, rather than its own issue. So, I write my test for a single intention: My container can Store a rule and when I ask for a Report of the size of the collection after giving it a rule, the size will be correct.

```
import static org.junit.Assert.*;
import org.junit.*;

public class RuleContainerTest {

     @Test
     public void testPutRule() {
          Rule testRule =
               new Rule("TestID", "TestSQL", Rule.LOW);
          RuleContainer testRuleContainer =
               new RuleContainer();
          testRuleContainer.putRule(testRule);
          assertEquals("Number of rules should increase",
                       1,
                       testRuleContainer.getSize());
     }

}
```

The imports, class declaration, and annotations are the same as before with RuleTest.

testPutRule() expresses my first intention. I want to be able to put a Rule into the RuleContainer, and see that the size of the RuleContainer is 1 as a result. To test this, I need my fixture, which in this case consists of one Rule and one RuleContainer.

Note that RuleContainer needs a bigger fixture than Rule did when we wanted to test it. Why? Because you cannot test the container meaningfully without an instance of the thing it is designed to contain. This is *coupling*, and you'll note that the test makes it clear. This is the first example of a test relating to the quality of the code.

I get to ask myself right now, early in the process, if I think this coupling is logical, sensible, and intended. It is, of course, but sometimes I catch weird coupling just this way.

Next, I call putRule() on my testRuleContainer and immediately assert that the getSize() method on it should return a 1.

This does not compile, of course. There is no `RuleContainer`, and so I must create one. I must also create it with a `PutRule()` method that takes a `Rule` object reference, and with a `getSize()` method that returns an integer. The test dictates this.

So, the public methods of `RuleContainer` appear as shown in the following:

```
public class RuleContainer {

      public void putRule(Rule aRule){
      }


      public int getSize(){
               return 0;
      }

}
```

These methods are stubbed out. There is just enough behavior to get them to compile. They take the right parameters. Where they have void return type, I just code no method guts at all. Where they return an object reference, I return null. Where they return a primitive, I return the default value (0 for the int).

That is all I am going to write for now. This class obviously will not pass my test, but it is my starting point.

I run the test, and it fails (see Figure 10.4). At this point, the failure is a good thing: It confirms that my test does work (I can make a mistake when writing a test, obviously), and also that it could fail. A test that could never fail is worse than no test at all!

Now, I change `RuleContainer` just enough to pass the test.

```
public class RuleContainer {
     private int ruleCount = 0;

     public void putRule(Rule aRule){
          ruleCount++;
     }
     public int getSize(){
          return ruleCount;
     }
}
```

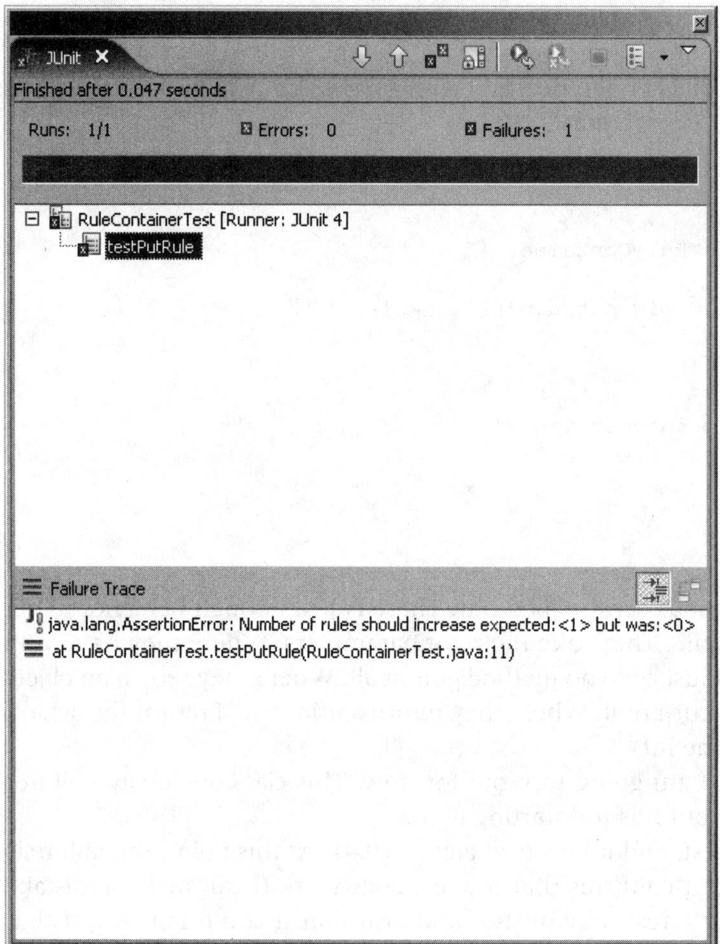

Figure 10.4 The test fails

I hear some groaning out there. I am not actually storing the `Rule` in `putRule()`, am I? I am just keeping track of the number of times it gets called, because that satisfies my test. Is this taking the idea to an extreme? Yes, I admit it is. To be honest, I would probably create a `Hashtable` or `Hashmap` member right now in `RuleContainer`, as a way of satisfying this test, because I know what is coming next.

I could also pass the test by just returning 1 at this point. How simply should I proceed? How much implementation should I put in now? The answer: It depends on your clarity and confidence level relative to the problem. If I'm really not sure where I am going, I will do the simplest thing I can, but I will write a lot more tests to help me figure things out. Here, I am pretty clear.

However, it is useful to look at this technique in its pure form. It is like the actor who needs to learn his lines before he can forget them and improvise "in character." I think it is important that I understand test-first in its pure form before I skip any steps.

Now, this passes, as shown in Figure 10.5.

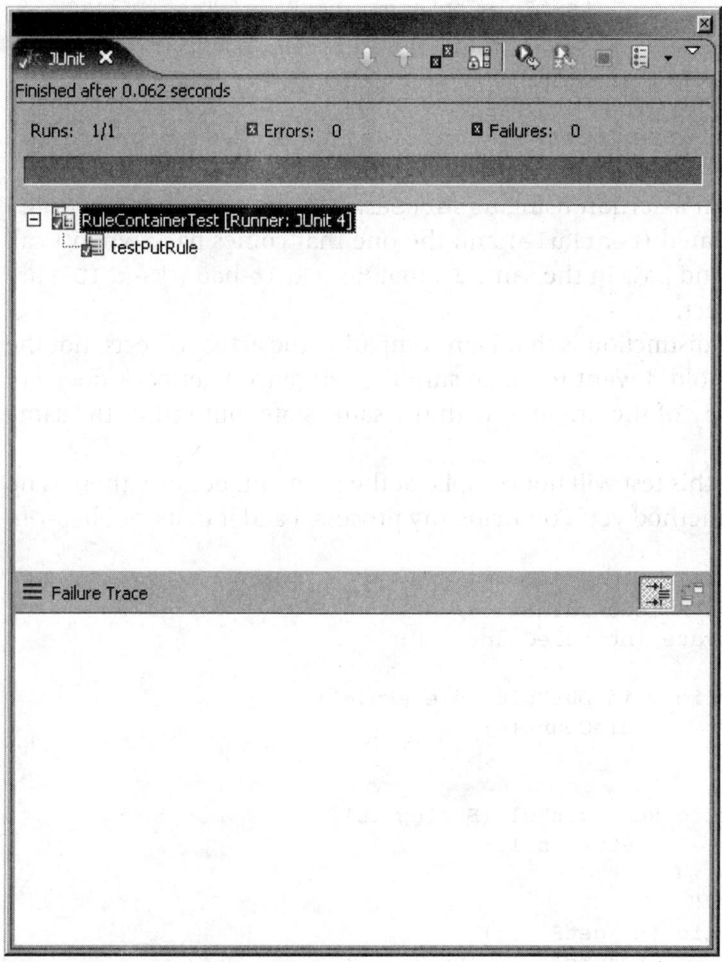

Figure 10.5 Now, the test passes

The next step is to identify another requirement/intention and write a test for it. I choose the *fetch a* `Rule` *by* `ID` requirement.

```
@Test
public void testGetRule() {
        Rule testRule =
        new Rule("TestID", "TestSQL", Rule.LOW);
        RuleContainer testRuleContainer = new RuleContainer();
        testRuleContainer.putRule(testRule);
        assertSame("Should get the same Rule",
                        testRule,
                        testRuleContainer.getRule("TestID"));
}
```

Each test method has to stand on its own, so I create my fixture objects anew. `testRule` and `testRuleContainer` are needed for this test, so I create them. Next, I use `putRule()` to store the rule, and then immediately create an assertion using `assertSame()`. This tests that the Rule I originally created (`testRule`) and the one that comes back when I call `getRule()` and pass in the same `ID` that `testRule` had (“`TestID`”) are the same object.

Again, the distinction is that I am comparing the actual objects, not the values they hold. I want to make sure the reference I get back does not point to a copy of the original, with the same state, but rather the same exact object.

Of course, this test will not compile at the moment, because there is no `getRule()` method yet. Following my process, I add it in its stubbed-out form.

```
public class RuleContainer {
        private int ruleCount = 0;

        public void putRule(Rule aRule){
                ruleCount++;
        }

        public Rule getRule(String ID){
                return null;
        }

        public int getSize(){
                return ruleCount;
        }
}
```

This will fail, of course; because getRule() is not implemented, it just returns a null. I fail the test anyway, of course. Then, we are back to RuleContainer with another modification.

```
import java.util.HashMap;
public class RuleContainer {
        private  HashMap myRules = new HashMap();

        public void putRule(Rule aRule){
                myRules.put(aRule.getID(), aRule);
        }

        public Rule getRule(String ID){
                return (Rule)myRules.get(ID);
        }

        public int getSize(){
                return myRules.keySet().size();
        }
}
```

Now, I am actually storing the Rule that is sent into putRule() by using an internal data member of HashMap type. I get the key out of the Rule by calling getID(), which nicely keeps Rule responsible for itself. When I need the size of the RuleContainer, I just return the size of the enumerator that I get when I ask the HashMap for its set of keys. Again, this passes nicely.

Looping back, I now want to deal with the duplicate ID situation. The requirements state that if a Rule is put into the container with an ID that matches a Rule that is already there, the new Rule will replace the old one, and the priority of the new Rule should be forced to high.

So, I write a new test method.

```
@Test
public void testDuplicateRule() {
    Rule testRule =
    new Rule("TestID", "TestSQL", Rule.LOW);
    Rule duplicateRule =
    new Rule("TestID", "TestSQL", Rule.LOW);
    RuleContainer testRuleContainer = new RuleContainer();
    testRuleContainer.putRule(testRule);
    testRuleContainer.putRule(duplicateRule);
    assertEquals("Duplicate should not increase size", 1,
                testRuleContainer.getSize());
```

```
        assertSame("New Rule should replace old",
                   duplicateRule,
                   testRuleContainer.getRule("TestID"));
        assertEquals("Priority should be set to High" +
                     "on replacement",
                     Rule.HIGH,
                     testRuleContainer.getRule("TestID").
                         getPriority());
}
```

Again, I need to make my fixture objects, and so I make `testRule`, `testRuleContainer`, and `DuplicateRule` (which has the same `ID` as `testRule`).

I add both rules to the `RuleContainer`, and then create the assertions I need to verify that

- The `RuleContainer` is size 1 after both `Rules` were put into it. This should be true, because the second `Rule` should have replaced the first.
- The `Rule` now stored under "`TestID`" should be the second `Rule`, `DuplicateRule`, not the original, `testRule`.
- The priority of the `Rule` now stored under "`TestID`" should be high, even though I created `DuplicateRule` with a medium priority.

Here is where it got a little interesting as I was writing this example. When people really get into automated unit testing, they have this tendency to compulsively hit the Run button just to see that green bar. It is a psychological thing, I suppose, but I have even caught developers who hit the Run button, get the green bar, and then hit it again when they thought no one was watching! Okay, sometimes I do that, too. It is comforting, a nice confirmation that you are doing okay.

I also like to compile a lot. When I coded the preceding test, I compiled it and ran JUnit after I had written only the first assertion, and before I had written the second and third assertions.

```
assertEquals("Duplicate should not increase size",
             1,
             testRuleContainer.getSize());
```

Of course, I knew it would fail. I had not written any logic to check for the existence of a duplicate `Rule ID`, replacing the old with the new, and so forth, so the size of the `RuleContainer` was going to be 2. The test would fail.

It passed!

Huh? Did I write the test wrong? I checked it immediately (here is one reason to run tests you "know" will fail—you might have written the test incorrectly). Nope, it looked fine.

Oh! Right! Java HashMaps already do this. They ensure that keys are unique, and if you store a new object with the same key as an existing one, the HashMap only keeps one of them and the number of keys stays the same. I was about to write code I did not need, because I had forgotten how Java's HashMap object handles this situation.

(Yeah, I forget things all the time. Another reason I like testing.)

This is another big reason that test-first can help you. When you are focused on the test, you are focused on the behavior you want, not how you will get it. The test expresses *the question* and writing it ensures that you understand it. But, you also then create *the answer* in the light of that understanding, and this can encompass many things: knowledge of the problem domain, knowledge of the objects others have written and you are using, knowledge of the language itself, and so forth.

The truth is that without writing the tests first, I would have created unneeded code, which would probably have never been weeded out of the project (assuming it worked, of course).

Now, back to Java HashMaps: When you try to store a duplicate key, does it throw out the old one or bounce the new one? If I cannot recall, I suppose I could go look it up in the JDK, as I would have in years past. But now, heck, let's just write the test and find out.

I coded the second assertion, compiled it, ran JUnit, and it passed as well. This confirmed that Java HashMaps do not simply throw away the new object when there is a duplication; they overwrite the original. That is what I wanted, so I got lucky there.

Of course, the third assertion does fail. The designers of HashMap were not prescient enough to anticipate the needs of my Rule objects to change priority. So, I need to make a change to RuleContainer.

```
import java.util.HashMap;
public class RuleContainer {
        private  HashMap myRules = new HashMap();

        public void putRule(Rule aRule){
                if (myRules.containsKey(aRule.getID())){
                        aRule.setPriority(Rule.HIGH);
                }
                myRules.put(aRule.getID(), aRule);
        }
```

```
    public Rule getRule(String ID){
        return (Rule)myRules.get(ID);
    }

    public int getSize(){
        return myRules.keySet().size();
    }
}
```

Eliminating Redundancy: @Before and @After

As I stated, each `testXXXXX()` method in a test class has to stand on its own. You cannot assume that any of other test methods have run, nor can you ensure the order the test will be run in. `JUnit` uses Java's reflection mechanisms to find the methods to run, and there is no guarantee in what order they will be found. Some unit testing frameworks allow you to specify a run order, but if you end up doing that a lot you should begin to wonder why there are so many order dependencies in your tests.

In my examples, we have been creating the fixture objects we need every time, in every test. This creates a lot of redundancy, and since eliminating redundancy is a first principle, we know for sure that we would rather eliminate it if possible.

Luckily, `JUnit` was invented by people who understand this principle very well, and so there are two annotations you can assign to methods: @Before and @After. You can call the methods anything you like, but to be consistent with other testing tools that dictate the method names, I like to call them `setUp()` and `tearDown()`.

Like the `testXXXXX()` methods, these two must have a void return type and take no parameters. However, the assurance is that `setUp()` is called right before each test method is called, and `tearDown()` is called right after. Each time.

So, if I have three test methods—`testOne()`, `testTwo()`, and `testThree()`—the IDE's testing mechanism will call

```
setUp() testOne() tearDown()
setUp() testTwo() tearDown()
setUp() testThree() tearDown()
```

However, again, the order of the actual test method calls may be different. So, I can refactor my `RuleTest` by putting the common fixture creation code into `setUp()`.

```
import static org.junit.Assert.*;
import org.junit.*;

public class RuleTest {
   private Rule testRule;
   @Before
   public void setUp() {
        testRule =
        new Rule("testID", "testSQL", Rule.HIGH);
   }

   @After
   Public void tearDown() {
        testRule = null;
   }
   @Test
   public void testRuleConstruction(){
        assertEquals("is Rule ID correct",
                     "testID",
                     testRule.getID());
        assertEquals("is Rule SQL correct",
                     "testSQL",
                     testRule.getSQL());
        assertEquals("is Rule priority HIGH",
                     Rule.HIGH,
                     testRule.getPriority());
   }

   @Test
   public void testSetPriority(){
        testRule.setPriority(Rule.MEDIUM);
        assertEquals("is Rule priority set MEDIUM",
                     Rule.MEDIUM,
                     testRule.getPriority());


        testRule.setPriority(Rule.LOW);
        assertEquals("is Rule priority set LOW",
                     Rule.LOW,
                     testRule.getPriority());
   }
}
```

Because Java has automatic garbage collection, is the `testRule = null;` in `tearDown()` really necessary? No, but it nicely documents my intentions, and it does not cost me much.

I can also refactor RuleContainerTest, although in the case of assertDuplicateRule(), I still have to make duplicateRule, because it is a fixture object needed only by the one individual test, so it is not redundant or common.

```
import static org.junit.Assert.*;
import org.junit.*;

public class RuleContainerTest {

     private Rule testRule;
     private RuleContainer testRuleContainer;

     @Before
     public void setUp() {
          testRule = new Rule("TestID", "TestSQL", Rule.LOW);
          testRuleContainer = new RuleContainer();
     }

     @After
     public void tearDown() {
          testRule = null;
          testRuleContainer = null;
     }

     @Test
     public void testPutRule() {
          testRuleContainer.putRule(testRule);
          assertEquals("Number of rules should increase",
                         1,
                         testRuleContainer.getSize());
     }


     @Test
     public void testDuplicateRule() {
          Rule duplicateRule =
          new Rule("TestID", "TestSQL2", Rule.MEDIUM);
          testRuleContainer.putRule(testRule);
          testRuleContainer.putRule(duplicateRule);

          assertEquals("Duplicate shouldn't increase size",
                         1,
                         testRuleContainer.getSize());

          assertSame("New Rule should replace old",
                       duplicateRule,
                       testRuleContainer.getRule("TestID"));
```

```
            assertEquals("should be set to High on " +
                         "replacement",
                         Rule.HIGH,
                         testRuleContainer.getRule("TestID").
                         getPriority());
      }

      @Test
      public void testGetRule() {
            testRuleContainer.putRule(testRule);
            assertSame("Should get the same Rule",
                       testRule,
                       testRuleContainer.getRule("TestID"));
      }
}
```

Automating Tests in Batches

My project now has two tests, one for each of my classes. As I move on, writing more tests and more classes, it becomes important that I have a way to run all the tests in one batch, conveniently.

Naturally, as I code, I am going to create as decoupled a design as possible; but I know that there will certainly be dependencies across the system, so I also want to make sure I test the entire system whenever I make a change to any part of it.

`JUnit` allows me to annotate a class to make it a suite, and then hand that class to the test-running mechanism of my IDE.

Here is the test suite for my current project.

```
import org.junit.runner.RunWith;
import org.junit.runners.Suite;

@RunWith(Suite.class)
@Suite.SuiteClasses({
      RuleTest.class,
      RuleContainerTest.class
      })
public class RuleTestSuite {

}
```

There are other ways of doing this, but I find this is the most straightforward, easy-to-maintain, and clearest way of creating a suite of tests, so it is my preferred usage (see Figure 10.6).

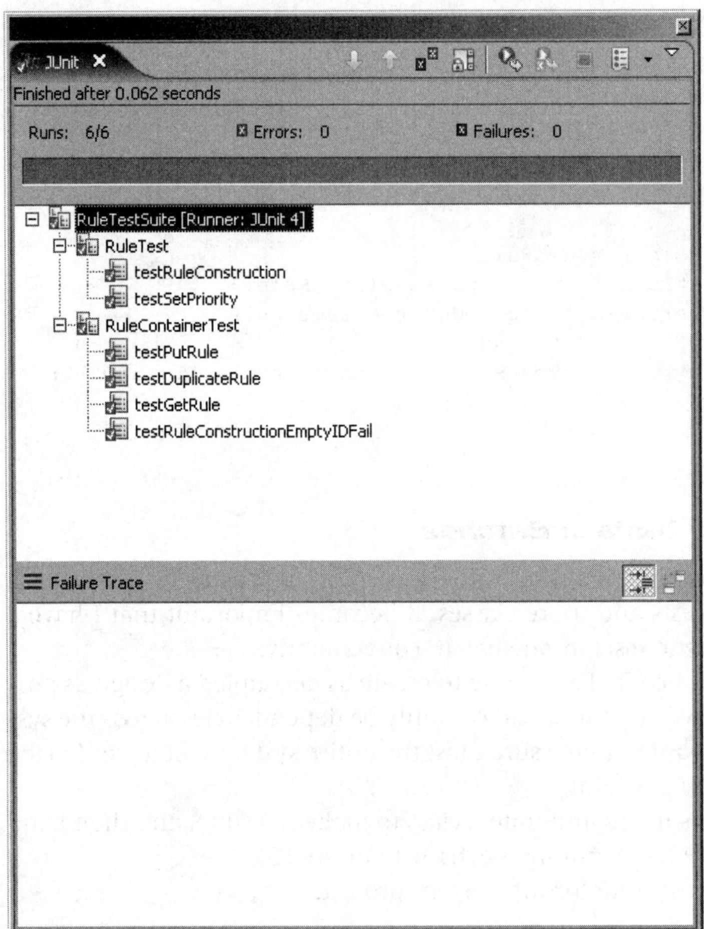

Figure 10.6 Testing the entire suite

Exceptions and Unit Testing

One wrinkle that you have to deal with in unit testing in Java comes from the fact that Java uses specified, checked exceptions. This means that a method that may throw an exception of some kind must specify this using the `throws` clause in the method declaration. Then, any method that calls the potentially throwing method must either place the call in a try/catch block, or must also declare that it throws the same exception.

Other languages don't necessarily require this, but even there you have to deal with the exceptions that your production code may throw, from the viewpoint of your tests.

In unit testing, I have two concerns regarding exceptions.

- I want to make sure that a method actually throws an exception under circumstances that warrant it. In other words, if I am using exception handling to deal with some issue in my design, I want to make sure it works when it should. A failure occurs when the exception is *not* thrown in a test such as this.
- I have to deal with exceptions that I do not expect to arise. The unit test should be able to catch and report these unexpected exceptions, and they should be distinct from the failure or success of the assertions I am intentionally making.

`JUnit` handles both of these quite nicely.

Take my `Rule` class as an example. Recall that the requirements stated that the `ID String` inside a `Rule` cannot be empty (the `SQL` String could be, but not the `ID`). I have not put any validation code in `Rule` to make sure that nobody tried to build one with an empty `ID String`. An exception in the constructor works nicely.

```
public Rule (String anID, String aSQL, int aPriority)
           throws InstantiationException{
    if(!anID.equals("")){
        myID = anID;
    } else throw new
        InstantiationException(
            "ID cannot be an empty String");
    mySQL = aSQL;
    myPriority = aPriority;
}
```

However, I have an immediate problem as soon as I do this: All the places in my code where I have `new Rule()` must now either be in a try/catch block, or called from a method that itself throws `InstantiationException`. Luckily, I can find all these by simply compiling the code; the compiler gives me a nice list to work from.

Also, luckily, I am using `setUp()` to create all my fixture objects, so I have one easy place to handle this. When creating my fixture objects, I do not expect to get the exception, so all I need to do is have setUp() rethrow the exception and let the test runner program handle it. JUnit reports any exception thrown in this as an *error* as opposed to a *failure*, which creates the distinction I was looking for. If an exception pops out in setUp(), something is probably wrong with my testing, since I did not expect this to happen.

```
// in RuleTest.java:

    @Before
    public void setUp() throws InstantiationException {
        testRule = new Rule("testID", "testSQL", Rule.HIGH);
    }

// in RuleContainerTest.java

    @Before
    public void setUp() throws InstantiationException {
        testRule = new Rule("TestID", "TestSQL", Rule.LOW);
        testRuleContainer = new RuleContainer();
    }
```

Alternately, I could simply have my setUp() methods throw Exception, which would cover all possible exceptions that might be thrown by any part of the fixture-creating process. I do not like this, however, because it side-steps another opportunity for me to document my intentions, and I like to capitalize on such opportunities whenever they arise. Also, catching Exception generically can break some of the test runners, including those that run JUnit tests.

I also create a new Rule in RuleContainerTest when I create the additional Rule for duplication testing, in testDuplicateRule. Again, I do not expect a problem (I am not passing in an empty ID), so I prefer to rethrow the exception if I get it, so it is reported as an error:

```
// in RuleContainerTest.java

@Test
public void testDuplicateRule()
                                throws InstantiationException {
    Rule duplicateRule = new Rule("TestID",
                                  "TestSQL2",
                                  Rule.MEDIUM);
    testRuleContainer.putRule(testRule);
    testRuleContainer.putRule(duplicateRule);
```

```
    assertEquals("Duplicate should not increase size",
                 1,
                 testRuleContainer.getSize());

    assertSame("New Rule should replace old",
               duplicateRule,
               testRuleContainer.getRule("TestID"));

    assertEquals("Should be set to High on replacement",
                 Rule.HIGH,
                 testRuleContainer.getRule("TestID").
                 getPriority());
}
```

This is all well and good, and everything should compile. My suite runs and reports no failures.

However, this is not quite enough. I want to make sure that an exception does get thrown if anyone tries to make a `Rule` with an empty `ID`. I need a new test method, and it should succeed if the exception gets thrown, rather than fail. To do this, I have to do something that looks rather odd at first.

```
// In RuleTest.java, add a new test method:

@Test
public void testRuleConstructionEmptyIDFail(){
    try {
        Rule failingRule =
        new Rule ("", "TestSQL", Rule.MEDIUM);
        fail("Rule instantiated with empty ID");
    } catch(InstantiationException ie){}
}
```

If I get past `Rule failingRule = new Rule ("", "TestSQL", Rule.MEDIUM);` without an exception being thrown, this is a failure of the `Rule` class to properly function. I can force a failure by calling the inherited `fail()` method I got from `TestCase`.

However, if an exception is thrown in this case, that indicates a success! So, I do that big, awful exception-handling no-no: I swallow the exception in a catch clause that does nothing. Normally, swallowing and ignoring an exception mean you have to wear the pointy hat and sit in the corner, but this is the one case where I get to do this and feel good about myself, so I will enjoy the moment.

I can go on now to create more validation, such as to assure that the priority integer is in the proper range, but I will use these same techniques throughout.

Mock Objects

It is all well and good for me to claim that untestable code is an indicator of poor quality, but the fact of the matter is that systems have coupling (no coupling, no system), and some forms of coupling do introduce difficulties for testing.

One very common problem comes up when the class I am trying to test has a dependency to an *ephemeral* object. An ephemeral object is one that has unpredictable state. For example:

```
public interface DataObject {
    float fetchRate();
}
public class DAO implements DataObject {
    public float fetchRate(){
        float rate = 0.0;
        // Code here to fetch current rate from database
        return rate;
    }
}
```

The class `DAO` is ephemeral because the value returned from `fetchRate()` depends on what happens to be in the database at the particular moment it gets called. This unpredictability affects the testability of any object that uses `DAO`.

```
public class BusinessRule {
    private float commissionRate = .10;
    private DataObject myDataObject;

    public BusinessRule(){
        myDataObject = new ConcreteDAO();
    }
    public float getRate(){
        float baseRate = myDataObject.fetchRate();
        return baseRate + (baseRate * commissionRate);
    }
}
```

Although BusinessRule has theoretically testable behavior (it returns something), it depends on DAO to get part of the information needed to fulfill the getRate() responsibility; and since DAO is ephemeral, I have no way to test getRate() against a predictable result.

One obvious solution to this is to create a version of DAO that does not actually contact the database, but rather reliably returns a well-known value. (A secondary advantage to this, by the way, is that I do not need access to the database when unit testing.) Such an object is called a *mock object*. These objects are typically used to enable testing on a class that has an ephemeral dependency.

Assuming there is some good, dependable, practical way of obtaining mock versions of my ephemeral object, I still have a problem.

How can I get BusinessRule to use my substitute version of DAO (once I have it) instead of the real DAO that makes it so untestable?

BusinessRule has fully encapsulated the creation of its DAO service object, and has also encapsulated the fact that it uses an instance DAO. This is a good thing, because no other entity in my design can ever become coupled to these things, if they are hidden like this. The constructor of BusinessRule builds its own instance of DAO privately, and then the class proceeds to use that instance without revealing this detail of its implementation. This is encapsulation of design, essentially, since the delegation itself is hidden from classes that interact with BusinessRule.

Also, if I start handcrafting mock objects to enable such classes to be testable, and I also make the unit tests themselves, it seems like I am creating a heck of a lot more classes than I was when I just wrote the production classes. Isn't this unit testing thing getting out of hand?

To summarize the issues

- BusinessRule secretly uses DAO. DAO is ephemeral, which makes BusinessRule untestable. I need to make a Mock version of DAO, but I would rather not actually make another whole class each time I do this.
- BusinessRule has no way to "switch" this Mock DAO for the real DAO. I like the fact that the relationship between BusinessRule and DAO is encapsulated, and I would like to keep their little secret under wraps. People will talk.

I will take these one at a time.

MockObject Frameworks

There are frameworks that can help you make mock versions of your ephemeral classes, in an automated fashion that requires you to create and maintain no additional classes in your project. One such, and the one I use for my example, is Tammo Freese's *EasyMock*.

There are others. EasyMock has strengths and weaknesses, as they all do, so you may prefer another tool. I just needed to settle on something to demonstrate the concepts here, and EasyMock suits my need. EasyMock is an open source project, available under the MIT license, and can be downloaded from www.easymock.org, as shown in Figure 10.7.

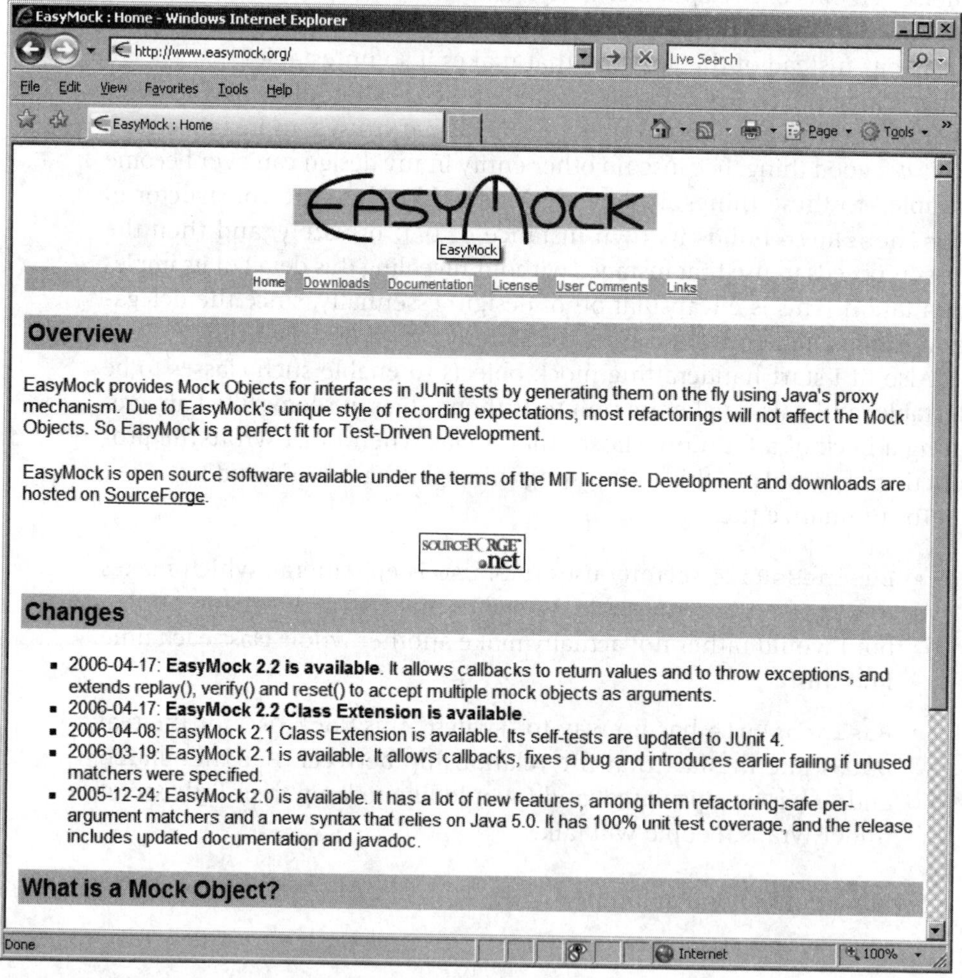

Figure 10.7 EasyMock Web site: www.easymock.org

> **EasyMock Is a Dynamic Tool**
>
> One critical distinction is that EasyMock and frameworks like it are dynamic tools. There are other mock-generating projects out there (such as Mock Maker) that do code generation and create mock classes that you compile and keep in your project.
>
> I prefer to avoid that if I can, and create the mocks on-the-fly as I need them. This way, when I pull the unit tests from a project, no traces remain behind.
>
> Your mileage may vary.

If you cannot use a mocking tool like this, or don't wish to, you can simply handcraft the mock object (usually by subclassing the real one)—that's what some people call a fake. Handcrafted mock is just as good a term. We'll do both the automated and handcrafted versions.

EasyMock is for Java only, and it can only mock an interface,[2] but as noted earlier, the preceding `DAO` implements the `DataObject` interface and (apart from the new `DAO()` code in the constructor) `BusinessRule` uses it as `DataObject`.

EasyMock allows the `TestCase` class to create, at testing runtime, a mock object that implements this same interface. The object it creates also has a mechanism that allows my testing code to condition it, to ensure predicable results.

Let's make a start.

```
import org.easymock.*;
import static org.junit.Assert.*;
import org.junit.*;

public class BusinessRuleTest extends {
    private BusinessRule testBR;

        public void setUp(){
            testBR = new BusinessRule();
        }
    }
}
```

2. At the time of this writing, mocking tools are very much "in play," and they change a lot. Also, most of them are open source. So, if you cannot use an open-source tool, or if tools that are not yet very stable are a problem, you might want to create you own tool or handcraft your mocks.

Hopefully, this is a familiar beginning for a unit test.

EasyMock enables this test to create the needed `DataObject` mock on-the-fly. We do not need to create (or maintain) any new classes; the mock is totally contained in the test.

```
import org.easymock.*;
import static org.junit.Assert.*;
import org.junit.*;

public class BusinessRuleTest extends TestCase {
    private BusinessRule testBR;
    private MockControl control;

    public void setUp(){
         testBR = new BusinessRule();
         control = EasyMock.controlFor(DataObject.class);
    }
}
```

In EasyMock, I begin by creating a control based on the interface I am going to mock. This control object can now be used to create the mock instance.

```
import org.easymock.*;
import static org.junit.Assert.*;
import org.junit.*;

public class BusinessRuleTest extends TestCase {
    private BusinessRule testBR;
    private MockControl control;
    private DataObject mockDAO;

    public void setUp(){
         testBR = new BusinessRule();
         control = EasyMock.controlFor(DataObject.class);
         MockDAO = (DataObject)control.getMock();
    }
}
```

Now I have `MockDAO`, which refers to an instance that is totally substitutable for any object that implements the `DataObject` interface, such as my `DAO` class.

But I cannot use the mock yet, at least with EasyMock. Instances created with this framework come into being initially in a *record* state. This allows me to record how I want `MockDAO` to behave after it is activated.

To do this, I can create a test method that conditions MockDAO to behave in a predictable way, and then activates it, so it can be used as any old DataObject implementation would be.

```
public void testGetRate(){
    mockDAO.fetchRate();
    control.setReturnValue(50.00);
    control.activate();
}
```

The line mockDAO.fetchRate();, issued when MockDAO is in the record state, basically tells the Mock that the test will call this method; and the control.setReturnValue(50.00); line says that when it does, return the value 50.00. The call to control.activate(); then puts the Mock into its active state, which means any further call to mockDAO.fetchRate(); will return a value, rather than just record the call.

There is more to EasyMock, but you get the idea. Other mocking frameworks do this differently, but this is a pretty common general approach.

Faking It

Another way to go, if you can't or don't want to use a mocking tool, is to write a handcrafted mock, or fake.

```
public class FakeDAO implements DataObject {
    float dummyRate = 0.0;
    public float fetchRate(){
        return dummyRate;
    }
    public void setRate(float newRate) {
        dummyRate = newRate;
    }
}
```

If the unit test holds a reference to this class as FakeDAO, it must have access to the additional method setRate(). If BusinessRule holds it in an up-cast as DAO, it does not. This allows the test to condition the fake behavior, but does not couple the production class to this only-for-testing version of DAO.

One problem still remains, of course: How can the test get testBR, the instance of BusinessRule it is testing, to use mockDAO or FakeDAO instead of the real DAO instance it builds for itself? We can do that, by injecting this dependency or by using a technique called endo-testing.

Dependency Injection and the Endo-Testing Technique

Your first reaction to this issue might well have been, as mine was, to either parameterize or overload BusinessRule's constructor.

```
public BusinessRule(DataObject aDAO){
    myDataObject = aDAO;
}

//...or...

public BusinessRule(){
    this(new DAO());
}

public BusinessRule(DataObject aDAO){
    myDataObject = aDAO;
}
```

In fact, this is a way to solve the problem, and is often called *dependency injection*. In some cases, it is fine to do this.

On the other hand, this might allow other objects to interfere with BusinessRule's behavior, and couple them to the specifics of its design, at least when instantiating it.

If you are using object factories, you might say, "Eh, that's okay; the factory is coupled to it anyway," and you would be right. But I get queasy whenever I weaken any aspect of my design solely to enable a test. Also, if I do not want to ship my mocks and tests with my production code, I have to maintain the factories when I pull these classes out. That makes me queasy, too.

Maybe you have a stronger stomach than I do, maybe not. But here is a technique you can sometimes use to avoid the issue entirely.

Endo-Testing

I am not sure who came up with the endo-testing technique, but it was not me. I came across it in an article by Alexander Day Chaffee and William Pietri, published on IBM's Developerworks Web site: www.ibm.com/developerworks/java/library/j-mocktest.html.

Endo-Testing

To enable endo-testing, we start with a minor change to BusinessRule.

Step 1: Use a Factory method in the constructor of BusinessRule.

```
public BusinessRule(){
    myDataObject = makeDao();
}

protected DataObject makeDao(){
    return new DAO();
}
```

Here, the constructor delegates the "build the DAO" issue to the protected method makeDao(), which can be overwritten (to return the mock instead) if we subclass BusinessRule; then I can test the subclass instead of the original.

But oy! I hear you cry. More classes! Not when we have inner classes, as we do in Java and similar languages. In fact, in Java, we have anonymous inner classes, so we can create our "BusinessRule version that uses the MockDAO" completely on-the-fly, and without creating another type to maintain and/or keep in synch with the original. Here is the whole thing, using an automated mock object, with the endo-testing stuff in bold:

```
import org.easymock.*;
import static org.junit.Assert.*;
import org.junit.*;

public class BusinessRuleTest extends TestCase {
    private BusinessRule testBR;
    private MockControl control;
    private DataObject mockDAO;

    public void setUp(){
        control = EasyMock.controlFor(DataObject.class);
        mockDAO = (DataObject)control.getMock();
        testBR = new BusinessRule(){
            protected DataObject makeDao(){
            return mockDAO();
        };
    }
```

```
    public void testGetRate(){
        mockDAO.fetchRate();
        control.setReturnValue(50.00);
        control.activate();

        assertEquals("Testing getRate()", 50 * .10,
                     testBR.getRate())
    }
}
```

Now `testBR` is set not to an instance of `BusinessRule`, but rather to an extending anonymous inner class, with the `makeDao()` method overridden to return the mock instead of a real `DAO` instance. In the assertion, `testBR's` overall behavior is tested, but the "ephemerality" of `DAO` no longer influences the results.

It is a neat little trick. It depends on the ability to create a class on-the-fly, and of course you cannot do it if the class needs to be `final` or `sealed`.

Summary

Unit testing is an essential tool in emergent design. It helps me in the following ways:

- Unit testing enables me to refactor confidently. If I refactor and then run my unit tests and they pass, I know that I have not inadvertently broken anything. Anticipating this benefit, I am more willing to refactor in the first place, even eager to do so, and will do it more often.
- Unit testing causes me to think about the nature of my problem domain and my design, especially if I write the tests before the code. If I try to write a test and I cannot, either I do not understand the problem as well as I thought (and I can immediately ask for more details from the customer) or I have a cohesion, coupling, or redundancy problem in my design that is making the test difficult (and I should change it now, before the problem mushrooms).

Mock objects can help greatly when certain objects in my design have ephemeral dependencies, and as in unit testing, automation makes this realistically doable. Finally, the endo-testing technique can allow the insertion of mocks into dependant classes, without breaking the encapsulation of their design.

CHAPTER 11

Paying Attention to Disciplines: Refactoring

Refactoring is not a new idea. I have been doing it, in one sense or another, for my entire career as a software developer, with neither a name for it nor any systematic way of describing it. I am "doing refactoring" whenever I am changing my code because I do not like how it is written, for whatever reason that is. I suspect this is true for you, too.

I have been doing refactoring in the chapters that precede this one—when I changed an example to make it more cohesive, or to decouple it, or to remove redundancy, or to make the code more readable. These were all refactorings because I was changing the code to make it better code, rather than to change its behavior.

In the year 2000, Martin Fowler wrote a very important book called *Refactoring: Improving the Design of Existing Code*, in which he took the process we had all been doing (with various degrees of efficiency and effectiveness) and gave it a structure and a set of rules to guide us. This turns out to be very important, because it is the *discipline* of refactoring that helps us to reduce the fear we normally feel when we make changes to code that currently seems to work properly.

You know the feeling. You are working on your code and you see a method or an entire class that is poorly designed, and you know that it really ought to be changed, but you are afraid that

- You will break it
- You will break something else that uses it
- Either way, it will be your fault

Emergent design is all about changing code, due to the need to improve it (in terms of, chant with me, "coupling, cohesion, redundancy, readability, testability"), because the requirements of the project have become clearer to me or have changed, or as part of the process of up-front testing. In other words, if I am going to work in an evolutionary way, I am going to be changing my code more than I have in the past, and so I need something in my process to make change less worrisome and more reliable.

But refactoring is more than this. I want to recast change from the traditional role it has played in software development—an opportunity to fail, a danger—to something more positive. I want to make change my ally, to alter the equation of change such that it becomes an opportunity to succeed, and a chance to improve my code.

I need to be able to make changes confidently, so I can concentrate on the goals I have in making the change, and less on the process of change itself. This concentration, combined with a good understanding of patterns, will give me the mental freedom and power to recognize the designs that are emerging from my process, and capitalize on the opportunities they represent.

For many years, I accepted the belief that code decays over time, that this is an inevitable reality in software development. I do not want to accept that any more. I want to see every change I make as a step along the way toward correctness and increased value, a moment of evolution in the lifecycle of my project. Typically, the need to make a change is motivated by one of two things:

- A bug has been found, or the system fails to meet a requirement
- A new requirement (or a better understanding of an existing requirement) has emerged

Either way, the motivation represents a pressurizing force that stresses the existing design, and in making a change to accommodate this force, I am not only improving the quality of the code, but also making the system more appropriate to the needs it is intended to address. In other words, each time I make a change because of a business need, the change tends to align the software with the real ways it will be used.

Thus, change can become an opportunity instead of a danger, if I can find a way to approach it with confidence and aggression.

This is what refactoring will do for me.

Refactoring Bad Code

Fowler says, "Refactoring is the process of changing a software system in such a way that it does not alter the external behavior of the code yet improves its internal structure." Just so. The question, of course, is what is meant by "improves." If we do not alter the external behavior of a class or method, how can we say we have improved it internally? What is the nature of the improvement?

Let's look at an example.

```
import java.util.*;
public class ReportCard {
   public String studentName;
   public ArrayList clines;

   public void printReport(){
       System.out.println("Report card for " + studentName );
       System.out.println("-------------------------------");
       System.out.println("Course Title                Grade");
       Iterator grades = clines.iterator();
       CourseGrade grade;
       double avg = 0.0;
       while(grades.hasNext()) {
          grade = (CourseGrade)grades.next();
           System.out.println(grade.title + "             " +
                                    grade.grade);
           if(!(grade.grade=='F')) {
               avg = avg + grade.grade-64;
           }
       }
       avg = avg / clines.size();
       System.out.println("-------------------------------");
       System.out.println("Grade Point Average = " + avg);
   }
}

class CourseGrade{
   public String title;
   public char grade;
}
```

There are a lot of things I do not like about this. Fowler says that my sense of smell is at work here. This code is "smelly" right off, and it is pretty easy to determine the source of the odor if I examine it carefully.

First, the `printReport()` method is far too complicated—it does too much, and it is not particularly readable. Right away, I can see that I should move some of this code into private methods that work on a more fine-grained level, and keep `printReport()` at the specification level of perspective (see Chapter 7, "Paying Attention to Qualities and Pathologies"). This will follow the principle that I want strong cohesion in my methods.

Also, I do not like that `CourseGrade` has public members rather than private members with `get()` and `set()` (accessor/mutator) methods to provide access to them. I also think it should have a constructor to ensure that I never accidentally get a `CourseGrade` instance without meaningful state. This helps to ensure that these classes are logically coupled (nothing is coupled to the "fact" that `CourseGrade` has these members per se, only that it has the responsibility of somehow tracking the title of the course and the grade received).

Similarly, I do not like that `studentName` and `clines` are public in `ReportCard`. They should be private, with accessor methods too. The name `clines` is not terribly descriptive either—it does not add to the readability of this code. I know that I want my code to be as readable as possible.

However, it runs. It works. If I change it to "improve" it and in the process damage it to the point that it no longer works, I will have essentially vandalized the code. I am sure to be unpopular for that! I will be accused of being a "purist" or being arrogant because I think I know better, and have broken the code as a result.

When I get to the mechanics of refactoring later in this chapter, I will show how I can improve the odor of this code without fear of harming it.

Refactoring Good Code

Fowler's emphasis is on refactoring code that works but could be implemented in a way that is easier to understand. After refactoring, the code is clearer in purpose, thus making it easier to change in the future. This is extremely powerful.

However, the same techniques that allow us to confidently make changes to poorly written code also allow us to change code that was well-written, but later needed changing due to a new or changed requirement. Or, sometimes code that *seemed* fine when I wrote it is revealed to be naive when I finally gain understanding of the nature of the problem being solved.

In other words, my code may be strong cohesive, intentionally coupled, free of redundancies, and clear as a bell, but still prove to be inadequate to address the problem domain sufficiently.

This can easily happen if I am trying to avoid waste in my design, for instance, if I make the `CourseGrade` in the code example above an interface instead of a class.

```
public interface CourseGrade {
     public String getTitle();
     public char getGrade();
}

public class BasicCourseGrade implements CourseGrade {
     // Implementation here
}
```

I could easily argue that this is decoupled to a greater degree than the previous design, even if I refactored the original code to use accessor methods. This is because `ReportCard` would not even have identity coupling to `BasicCourseGrade`, and I would be free to add other specialized implementations to the system—`ProbationaryCourseGrade`, for instance—without having to modify `ReportCard`.

But if my requirements state that there are `CourseGrades` and only `CourseGrades`, then using an interface at this point is wasteful of my time, wasteful of the process by which this code is stored, version controlled, and so forth, and creates more complexity than is required to solve the problem.

And requirements, of course, never change.

(I will let you mop up your coffee and dry your tears of laughter before I proceed.)

Yes, of course, the problem is that the very same domain expert who was absolutely certain there was only one kind of course grade may very well come back later and change his tune. This is because

- He may not understand the implications, in the software development sense, of the word *never*. Software development is more exacting than many other professions, requiring more precise language than most people are accustomed to using.
- You may not have asked the question you meant to ask, given your limited understanding of his problem domain and its traditions.

- You may have misunderstood his answer when you asked the question in the first place.
- Things may have changed since his first answer.

So, we can do the following:

- Complain and commiserate about the fact that requirements always seem to be in flux.
- Over-design everything to allow for any possible change we can imagine.
- Assume that this is a reality of the business we are in and prepare ourselves to deal with it.

We are back to the overall nature of our profession again. We do not plan, do, test, and ship; we code what we know and expect it will evolve.

Structural Changes Versus Functional Changes

One of the reasons that changing code is so fraught with danger is that our tendency is to change too much simultaneously. I know that my mind is capable of multiple modes of thought, but if I try to engage too many of them at once, chaos ensues.

So, I never bathe the baby while I am cooking the stew. I do not want to end up with onions in the shampoo.

Similarly, when refactoring code I want to make changes to structure and changes to function in separate steps. When I am thinking about, say, adding a new method to my class, I find that this is a different mode of thought for me than when I consider the code that should be moved into it, at least in any detailed sense. I will know that I want to move "that loop and stuff," but that is about all the detail I will consider as I think about naming the method, what its signature should be, and so forth.

Then, once the new method is in place, I can consider how to extricate the code from its original spot without disturbing anything. My mental discipline will be stronger, and since I am not what-if-ing anymore, I can focus myself more thoroughly on the care with which I make the change.

Moving in little steps, compiling (and unit testing, of course) between each change, gives me a lot of confidence. If something goes afoul, it will almost certainly be the very last *little* thing I did, which I can easily back out, and probably just as easily fix.

Refactoring Helps You Choose Your Battles

I have been using, studying, and teaching the refactoring discipline for quite a while now. At first, the main value it gave me was an increased sense of confidence when making changes.

It still does that, but now that most of the refactorings are second nature to me, they help me in a way I never anticipated: They tell me when to yield to the views of others, and when to stand my ground.

We have all been there. There is a design decision before the team, and the way you want to solve the problem is different from the majority. You are pretty sure you are right, but you cannot seem to make any headway with the rest of the group.

Do you give up, or fight it out?

Well, some things are always worth fighting for. "Do no harm" is essential to an evolutionary process, so if I am sure we are heading for decay by doing whatever it is the rest of the team wants to do, I am gonna strap on the six-guns and hold my ground.

But, on the other hand, some things are relative, and subtle. So, when I find myself in a situation that is not so clear, I find it very helpful to ask the refactoring question:

If I do it their way, and later I am proved right, what is the refactoring we will need to perform to get from their design to mine?

The refactoring moves are not all equally difficult, and in knowing them well I also know which ones are expensive to accomplish, in terms of time and effort. Move Method, for instance, is easier than Extract Method. Replace Conditional with Polymorphism can be a bear, but Pull Up Method is not so bad. Also, some of the refactorings can be automated more easily than others, and the tools we use reflect this.

So, when I cannot convince my colleagues of the wisdom of my position, I ask myself the refactoring question. If the answer is that the refactoring will be simple, I yield. If it is going to be a toughie, however, then it's go time!

This also means I fight fewer battles, which I have found increases my chance of winning the ones that remain.

Patterns Can Be Targets of Refactoring

Some of the refactoring moves are, in fact, named for the patterns they result in. Form Template Method and Replace Type Code with State/Strategy are good examples.

Patterns represent examples of good design, and refactoring is about changing an existing design into a better one. If we did not find some confluence between patterns and refactoring, I would have to suspect that one or the other was misbegotten.

However, even the refactorings that are not specifically attached to patterns can be used to find them in an existing design. In his splendid book, *Refactoring to Patterns,* Josh Kerievsky outlines this nicely. It is a worthwhile read in my opinion.

Later in this book, we are going to examine how designs can evolve, and how refactoring, in all of its forms, contributes to this process.

Avoiding Refactoring: Prefactoring

Knowing how to refactor is extremely helpful, and learning it as a discipline is especially important in an evolutionary process. However, it does take time and is not always what I would call *fun*.

Where I can avoid it, I do.

For instance, in Chapter 9, "Paying Attention to Practices," I outlined the practice of programming by intention. If you examine the results of the refactoring Extract Method (demonstrated later in this chapter), it might occur to you that the code would have already been in the refactored form if the programmer had simply followed this practice in the first place.

Precisely.

You might also note that the practice of encapsulating constructors means that changes will be very limited when polymorphism shows up late in a design, and that therefore less refactoring will be needed when that happens.

Indeed.

Furthermore, you might suggest that refactoring moves like Form Template Method would not be needed if the Template Method was "noticed" in the first place, if one was designing with the patterns in mind all along.

Agreed.

Do we need to know the refactoring moves after all? No, unless

- You are imperfect
- You have to work with other people's code
- You are not writing your very first piece of code tomorrow
- You never have a changing requirement that totally throws your design a curve

In other words, yes.

The Mechanics of Refactoring

I will end this chapter by demonstrating a bit of refactoring. If you have done Extract Method and Split Loop before, you probably do not need to read this section. However, if you find my prose too scintillating to resist, read on anyway.

In Fowler's book, he provides a catalog of refactorings (named for what they do), and for each refactoring he provides a list of mechanics. These are the discrete steps you should follow in performing the given refactoring.

One of the more common refactorings is called Extract Method. I find that I often encounter methods that are not as cohesive as I would like, and thus I end up breaking them into lots of smaller methods, which is what Extract Method helps me to do safely.

In *Refactoring*, Fowler gives us the following mechanics for Extract Method:

- Create a new method, and name it after the intention of the method (name it by what it does, not by how it does it).
- If the code you want to extract is very simple, such as a single message or function call, you should extract it if the name of the new method will reveal the intention of the code in a better way. If you cannot come up with a more meaningful name, do not extract the code.

- Copy the extracted code from the source method into the new target method.
- Scan the extracted code for references to any variables that are local in scope to the source method. These are local variables and parameters to the method.
- See whether any temporary variables are used only in this extracted code. If so, declare them in the target method as temporary variables.
- Look to see if any of these local-scope variables are modified by the extracted code. If one variable is modified, see whether you can treat the extracted code as a query and assign the result to the variable concerned. If this is awkward, or if there is more than one such variable, you cannot extract the method as it stands. You may need to use *Split Temporary Variable* and try again. You can eliminate temporary variables with *Replace Temp with Query* (see the discussion in the examples).
- Pass into the target method as parameters local-scope variables that are read from the extracted code.
- Compile when you have dealt with all the locally scoped variables.
- Replace the extracted code in the source method with a call to the target method.
- If you have moved any temporary variables over to the target method, look to see whether they were declared outside of the extracted code. If so, you can now remove the declaration.
- Compile and test.

For each refactoring move, Fowler is giving me steps to follow that are discrete To Do's and that also encapsulate the wisdom he and his coauthors have gleaned from their experiences and investigations. One of the values, for me, of Fowler's book is that it is not just a cookbook of solutions, but also a detailed investigation of the principles behind those solutions.

Refactoring is at your elbow at all times when you are evolving a design.

To show this in action, I will try improving the smelly code I created earlier in the chapter by using Extract Method. This is just a brief example, however. I think Fowler's book is an absolutely essential tool for any serious professional developer.

```
import java.util.*;
public class ReportCard {
    public String studentName;
    public ArrayList clines;

    public void printReport(){
        System.out.println("Report card for " + studentName );
        System.out.println("-------------------------------");
        System.out.println("Course Title                Grade");

        Iterator grades = clines.iterator();
        CourseGrade grade;
        double avg = 0.0;
        while(grades.hasNext()) {
           grade = (CourseGrade)grades.next();
            System.out.println(grade.title + "              " +
                                             grade.grade);
            if(!(grade.grade=='F')) {
                avg = avg + grade.grade-64;
            }
        }
        avg = avg / clines.size();
        System.out.println("-------------------------------");
        System.out.println("Grade Point Average = " + avg);
    }
}

class CourseGrade{
    public String title;
    public char grade;
}
```

One of the problems I notice right away is that `printReport()` is too complex and weakly cohesive. Extract method, applied a few times, should help to clean this up.

Those first three `System.out.println()` calls seem like a good place to start. They are clearly intended to print the header of the report, so I make a new method, as Fowler suggests, named for that function.

```
    private void printReportHeader(){
    }
```

Note that this is a private method. Extract Method usually results in private methods, because I do not want any other part of the system coupled to the fact that printReport() calls other methods, or what they are or how they work. I may want to change it later, and what I hide I can change.

The next step is to copy the extractable code from its current position into the new method.

```
private void printReportHeader() {
    System.out.println("Report card for " + studentName );
    System.out.println("-------------------------------");
    System.out.println("Course Title                Grade");
}
```

Note that I am *copying* this code, not *moving* it. The old code is still just as it was. Do one thing at a time, in very small steps.

Next, Fowler tells me to look for locally scoped variables and gives me rules for dealing with them. There are not any in this case, so our refactoring is going to be pretty simple.

Given this, the next step is to replace the copied code with a call to the new method. Here is the resulting class:

```
import java.util.*;
public class ReportCard {
    public String studentName;
    public ArrayList clines;

    public void printReport(){

        printReportHeader();

        Iterator grades = clines.iterator();
        CourseGrade grade;
        double avg = 0.0;
        while(grades.hasNext()) {
            grade = (CourseGrade)grades.next();
             System.out.println(grade.title + "          " +
                                             grade.grade);
             if(!(grade.grade=='F')) {
                 avg = avg + grade.grade-64;
             }
        }
        avg = avg / clines.size();
        System.out.println("-------------------------------");
        System.out.println("Grade Point Average = " + avg);
    }
```

```
    private void printReportHeader() {
        System.out.println("Report card for " + studentName );
        System.out.println("--------------------------------");
        System.out.println("Course Title                Grade");
    }
}

class CourseGrade{
    public String title;
    public char grade;
}
```

I have a similar opportunity with the footer-printing code. It is a little bit more complex because I have to pass in the double avg as a parameter, since it is calculated by the segment of the code that prints the individual grade lines.

Still, that is not too hard. I make the method.

```
    private void printReportFooter(double gradePointAverage){
    }
```

Because I have my refactoring hat on, I have decided to give the parameter a more descriptive name—`gradePointAverage`—since the method can use any parameter name it likes.

Now I grab the code and copy it in.

```
    private void printReportFooter(double gradePointAverage){
        System.out.println("--------------------------------");
        System.out.println("Grade Point Average = " + avg);
    }
```

Uh oh. This breaks because I refer to `avg` inside the code, and not `gradePointAverage` as I have named the parameter. Here, this is plain to see, but in a complex bunch of code, I would probably miss it.

One thing at a time is better.

```
    private voide printReportFooter(double avg){
        System.out.println("--------------------------------");
        System.out.println("Grade Point Average = " + avg);
    }
```

Now, I replace the code in the original method with a call to this new method, and the class is beginning to shape up.

```
import java.util.*;
public class ReportCard {
    public String studentName;
    public ArrayList clines;

    public void printReport(){

        printReportHeader();

        Iterator grades = clines.iterator();
        CourseGrade grade;
        double avg = 0.0;
        while(grades.hasNext()) {
            grade = (CourseGrade)grades.next();
             System.out.println(grade.title + "              " +
                                              grade.grade);
             if(!(grade.grade=='F')) {
                 avg = avg + grade.grade-64;
             }
        }
        avg = avg / clines.size();
        printReportFooter(avg);
    }

    private void printReportHeader() {
        System.out.println("Report card for " + studentName );
        System.out.println("-------------------------------");
        System.out.println("Course Title                Grade");
    }

    private void printReportFooter(double avg){
        System.out.println("-------------------------------");
        System.out.println("Grade Point Average = " + avg);
    }
}

class CourseGrade{
    public String title;
    public char grade;
}
```

It seems pretty logical that next I would like to pull out the part of the `printReport()` method that creates the individual lines that show the grades that are in the `ArrayList` collection grades. However, the problem is that the same code that prints the grade lines out also calculates the grade point average and assigns it to `avg`.

Should I make a method called `printGrades()` that returns the average? I do not like that either, because it is weakly cohesive. Printing grades and calculating an average are different things, so I would like to do them in separate methods.

How can I split the while loop into two different pieces, so I can extricate the one issue from the other?

I do not find anything that specifically addresses this in *Refactoring*, but if I pay a visit to www.refactoring.com I find that Fowler is maintaining an ever-growing list of new refactorings that developers like myself have contributed to the community. One of them, Split Loop, which Fowler contributed himself, seems perfect for my situation.

Our profession is a living thing, growing and changing all the time. The efforts of Fowler and people like him are essential if we are all to move forward together, and to benefit from what each of us discovers.

The mechanics of Split Loop are

- Copy the loop and remove the differing pieces from each loop
- Compile and test
- Reorganize the lines to group the loop with related code from outside the loop
- Compile and test
- Consider applying Extract Method or Replace Temp with Query on each loop

I have not done this one before! But I will give it the old college try. Copy the loop and remove the differing pieces. This gives me the following:

```
Iterator grades = clines.iterator();
        CourseGrade grade;
        double avg = 0.0;
        while(grades.hasNext()) {
           grade = (CourseGrade)grades.next();
            System.out.println(grade.title + "              " +
                                              grade.grade);
            if(!(grade.grade=='F')) {
                avg = avg + grade.grade-64;
            }
        }
```

And this becomes

```
Iterator grades = clines.iterator();
        CourseGrade grade;
        double avg = 0.0;

        while(grades.hasNext()) {
           grade = (CourseGrade)grades.next();
            System.out.println(grade.title + "              " +
                grade.grade);
        }

        while(grades.hasNext()) {
           grade = (CourseGrade)grades.next();
            if(!(grade.grade=='F')) {
                avg = avg + grade.grade-64;
            }
        }
```

This is not quite right. The `Iterator` grades are exhausted after the first loop. That is okay; I can just refresh it before the second loop.

```
        Iterator grades = clines.iterator();
        CourseGrade grade;
        double avg = 0.0;

        while(grades.hasNext()) {
           grade = (CourseGrade)grades.next();
            System.out.println(grade.title + "              " +
                grade.grade);
        }

        grades = clines.iterator();
        while(grades.hasNext()) {
           grade = (CourseGrade)grades.next();
            if(!(grade.grade=='F')) {
                avg = avg + grade.grade-64;
            }
        }
```

`avg` is now not needed until the second loop executes, so, as Fowler suggests, I rearrange the order of the surrounding lines of code.

```
Iterator grades = clines.iterator();
CourseGrade grade;

while(grades.hasNext()) {
   grade = (CourseGrade)grades.next();
    System.out.println(grade.title + "               " +
        grade.grade);
}

grades = clines.iterator();
double avg = 0.0;
while(grades.hasNext()) {
   grade = (CourseGrade)grades.next();
    if(!(grade.grade=='F')) {
        avg = avg + grade.grade-64;
    }
}
```

The next step in the mechanics of Split Loop says to consider the Extract Method! Well, that is what I was doing this for, so that is a nice confirmation from Mr. Fowler.

I can extract the code that prints the grades, and it will not disturb the part that calculates the average. Then, I can extract the part that calculates the average in a method, letting it return the average as part of its function, and that will be strongly cohesive. Can you see the steps?

- Make a new method called `printReportLines()` that takes no parameters and returns void.
- Copy the loop into the new method.
- Replace the loop in the original method with a call to `printReportLines()`.

And then do the following:

- Make a new method called `calculateAverage()` that takes no parameters and returns a double.
- Copy the loop into the new method.
- Replace the loop in the original method with a call to `printReportLines()`. This call should be a query that sets the double `avg` to its return value.

Here is the resulting code.

```
import java.util.*;
public class ReportCard {
    public String studentName;
    public ArrayList clines;

    public void printReport(){

        printReportHeader();

        printReportLines(clines);

        double avg = calculateAverage(clines);

        printReportFooter(avg);
    }

    private void printReportHeader() {
        System.out.println("Report card for " + studentName );
        System.out.println("-------------------------------");
        System.out.println("Course Title                Grade");
    }

    private void printReportFooter(double avg){
        System.out.println("-------------------------------");
        System.out.println("Grade Point Average = " + avg);
    }

    private void printReportLines() {
        Iterator grades = clines.iterator();
        while(grades.hasNext()) {
            grade = (CourseGrade)grades.next();
            System.out.println(grade.title + "               " +
                                          grade.grade);
        }
    }

    private double calculateAverage() {
        Iterator grades = clines.iterator();
        double avg = 0.0;
        while(grades.hasNext()) {
           grade = (CourseGrade)grades.next();
           if(!(grade.grade=='F')) {
                avg = avg + grade.grade-64;
           }
        }
```

```
        avg = avg / clines.size();
        return avg;
    }
}

class CourseGrade{
    public String title;
    public char grade;
}
```

Much, much more readable, wouldn't you say? Look at `printReport()` now: It is four method calls, each clearly spelling out what it does. This is practically documentation! Each of the private methods we have created is simple and straightforward, and since they are private they have added no complexity or possibility of side effects to the system overall.

There is much more to do with this code, but even this brief session of refactoring has improved it immensely. I would do a global find-and-replace on that awful clines member, giving it a more descriptive name like `courseGrades` or `gradeList`. I would use Encapsulate Field (per Fowler's *Refactoring*) to get rid of the public data members of `CourseGrade`, replacing them with public methods instead.

And so on. I will leave the rest as an exercise for you.

Refactoring Legacy Code

We do not only work on our own code, and we do not only work on modern code. A lot of the code in our lives (for many of us, *most* of the code in our lives) is legacy code, or code that we inherited from other developers and other times.

One thing we have to acknowledge is that legacy code is still around because it has value to the business, and that means we have to be sure not to reduce that value when we have to change it.

Michael Feathers, in his wonderful and courageous book, *Working Effectively with Legacy Code*, addresses this issue thoroughly, and so I primarily refer you to that book for a full treatment of the issue; it is definitely worth your time. However, I will hit the high points.

General approaches to refactoring legacy systems:

- *Throw away the system and rewrite it.* This is the position many organizations have taken with their legacy code base, and for some it is the right decision. However, as we continue to create more software in the world, and as its importance increases, I think this will diminish as a viable approach. We simply cannot afford to continue revisiting the same old problems endlessly while new needs and roles for software continue to proliferate. Also, when a system is "trashed" like this, we often have to ask the business to halt its forward progress until the new system is ready.

- *Refactor the systems safely*. This is the thesis of Feathers' book, and he suggests a number of surprisingly effective techniques for bringing a troublesome legacy under test, or at least under *enough* tests that we can change the system in a fundamentally safer way. I have touched a bit on the use of mock objects to break dependencies and create an inner view of monolithic code, from a testing perspective, but Feathers expands on these ideas fundamentally and realistically.
- *Incrementally replace the system*. This is something of a middle ground, and is termed *strangling* the system by Martin Fowler. The basic idea is that you create new modules incrementally, where the new code is solid, tested, high-quality stuff, and create references to the new code from the old legacy code, eliminating sections of the legacy code as you go. At some point, you discover that the entire legacy system is nothing but a set of delegations into new code, and so you can collapse it out, or simply leave it in place as a delegating layer (depending on the complexity of the systems that consume its behavior).

The most typical approach is usually a combination of the second and last options, where we improve the existing system using Feathers' techniques where that seems most efficient, and replace sections where the code is so bad that we sense it will take more time to improve it than to rewrite it.

Of course, job one is almost always to create a Façade for the legacy system, to prevent any new development from becoming coupled to it before it gets replaced. See Appendix B, "Overview of Patterns Used in the Examples," on patterns if you are unfamiliar with the Façade.

Using the Façade can help to eliminate the primary reason that legacy systems are not refactored: Enough time cannot be given to the team to fix the legacy system, because there is pressure to deliver new business value on an ongoing basis. This is a reasonable expectation of those who pay for what we do, but the problem is that ignoring legacy problems puts us on that constantly downward slope we can no longer afford to accept.

Using a Façade means you can stop the negative effects of legacy code without having to refactor it first. Once the Façade is in place, you can refactor the legacy system gradually, as time permits, thinning out the Façade over time until it is merely a thin architectural layer.

Of course, after the Façade does nothing, it could arguably be eliminated. I prefer not to eliminate it, however. Even if a Façade does nothing, it can be used to encapsulate the legacy system, even after it has been refactored into beauty.

Why might that matter?

What you hide you can change. No big surprise there.

Summary

Disciplines are like practices in that they are much more valuable when they are ubiquitous, when everyone understands them and follows them.

Refactoring has a special challenge attached to it, however. Some developers find themselves in the position of being discouraged from refactoring code at all. The argument is this: Because refactoring preserves existing behavior, it adds no business value and thus represents nothing more than developers being obsessed with the quality of their code.

This can be a hard attitude to overcome, especially since there is an element of truth to it. If we spent our days endlessly refactoring our code, we would not add any business value and would not be doing our jobs.

The best way I've discovered to deal with this is to cast refactoring this way: Well-factored code is easier (takes less developer time) to change, and therefore is less expensive/risky to change. When I refactor code, I am making an investment in it that will pay off in the future to the extent that changes in the future will cost less.

On the other hand, if I do not refactor a code quality problem when I see it, I am accepting a kind of debt in the code, and like most debt, it will be more costly to pay back in the future than it would be to do so now. In the future, the code will not be as fresh in my mind, it may have decayed further, and in fact it may have passed out of my hands into others who are less familiar with it. It's sort of like interest on a loan.

The notions of debt and investment are very familiar to the people who pay for software to be developed, and most would rather have a valuable investment paying off over time than a debt that burdens their business.

There is another way to put this. When we look at the open-closed principle, we know that no matter how open-closed our code is, it could theoretically be more so. That's the way principles are. Trying to make code perfectly open-closed is pointless. But when a new requirement arises, and the code is not open-closed to that new requirement, we can fix the problems in two steps:

1. Refactor the code to make it open-closed to the issue in question.
2. Add the new requirement.

In fact, this notion of *refactoring to the open-closed* was the initial clue that led me to consider that designs could emerge over time, rather than be planned. But before we can take it that far, we need a few more concepts under our belts.

Chapter 12

Test-Driven Development

One of the most popular and energized movements in software development, as of this writing, is test-driven development, or TDD.

I have to admit that I was pretty skeptical of the whole notion of "letting tests drive," probably because it seemed such an odd idea to me at the time. Like most developers (especially those from an earlier era), I considered testing to be someone else's job: the Quality Assurance department. In fact, I generally considered myself unqualified to do proper testing. QA is a study and perhaps a profession in and of itself.

Also, I have come to suspect "cool ideas" generally. It seems like every so often, on a regular basis, someone comes along and offers our profession a "silver bullet" that is supposed to solve all of our problems. I suppose this is partly our fault; we seem to want such things, and are hopeful about finding them. This makes us vulnerable to those who offer these magic tricks.

Frankly, I do not believe such universal answers exist. Software development is hard. That said, I do believe in TDD. In this chapter, I want to suggest some of the benefits of TDD for emergent, evolutionary design. I hope you will be inspired enough to want to learn TDD yourself. At the end of this chapter, I will suggest some books I have found to get started.

What Makes Development Test-Driven?

Test-driven development is definitely a topic of frequent discussion across our industry. TDD, like automated unit testing for developers, is something I personally took some time to warm to. Also, I still have clients who don't accept that they should devote up to half of their developers' time to writing tests, especially when they have full-time testers assigned to do it.

I like to characterize test-driven development as a way of thinking, rather than a specific practice. There are specific practices for us to consider when we learn TDD, but TDD is something higher level. This is what I hope to make clear in this chapter.

Test-Driven Versus Test-First

What makes development test-driven? The usual answer is "when you write the test before you write the actual production class."

I disagree. The way I think about test-driven development, it is possible to work in a test-driven way without actually writing a single test.[1] This is good news because many developers still work in organizations where testing is not considered to be a part of their job and may even be something they are not allowed to do. Even so, they can still get many of the benefits of TDD.

When someone says, "Write the test before you write the actual production class," what they are talking about is something called the test-first technique. Test-first is a very powerful technique and it *is* a good way to enable TDD. Here are the important points about test-first:

1. Write a test that expresses one of the intentions driving the creation of a production class.
2. Get the test to compile (you will have to stub out the production class to do this).
3. Fail the test (proving that the test works, and could possibly fail).
4. Get the test to pass by changing the production class.
5. Refactor the quality of the production class, using the tests to cover the refactoring.
6. Return to step 1 until all intentions are satisfied.

There are many advantages to a test-first approach. First, writing the tests before you write code to satisfy them is a nice way to ensure that you

1. Don't get me wrong. I think it is better to actually write the tests. But I do not want to leave our colleagues behind if this is something they cannot do because of a policy or restriction that they cannot control.

have very good code coverage when you are done. After all, if you only write code to make tests pass, you will not have much untested code when you are done. Ideally, you will not have any at all.

Second, as I mentioned earlier, it is very difficult to write a test for something that you do not understand well and so trying to write a test is a good way to test yourself on your knowledge of how a production class is supposed to work before you try to write it. That is a good sequence: make sure you understand what you are going to try to do before you actually try to do it. In fact, putting it that way seems much more natural to consider tests as Job One and creating the code as Job Two.

You will note that getting the test to pass and refactoring the production class for quality are discrete, separate steps in this process. This separates the "does it work?" question from the "is it any good?" question, which are two distinct questions we should always ask of our code, and ensures that the second one does not get overlooked.

Third, the test-first technique generally leads us to work in small steps, and so the tests are rarely hard to write, the refactorings we do are generally small, and therefore it is much less likely that we will be blocked and unable to move forward.

Because of these positive side effects, I like writing code in a test-first way. However, the *real* value of TDD goes beyond these points. And it starts with a bias toward thinking about the testability of a class or a design before I implement it.

Designing from the Perspective of the Unit Test

In my view, you are working in a test-driven way if you allow the point of view of a test to inform the decisions you make about a design. For example, one of the design decisions you frequently have to make has to do with the public interface of a class. The goal is to design interfaces that will endure over time because changing an interface often causes lots of maintenance.

Consider the relationship in Figure 12.1, arguably the most common and fundamental in OO.

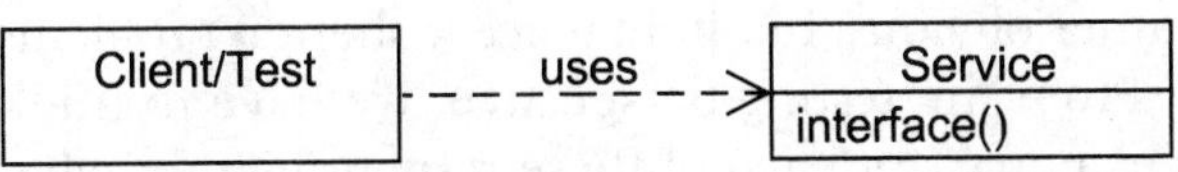

Figure 12.1 Design interfaces

In Chapter 8, "Paying Attention to Principles and Wisdom," I talked about this issue in terms of the dependency inversion principle. What is interesting here is that the unit test has the same relationship to the `Service` class that the client has (or will have), and that the point of view that the test has on the service is therefore the same or extremely similar to the client.

This is not an absolute but is a strong tendency. It is also an example of how the testing point of view can inform design, because the test of a class is also the first client of the class, and so the interface that the test would suggest is a client-driven interface, and thus will generally be more stable.

Testing and Quality

In the earlier chapter on the discipline of unit testing, I mentioned that testing helps to keep us honest on the basic code qualities that we believe will make our code easier to maintain, thus, to "live on" into the future, continuing to deliver a return on the initial investment it took to create it.

I would like to give you a few concrete examples of what I mean and how this plays out in the notion that tests can *drive* the development process, in an intellectual way.

Testing and Cohesion

Strongly cohesive classes are easier to test. This is because

- A strongly cohesive class has a single responsibility. Therefore, the test only needs to test a single responsibility.
- When an issue is separated into its own class, the class represents an opportunity to encapsulate the issue, and thus we have fewer side effects to test for.

For an example of the second point, consider Figure 12.2.

This object has two orthogonal responsibilities and is therefore weakly cohesive. Here, this is rather obvious, but in practice, cohesion problems can be far more subtle. From the testing perspective, we have to think about the variants. For example, for each of these responsibilities, what are the different possible results or outcomes that we should test for to ensure that they are all working correctly? Supposing there are 7 different variants for responsibility A and 5 different variants for responsibility

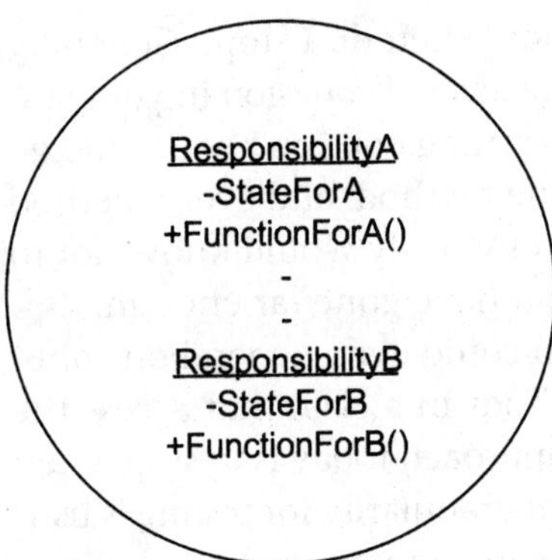

Figure 12.2 Two orthogonal issues

B, a robust, thorough test requires testing every combination: 35 tests, and even more if there are sequential variations. Why? Because there can be *side effects* between these two responsibilities and we have to account for them for complete coverage. QA folks understand these combinatorial problems well, I would imagine.

Now, I can make this easier to test by putting these two responsibilities into separate, cohesive objects, as shown in Figure 12.3. When I do, such side effects are not possible or are only possible where the design allows for it, through the interfaces of these objects. `+functionForA()` cannot change `StateForB` unless we allow for it in B's interface, and therefore we do not have to test for that possibility. This yields 12 tests (7 for A, 5 for B) plus a few more if these classes are designed to interact in some defined way. That is a lot easier to write than all of those combinatorial tests!

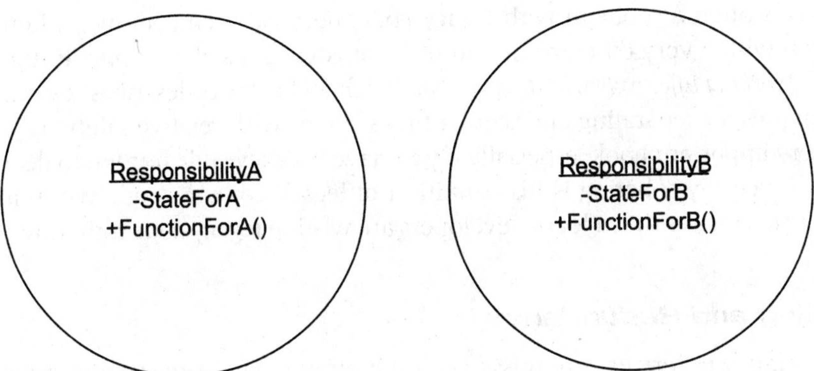

Figure 12.3 Separate, cohesive objects

Testing helps to answer a tricky question: When do I stop? Generally speaking, you can almost always improve the level of cohesion in your system. How far should you go? How strong is strong enough? You could go to ridiculous extremes, giving every class one method, and every method one line of code, and so on. Although you obviously would know not to go *that* far, you still have to know when you have gone far enough.

There are many theoretical answers. You could even depend on cohesion metrics to specify the number of methods in a class that access the same state variable. However, my general approach today is to stop when I have made the system easy to test. The right granularity for testing is usually the right level of granularity for objects in general.

Testing and Coupling

One of the issues I often hear that causes people to push back on the notion of unit testing is that it places a large burden on developers and is therefore too costly for the team to embrace.

However, this push-back often reveals that their system is too tightly coupled. When objects are intertwined with each other, you find that you have to instantiate a lot of the system in order to test any part of it; the tests therefore become difficult to write, and will also be slow and cumbersome to run.

Here is a trick that can help you quickly determine the general degree of coupling in a system, if there are unit tests in place: Count the number of objects instantiated in the fixture of each unit test, and take an average. If the number is high, you have a lot of coupling, because it indicates that in most cases a test of class X requires instances of other classes to test it, and therefore these classes are coupled to each other.

This is often a problem with legacy code, because such code was often written with a very different notion of what is virtuous about code. In the book, *Working Effectively with Legacy Code,* Michael Feathers describes several techniques for separating and segmenting systems with relative safety. This is a very important book, especially if you have a legacy code burden to deal with. Especially sobering is his definition of legacy code as "code without tests." This means that a lot of developers are writing legacy code right now!

Testing and Redundancy

Redundancy is very easy to miss because it often creeps into systems over time and because of the parallel efforts of different developers. You might notice that a redundant system requires redundancy in its unit tests if you are trying to keep your code coverage high. Tests offer a *second chance* to see the redundancies in a system.

Of course, this means you have to consider the quality of your tests in the same way you have to consider the quality of your production code: You have to maintain your tests, too. Redundant, accidentally coupled, and weakly cohesive unit tests are as unacceptable as any other bad code.

Test-Driven Development and Patterns

One of the important qualities of patterns is that they reflect the essential qualities of good object-oriented design. In the same way, patterns reflect the essential qualities of good testing. This is true, but is rarely discussed in books on patterns. I suppose this is because patterns have been around for quite a while, whereas the idea of unit testing as a design paradigm is relatively new. This is a gap that needs to be filled. Guidance for testing should become part of the general description of patterns.

For example, let's think about the Strategy pattern. Figure 12.4 illustrates the pattern and Appendix B, "Overview of Patterns Used in the Examples," describes it in detail.

The Strategy Pattern

As shown in Figure 12.4, the two classes that implement the varying algorithm (`Strategy_V1` and `Strategy_V2`) are nicely testable on their own. A unit test could instantiate either class individually and test its behavior in a way that is totally separate from the `Context` object and how it uses them. This is because one consequence of the Strategy pattern is strengthened cohesion.

However, how can we test the `Context` object by itself? By creating a reference to the `Strategy` abstraction, we have introduced a dependency. Do we need to test the `Context` object with each of the possible `Strategy` implementations? How can we know how the `Context` interacts with them, to ensure it does so properly? The test of `Context` occupies the same position as `Client` in Figure 12.4. The `Client` cannot detect the interaction between `Context` and `Strategy`. Also, if we add a new `Strategy` implementation to the system in the future, won't the test of the `Context` object have to change? This means the test of `Context` has subclass coupling to the `Strategy` polymorphic set, which seems very unfortunate.

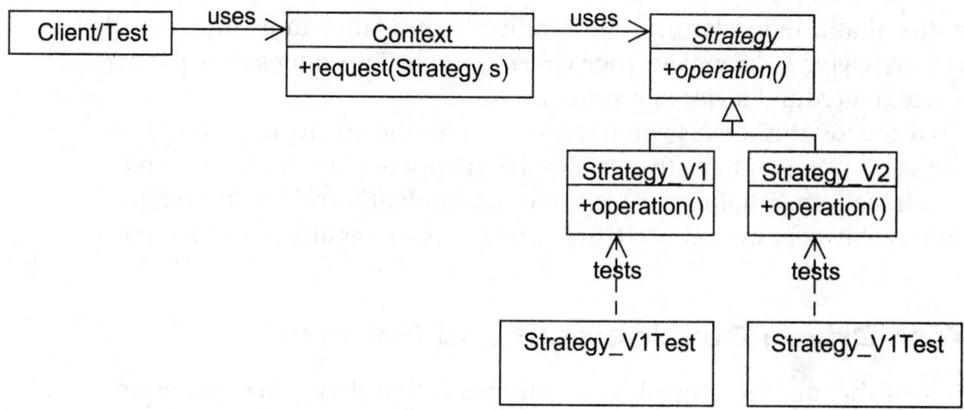

Figure 12.4 The Strategy pattern

I have said that testability is a clue to quality and here we seem to have created a testing *problem* by using a pattern. If patterns reflect the same qualities that testing is supposed to lead us toward, why has the use of this pattern made testing harder?

Turtles All the Way Down

I remember reading this story in Steven Hawking's *A Brief History of Time*. Here, I am quoting the version from Wikipedia[2]:

> A well-known scientist (some say it was Bertrand Russell) once gave a public lecture on astronomy. He described how the Earth orbits around the sun and how the sun, in turn, orbits around the centre of a vast collection of stars called our galaxy.
>
> At the end of the lecture, a little old lady at the back of the room got up and said: "What you have told us is rubbish. The world is really a flat plate supported on the back of a giant tortoise."
>
> The scientist gave a superior smile before replying, "What is the tortoise standing on?"
>
> "You're very clever, young man, very clever," said the old lady. "But it is turtles all the way down."

2. http://en.wikipedia.org/wiki/Turtles_all_the_way_down

Sometimes, good object-oriented design feels like this. There is a lot of delegation and a lot of complexity. It seems that whenever we look for behavior, there is a delegation of responsibility to somewhere else. Delegations all the way down. From the point of view of maintenance, this approach tends to produce more encapsulation, stronger cohesion, and so forth, and that is good. However, from the point of view of testing, it seems that these benefits are gained at the expense of greater complexity. That cannot be good!

Are patterns right, or is TDD right? My answer is, "both." What if we need to be able to test the `Context` object separately from *any* of the `Strategy` implementations? What if our view is that the `Context` object has *no business* containing knowledge that is specific to the `Strategy` implementations and that, therefore, the test for the `Context` object should be decoupled from the `Strategy` specifics?

Put another way, one purpose of the `Strategy` abstraction in the Strategy pattern is to allow the `Context` to couple *abstractly* to the service it uses. Therefore, the test should reflect this. Mock objects (objects used to replace dependencies for testing) can help us here. Let me show you a simple example of what I mean by this.

Mock Object/Mock Turtles

Let's reexamine our `Strategy` example. Figure 12.5 shows the Strategy pattern with testing issues included.

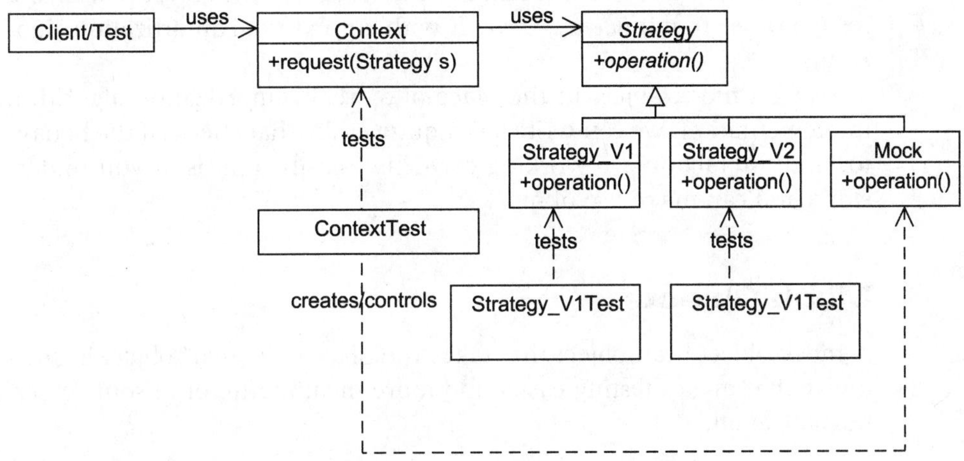

Figure 12.5 The Strategy pattern with testing issues

Four classes have been added:

- `Strategy_V1_Test`
- `Strategy_V2_Test`
- `Context_Test`
- `Mock`

The first two classes demonstrate again the value of testing in keeping classes *cohesive* and *decoupled*. Each of the `Strategy` implementations is a single algorithm. Therefore, each can be tested in isolation for the particular way the `Context` object will use them. That also means that the code in each `Strategy` implementation is covered by its own test and does not need to be tested by the test for the `Context` object.

For example, let's say that the `Context` object represents an `Asset` and the `Strategy` represents two different `Amortization` algorithms: `Straight_Line` and `Double_Declining`. To determine if the `Straight_Line` object can calculate the amortization of a value correctly, write a unit test. This is very straightforward and totally isolated from `Asset`. The same is true with `Double_Declining`.

Testing the `context` (`Asset` itself) might seem a little daunting at first, since you would have to test it in the presence of each of the possible `Amortization` implementations. You would also have to upgrade the test if/when a new algorithm was added to the pattern later.

However, because the algorithms will already be tested on their own, the only testing we need is of `Asset`'s core behavior (whatever that is) and testing to see that it *interacts correctly* with *any* external amortization algorithm.

Using a mock object in the place of a "real" amortization algorithm implementation, we can write a test quite easily that checks if the behavior and interaction are working correctly—easily, that is, if you understand and can make use of mocks.

Mock Objects

A mock object is an object that takes the place of a "real" object in such a way that makes testing easier and more meaningful, or in some cases, possible at all.

We substitute a mock for a real object in order to eliminate it as a dependency that might make testing difficult. Mock objects can be created by hand or, more typically these days, can be generated by a tool. We discussed mocks a bit in Chapter 10, "Paying Attention to Disciplines: Unit Testing," but they definitely deserve a second look here. I also want to give the C# folks a few concrete examples to look at.

Mocks are definitely congruent with the Gang of Four (GoF) notion of *designing to interfaces,* because a mock is essentially the interface without any real implementation. From the testing point of view, the mock is something that the test itself can generate, control, and inspect during the testing process. The test uses the mock to make *another object* more testable.

Here is a code[3] example of this Asset/Amortization Strategy pattern using C# and, later, a mocking tool called `NMock`.[4]

```
// The Context object in our Strategy pattern
public class Asset {
     private double myValue;
     private int myTerm;
     public Asset(double aValue, int aTerm) {
          this.myValue = aValue;
          this.myTerm = aTerm;
     }

     // This method takes "some" Amortization Strategy
     // implementation and delegates to it blindly
     public double GetRemainingValue(Amortization
                                        anAmortization) {
          return myValue -
                 anAmortization.GetAmortization(
                 myValue, myTerm);
      }
}

// The Strategy interface (abstract class)
public abstract class Amortization {
      public abstract double GetAmortization(double val,
                                            int term);
}
```

3. Yes, this code compiles and runs. ☺

4. http://www.nmock.org allows you to download this open-source tool, and provides details. Also, visit http://www.mockobjects.org to peruse other mocking frameworks for .Net and other languages.

We have not specified any actual Amortization implementations because ideally we want to be able to test Asset in isolation. However, Asset depends on Amortization in the way GetRemainingValue() is implemented, so it seems difficult to test on its own.

Ironically, the design pattern's view on object orientation seems to lead us into this problem because we are trying to ensure that each little part of a pattern is as independent (decoupled) and straightforward (cohesive) as possible. Every time we favor aggregation, we create a delegating pointer. This can introduce dependency problems when testing.

However, the GoF design to interfaces point of view saves us because that is the genesis of the mocking concept. The very presence of an interface gives us a place to insert the mock.

```
using NUnit.Framework;
using NMock;

//This is the unit test for the Context object (Asset) in
//our Strategy pattern
[TestFixture]
public class AssetTest {
      private Asset testAsset;
      private NMock.DynamicMock control;                       //(1)
      private Amortization mockAmortization;                   //(2)
      private const double testValue = 1000.00;
      private const int testTerm = 10;
      private const double mockedReturn = 100.00;              //(3)

      [SetUp]
      public void init() {
            control = new
                 DynamicMock(typeof(Amortization));            //(4)
            mockAmortization =
                 (Amortization)control.MockInstance;           //(5)
            testAsset = new Asset(testValue, testTerm);
      }

      [Test]
      public void testGetRemainingValue() {
            control.ExpectAndReturn("GetAmortization",
                                    mockedReturn,
                                    testValue,
                                    testTerm);                 //(6)
            double result =
               testAsset.
               GetRemainingValue(mockAmortization);            //(7)
```

```
            Assert.AreEqual(testValue-mockedReturn,
                            result);                        //(8)
            control.Verify();                               //(9)
        }
}
```

The lines marked (1) and (2) in the code establish the control and the mock, respectively.

The control is like one of those little joystick boxes that they use to control the robots that are sent into nuclear reactors or other hazardous areas. The mock is the object that will "act like" an amortization implementation. It really only represents the interface and can be used to simulate and/or record behavior. They are instantiated in lines (4) and (5)—I am using NMock here. Other mocking frameworks might do this differently, but the concepts are the same.

Line (3) establishes the value that I want my mockAmortization to return to when asked. It does not really have any implementation but I can simulate a result by essentially "programming" the mock to behave as if it did.

Line (6) is where I use the control to "condition" the mock, telling it what to expect Asset to do to it (call the GetAmortization() method with the specified parameters), and what it should return to Asset at that time. This is one of many such conditioning methods that NMock places on the control—one of the joysticks, if you will.

Line (7) is where the action is. This is a call to Asset (which is what I am testing, remember), passing in the strategy object; but I do not really even *have* any strategy objects yet. The mock takes the place of them all, acting as a placeholder for the *concept* of Amortization. This is what I meant when I said that mocks are a natural outgrowth of the design to interfaces GoF advice.

The test is essentially acting as the Client in the pattern, asking for the Asset to behave and to return a result. In line (8), I use a standard assertion to check this return against what I would expect to come back, given how we conditioned the mock to behave.

Obviously, this behavior could be (and would be) much more complex, but this technique puts it under the control of the test. This is the point. As I said earlier, frameworks like NMock provide a broad set of conditioning methods to create complex simulated behavior in the mocks without putting a lot of burden on the developer.

Line (9) is optional and somewhat controversial. The `Verify()` behavior of most mock frameworks basically says that it will "fail the test if the class we are testing did not interact with the `mock` the way we expected it to."

The argument against this is that it couples the test to the implementation of the class it is testing, rather than just the desired result. The argument in favor is that sometimes, as we will see with our test for a Decorator pattern, this is the only way to make something testable. Use it with caution.

Mock Turtles

Designing to interfaces and the use of automated `mock objects` allows us to break dependencies when testing without creating unrealistically simple testing scenarios.

This has implications for testing patterns because, as I have said, patterns tend to lead us toward *more* delegation in design in order to create clean seams for future integration as well as to encapsulate concepts.

I call the `mock` itself a *mock turtle* when I talk about creating a `mock` for a dependant object *within a design pattern* that I have to separate from the object that I am trying to test (another object in the same pattern). This is because it eliminates the "delegation leading to delegation" problem. I like specific words for specific things, and I admit this one amuses me.

Let's look at another example.

Testing the Decorator Pattern

The Decorator pattern, shown in Figure 12.6, allows you to add behaviors to an object dynamically without changing the class of the object in question. If you are not familiar with the Decorator pattern, I suggest you review the summary in Appendix B.

A `Client` sees the `Concrete_Component` or any `Decorator` as the same because the design is to the abstraction (interface) `Component`.

If a `Client` (or, as we will see, the unit test) is given the `Concrete_Component` to interact with, the behavior is predictable. The service class behaves in a defined, nonvarying way.

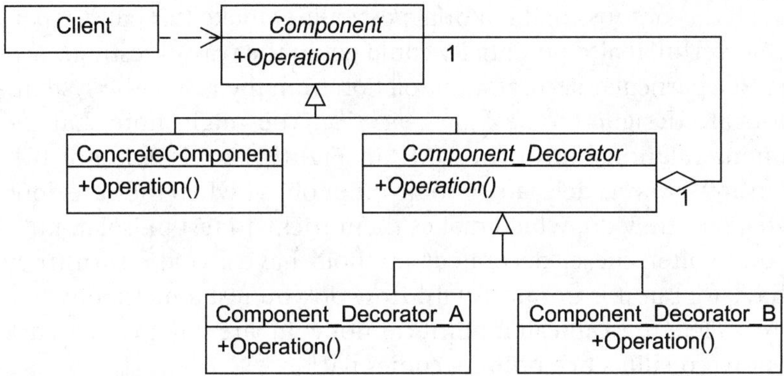

Figure 12.6 The Decorator pattern

However, if the `Client/unit` test is given `Component_Decorator_A`, for example, we know that more is involved because of the containment reference back to `Component`. This means, at runtime, that there are at least two possible behaviors we can expect (see Figure 12.7). This depends on what our decorator points to (another decorator, or the concrete version, or both).

In Case A, we get the behavior of `DecoratorA` plus the behavior of the `ConcreteComponent`. In Case B, we get both decorators plus the `ConcreteComponent`. Given that we can add more decorators later and that we can, if we choose, reverse the order of A and B, you can see that the decorator provides a lot of flexibility.

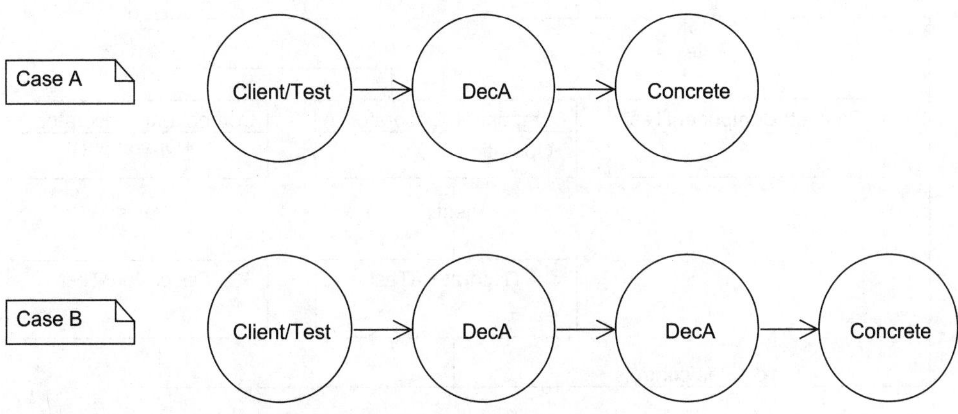

Figure 12.7 The Decorator pattern at runtime

Although the various combinatorial possibilities make this pattern particularly powerful, it also potentially could get in the way of testing. How can you test a particular decorator in isolation from the rest of the system? Decorators are designed to *decorate something*. You might note that the containment relationship in the UML in Figure 12.6 is 1:1, not 0:1. Decorators must *always* delegate to some other object when they are done doing whatever they do, which makes them tricky to test in isolation.

Also, quite often these "decorated" methods have a void return (they do not have to, but it is not unusual). How do you test a method with a void return? The test can call it but it cannot compare what comes back with a known result, since nothing comes back.

Mock objects can help us solve both problems and are part of the testing best-practice (mock turtle) for the Decorator pattern, as shown in Figure 12.8.

The problem is sort of the opposite of the `Strategy` situation. Here, the `ConcreteComponent` is the easier thing to test, whereas the various decorators (which encapsulate the variation of behavior) are the challenge.

The `concrete` version can simply be tested in its own right because it is not coupled to anything.

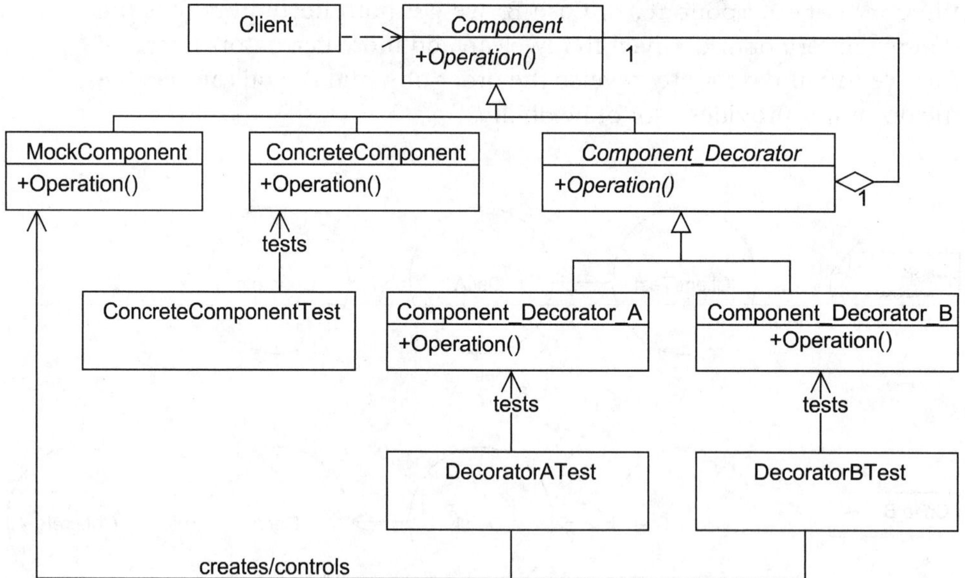

Figure 12.8 The Decorator pattern with unit tests

To test each decorator individually, however, it must be given a link to something predictable/controllable, and here is where the mock object really helps.

Also, if the Operation() type method being tested has a void return, we can use the control to "program" the mock to expect certain values to be sent to it by the decorator being tested in each case. We can then use that optional Verify() method on the control to check and see if what we expected has happened.

As an example, let us say that the design in Figure 12.8 is for processing Strings. The ConcreteComponent simply writes the String to an output stream, whereas the decorators do various things to alter it (convert it to uppercase, compress it, encrypt it, and so on).

Using a mock for the ConcreteComponent, we could test any of the decorators (we will focus on the one that converts to uppercase) individually.

Here is the code for the base types and that one decorator:

```
//This is the base abstraction for the Decorators
//and Concrete Components
public abstract class StringProcess {
      public abstract void ProcessString(String s);
}

//This is the base type for all specific Decorators
public abstract class StringDecorator : StringProcess {
      private StringProcess myNextProcess;
      public StringDecorator(StringProcess aNextProcess) {
            this.myNextProcess = aNextProcess;
      }
      public override void ProcessString(String s) {
            this.myNextProcess.ProcessString(s);
      }
}

//This is one particular Decorator,
//The one that converts the String to uppercase
public class UpperDecorator : StringDecorator {
      public UpperDecorator(StringProcess
            aNextProcess):base(aNextProcess){}
      public override void ProcessString(String s){
            s = s.ToUpper();
            base.ProcessString(s);
      }
}
```

And here is the code to test the `UpperDecorator` all by itself:

```
using NUnit.Framework;
using NMock;
// Test for an individual decorator
[TestFixture]
public class UpperDecoratorTest      {
     private UpperDecorator testDecorator;
     private DynamicMock control;
     // Mock turtle for the concrete StringProcess
     private StringProcess mockConcreteProcess;

     [SetUp]
     public void init() {
          control = new DynamicMock(typeof(StringProcess));
          mockConcreteProcess =
               (StringProcess)control.MockInstance;
          testDecorator =
          new UpperDecorator(mockConcreteProcess);
      }

     [Test]
     public void testUpperDecoration() {
     control.Expect("ProcessString", "AAA");
          testDecorator.ProcessString("aaa");
          control.Verify();
     }
}
```

You will note that I have been able to successfully test a decorator without the presence of the `ConcreteComponent` (in fact, I have not even created the `ConcreteComponent` yet!). This illustrates the value of a mock turtle.

Of course, often, there are combinations of decorators that need to be tested as well. However, with the `mock` in place:

- You *can* test each decorator individually, which gives you very helpful information when the test for a given decorator fails.
- You only need to test the combinations that are allowable or interesting. This is part and parcel of "letting tests drive."

There is much more to be done here, but I hope the idea is clear.

Among the many things that patterns offer is specific guidance about how to test them and how to capitalize on the value and quality of the patterns to drive toward tests that give us the maximum possible benefit.

Summary

Test-driven development is a new point of view on design. What it promotes is not new at all; it promotes high-quality, maintainable code that will continue to deliver a return on its investment for a long time. It is not some cool idea, but rather an extremely practical, grounded point of view on design.

That said, TDD does offer us an interesting opportunity. Design is often difficult to quantify. Yet if tests are a reflection of design, it is interesting that they are in and of themselves very concrete.

Tests are code, after all. Writing a test, or thinking about how you *would* write a test, is essentially thinking in code.

I said earlier that I am skeptical when it comes to new, supposedly cool ideas in development. I've been down too many roads that ultimately led nowhere, so that these days I expect a tool or technique to really *prove* its value to me before I will embrace it.

Try TDD. If your experience is like mine, you'll find that it proves itself amazingly quickly. Also, remember: It's the *thinking in code* and *thinking from the client's perspective* that really delivers a lot of the value of TDD, so if you're thinking, "This is great, but in my job, I am not allowed to do this," remember that you can still derive value from TDD simply by knowing how testing works, and what it would lead you to do if you could do it.

Nobody can tell you how to think, after all. ☺

CHAPTER 13

Patterns and Forces

Design is a mental process, a decision-making process. It's a way of organizing your thinking about how you will solve a given problem using software, and in doing so you reduce risks, allow for changes without overdesign, add clarity, and in general produce value that will represent a persistent return on investment.

In this book and in my career generally, I hope to find ways to help us all make these decisions better. I don't want to take those decisions away from you (any more than I want them taken away from me); I want to find ways to empower us to make them better.

Even if the notion that "patterns are collections of forces" makes sense to you, I would not be surprised if you were dubious as to how useful all this really is. It can seem awfully theoretical especially when using terms like forces and ephemerality and so forth.

What I want to do here is show you how looking at patterns in this way can help you to make better decisions, more reliably.

Making Decisions in an Evolving Design

In Chapter 9, "Paying Attention to Practices," I investigated the practice of *encapsulating construction* as a way of handling unforeseen variation without excessive risk and with a high degree of efficiency. In general, the idea was that by wrapping the `new` keyword in a method, and then using that method in place of the `new`, we could vary what was actually instantiated. We cannot do this with `new` in Java or C#, nor any other language in widespread use.

I have also outlined the notion that patterns are not reusable solutions so much as they are collections of wisdom from the incipient profession of software development. Their value lies in how they can help us to understand the problem we are solving, how to prioritize what we know, and the critical distinctions we should consider when working out a design.

So, there are *practices* that can help us in terms of accommodating possible, future, and unforeseen change. There are *patterns* that can help us in terms of making good decisions about handling that change when it occurs.

Often, however, there is more than one way to skin a particular cat. Often (dare I say, usually?), there is more than one pattern that could possibly be at play in a given situation, and we need a good approach to help us decide which way to go.

In other words, sometimes the connection between the motivation of a pattern and the nature of the problem we are trying to solve leads us in more than one potential direction, toward more than one design. How do we pick the right path?

Christopher Alexander and Forces

Christopher Alexander, in his seminal book, *The Timeless Way of Building*, outlined the Courtyard pattern as a way of demonstrating how repeated patterns of quality are found in architecture. It was primarily his work that led to the patterns movement in software.

However, there were some subtleties in Alexander's work that did not initially make the transition to pattern-thought in software design, or at least did not achieve the emphasis that he probably intended for them.

In describing the Courtyard pattern, Alexander said, "consider the forces at work in a courtyard." He then went on to show that some forces are obvious (courtyards are open to the sky); whereas others are more subtle; these are things that we learn only by building a few courtyards and noticing which ones tend to be more successful. Examples of these more subtle forces in a courtyard include a view out to the horizon and the presence of multiple crossing paths that lead in and out of the space.

Here, we see a major value of patterns in terms of how they elevate our decisions to a higher professional level and tend to make our designs more predictably successful. Patterns capture both the obvious and the *subtle* forces that can determine whether a given design succeeds or not. They also allow us to communicate our intentions to other developers with a high degree of fidelity.

The forces provide *guidance*. Alexander said, "consider the forces." If we follow his advice, perhaps we can make better decisions in software design.

What does that mean, exactly? If I consider the forces, what am I actually doing?

The Signal Processor Example

Let's go back to the problem that I talked about when investigating the principle of separating use from construction. Recall that the idea is this: By wrapping the constructor of `ByteFilter` in the static `getInstance()` method, it is easier for `ByteFilter` to *evolve* into an abstract class and then for `getInstance()` to return a subclass, perhaps one of many possible subclasses, without changing the client object `SignalProcessor`.

Here is the code, just to refresh your memory:

```
public class SignalProcessor {

      private ByteFilter myFilter;

      public SignalProcessor() {
            myFilter = ByteFilter.getInstance();
      }

      public byte[] processSignal(byte[] signal) {
            // Do preparatory steps
            myFilter.filter(signal);
            // Do other steps
            return signal;

      }

}

public class ByteFilter {
      private ByteFilter() {
          // do any construction set here
      }
```

```
    public static ByteFilter getInstance() {
          return new ByteFilter();
    }

    public byte[] filter(byte[] signal){
          // do the filtering here
          return signal;
    }

}
```

Encapsulating the constructor allows the design to evolve without great risk or cost. The question: What should it evolve *into*?

After we determine that there is now more than one kind of `ByteFilter`, what we have found is a *variation*, and we want to handle it well. Our profession has discovered patterns that can help us to make a good call here (refer to *Design Patterns: Elements of Reusable Object-Oriented Software*). I can see at least two patterns that *could potentially* solve the problem: The Strategy pattern and the Chain of Responsibility (CoR) pattern.

If we determine that the `getInstance()` method really belongs in a separate object (a factory), which is a pretty common thing to do, the Strategy solution would look like Figure 13.1.

Here, the factory builds *either* the `HiPassFilter`, which implements the `filter()` method one way, *or* the `LoPassFilter`, which implements the `filter()` method another way. The `SignalProcessor` cannot tell which one it is using and so future `ByteFilter` implementations can be plugged in later without changing it.

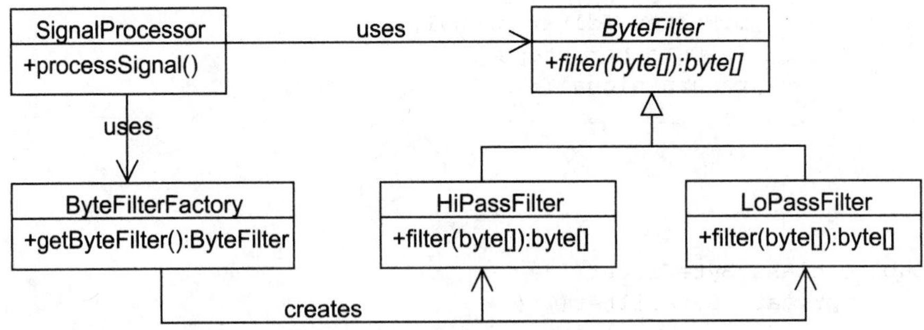

Figure 13.1 The Strategy solution

We get this because the Strategy pattern tells us that a varying algorithm, which is what we essentially have here, can be dealt with in this way. It is a general solution that we have implemented in a way that we feel is appropriate under the circumstances. We are not matching the Gang of Four's[1] solution precisely. They would have the `processSignal()` method take a `ByteFilter` reference as a parameter to be passed in, whereas we are having `SignalProcessor` use a factory to build the right one instead.

However, it is not the only way to go. I could suggest, just as easily and convincingly, that the `ByteFilter` implementations should be chained together in a linked list to allow the `filter()` request to be passed down that chain until one of the `ByteFilters` determined that it was the right one to handle the request. This is called the Chain of Responsibility and the design looks like Figure 13.2.

This looks remarkably similar in the class diagram, except for the containment relationship (see the dotted circle above) that the `ByteFilter` abstraction now has to itself and the slight difference in the behavior of the factory. As shown in Figure 13.3, it is easier to see the critical difference when one looks at the object (instance) diagram.

Here, it is clear that these two designs will behave very differently at runtime. In the case of the Strategy, the factory will make a decision between the two possible `ByteFilter` implementations (`HiPass` *or* `LoPass`). It will then hand the right one to the `SignalProcessor` which will use it blindly.

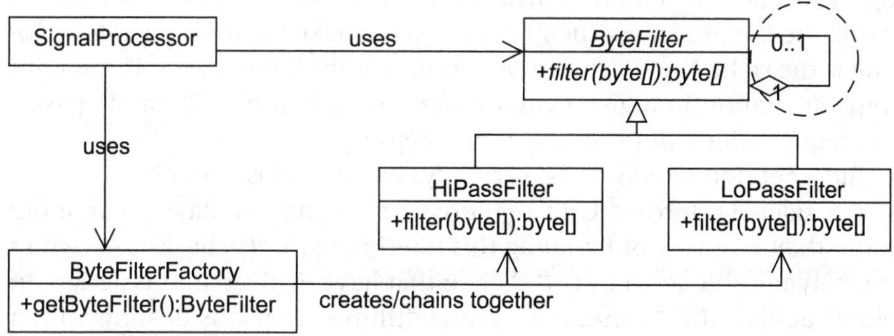

Figure 13.2 The Chain of Responsibility

1. The Gang of Four is an affectionate reference to the authors of the *Design Patterns* book mentioned earlier and listed in the Bibliography.

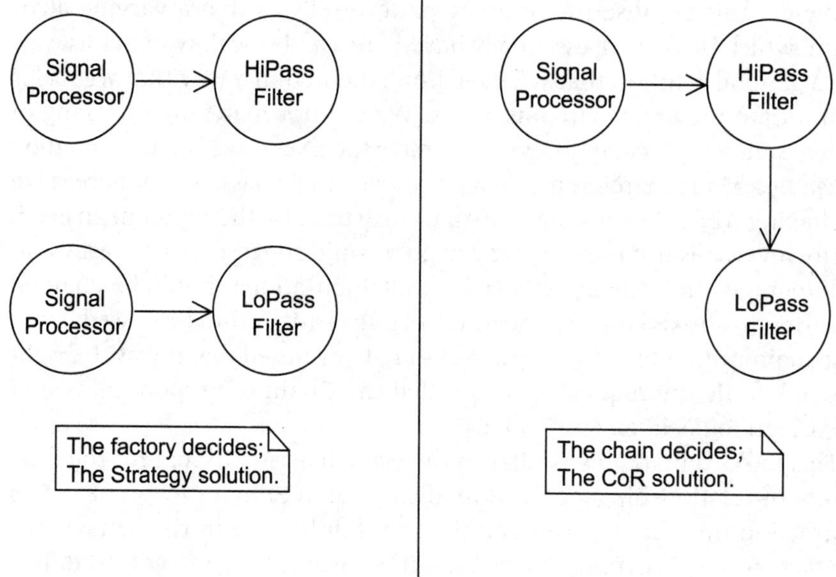

Figure 13.3 The object diagram

In the case of the CoR (Chain of Responsibility) pattern, the factory will build the same chain regardless of the circumstance. Then, when the `SignalProcessor` asks the first `ByteFilter` implementation in the chain to deal with the issue (filtering), it may do so, or it may delegate to the next one and simply return what it returns, and so on. For this to work, the `ByteFilters` themselves have to make the decision as to *which* one is the right one. Each can determine for itself whether it is the right implementation in a given circumstance or not. If not, it simply passes the request along until one of them "steps up."

Either option would work, certainly. Which one is better?

Consider the forces.[2] One key force here is that we have a variation: more than one way of handling this filtering request. This is reflected in the polymorphic set of `ByteFilters` that have evolved in this design. In either design, the `SignalProcessor` "thinks" that it is dealing with a single object, so this force of variation will not affect it.

---

2. This whole notion of focusing on the forces behind the patterns is something I learned from our fearless leader at Net Objectives, Alan Shalloway. Early in my relationship with him, listening to him speak and teach on patterns, I was introduced to this notion, which has become more clear to me lately. For more on this, see the article Alan wrote for the Net Objectives ezine: http://www.netobjectives.com/ezines/ezine_2004_01.pdf.

What *will* this decision affect? It will affect the design of the factory and the `ByteFilter` implementations.

In the Strategy solution, the factory may be more complex because it must make a decision. In the CoR, the factory simply builds the chain and returns it. If we get new variations in `ByteFilter`, the factory must make further decisions in the Strategy solution. In the CoR, it simply builds a longer chain. The maintenance on the factory, given future change, is simpler with the CoR solution.

On the other hand, in the CoR solution, the `ByteFilter` implementations have to be more complex: They not only filter the bytes, but also decide whether or not they are the appropriate filter under a given circumstance. In the Strategy solution, they only filter. So, the Strategy may create stronger cohesion in the `ByteFilters`.

These are forces too; they are the more subtle forces in the problem that reveal themselves when we consider one approach versus another. They are the forces of *context* and they are different under different circumstances.

For instance, how do we know which `ByteFilter` implementation to use at runtime? There must be a rule about this, something from the problem domain that is critical in making this decision. That is part of the problem, too.

Given this, we realize that we do not have enough information to make this decision.

- How complex is the logic required to determine which `ByteFilter` is the right one?

  If it is simple, perhaps the factory can handle it well.

- How related is this decision to the filtering algorithm?

  If it is highly related, maybe it is the `ByteFilter's` "business" to know if it is the right one.

  If it is unrelated, we would be weakening the cohesion of the `ByteFilter` to put the deciding logic within it.

Also, *where* is this decision to be made? If the rule centers on something other than the nature of the signal being filtered, the Strategy pattern is probably more appropriate. However, if something about the signal data itself can be used to determine which filter to use, the CoR is probably more appropriate.

Assume for this exercise that the application in question will have a graphical user interface (GUI) and that there will be a pull-down menu from which the user can select the sort of filtering desired. Therefore, the issue is

- *Simple*. The factory or the `ByteFilters` can simply query the GUI widget involved (actually, I would decouple the issue using the Mediator pattern, but at least we're limiting the coupling to the GUI to one place) and make the decision according to which one is "checked."
- *Not related to filtering*. Which one the user checks depends on the effect he desires, not on the nature of the signal itself per se.

In this case, the CoR solution, which would put the selection logic in the `ByteFilters` themselves, would weaken the cohesion of the `ByteFilters` (they would contain "stuff about the GUI" as well as "stuff about filtering"). Also, it would not create much value in terms of simplifying the factory since the decision is an easy one to make.

By paying attention to forces like these

- How does the use of one solution versus another affect the overall quality of the software?
- How well will one versus the other handle possible future variations?

We can gain a great deal of clarity on which way to go, either as an individual developer, or as a team.

Could this have gone the other way? Certainly, if the *forces in the problem* were different.

The PKZip Example

Consider Figure 13.4, a rather similar problem.

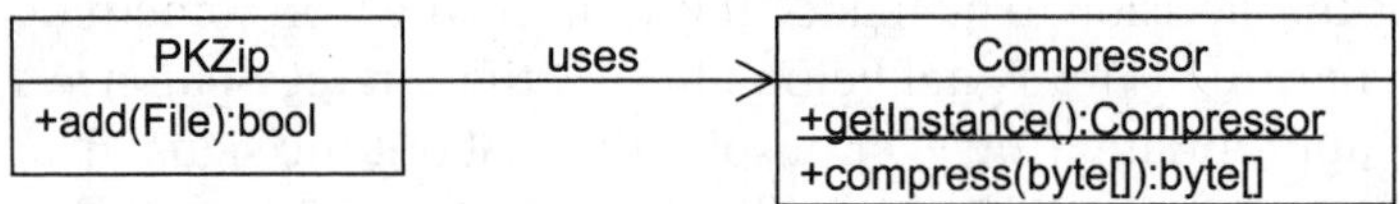

Figure 13.4 The PKZip example

Here, we have a data compression[3] utility that delegates the actual compression algorithm to a `Compressor` object. Again, we have encapsulated the constructor to allow for a possible future when there will be more than one way to compress data.

Once this `Compressor` starts to vary, once we get more than one possible `Compressor` implementation that we might use, the *motivation* is the same as it was when the `ByteFilters` started to vary in the previous problem: We have a varying algorithm. Again, as shown in Figure 13.5, we have a similar decision to make: Should we use a Strategy pattern and have the factory decide which `Compressor` to use, or should we have that factory build a Chain of Responsibility and allow the chained objects to self-select?

Again, the general motivation is the same as with our `SignalProcessor/ByteFilters`, but a key force is different: how and where we determine the right way to compress this data.

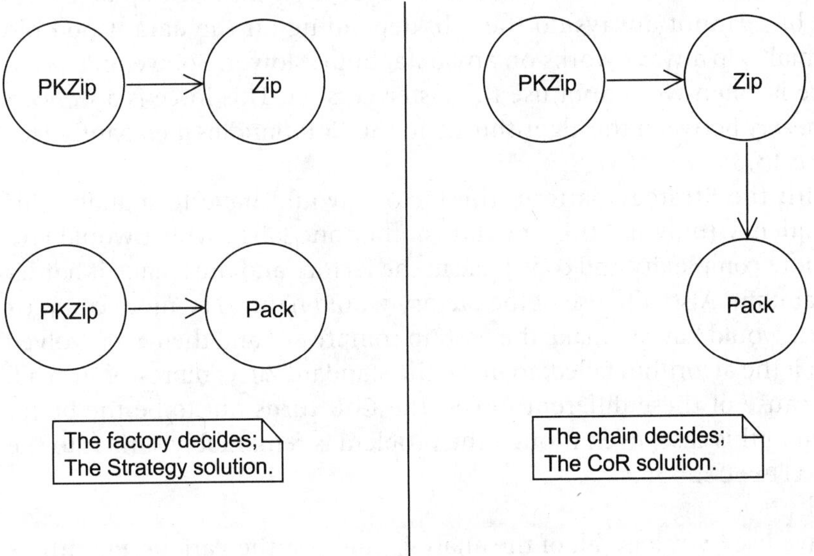

Figure 13.5 A decision to make

3. Phil Katz (the PK in PKZip) was a great guy who passed away a few years back. He created PKZip back in the days of BBS's, before the Internet, and released it to the world. Katz was an awfully clever guy, so I would not be surprised if he took an approach like the one that we are imagining here. At any rate, this is a bit of homage to him.

Those of you who remember PKZip know that over the years Phil Katz added many, many different compression/decompression algorithms as he continued to research and experiment with various techniques. He gave them names like Zip (the original, based on Huffman codes), Pack, Squash, and so forth.

The reason PKZip evolved in this way is that different types of data compress better with different algorithms. For instance, textual data with lots of spaces (or other repeating characters) compresses best with the Zip algorithm[4] whereas denser binary data compresses better if it is Packed (or Squashed, or whatever). In other words, the selection is

- Complex, based on an analysis of the data being compressed
- Completely related to the compression algorithm in each case

Also, there is another potential force here, due to the nature of data compression. We might actually have two objects, Zip and FastZip, which work in a similar way. This is with the exception that FastZip takes less time but cannot always do the job, depending on the data. Good old "normal" Zip always works on any data, but is slower. So, we only want to use it when we cannot use the faster version. This force is a *sequence dependency* between the algorithms and the CoR handles it elegantly (see Figure 13.6).

With the Strategy pattern, the factory would have to manage this dependency (only use this one if this other one fails), which would create more complexity and code logic in the factory and thus make it harder to maintain. Also, the use of the factory would have to be more complex since it would have to make the FastZip compressor and then get involved again if the algorithm failed, to make the standard Zip compressor instead.

Because of these different forces, the CoR turns out to be the better design in this case, even though the problem is remarkably similar to the `SignalProcessor`.

Why?

If we used Strategy, all of the analysis rules for the various algorithms would be in the factory. This would make it highly complex, weakly cohesive, and hard to maintain when new compressors are added.

---

4. I am no compression expert, but my point is that different data compresses more efficiently depending on the algorithm used.

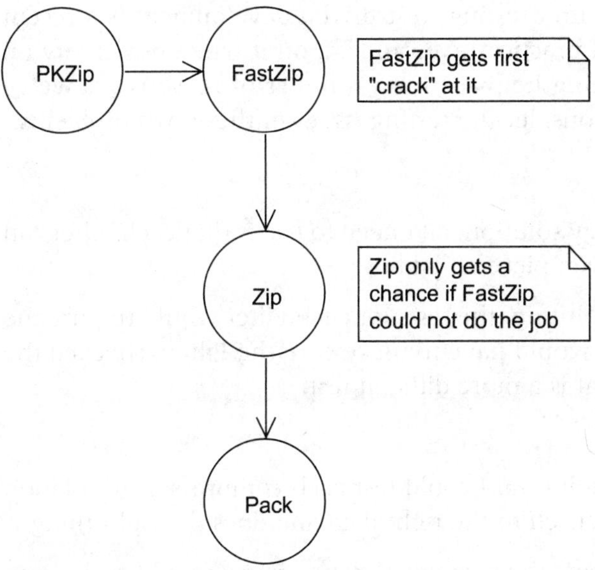

Figure 13.6 Sequence dependency

With the CoR, the analysis algorithms are paired with the compressors that need them, so adding a new compressor means we just make a new subclass of `Compressor` that "knows everything" about the kind of compression it is responsible for. Then, we change the factory only slightly: We add one instance to the chain it builds, that is all.

Testing and Forces

Consider that these forces can help us to make these decisions in a more reliably correct way. Of course, we do not always have this level of clarity on what we are doing. We know that paying attention to *encapsulation, coupling, cohesion,* and *redundancy* usually keeps us honest in terms of the general quality of the code, but sometimes this is simply not enough either.

As professionals, we need a suite of tools, like the tool belt a master carpenter wears. Ask him which tool is best, and he will say that it depends. It depends on what he is doing, what the situation is, the time available, and a host of other factors.

Our tools include technologies, qualities, principles, practices, patterns, and so forth.

One such practice is unit testing. Test-driven development is a recent addition to our suite of practices; we can lean on it when our clarity on a situation is low. Testing helps us for a number of reasons (as we've already covered), but consider the testing issues in these two problems:

- SignalProcessors

  If I use the Strategy solution, all I need to test is that each Filter can do its job on a given piece of data.

  If I use the CoR solution, the tests for each Filter would require the GUI, because we would have to make sure the Filters checked the GUI properly. That is a more difficult test.

- PKZip

  If I use the CoR solution, I could test each compressor in isolation to see if it applies itself to the right data and does the right thing.

  If I use the Strategy, the sequential dependency would be hard to test, since it involves more than one `Compressor` implementation.

  The Chain is also a testable entity: Give it different data and see if it ends up with the right result.

Considering these designs from the perspective of *testability* can also lead us to the same conclusions we arrived at when we looked at the problem in terms of the forces.

This is because testability, the forces, the practices, and our design principles are all rooted in the same things: What makes software maintainable?

More Choices, More Forces

In Chapter 4, "Evolution in Code: Stage 1," I pointed out that many object-oriented techniques (patterns being good examples) stem from earlier, procedural mechanisms that were used to solve the same problems, albeit with fewer advantages and less maintainability. In fact, one of the contextual forces that I list for each pattern in Appendix B is the *procedural analog* to each pattern. This can be a useful way to think about patterns, because for many of us the purely algorithmic, code-based solutions to problems are readily available to our thinking, and we can leverage this aspect of our minds to help us find a pattern we may believe is appropriate to the problem we are solving.

For example, let us say that we are selling things on the Web via an e-commerce Website; because we need to handle various currencies, impose differing taxes, and evaluate the formats of addresses in different ways, depending on the country that the buyer lives in, we decide that, in the procedural sense, we could use a series of switches to solve each of these variations.

```
switch(nationality){
      case US:
      //US Dollars

      case Mexico:
      //Pesos

      case Denmark:
      //Danish Kroners
}

switch(nationality){
      case US:
      //US Taxes

      case Mexico:
      //Mexican Taxes

      case Denmark:
      //Denmark Taxes
}

switch(nationality){
      case US:
      //US Address Ver.

      case Mexico:
      //Mexican Address Ver.

      case Denmark:
      //Danish Address Ver.
}
```

I am not recommending this as a good solution, only pointing out that this *set of switches* might be one way, procedurally, to accomplish our goal here. If we turn to object orientation (OO), using this as an analogy, we might be able to discover a pattern that could solve the problem in a way with better encapsulation, more open-closed-ness, and in general with less risk of decay.

Indeed. Check Appendix B and you'll find *three different patterns* that could apply: The Abstract factory (with Strategies), shown in Figure 13.7, the Template Method, shown in Figure 13.8, and the State, shown in Figure 13.9.

Here, depending on which factory we inject into the system at runtime, the call for the creation of our service objects (each a Strategy pattern) gives us the set of US objects, or Mexico objects, or Denmark objects, and we can rest assured that we'll never try to pay Mexican taxes with U.S. dollars, and so on.

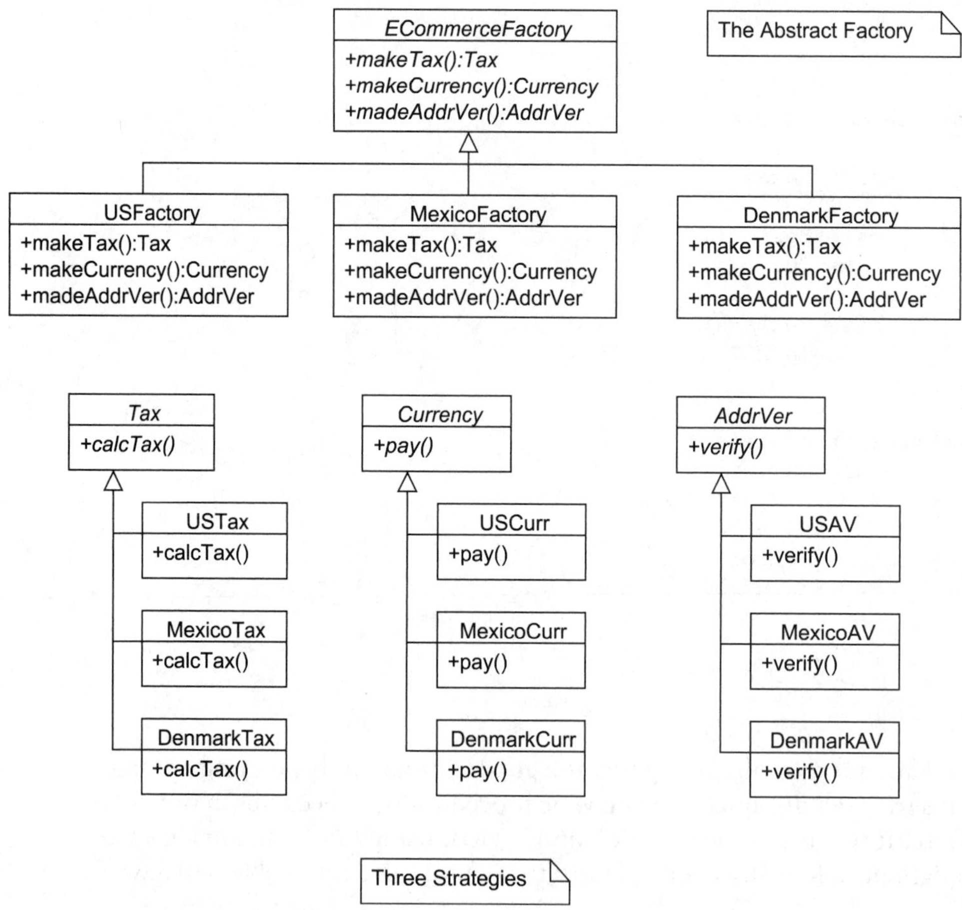

Figure 13.7 Solution #1: Abstract Factory pattern with Strategies

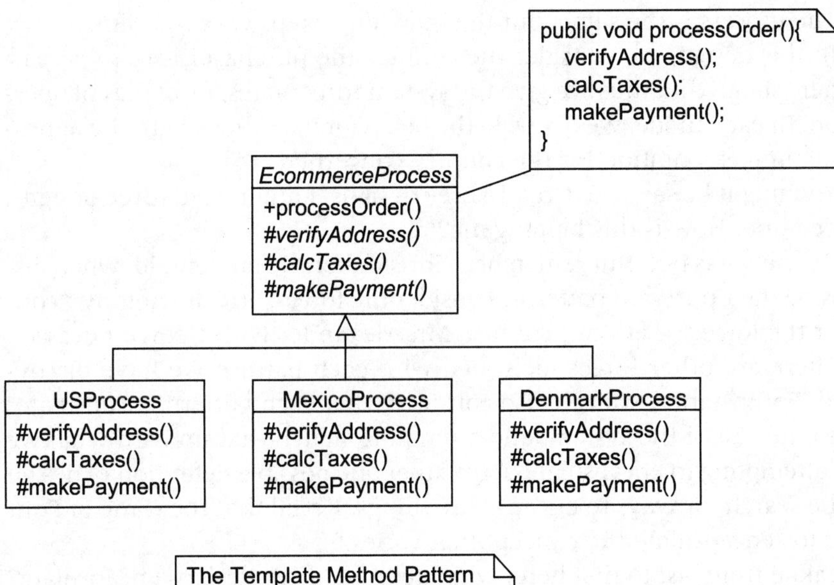

Figure 13.8 Solution #2: The Template Method pattern

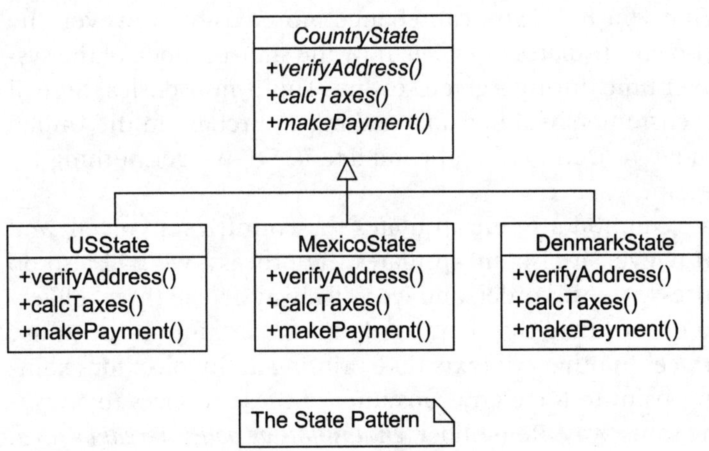

Figure 13.9 Solution #3: The State pattern

This pattern provides a single public method in the base class, which is implemented to call a series of other methods, each of which is abstract. Then, we create subclasses for each possible case, US, Mexico, and Denmark, and override the abstract methods with the logic appropriate to the country we're doing business in.

The process is the same, but the individual steps vary by country.

In this design, we consider the country the purchaser is in to be part of her "state," and thus we give the system three states, or modes of operation. In each mode, we override the behavioral methods with the appropriate implementation for the country concerned.

You might be saying, "Great! Three designs. I don't need three designs. I need one! How is this helping me?"

By itself, it is not. But remember, Christopher Alexander said, when discussing the Courtyard pattern, "consider the forces." He did not say, "consider the force." (Let's not confuse Mr. Alexander with George Lucas.)

There are other forces identified with each pattern we have discovered. For instance, we can also consider what each pattern encapsulates from the rest of the system, and attempt to match that up with what we are attempting to encapsulate. Recall that one possible definition of design is the search for ways to encapsulate things. Recall that the Gang of Four said to "encapsulate the concept that varies."

Taken from last to first here, what do these three designs encapsulate?

The State pattern encapsulates the states themselves, the countries involved. This is good: We could easily start doing business in other countries in the future, and we'd like as little change to the rest of the system as possible. What you hide, you can change more easily. However, the State pattern also encapsulates *transition*, how the state or mode of the system changes over time during a given session. This is nonsensical here; if we believe our customers will not start making a purchase in the United States, them move to Denmark and complete it. So, we get nothing for that encapsulation.

The Template Method also encapsulates the countries involved, and that is good. However, it also encapsulates the process; we will also do these three processes in this order, and we will always do all three. I likely do not *want* to encapsulate this, because I almost certainly want to use these same services in other contexts (like printing an invoice, for example), and I don't want to force any consumer of these services to always use them in the same way. Remember, *encapsulate by policy, reveal by need.* I need the process revealed here, and this pattern hides it.

The Abstract Factory also encapsulates the countries, just like the other two did, but it adds a level of encapsulation they did not: Because it separates the service objects into their own structures (Strategies, in this case), it encapsulates the implementations of these services from *each other*, which means they can all be tested on their own, and we do not have to worry about side effects, one upon the other. In both the State and Template Method solutions, the implementing method for Tax, Currency, and Address Verification were always together in the same class, and thus were not encapsulated strongly from each other. Any test would likely have to include all possible variations of their use, and this would be more complicated than necessary.

We use these forces, and the others that we identify for each pattern, *together* to help us make these decisions. I submit, this is a major reason why patterns are useful, and why they are so attractive to us. This kind of guidance can be invaluable.

Summary

I have said in this chapter and throughout this book that I believe that software development is going the last mile toward becoming a true profession, with all of the benefits and support that professions provide to the professionals that practice them.

As Alexander so eloquently said in *The Timeless Way of Building*, "At this final stage, the patterns are no longer important: the patterns have taught you to be receptive to what is real."

Sometimes, it can seem like studying patterns, testing, practices, and the like is a rather academic, theoretical pursuit and that we are sticking our heads into the clouds when we investigate and discuss these things.

I don't think so.

I think that trying to make code more maintainable and to help keep it from decaying as it evolves means

- An increased return on investment for the customer (architectures that survive for years continue to pay back on the cost encountered to build them).
- That developers will not burn out as frequently as they otherwise do. Decaying, hard-to-maintain software will disable a development team faster than anything I know of.

These are completely pragmatic concerns in my view, which is why these issues interest me in the first place.

Chapter 14

Emergent Design: A Case Study

The essential thesis of this book is that developing software, by its nature, is an evolutionary process. What we eventually build is almost always different than what we believe we will build when we start. If this is so, there is great value to the developer to establish principles, practices, and disciplines that will enhance his ability to capitalize on what is known, at any point, and to benefit from the ability to change when new truths emerge over time.

All of the "Paying Attention to" chapters have been intended to establish a list of practices and principles that, at least in my opinion, all contribute in this way. Now, I want to illustrate their value by walking through an evolving project. This case study is simplified, but it is typical of the sorts of problems we solve day-in and day-out. My focus is on helping you see the flow of the process. Thus, I have tried to keep it to a reasonable size so that the details do not get in the way of helping you see the flow. Also, I have minimized the number of code examples being shown so that coding techniques do not interrupt the narrative.

The Problem Domain: The MWave Corporation

MWave is a company that makes microwave transceivers (hardware sets) that allow its customers to link several buildings on a campus or similar environment. This forms a wide-area network (WAN) without pulling cable through the ground between them. As shown in Figure 14.1, these

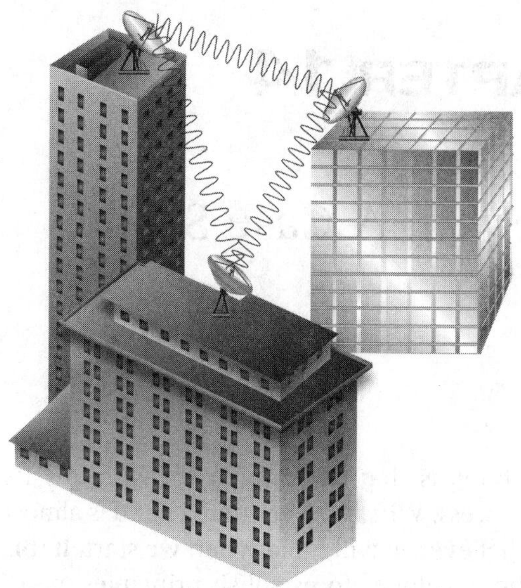

Figure 14.1 Buildings connected by WAN

devices are mounted on the tops of the buildings and can operate in virtually all weather conditions. Our team writes and maintains software that is used to run, configure, and maintain the transceiver hardware.

Rumors have been circulating that MWave is on the brink of signing a huge new client, a string of private hospitals. The hospitals will use these microwave transceivers to link the computer networks in various buildings within a complex into one large WAN so that surgeons can pull up patient history while in the middle of an operation, specialists can access complete patient histories without having to pull files, and so forth.

Because these customers are hospitals, there is a very stringent requirement from the FDA (which regulates all medical facilities) in terms of guaranteed uptime. Not only do we need to show, historically, a strong record of continuous uptime, but we need to demonstrate due diligence on the issue. This means that we need to create a monitoring framework to constantly query and verify the "health" of the components in the system. The components are, in general, VLSI (very large-scale integration) chips that were custom-made for this application.

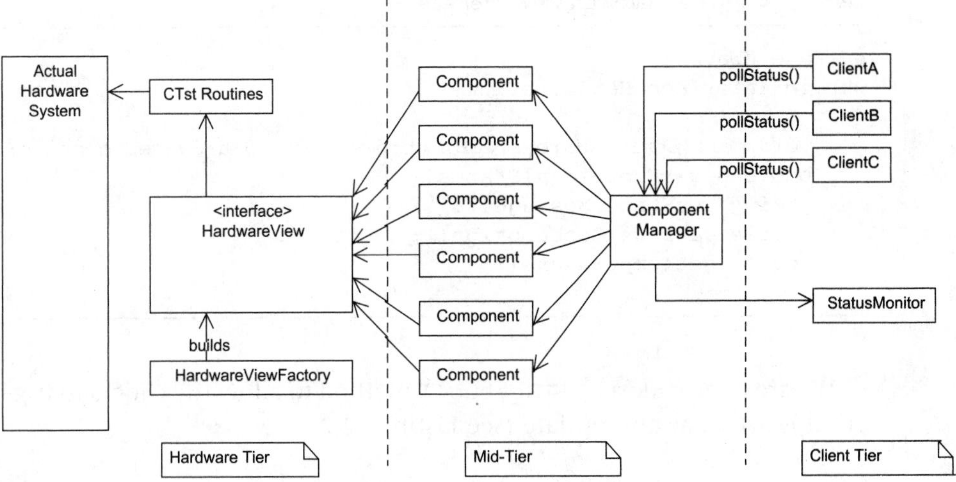

Figure 14.2 The three tiers for monitoring hardware

The Teams

The architecture for monitoring this hardware consists of three tiers, as shown in Figure 14.2. The three tiers include the hardware and low-level drivers, the middle tier (business logic), and the client tier, where the actual client(s) and monitor(s) will reside.

Consequently, there are three teams. The hardware team is in charge of the actual device drivers and firmware and has written a native-language interface (CTst, in Figure 14.2). This allows access to these VLSI components to query them for temperature, power consumption, checksums, and so on. There is also a `HardwareView` wrapper interface in Java that this team is responsible for creating and updating. The hardware team has implemented this interface but has asked us to use their supplied factory to get a referent to their implementation (via the static method `getHardwareView()`) rather than instantiating it directly.

We are working on the mid-tier. Our job is to model the various hardware systems in objects and to respond to requests from various monitoring clients. This obtains the needed information and forwards it on to a status monitor. The `HardwareView` interface (see Listing 14.1) represents our interface to the hardware, and the `StatusMonitor` class is what we must drive our results into whenever we are polled.

Listing 14.1 The HardwareView Interface

```
package MWaveNI;
public interface HardwareView
{
    void poll(String HardwareID) throws InvalidHardwareException;
    boolean getFunctionalStatus();
    String getStatusMessage();
    double getPowerConsumption();
    double getTemperature();
}
```

We are to provide a `pollStatus()` method to allow the clients to trigger this action as appropriate (see Listing 14.2).

Listing 14.2 The StatusMonitor Class, Interface Only

```
package MWaveMon;
public class StatusMonitor
{
    void showStatus(String statusDetail, bool ok){}
}
```

MWave makes more than one type of hardware box. Each has a different set of components to monitor. Therefore, we need a resource that lists all the Hardware IDs for a given piece of hardware. We are told, at least initially, that this is a straightforward ASCII text file. A given runtime instantiation of the system is for a single hardware box.

Polling the machine means to visit each component in the collection and to poll it individually. Polling an individual component means to do three things:

1. Get the actual status of the VLSI chip in question. Note that the `HardwareID` is used to "talk to" the right chip in each case through the supplied `HardwareView` mechanism.

2. Encrypt the status information (the FDA requires all information that flows across a medical network to be encrypted, though they do not specify how).

3. Send the encrypted status on to the client tier, via the `StatusMonitor` class, along with an unencrypted boolean indication of general health (true) or failure (false).

We are also told that the components need to be managed from a single place to make sure we do not redundantly monitor or fail to monitor any component.

Finally, all testing is to be done by the Quality Assurance group, a totally separate team. We have argued that the developers should be writing tests here, but the organization has a different view of this[1] and we have essentially lost the battle on this one.

However, nobody has said that we cannot *think about the testability* of our design. So, even though we are not writing the tests, the knowledge we have of how testing works at the unit level will help us keep our quality high anyway.

The Simplest Thing That Could Possibly Work

"Do the simplest thing that could possibly work" is a fairly popular point of view these days, and I fully understand where this comes from. The realization that maintenance issues can get ridiculously out of hand in software has led us, in many cases, to over-design systems in an effort to make *anything* possible.

Over-designed systems can be unmaintainable for a different reason: complexity.

However, *simplest* can mean many different things. To a procedural programmer, the simplest thing is to write a straightforward, structured program. If forced to work in an object-oriented language, this means a single static method, perhaps the static `main()`, which contains all the behavior in structured logic.

To an object-oriented programmer, the simplest thing is to create a simple relationship, as displayed in Figure 14.3, between the objects that monitor the individual components and the manager of those objects.

1. There are many organizations that still believe that a legitimate test must be done by someone other than the developer that wrote the code. The idea is that the coder knows the code too well and will make certain assumptions rather than test everything. I do not agree, but so far nobody has given me control of the universe, so . . .

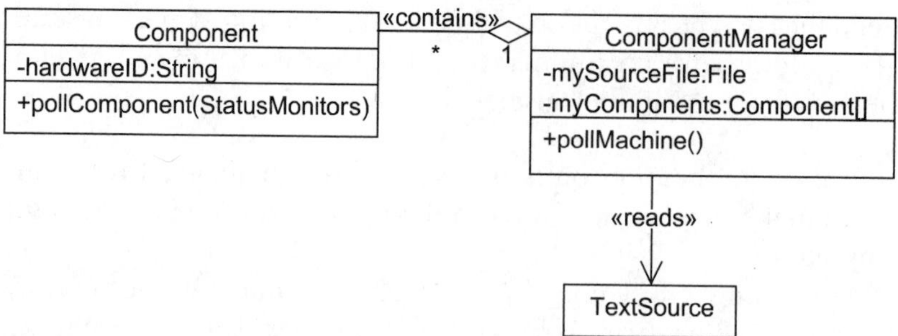

Figure 14.3 Relationship between objects and manager

That is pretty simple. It could be simpler, I suppose, and it could certainly be more complex. How do I know how far to go? How much design is too much design? How much is too little? What is design for, anyway?

One thing that design is meant to do is to protect us from change. Change can mean new requirements, taking advantage of innovations in technology, tuning for performance and resource (memory/disk) usage, and so on. I know that my ability to *predict the likelihood* of these changes is, well, terrible. I'll bet yours is terrible as well.

How do we know how much design is needed? We don't. But the nice thing about being in a profession is that *the profession knows* at least some things that we can depend on to help us make these decisions.

In other words, are there principles and practices that I am failing to follow here? If so, I have not done enough, and this guidance can help me see what I should do.

Note:

- The encapsulation of construction practice is not being followed. An entity wanting to interact with `ComponentManager` must instantiate it with the `new` keyword. Similarly, when `Components` are instantiated, `new` will be used directly.
- The programming by intention practice is not being followed in either class. `pollMachine()` and `pollComponent()` do everything themselves; they do not delegate to other, helper methods. Therefore, they are weakly cohesive.

- The use of the Singleton pattern is suggested by the forces in the problem (the components need to be managed from a single place), but it is not being used.
- This does not seem very easy to test (all of the testable behavior is glommed together into the `pollComponent()` method).

Maybe this is simple, but it does not work from our point of view as professionals. It does not rise to a minimal standard, and therefore it will be hard or impossible to "Do no harm" when unforeseen changes come along. If we do enough to follow our standards, our design might look something like Figure 14.4.

The `pollComponent()` method now explains the private methods `getStatus()`, `encryptStatus()`, and `sendStatus()` as programming by intention. These methods are, of course, more cohesive because of this and cohesion is something we know to pay attention to.

We have encapsulated the constructor of `Component` by using a static `getInstance()` method rather than using its constructor directly, with `new`. We could have encapsulated the *destruction* of `Component` by using a static `releaseInstance()` method as well. Yet, we are working in an environment with an automatic garbage collector and the issue is not critical, so we do not need to.

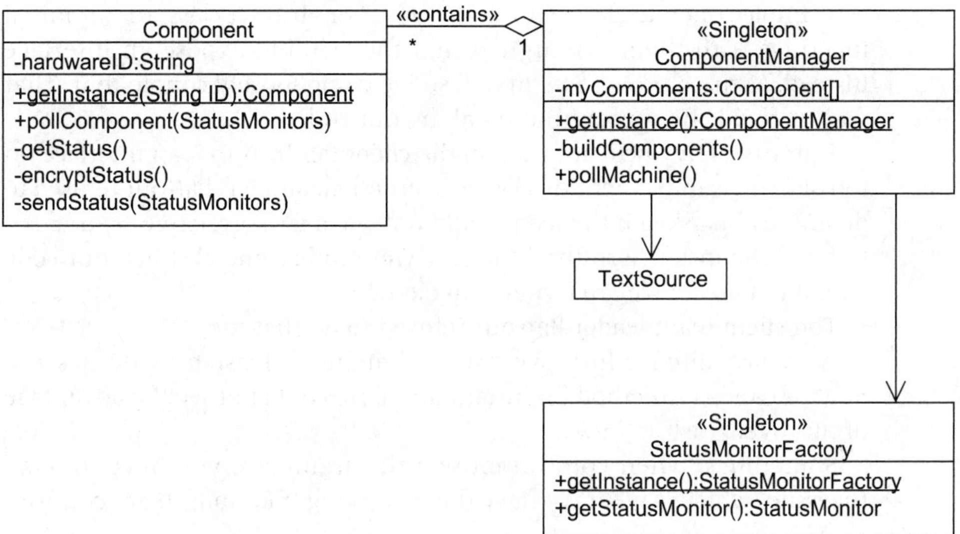

Figure 14.4 The design if we follow standards

The constructor of `ComponentManager` is also encapsulated, as we are making it a Singleton. It also delegates to a `buildComponents()` method to read the text source and call `getInstance()` on `Component` to create each instance. Constructors should be programmed by intention too.

But have we made this more testable? In a sense, yes. The various behaviors involved in polling a component have been broken out into individual methods, but they are private methods. Perhaps we should be pulling them out into separate classes?

Perhaps. If you think that, I do not disagree with you. However, that is another example of the "How far do we go?" question. Maybe we just need to make the methods *package private* and put the test into the same package. Maybe we just need to make them protected methods and derive the test from the class. In .Net, we might be able to use a delegate wrapper to test the private methods.

The main point is that, because we followed the programming by intention practice, we can pull each behavior into a separate class later if we do not do it now. This is because they are in separate methods and thus will not have to be detangled from each other.

If we ever need to refactor this code, we will have to do Move Method or Extract Class rather than Extract Method. Therefore, we are staying away from the thornier change. Not all refactorings are created equal in terms of their difficulty.

One last issue: The client tier team created the `StatusMonitor` class as a simple concrete class with no interface or abstract class. In our initial meetings with them, we argued that they should expose an interface instead, as the hardware team did, so we could loosely couple to it. That way, it could change without breaking our code.

Unfortunately, the team lead on the client tier feels that an interface on top of a single implementing class is overdesign, and has flat-out refused to do it. We also asked if the team could provide a `StatusMonitorFactory` to build the instance so that if it ever were to become abstract, our code would not break; we are trying to avoid `new`.

The client team leader flat-out refused to do that too.

As a last ditch effort, we asked that he at least provide a static `getInstance()` method for instantiation. He could not see the advantage of this over "just use `new`."

Sometimes, when you cannot win the argument, you have to wrap the issue, which is what we have done. Varying traditions, team cultures, and strong personalities can get in your way at times because many software organizations lack the kind of professional standards we are discussing in this book. The degree to which you can depend on other teams to follow practices that you feel are essential will vary from case to case.

Imagine this: You are a doctor, traveling across the country on vacation, and a hurricane hits. Because many people have been injured, you go to the closest hospital and offer to help. You have never been in this hospital before, and you know none of the people who work there. I submit that you would not walk through the door with any concern that this hospital might not "believe in" sterilizing their instruments or taking medical histories before giving medicines. One advantage of an established profession is that the critical issues are often off the table, reducing risks and empowering the professional.

Ideally, all client issues should remain in the client tier, but because we feel it is critical to avoid coupling to a specific concrete class in another tier, and because we cannot get the client team to encapsulate it, we are making a compromise by putting the factory we need in our own tier.

A New Requirement: Complex Machines

New requirements are extremely common in our business. That is because requirements reflect the world, and the world changes, frequently.

The hardware group lets us know that because of a recent decision regarding its architecture, we will need to be able to monitor more complex machines. The basic units we have modeled thus far are simply flat collections of VLSI components; but these new, more complex machines have units called boards. `Boards` are pluggable modules that mount within the machine.

What makes these boards complex is that they have VLSI chips mounted on them. They can also contain sub-boards, which also contains chips and so forth, to an arbitrarily deep level. In other words, the simple collection that we currently have is inadequate to capture the complex relationships between components when we are monitoring a more complex machine. It also means the flat text file will no longer work. They have changed their minds and now want all machines to be modeled in XML, even the simple ones.

Luckily, we know design patterns and we practice commonality-variability analysis. If we want to keep the `ComponentManager` simple, we will want to hide (encapsulate) the difference between the `Chip` component and the `Board` component. We know that difference is a hierarchical relationship in `Board`.

Conceptually, `Chips` and `Boards` are the same thing; they are `Components` in the system. If we create an abstraction to model this commonality, the way they vary has to do with the fact that `Chips` are simple, but `Boards` contain other `Components` on them.

This is the motivation of the Composite pattern (see Appendix B, "Overview of Patterns Used in the Examples"), so we can use what our profession already knows and has codified into a pattern to help us.

Furthermore, the construction of `Components` is not as simple as it once was. We need to build `Chips` and `Boards`, and add `Components` to the `Boards`, and the resource we will use (which used to be a flat ASCII file) is now going to be an XML file.

Luckily, we followed a good practice. The construction of `Components` is currently in a single method in `ComponentManager`, namely `buildComponents()`. Although we cannot avoid changing this, at least the change is in a single, relatively simple place. Because the issue of construction is now nontrivial, we will move it into a separate factory, and delegate to it from `buildComponents()`. As shown in Figure 14.5, the factory is designed to read the XML file.

Note the following:

- It was relatively easy to transition to the Composite pattern because of the encapsulation of construction. It turned out that the `getInstance()` method in `Component` was actually unnecessary because the `buildComponents()` method in `ComponentManager` was already encapsulating the construction of `Component` (due to programming by intention). This caused no harm, however. It is always better to be over-encapsulated than under-encapsulated because it is easier to break encapsulation later than to add it.
- It was also easy to change the simple text source to an XML source because we had programmed by intention, keeping the issue in a single place.
- `Chips` and `Boards` can be tested individually (we can give a mock `Component` object for the `Board`, to allow us to test how it interacts with its "child" objects).

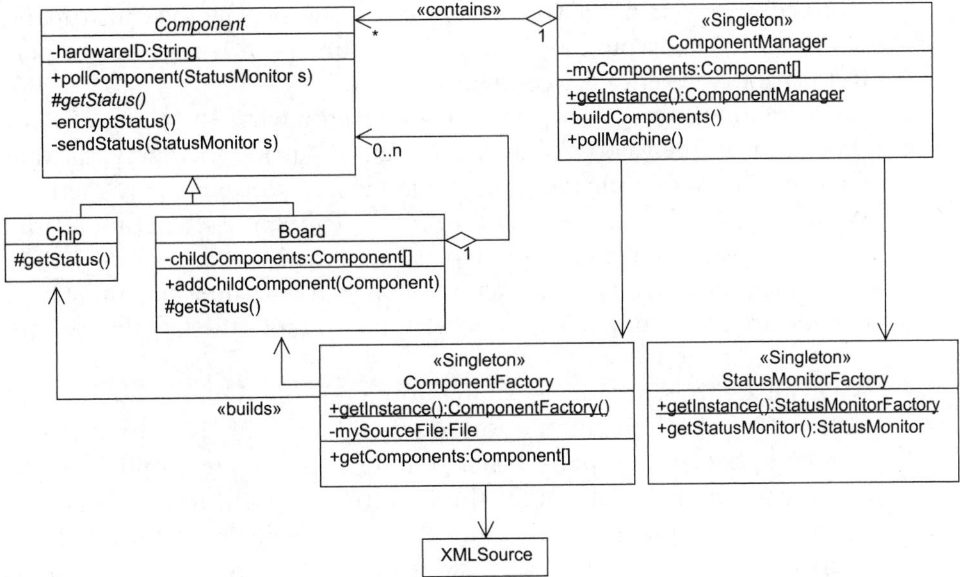

Figure 14.5 The factory designed to read the XML file

Oh, By the Way

Vic, an enterprising young man in the sales department, has scored a really big win; he has landed a Navy hospital as a client. This is very good news for MWave because once you get your product into one military facility, it is very likely that you will make more sales to the military. The dollar signs are evident in everyone's eyes at our morning meeting.

The bad news, however, is that the military cannot allow the use of the encryption mechanism we have been using because it is not up to Mil-Spec. The Department of Defense mandates that any installation into a military hospital has to use a special encryptor, one that can *only* be used in a military installation (it is a classified algorithm).

Now we need to vary the encryption mechanism. We know that the issue will be static, not dynamic (meaning hospitals do not change from civilian to military and back again), so we can create a configuration file that stores the information about which encryptor to use.

Good thing we programmed by intention! The code that used to be in the `encryptStatus()` method will now move into a class (the *extract class* refactoring), which will be one of two implementations of the abstraction Encryption. Of course, we will encapsulate the construction of the "right" encryptor, as displayed in Figure 14.6. This gives us a perfect place to reference the configuration file.

This is the Strategy pattern. It is not *exactly* what the Gang of Four showed us in their book because we are not passing the encryptor that we want to use into the Component via the pollComponent() method. We are encapsulating the issue in the getInstance() method of the Encryption abstract class. This avoids coupling the ComponentManager to the fact that there are two encryptors, which ones they are, and which one we are using for a particular client. It also hides the fact that we are using a Strategy pattern at all!

Because the issue does not have to be terribly dynamic, we would rather keep the implementation more hidden. This is a force in the Strategy pattern. The pattern tells me to consider these options right away, as soon as I realize that the pattern is present in my situation. Again, if you do not know the Strategy pattern well, visit Appendix B for a few minutes.

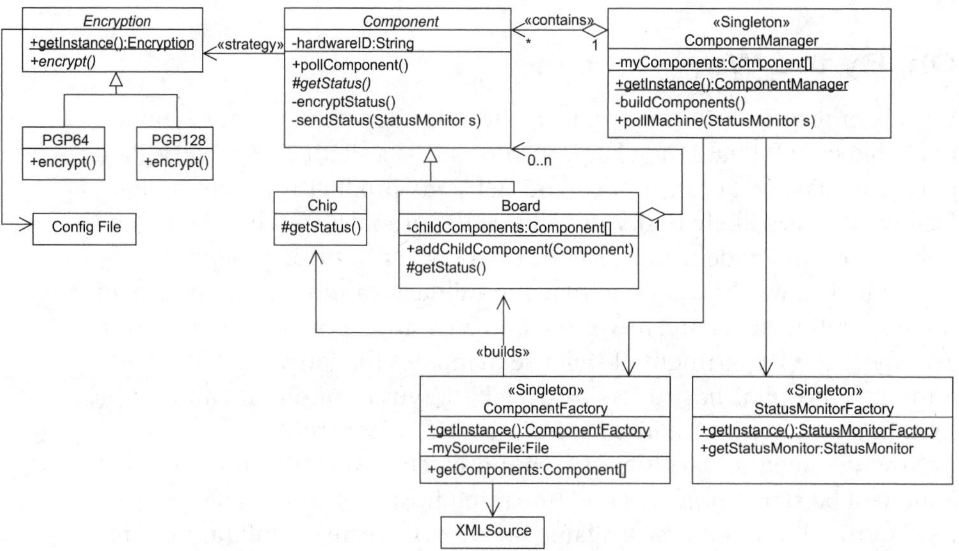

Figure 14.6 The construction of the right encryptor

Notes:

- Pulling the `encryption` out of `Component` now is not especially difficult because the original encryption algorithm was in a separate method already. Programming by intention did this for me.
- We pulled `encryption` out rather than subclassing the `Component` class and specializing it. This is one of the main pieces of advice from the Gang of Four: to favor delegating to a service over specializing the consumer of that service.
- Testability is enhanced! We can now write individual unit tests for each version (subclass) of the `Encryption` service. I guess we were right all along, but you cannot always win such a battle. Now that we have a variation, it is hard to argue that `Encryption` should not be in a class by itself since leaving it in `Component` requires procedural logic to contain the variation and this degrades cohesion. Do no harm!
- We need a mock version of `Encryption` to test `Component` implementations (`Chip` and `Board`).
- We could have created an `Encryption` factory. If you chose that, I would not argue with you. However, since the issue is really very simple, at this point, we do not have to. If a separate factory ever becomes warranted, we can delegate to it from the static `getInstance()` method that we have provided in the `Encryption` base class, so we have not painted ourselves into a corner here.

More Good News

Ah, Vic. What would we do without him?

Right after landing the Navy hospital's business, Vic ran right out and signed another client: The Emperor Adamantine Hospital Consortium. Although this represents another great revenue opportunity for MWave, it does put another fly into the ointment for us.

Emperor Adamantine does not particularly care what encryption algorithm we use, so long as the FDA is satisfied. However, it prefers to mange things centrally, and so groups of Emperor hospitals will all report their hardware status to the management hub for their districts. This means that the straightforward TCP socket that `StatusMonitor` has been using to send the status reports will not work for Emperor.

```
package MWaveMon;
public class RemoteStatusMonitor
{
    void open() {
         //Opens the connection to an Empire Adamantine hub
    void sendStatus(String statusDetail, bool ok){
         //Client tier implementation here
    }
    void queueStatus(String statusDetail, bool ok){
         //Client tier implementation here
    }
    void close(){
         //Closes the connection to the hub
    }

}
```

The client tier has been working with the developers from Emperor. Together, they have come up with a different service for monitoring where Emperor's hospitals are concerned.

When sending status reports via this class, we have to open the connection before using it, and close it afterward. In addition, for efficiency, the more complex machines (the `Board` components, specifically) should be coded to send their status to the `queueStatus()` method until all of their child components have been polled. Then, they should call the `sendStatus()` method with their own status, causing a single call across the network boundary.

Which monitor (`StatusMonitor` or `RemoteStatusMonitor`) we use is also based on the configuration file and is set at install time.

One thing that bothers us right away is that the two monitors do not have the same interface. In looking at the problem, we see that we have

- A variation of the sort of entity that we are monitoring: `Cards` versus `Boards`.
- A variation in the implementation of the monitoring itself: `Local` versus `Remote`.
- The different entities use the monitoring services in different ways: `Boards` use the queuing capability; `Cards` do not.

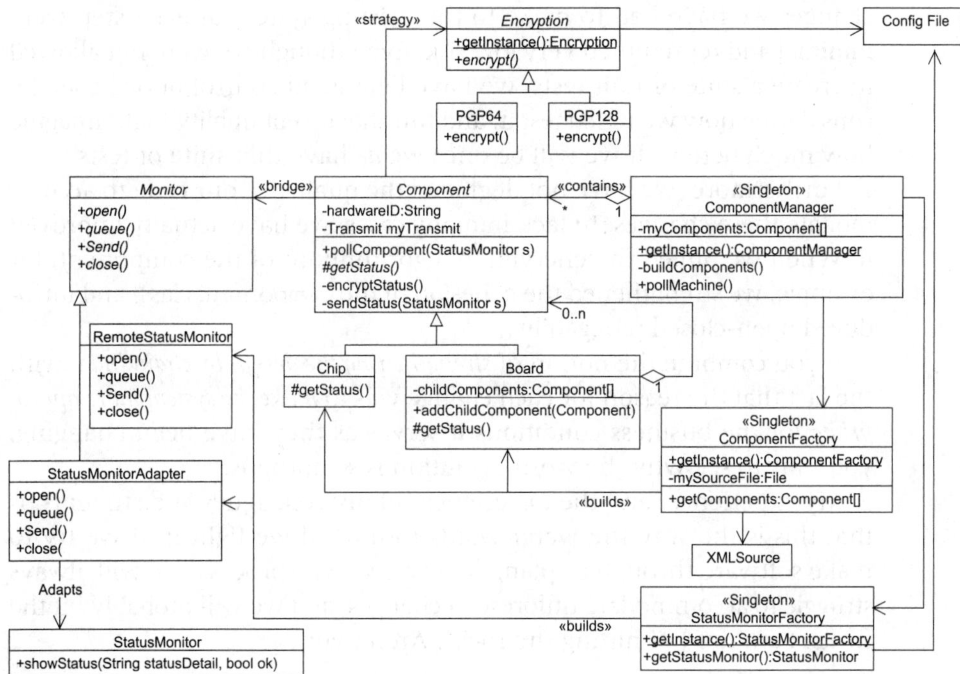

Figure 14.7 The Adapter pattern

To keep these variations independent, we might well decide to use a Bridge pattern (see Appendix B if you are unfamiliar with the Bridge). However, one of the issues that the Bridge tells me to investigate right up front is how difficult will it be to make the implementations (the monitors) work the same way?

If the client tier would resolve them to a single interface, we would have no problem. But they cannot do this because it would break a lot of other code that also sends monitor reports via the old interface. So, it is up to us to solve this problem if we want to be able to keep these variations independent.

Luckily, as shown in Figure 14.7, we know the Adapter pattern (Appendix B explains the Adapter pattern), so it is not such a big deal.

Summary: What a Long, Strange Trip It Has Been

If you look at the design we started with and compare it to what we have now, the difference is rather striking. You will note, however, that the changes we have had to make to the existing system at each step were minimal and represented very low risk. Even though we were not allowed to create a suite of unit tests, we have kept good control of our code by considering how we *would* test it, and thus have kept quality high. Imagine how much better off we will be once we *do* have that suite of tests.

Furthermore, we have not degraded the quality of our code to accommodate these changes. In fact, in many cases, we have actually improved it. When we pulled the encryption algorithm out of the component, for example, we strengthened the cohesion of the `Component` class, and introduced open-closed pluggability.

If you combine the notion of *strengthening the design by changing it* with the fact that the reason for each change was to *make the system more appropriate* for the business conditions it serves as they have been changing, you start to see why the word evolution is so apropos.

My experience, and the experiences of my colleagues and students, is that this is the way the water wants to flow. If we fight it, if we try to make software through a "plan, do, review" type process, we will always struggle to accommodate unforeseen changes, and we will probably hit the rocks. I am tired of hitting the rocks. Aren't you?

Chapter 15

A Conclusion: 2020

I want to make a prediction, and I like to think it is not too far off the mark.

It is 2020. The world has continued its technological upswing, but the pace of change has slowed somewhat due to the diminishing returns that innovation is providing. People are settling into a lifestyle that relies increasingly upon technology, but much of it has become relatively invisible to them.

Software is, of course, everywhere. It is in our televisions and toasters, in our cell phones and sliding-glass doors. Maybe it is in our shoelaces. And all of this software has been created by professionals.

People no longer talk about "crashing" software systems any more than they would have, in the good old days of 1995, talked about "not having enough bandwidth" for their cable TV to deliver a baseball game in real time. People depend upon technology, and therefore upon software in profound and fundamental and unspoken ways; and they can, because the software works reliably, can be changed as needed, and is affordable. Software is so good that it is rarely a topic of conversation outside the development field itself.

I am 60 years old. I am still teaching, writing, and contributing whatever I can to my profession. I work in an institution that did not, when I wrote my first book, exist in its current form. It is an institution that teaches software developers the real-world practices, principles, and disciplines that will make them into successful professionals. Perhaps it is sponsored by large companies that see the orderly creation of true software professionals to be in their best interest. Perhaps my students are like residents at a hospital, paid a relatively lower wage than they eventually will be, but in exchange they are learning from experienced gray-hairs like me, and Alan, and Rod, and Rob, and David, and . . .

Sometimes, over lunch, students ask me what it was like to be working in the field when things really started to change.

"It was an interesting time," I say, "and in lots of ways it was really, really hard. Change always is."

They go on to tell each other the stories they have heard about the days when people tried to build software like they built bridges or skyscrapers, before we really understood what software development was, before we committed to an evolutionary process, before we admitted to ourselves that we could *never* predict what software would need to do before we finished it. They laugh about this, tell their war stories, and remark how glad they are that things have changed.

I listen to them, and enjoy their enthusiasm.

What I do not say is how terrifically proud I am that I contributed to that change, even if only in some small way. Pride is vanity, so I keep it to myself.

But it feels good to know that "I was there" and that some part of the improvements we have seen since those days has come from my effort and the efforts of my colleagues. I know that there is more to learn, more to discover, and more to share with the other professionals making the software that will constitute the next wave of innovation and empowerment in human society; and I look forward to being a part of that, too.

Of course, I am probably describing you, too. You are part of this change, and if you choose, you will be part of the future "old guard" that the next generations of developers will look to for guidance and knowledge.

So, welcome. Welcome to the *profession* of software development. Let's work together to promote the qualities, principles, practices, disciplines, and patterns that will get us to that day in 2015, or sooner if we can manage it. Let's encourage the organizations we work for to *see us as professionals* and then let's make sure they benefit from that attitude, that they never regret relinquishing control of our profession to us.

Designing and creating software is hard. It is never going to be easy. But it is important, and will be more important tomorrow than it is today. Let's work together to learn how to do it right and then contribute this knowledge to our profession, and the world.

Appendix A

Evolutionary Paths

Chapter 14, the case study chapter, demonstrated by example the evolution of a relatively simple design into a much more complex one. Such examples are useful and informative, and of course, there are many of them we could look at.

This appendix shows various examples of simple designs evolving to more complex (pattern-oriented) designs, illustrating the value of simple practices like programming by intention and encapsulating construction.

No claim is (or can be) made that this is a comprehensive list, or even that these illustrations represent the more common evolutionary paths. This is simply a set of examples to elucidate the concept of design evolution.

Encapsulated Constructor to Singleton

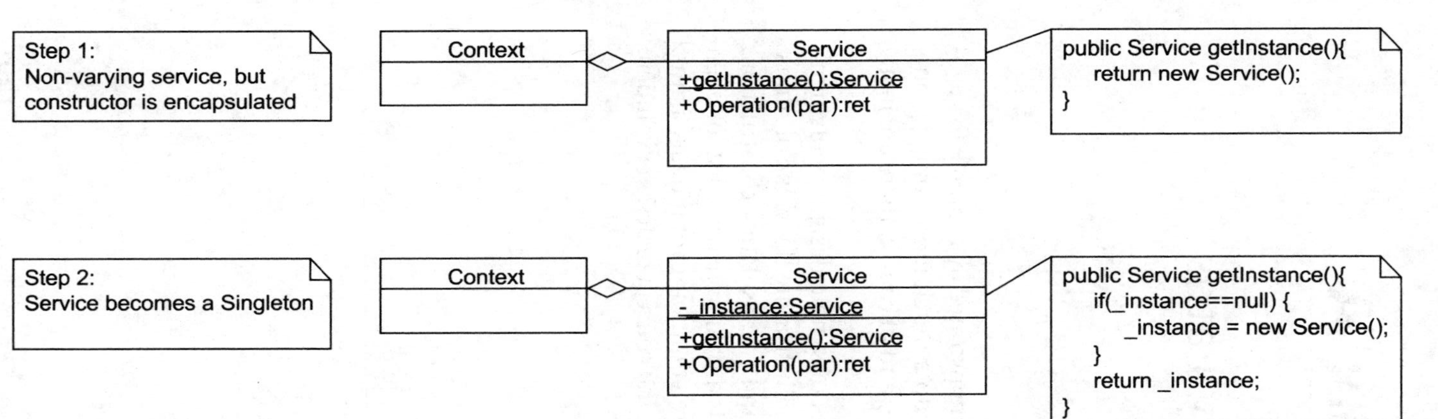

Figure A.1 Encapsulated constructor to Singleton

Programming-by-Intention to Encapsulated Constructor to Strategy (Varying on an Issue Extrinsic to the Client)

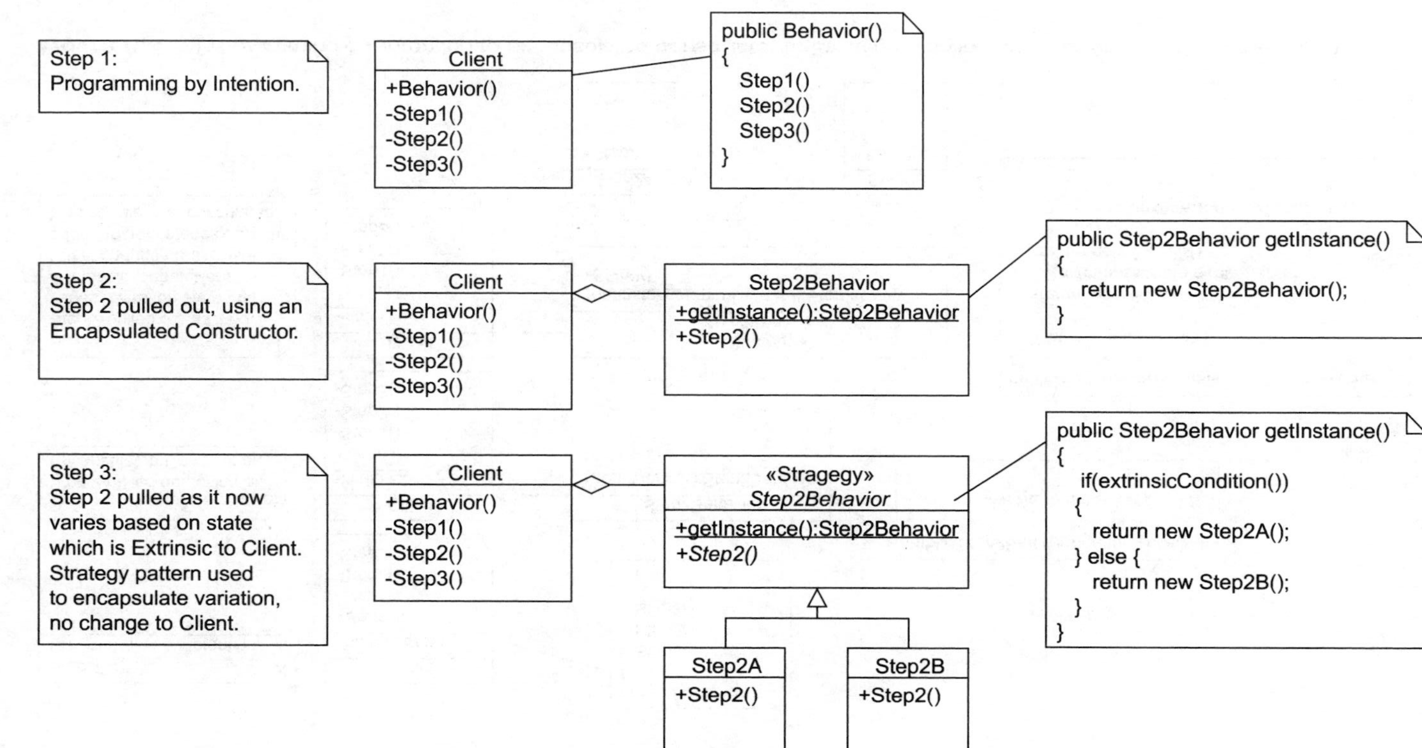

Figure A.2 Programming-by-intention to encapsulated constructor to Strategy (varying on an issue extrinsic to the client)

Programming-by-Intention to Encapsulated Constructor to Strategy (Varying on an Issue Intrinsic to the Client)

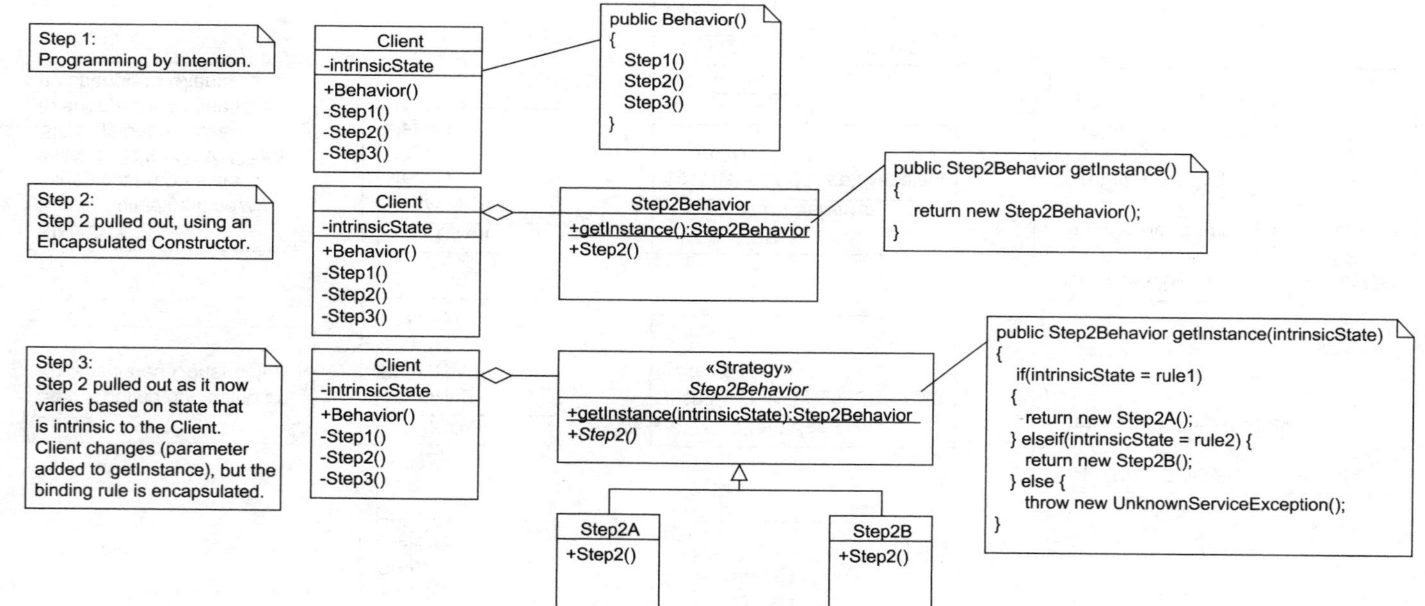

Figure A.3 Programming-by-intention to encapsulated constructor to Strategy (varying on an issue intrinsic to the client)

Programming-by-Intention to Encapsulated Constructor to Chain of Responsibility (Varying on an Issue Extrinsic to the Client)

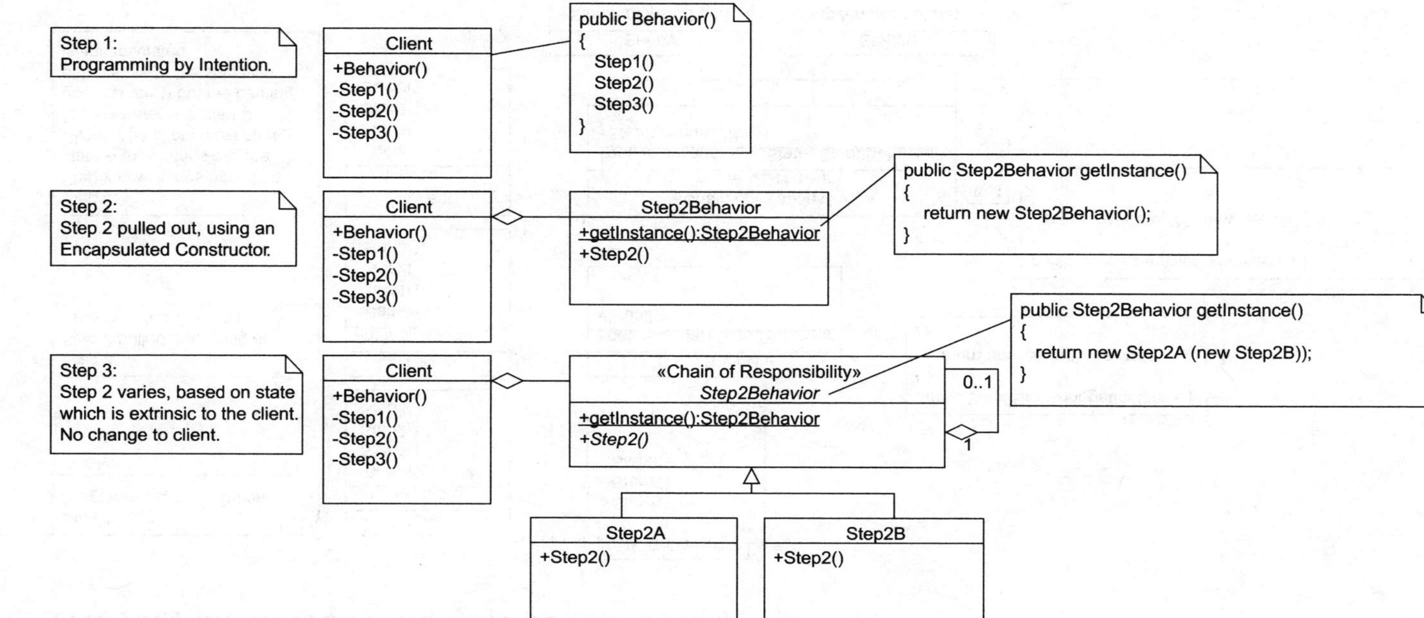

Figure A.4 Programming-by-intention to encapsulated constructor to Chain of Responsibility (varying on an issue extrinsic to the client)

Programming-by-Intention to Encapsulated Constructor to Chain of Responsibility (Varying on an Issue Intrinsic to the Client)

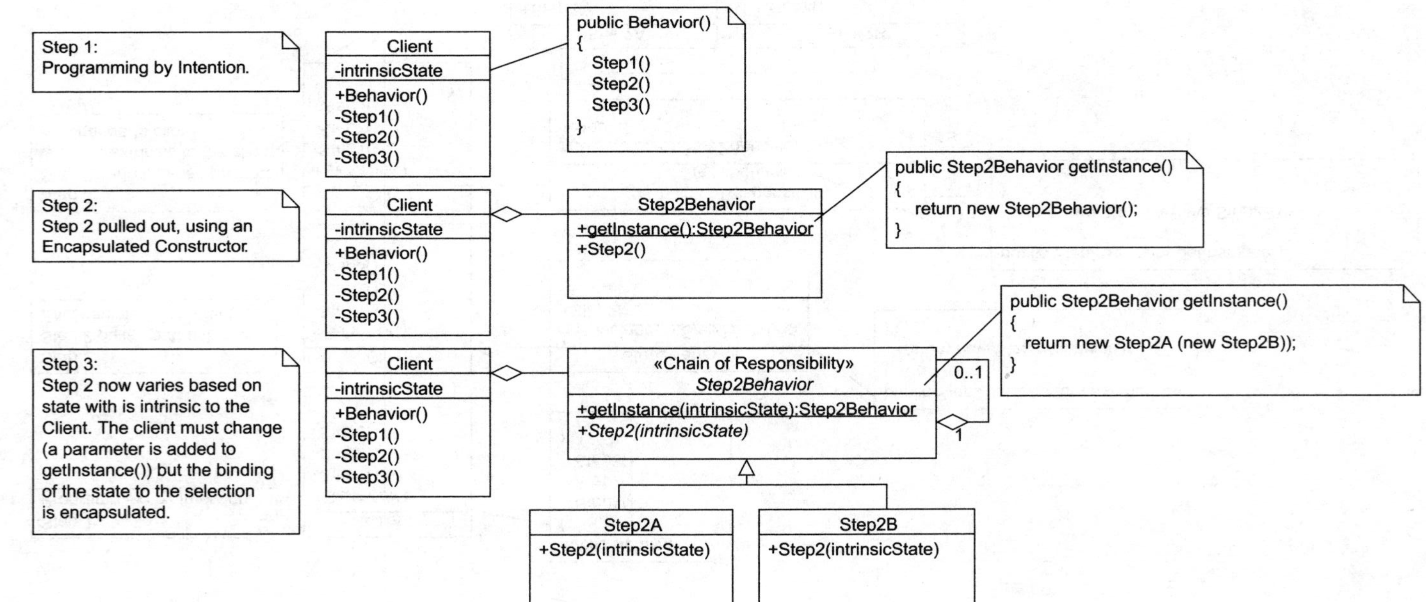

Figure A.5 Programming-by-intention to encapsulated constructor to Chain of Responsibility (varying on an issue intrinsic to the client)

From this point forward, we will assume programming by intention as a basic practice.

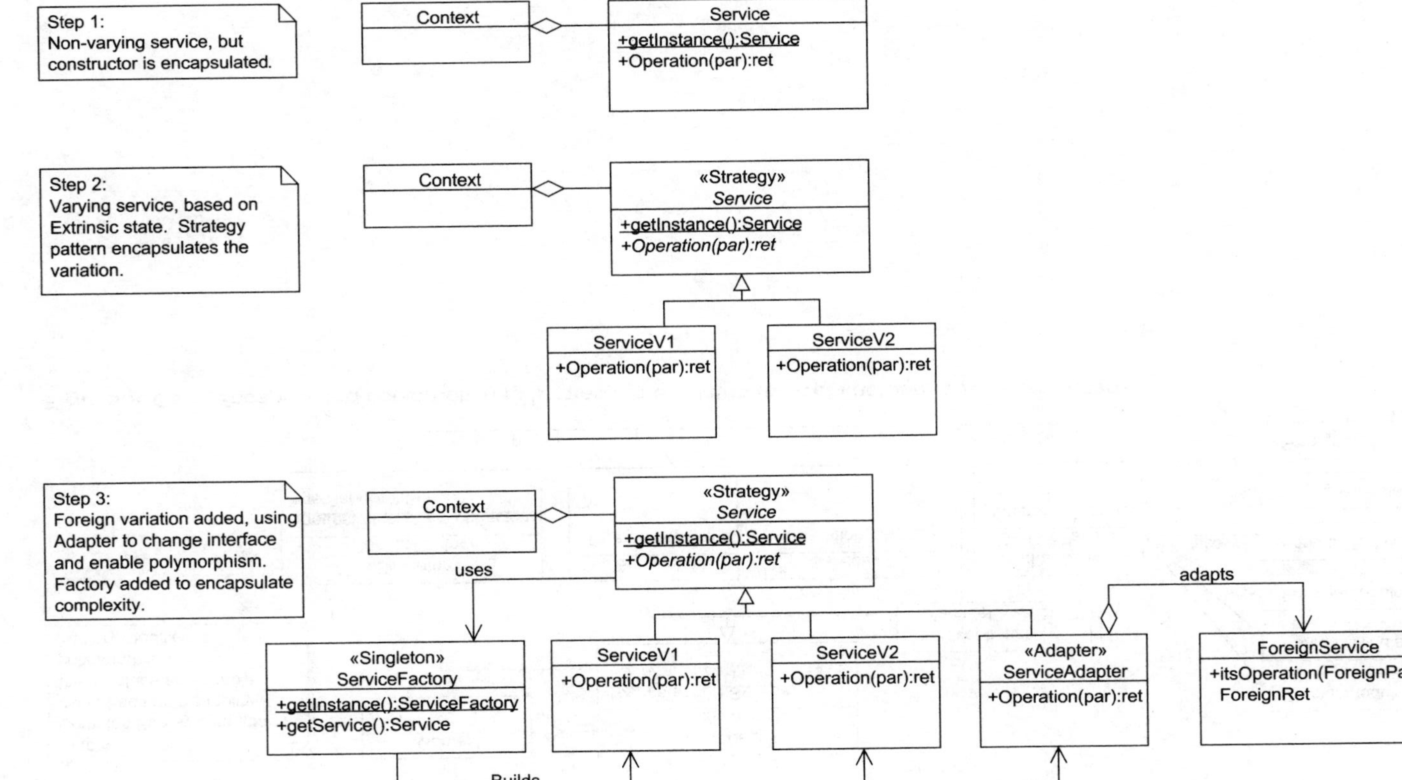

Figure A.6a Encapsulated construction to Strategy to Singleton (Object Factory) to Adapter/Façade

Encapsulated Construction to Strategy to Singleton (Object Factory) to Adapter/Façade

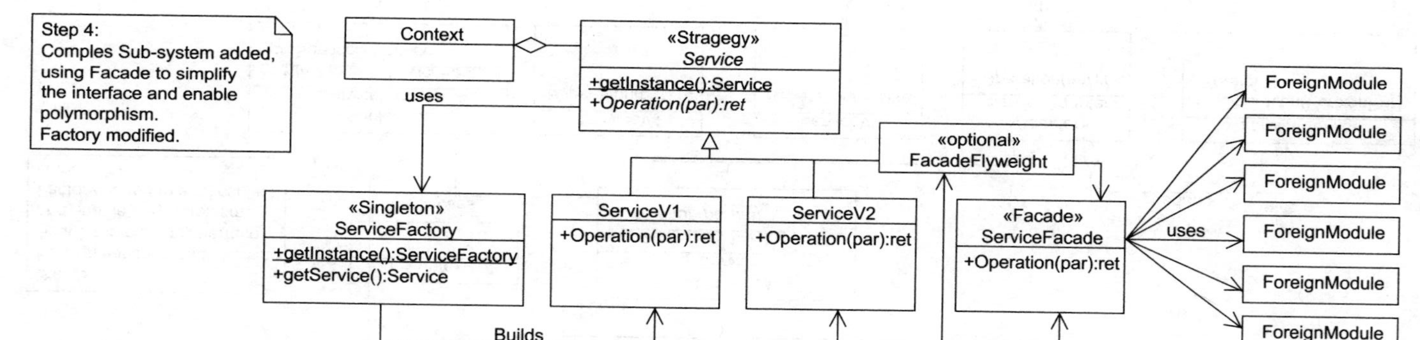

Figure A.6b Encapsulated construction to Strategy to Singleton (Object Factory) to Adapter/Façade

Encapsulated Constructor to Proxy to Decorator with Singleton (Object Factory)

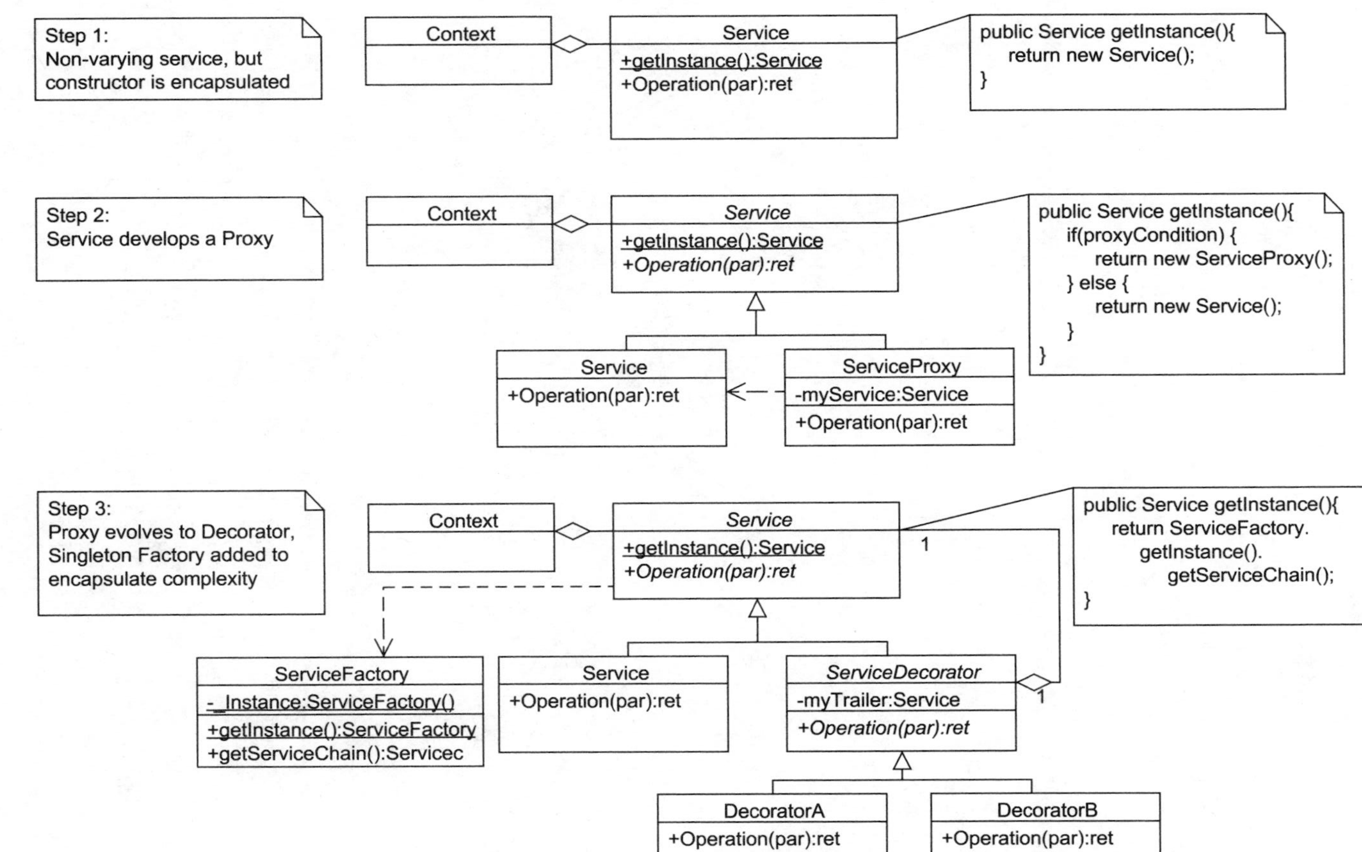

Figure A.7 Encapsulated construction to Proxy to Decorator with Singleton (Object Factory)

Appendix B

Overview of Patterns Used in the Examples

There are many books on patterns. In fact, as our profession matures, we will probably identify many more patterns than those we have identified to this point in time. Perhaps you will discover a few. Because of this, I think that it is a forlorn hope to try to cover "the right set" of patterns in software development at this point. However, we can derive a lot of value if we discuss the forces behind the patterns. In doing so, we can use a number of very common patterns as examples for our discussion.

This, I hope, is one of the things I have achieved in the book overall.

The purpose of this appendix is to allow you to look up the patterns mentioned in the book when you do not know them or if you feel that your understanding of one pattern or another is lacking detail.

I present the patterns here in the way that I think of them and in the way that they have been the most useful to me: as collections of forces.

By *forces,* I mean the knowns, the driving issues, the critical decisions, and the understood effects of what we do. I divide these forces for each pattern to be discussed into three categories:

- ***Contextual forces*** (how we know to consider a given pattern)
  - *Motivation*. Why this pattern is used, what it is for, and the domain problem it solves.
  - *Encapsulation*. What the use of this pattern hides from other entities in the system.
  - *Procedural analog*. How we would have solved this same problem procedurally.

    - *Non-software analog*. A way of seeing the pattern conceptually, from life experience.
- ***Implementation forces*** (how to proceed once we decide to use a pattern)
    - *Example (UML and pseudo-code)*. A concrete instance of the pattern (which is not the pattern, but only an example).
    - *Questions, concerns, credibility checks*. Those issues that should come into the discussion once the pattern is suggested as a possible solution.
    - *Options in implementation*. Various options that are well-known in implementing this pattern. Often, the various implementations arise out of the questions and concerns that accompany the pattern.
- ***Consequent forces*** (what happens if we use a pattern)
    - *Testing issues*. Testing wisdom that accompanies the pattern. These are hints, tricks, and tips that can make patterns, which usually depend heavily on delegation, easier to test. They depend on a reasonable knowledge of mock and fake objects, which are covered in the sections on testing and test-driven development.
    - *Cost-benefit (gain-loss)*. What we get and what we pay when we use this pattern. Understanding these issues is a key aspect of making the decision to use or not to use a pattern. Patterns are as just valuable to us when they lead us *away* from themselves.

Code examples will be presented in a Java-like, C#-ish pseudo-code style that hopefully will be readable by all. The purpose of both the code and UML examples is to *illustrate*, not to *define*. Patterns are not code, nor are they diagrams; they are collections of forces that define the best-practices for solving a recurring problem in a given context. We provide code and UML examples because many people understand concepts better when they are accompanied by concrete examples.

Similarly, the procedural analogs are not meant to be literally applied: you would *not* use a Strategy pattern every time you see a branching conditional in procedural code. The purpose of the analog is to allow us to use the part of our brains that understands procedural/algorithmic programming to suggest a possible pattern alternative, but only to ensure that we consider all of our options before making an implementation decision. The decision is, and in my opinion always will be, a human one.

The patterns that help to define our profession are not static, but are rather a living, changing thing that we must always seek to improve and expand upon. This must be a community effort.

To this end, my organization has started an online pattern *repository*. If you wish to participate and contribute, visit us at **http://www.netobjectives.com/resources** to find a link to the repository and to other tools we will develop to support this effort. The pattern appendix presented here also served as the starting content for this repository.

The Abstract Factory Pattern

Contextual Forces

Motivation

Create an interface for creating sets of dependant or related instances that implement a set of abstract types. The Abstract Factory coordinates the instantiation of sets of objects that have varying implementations in such a way that only legitimate combinations of instances are possible, and hides these concrete instances behind a set of abstractions.

Encapsulation

Issues hidden from the consuming (client) objects include

- The number of sets of instances supported by the system
- Which set is currently in use
- The concrete types that are instantiated at any point
- The issue upon which the sets vary

Procedural Analog

A fairly common need for something like the Abstract Factory arises when supporting multiple operating systems in a single application. To accomplish this, you would need to select the right set of behaviors: a disk driver, a mouse driver, a graphics driver, and so forth, for the operating system that the application is currently being installed for.

In a non-object-oriented system, you could accomplish this via conditional compilation, switching in the proper library for the operating system in question.

```
#IFDEF Linux
    include Linux_Drv.lib
#ENDIF

#IFDEF Windows
    include Windows_Drv.lib
#ENDIF
```

If the libraries in question contained routines that were named the same, and worked the same as other libraries for other operating systems, such that the consuming application code could reference them without regard to the particular operating system in use in a given case, it would simplify the code overall, and allow for a smoother transition between operating systems and in supporting new operating systems in the future. The Abstract Factory performs a similar role, but using objects, abstractions, and instantiation.

Another procedural form would be a set of switch/case statements, all based on the same variable, each of which varied a different service. The services in question would likely be implemented with patterns that hid their variations, such as the Strategy pattern, and would transition together when the value of the variable changed.

Non-Software Analog

I have two toolkits in my main toolbox.

One contains a set of wrenches (box-end wrenches, socket wrenches, closed-end wrenches) that are designed to work on a car that comes from overseas, and thus has metric measurements (centimeters, millimeters, and so forth).

The other contains an identical set (box-end, socket, closed-end) that is designed instead for an engine with English measurements (inches, quarter-inches, and so forth).

I do not have engines that have both metric and English bolts, and therefore I only use one set of wrenches or the other. The two toolkits encapsulate the difference: I choose the toolkit that applies to a given engine, and I know that all the wrenches I pull from it will be appropriate, making my maintenance process much simpler and allowing me to concentrate on the tune-up or other process I am trying to accomplish.

Implementation Forces

Example

Let's assume we are doing business in two countries, the United States and Canada. Because of this, our application must be able to calculate taxes for both countries, as we as calculate freight charges based on the services we use in each case. Also, we must determine that an address is properly formatted given the country we're dealing with at any point in time. To support this, we have the abstractions in place CalcTax, CalcFreight, and AddressVer, which have implementing classes for each country in each case.

The client would be designed to take an implementation of Abstract Factory in its constructor, and then use it to make all the helper objects that it needs. Note that since the client is designed to work only with a single factory, and since there is no factory version that produces, say, a USTax object and a CanadaFreight object, it is impossible for the client to obtain this illegitimate combination of helper objects (see Figure B.1).

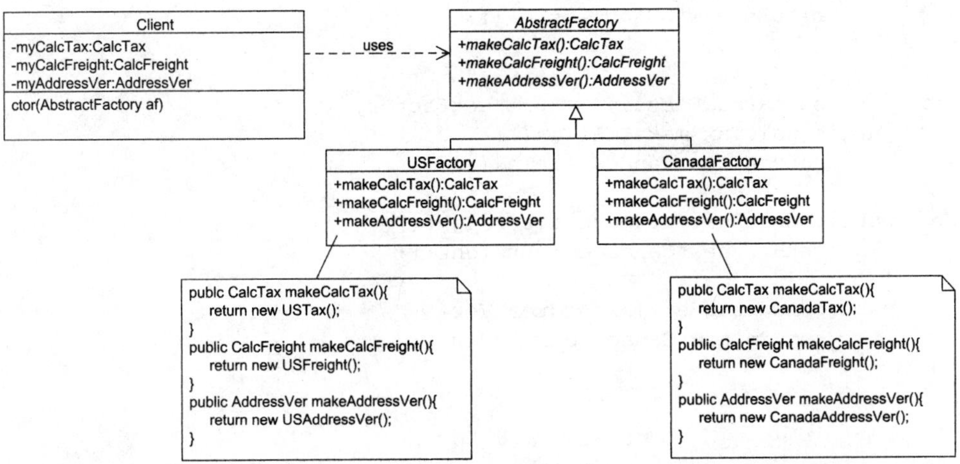

Figure B.1 A typical Abstract Factory, in this case, varying services that discreetly bind to a given nation

```
public class Client{
     private CalcTax myCalcTax;
     private CalcFreight myCalcFreight;
     private AddressVer myAddressVer;

     public Client(AbstractFactory af){
          myCalcTax = af.makeCalcTax();
          myCalcFreight = af.makeCalcFreight();
          myAddressVer = af.makeAddressVer();
     }

     // The rest of the code uses the helper objects generically
}

public abstract class AbstractFactory{
     abstract CalcTax makeCalcTax();
     abstract CalcFreight makeCalcFreight();
     abstract AddressVer makeAddressVer();
}

public class USFactory : AbstractFactory{
     public CalcTax makeCalcTax(){
        return new USCalcTax();
     }
     public CalcFreight makeCalcFreight(){
          return new USCalcFreight();
     }
     public AddressVer makeAddressVer(){
          return new USAddressVer();
}

public class CanadaFactory : AbstractFactory{
     public CalcTax makeCalcTax(){
          return new CanadaCalcTax();
     }
     public CalcFreight makeCalcFreight(){
          return new CanadaCalcFreight();
     }
     public AddressVer makeAddressVer(){
          return new CanadaAddressVer();
}
```

Questions, Concerns, Credibility Checks

For the Abstract Factory to be effective, there must be a set of abstractions with multiple implementations; these implementations must transition together under some circumstance (usually a large variation in the system); and these must all be resolvable to a consistent set of interfaces. In the preceding example, all tax systems in the supported countries must be supportable by a common interface, and the same must be true for the other services.

An obvious question arises: What entity determines the right concrete factory to instantiate, and deliver to the client entity? As this is an instantiation issue, the preferred approach is to encapsulate this behavior in an entity that is separate from any consuming object (encapsulation of construction). This can be done in an additional factory (arguably a Factory factory), or as is often the case, in a static method in the base (Abstract) class of the factory.

```
public abstract class AbstractFactory{
     abstract CalcTax makeCalcTax();
     abstract CalcFreight makeCalcFreight();
     abstract AddressVer makeAddressVer();
     public static AbstractFactory getAFtoUse(String customerCode){
          if(customerCode.startsWith("U")){
               return new USFactory();
          } else {
               return new CanadaFactory();
          }
     }
}
```

Note that I am not overly fond of this approach (it creates a mixture of perspectives in this abstract type; it is both a conceptual entity and an implementation of a factory), but it is nonetheless quite common.

Also, you must ask how often and under what circumstances does the proper set of objects change? The preceding example sets the factory implementation in the client's constructor, which implies little change during its lifetime. If more flexibility is required, this can be accomplished another way.

In determining many how object types are in each set, how many sets there are, and the resulting number of combinations, you can get an early view of the complexity of the implementation. Also, there are sometimes objects that can be used in more than one family, such as a Euro object that might be used as a Currency implementation for many different countries in the European Union, though their Tax object might all be distinct. The degree to which implementations can be shared, and intermixed, tends to reduce the burden on the implementing team, and is an early question to be asked.

Options in Implementation

That fact that the Gang of Four example, and the example shown earlier, uses an abstract class with derivations should not mislead you to assume that this is required for an Abstract Factory. The fact that abstract class may be used is not the reason the pattern is named *Abstract* Factory; in fact, it is simply one way of implementing the pattern.

For example, you could create a single concrete factory implementation, and for each method (`makeCalcTaxI()`, for instance) simply use a procedural switch or if/then logic to generate the correct instance. Although this would not be particularly object-oriented (and probably not ideal), it would still be rightly termed an Abstract Factory.

The term Abstract Factory indicates that all the entities being created are themselves abstractions. In the preceding example, `CalcTax`, `CalcFreight`, and `AddressVer` are all abstractions.

Another very popular way of implementing an Abstract Factory is to bind the factory to a database table, where fields contain the names of the proper classes to instantiate for a given client, and dynamic class loading is then used to instantiate the proper class. The advantage here is that changes to the rules of instantiation can be made simply by changing the values in the table.

```
//Example is in Java
//Assumes myDataSource and ID are set elsewhere. ID reflects
//the current customer.

CalcTax makeCalcTax () {
    String db = "jdbc:odbc:"+ myDataSource;
    Class.forName("sun.jdbc.odbc.JdbcOdbcDriver");
    String query = "SELECT CALC_TAX FROM mytable WHERE ID = "
                  + ID;

    Connection myConn = DriverManager.getConnection(db, "", "");
    Statement myStatement = myConn.createStatement();
    ResultSet myResults = myStatement.executeQuery(query);
```

```
    String classToInstantiate;
    classToInstantiate= myResults.getString("CALC_TAX");
    return Class.forName(classToInstantiate);
}
```

Consequent Forces

Testing Issues

As with factories in general, the Abstract Factory's responsibility is limited to the creation of instances, and thus the testable issue is whether the right set of instances is created under a given circumstance. Often, this is covered by the test of the entities that use the factory, but if it is not, the test can use type-checking to determine that the proper concrete types are created under the right set of circumstances.

Cost-Benefit (Gain-Loss)

When we use the Abstract Factory, we gain protection from illegitimate combinations of service objects. This means we can design the rest of the system for maximum flexibility, since we know that the Abstract Factory eliminates any concerns of the flexibility yielding bugs. Also, the consuming entity (client) or entities are incrementally simpler, since they can deal with the components at the abstract level. In our preceding e-commerce example, all notion of nationality is eliminated from the client, meaning that this same client will be usable in other nations in the future with little or no maintenance.

The Abstract Factory holds up well if the maintenance aspects are limited to new sets (new countries), or a given set changing an implementation (Canada changes its tax system). On the other hand, if an entirely new abstract concept enters the domain (trade restrictions to a new country), the maintenance issues are more profound as the Abstract Factory interface, all the existing factory implementations, and the client entities all have to be changed.

This is not a fault of the pattern, but rather points out the degree to which object-oriented systems are vulnerable to missing/new abstractions, and therefore reinforces the value of analysis practices like commonality-variability analysis.

The Adapter Pattern

Contextual Forces

Motivation

There are two primary reasons to use an adapter:

- To use the behavior of an existing object, using a different interface than it was designed with.
- To make an existing object exchangeable with a polymorphic set of objects.

The Adapter pattern is generally used when one or both of these motivations exists but the existing object cannot be changed.

Encapsulation

The Adapter encapsulates the *differentness* of the object being adapted. It hides the fact that the adaptee has a different interface, and also that it is of a different abstract type (or is purely concrete and has no abstract type).

Also, since the client would deal with a nonadapted (local) object and an adapted (foreign) object in the same way, the fact that the client is using one object in the first case and two in the second case is encapsulated. This is shown in Figure B.2. This is a limited form of the encapsulation of cardinality (see the Decorator pattern).

Procedural Analog

A method, function, or other code segment that redirects behavior to another method, function, or code segment hiding this redirection from the consuming code.

```
rval m(para p) {
      c = (cast)p;
      x = n(c);
      return (cast)x;
}
```

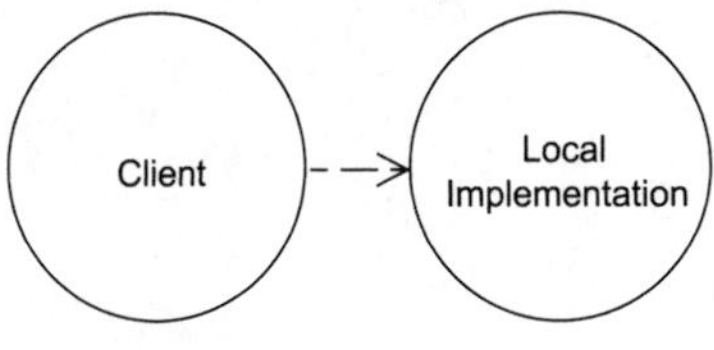

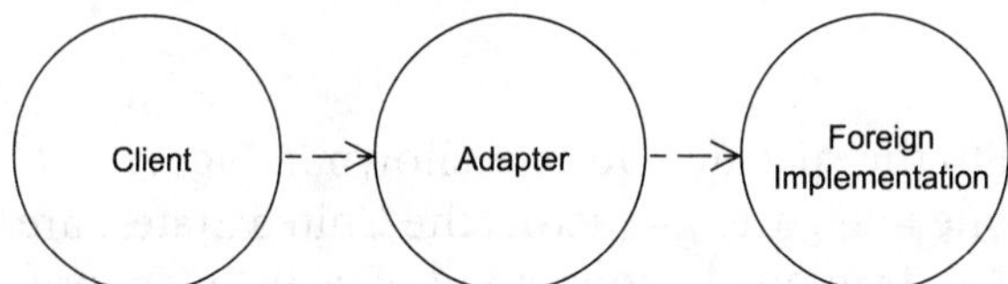

Figure B.2 Case 1: Local implementation, one object used by the client. Case 2: Foreign implementation with Adapter, two objects used by the client.

Non-Software Analog

Since I travel a lot, my primary computing device is a laptop. I notice that even though laptop batteries have improved dramatically (lithium-ion or nickel-mental-hydride as opposed to nickel-cadmium), they still seem to quickly lose their capability to hold a charge for very long.

As a result, when I am at a coffee shop, airport terminal gate, or hotel lobby, I am always "on the hunt" for a wall outlet to plug my power brick into. Unfortunately, I am rarely the only person on this hunt, and typically someone else will have found the one outlet, and is "hogging" it.

My solution is to look for a lamp. A lamp has what I need: 110 volts at 60 cycles, paid for by somebody else! It does not present it in the form that I need it, however (two little slots that my power brick plug will fit into), but in a form that is appropriate for a light bulb (a threaded socket and a copper tab in the bottom).

So, I carry one of these (see Figure B.3) in my laptop bag.

I (quietly) unscrew the light bulb from the lamp, screw in my adapter, and plug my laptop into it.

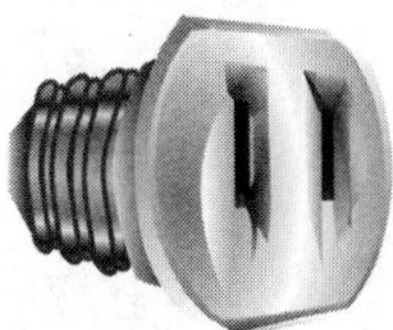

Figure B.3 Adapter for socket

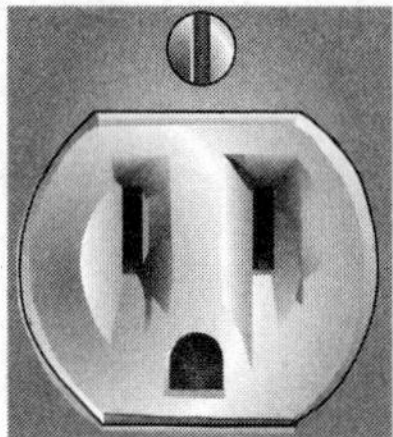

Figure B.4 Wall socket

My laptop was designed to the specific interface shown in Figure B.4.

All wall sockets like the one in Figure B.4 (across the United States) are exchangeable for one another, from my laptop's point of view. In a sense, they are a polymorphic set. The lamp socket is not exchangeable because its interface is not acceptable, even though the "stuff it has to offer" is just what I need.

The adapter allows my laptop to consume the electricity the way it was designed to, and makes the lamp socket interchangeable with the wall sockets of the world.

Implementation Forces

Example

See Figure B.5.

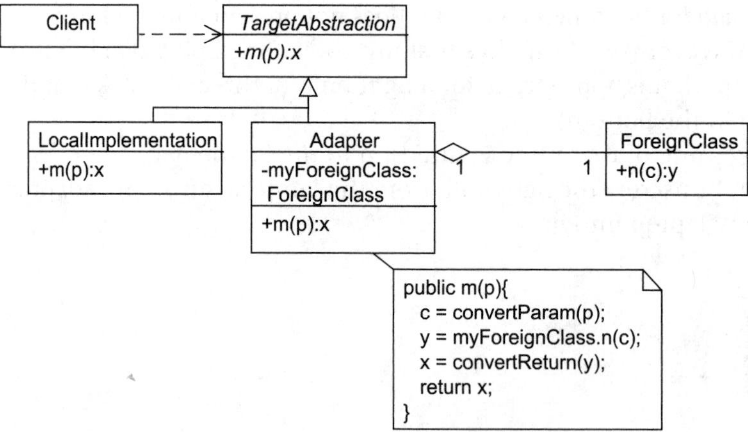

Figure B.5 Implementation forces

Code

```
public class TargetAbstraction {
      public abstract ret m(par p);
}

public class Adapter extends TargetAbstraction {
      private ForeignClass myForeignClass();
      public Adapter() {
            myForeignClass = new ForeignClass();
      }
      public ret m(par p) {
            var y = myForeignClass.n((cast)p);
            return (cast)y;
      }
}
```

Questions, Concerns, Credibility Checks

- How large is the delta (difference) between the interface that the foreign class offers and the interface of the target abstraction? If it is very large, this may be difficult to accomplish with a simple adapter. The Façade pattern should be considered in this case.
- If the foreign class throws exceptions, should the adapter rethrow them directly, rethrow them as a different exception, or deal with them by itself?
- How will the adapter obtain the instance of the foreign class? Direct instantiation (shown in the code) is actually not preferable, as it violates the encapsulation of construction principle; but the foreign class may not have been designed with this principle in mind. If this is the case, we may need to create an object factory to encapsulate the instantiation.
- Will the adapter need to add functionality to the foreign class? In other words, is the foreign class feature-poor to some degree?
- Will the adapter need to be stateful?

Options in Implementation

The preceding form uses delegation from the adapter to the foreign class to reuse the preexisting behavior. As shown in Figure B.6, another form of the adapter (called the *class adapter*) uses inheritance instead.

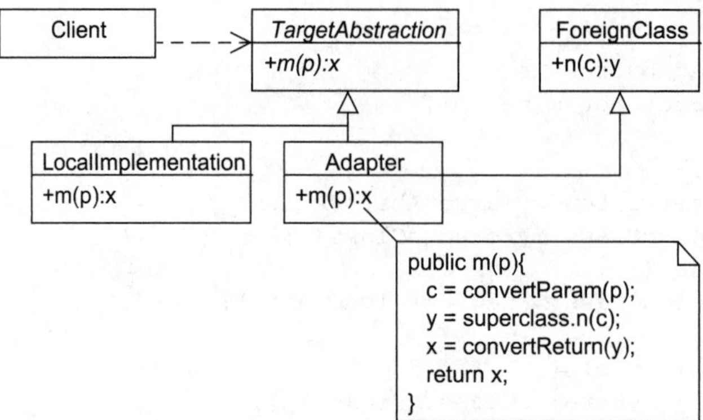

Figure B.6 Class adapter with inheritance

This implementation is more common with languages that support multiple inheritances, but it is also possible in single-inheritance languages if the `TargetAbstraction` is an Interface type.

Consequent Forces

Testing Issues

To test the adapter, you can use a mock or fake object in place of the foreign object (which would normally be adapted). The mock or fake can return predictable behavior for the adapter to convert, and also can record the action the adapter takes with the adaptee if this is deemed an appropriate issue to test.

Cost-Benefit (Gain-Loss)

The adapter is a low-cost solution and is therefore quite commonplace. The cost is the creation of an additional class, but the benefits are

- Encapsulated reuse of existing behavior
- Polymorphism (through an upcast) with a foreign class
- Promotes the open-closed principle
- If the construction of the foreign class was not encapsulated (which is common), the adapter can encapsulate it in its constructor. However, an object factory is preferred.

The Bridge Pattern

Contextual Forces

Motivation

Separate a varying entity from a varying behavior[1] so that these issues can vary independently. Sometimes, we say it this way: separate what something *is* from what it *does*, where both of these things vary for different reasons.

Encapsulation

The entity variation, the behavior variation, and the relationship between these variations are encapsulated. Also, we may wish to encapsulate that the Bridge pattern is being used at all.

Procedural Analog

Similar to a Strategy, a Bridge is analogous to the use of branching, conditional logic. However, in this case the logic is nested.

```
if(entityConditionA) {
     if(behaviorCondition1){
          // Algorithm A1
     } else {
          // Algorithm A2
     }
} else {
     if(behaviorCondition1){
          // Algorithm B1
     } else {
          // Algorithm B2
     }
}
```

1. The Gang of Four (Gamma, Helms, Johnson, Vlissides) said it this way: "Separate an abstraction from its implementation so the two can vary independently." Because most people use these words to mean "abstract superclass" and "implementing derived class," this can be a confusing motivational statement and does not reflect the original intent of the GoF. However, this wording is quite accurate given that these terms are being used in a different way. Abstraction = Entity, Implementation = Behavior or Action.

Non-Software Analog

My friends and I like to go to dinner together a lot. From the waitress' point of view, we are all the same—she considers us to be *patrons*, and she wants the same question answered no matter which of us she is speaking with: "whatlyahave?"

We are actually all different, of course, but that is not her concern. One difference that influences the outcome of this interaction is our ordering preference.

I usually get what is on special for the day. I like adventure. My younger brother, Christopher, says that I am crazy, because he says everyone knows "the special" is the thing that is just about to go bad. He says, "Get the specialty of the house; they take pride in doing that right." "Sure," I say, "but you always get the same thing if you do that." It is an old argument.

Andrea, my wife, likes salads and usually orders one. However, some places do not have them, so then she needs to get something meatless, whatever that might be.

Brenner always gets the most expensive thing on the menu. He has noticed that we always divide the check equally . . . and, well, that is Brenner.

That is one variation, or really, two: the variation of who we are and the variation of how we order food. These do not vary independently, however. The variation in our ordering preferences is what makes us different, in the context of being restaurant patrons.

The independent variation has to do with the restaurant we are currently visiting on a given evening. For example

Ocean Breeze: Seafood, primarily, and very experimental cuisine

RedRocks: Barbecue, mostly meat, very large portions: not Andrea's favorite place

Who we are varies and the food available varies, but each of us can use the menu in our own way to get what we want. From the waitress' point of view, she just wants an answer.

Implementation Forces

Example

See Figure B.7.

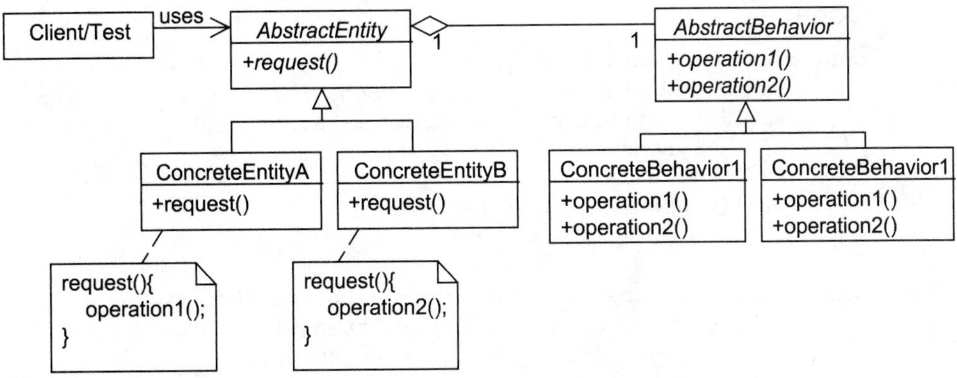

Figure B.7 Generic example of a Bridge implementation

The Bridge can be tricky, so Figure B.8 shows the same example using my non-software analogy.

Note that Andrea has to take some extra actions because `getSalad()` is not reliable across all restaurants. Because she is isolated from everyone else, only she has to be so high-maintenance. ☺

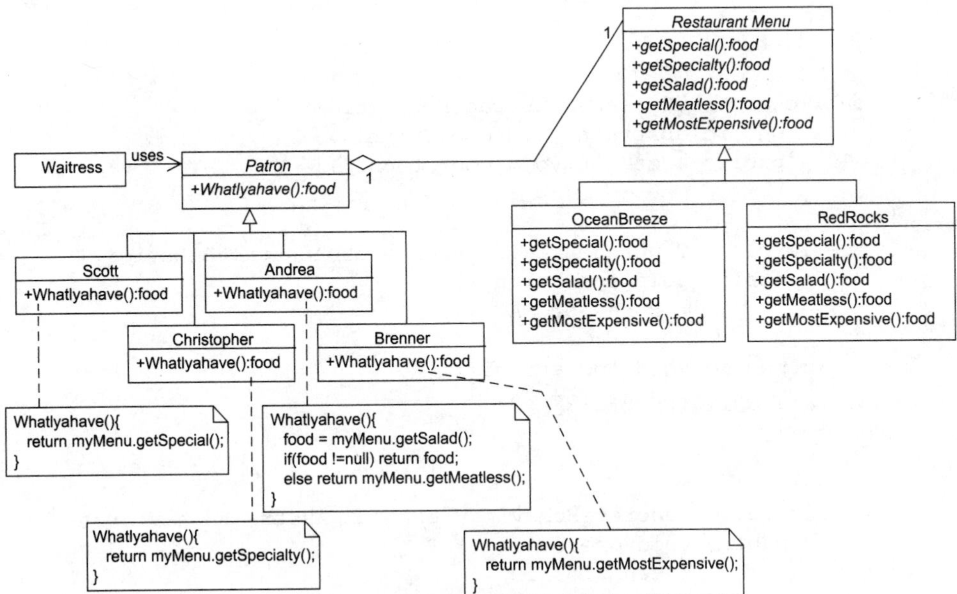

Figure B.8 Restaurant example with non-software analogy

Code

```
public class AbstractEntity {
      protected AbstractBehavior myBehavior;
      public AbstractEntity(AbstractBehavior aBehavior) {
            myBehavior = aBehavior;
      }
      public abstract void request();
}

public class ConcreteEntityA extends AbstractEntity {
      public ConcreteEntityA(AbstractBehavior aBehavior) {
            superclassConstructor(aBehavior);
      }
      public void request() {
            myBehavior.operation1();
      }
}

public class ConcreteEntityB extends AbstractEntity {
      public ConcreteEntityB(AbstractBehavior aBehavior) {
            superclassConstructor(aBehavior);
      }
      public void request() {
            myBehavior.operation2();
      }
}

public abstract class AbstractBehavior {
      public abstract void operation1();
      public abstract void operation2();
}

public class ConcreteBehaviorA extends AbstractBehavior {
      public void operation1() {
            // Behavior 1A
      }
      public void operation2() {
            // Behavior 2A
      }
}

public class ConcreteBehaviorB extends AbstractBehavior {
      public void operation1() {
            // Behavior 1B
      }
      public void operation2() {
            // Behavior 2B
      }
}
```

Questions, Concerns, Credibility Checks

- How likely is it that all of the entities can share the same interface without giving up any key capabilities?
- How likely is it that behaviors can share the same interface without giving up any key capabilities?
- How consistently do the entities use the behaviors? If they are very orthogonal, the interface of the `AbstractBehavior` will tend to be broad.
- How likely is it that new entities that may be added later will be able to use the existing `AbstractBehavior` interface? If this is unlikely, the interface will tend to grow, and perhaps bloat over time.
- Are the behaviors likely to be stateful or stateless? If they are stateless, they can be shared to increase efficiency and performance.

Options in Implementation

Because the Bridge requires that all behaviors must share the same interface and because it is quite common for these behaviors to come from foreign classes (device drivers, APIs from other systems, and so on), Bridges often use Adapters and Façades to bring the behaviors to a common interface. See Figure B.9 for an example.

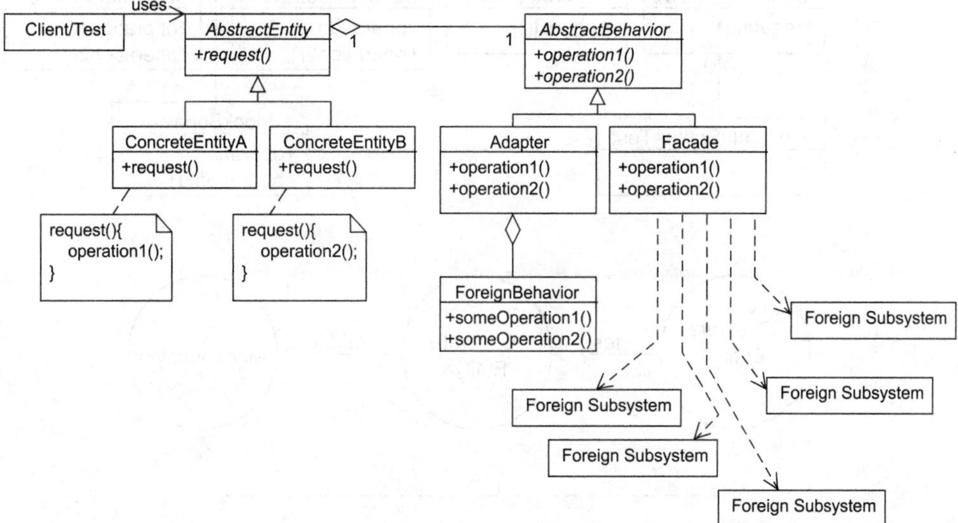

Figure B.9 Bridges using Adapters and Façades

Consequent Forces

Testing Issues

As shown in Figure B.10, the behavior classes are probably testable on their own (unless they are Adapters and/or Façades, in which case, see the testing forces accompanying those patterns). However, the entity classes are dependant upon behaviors and so a mock or fake object can be used to control the returns from these dependencies. It can also check on the action taken upon the behavior by the entity, if this is deemed an appropriate thing to test.

Cost-Benefit (Gain-Loss)

- The Bridge creates flexibility because the entities and behaviors can each vary without affecting the other.
- Both the entities and behaviors are open-closed, if we build the bridge in an object factory, which is recommended.

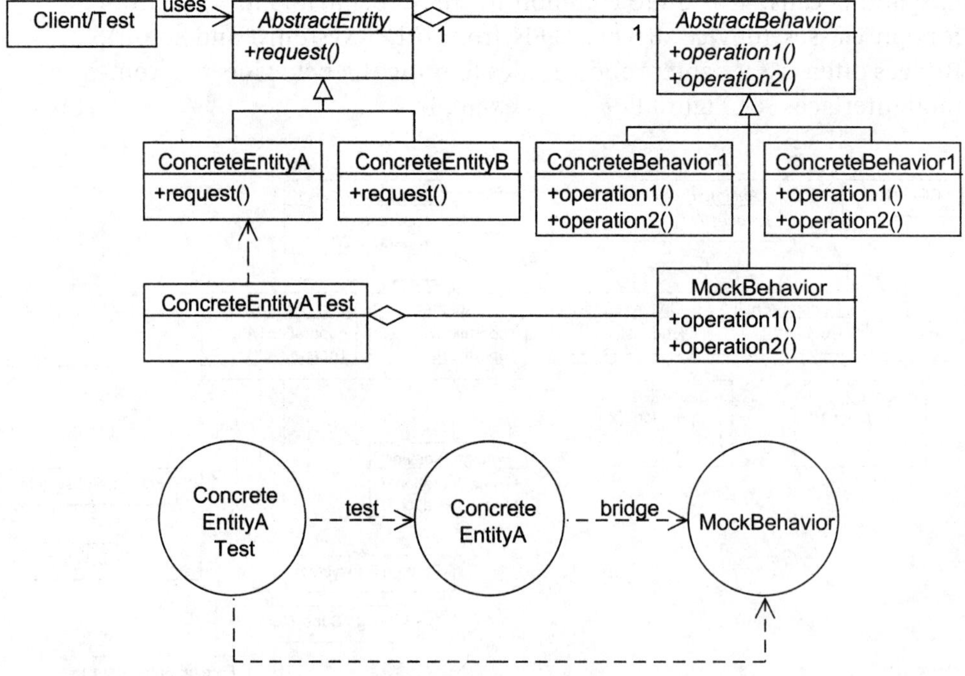

Figure B.10 Behavior classes testable on their own

- The interface of the behavior can require changes over time, which can cause maintenance problems.
- The delegation from the entities to the behaviors can degrade performance.

The Chain of Responsibility Pattern

Contextual Forces

Motivation

Where there are a number of different entities that handle the same request, and where only one of them will be the correct entity in a given circumstance, we can decouple the client (requester) from the entity that will handle the request in a given case.

Encapsulation

The client cannot see

- How many different entities there are that may handle the request (cardinality)
- Which entity actually handles any given request (variation)
- The order that the entities are given their chance (sequence)
- How the selection is achieved (selection)

These issues are all encapsulated by the pattern, especially if the chain itself is created in an object factory.

Procedural Analog

Each entity will be given *a chance* to handle the request until one of them elects to handle it. Once the request is handled, no further entities are given a chance to handle it. Any entity will self-select (or not), and therefore the selection is done from the point of view of the entity.

A clear procedural analog to this is the switch/case statement.

```
switch(condition) {

      case A:
      // Behavior A

      case B
      // Behavior B

      case C:
      // Behavior C

      default:
      // Default Behavior
}
```

The condition is evaluated from the point of view of each behavior, not from the point of view of the client or system (see the Strategy pattern).

Non-Software Analog

Imagine you have a large number of coins that you need to sort. A simple (old-fashioned) way of doing this is to create a stack of trays, each one with holes in it that match the size of a given coin (one for half-dollars, one for quarters, one for nickels, and so on).

In this stack, as displayed in Figure B.11, the tray with the largest holes will be on top, the next largest will be underneath that, and so on until you have a tray with no holes at the bottom. Only the dimes (which have the smallest diameter) fall all the way to the bottom tray. The pennies (next smallest) are caught one tray up, and so forth.

Implementation Forces

Example

See Figure B.12.

Figure B.11 Coin-sorting tray design

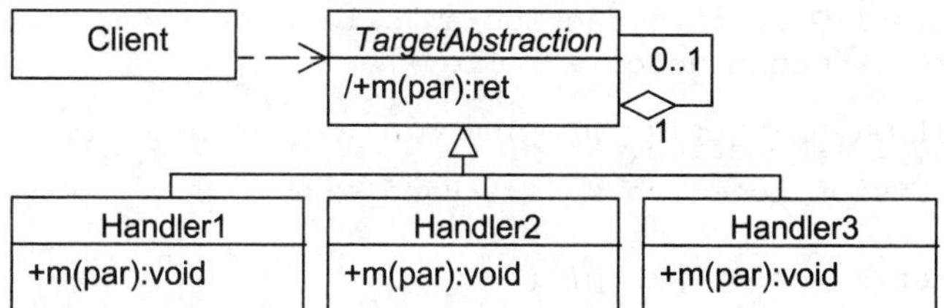

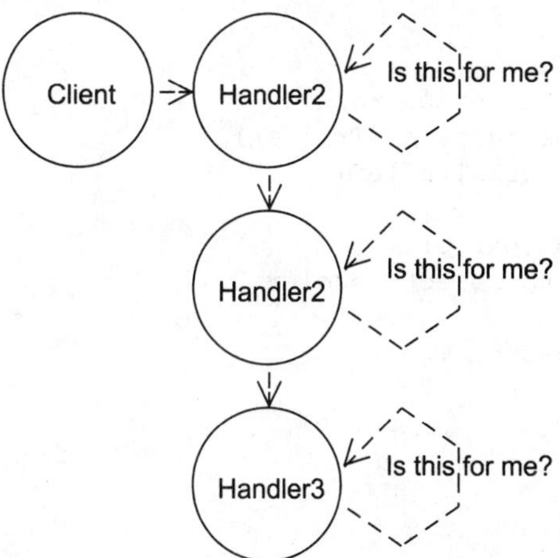

Figure B.12 Implementation forces

Code

```
public abstract class TargetAbstraction {
      private TargetAbstraction myTrailer;
      public TargetAbstraction(TargetAbstraction aTrailer) {
            myTrailer = aTrailer;
      }
      public ret m(par p) {
            if (isMyAction(p)) {
                  return myAction(p);
            }
            if(myTrailer != null {
                  return myTrailer.m(p);
            }
            throw new EndOfChainReachedException();
      }
      protected abstract bool isMyAction(par p);
      protected abstract ret myAction(par p);
}

public class Handler1 extends TargetAbstraction {
      public Handler1(TargetAbstraction aTrailer) {
            superclassConstructor(aTrailer);
      }
      protected bool isMyAction(par p) {
            // Decision logic to select Handler 1
      }
      protected ret myAction(par p) {
            // Handler 1 behavior
            return ret;
      }
}

public class Handler2 extends TargetAbstraction {
      public Handler1(TargetAbstraction aTrailer) {
            superclassConstructor(aTrailer);
      }
      protected bool isMyAction(par p) {
            // Decision logic to select Handler 2
      }
      protected ret myAction(par p) {
            // Handler 2 behavior
            return ret;
      }
}
```

```
public class Handler3 extends TargetAbstraction {
      public Handler1(TargetAbstraction aTrailer) {
            superclassConstructor(aTrailer);
      }
      protected bool isMyAction(par p) {
            // Decision logic to select Handler 3
      }
      protected ret myAction(par p) {
            // Handler 3 behavior
            return ret;
      }
}
```

Questions, Concerns, Credibility Checks

- All handlers must have a common interface. How difficult will this be to achieve without sacrificing any key distinction in one or more of the handlers?
- Is there significance in the order of the chain?
- Will different chain sequences affect performance in beneficial or harmful ways?
- How many handlers are there, as a performance issue?
- What should happen if none of the handlers elects? Is there a default case? Should an exception be thrown (as shown in the code example)?

Options in Implementation

As with the Decorator pattern, the Chain of Responsibility can be implemented with any desired collection. The advantage of the linked list is that it entirely encapsulates the handlers, and the selection of the correct handler under a given circumstance. However, a manager can be added to any collection in order to hide these issues.

Thus, a Chain of Responsibility can be implemented in an array, array list, vector, or any desired collection.

The Chain of Responsibility is also a good example of the capability of object-oriented designs to replace procedural logic with structures of objects. See the upcoming section, "Chain of Responsibility: The Poker Example," for more details.

Consequent Forces

Testing Issues

Testing each chain implementation is simply a matter of giving it the right and wrong state, to see if it responds by returning a correct value, or delegating to the next implementation. To test this second issue shown in Figure B.13, a mock or fake object should be used.

Cost-Benefit (Gain-Loss)

- The client is freed from containing the selection logic, strengthening its cohesion.
- The selection logic is spread out over many objects, and is therefore hard for the developer to see.
- Business logic regarding ordering dependencies is captured in the ordering of the chain rather than expressed in code (see the following poker example).
- If the chain is added to, it may get lengthy and may introduce performance problems.

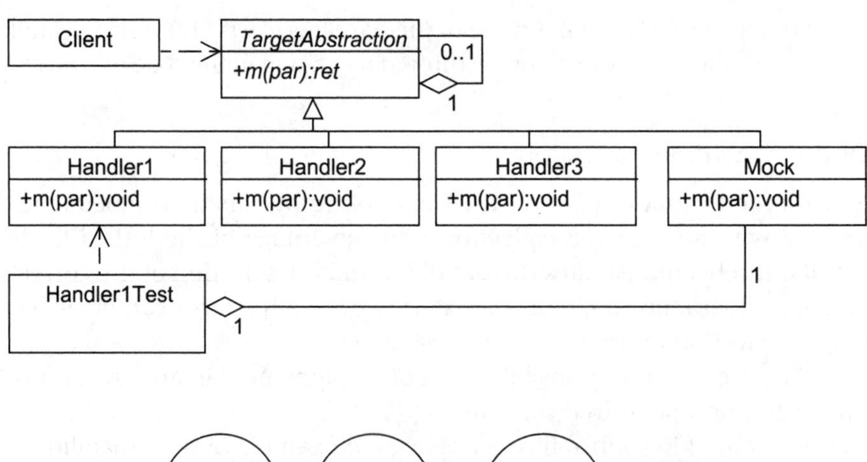

Figure B.13 Testing a chain implementation with a mock or fake object

Chain of Responsibility: The Poker Example

The Chain of Responsibility gives us an opportunity to demonstrate how various, sometimes surprising, issues can be composed into objects, rather than rendered into procedural code. This is not to say that *all* issues that were once dealt with procedurally should now be dealt with in an object-oriented way, but rather that it is helpful to know that such options exist, to allow the development team to make the most advantageous decision.

Our example here is the game of poker. If we were creating a software version of this game, one issue we would have to deal with is the rules that specify what hand beats what.

In poker, the hand with the highest card wins, unless one hand has a pair. The highest pair wins unless one hand has two pair. The hand with the highest "higher pair" wins unless one hand has three of a kind. Three of a kind is beaten by a straight (five cards in sequence, like 5, 6, 7, 8, 9). A straight is beaten by a flush (five cards in the same suit). A flush is beaten by a full house (three of one kind, a pair of another). A full house is beaten by four of a kind. Four of a kind is beaten by a straight-flush (five cards in sequence, all of the same suit), and the highest hand is a royal flush (the ace-high version of the straight flush).

These are business rules, essentially. Imagine that we decide to assign each of these hand types a numeric value so that once we determine the value of two or more hands, we could easily determine the winner, second place, and so forth. The Chain of Responsibility, as shown in Figure B.14, could be used to capture the rules that bound each hand type to a specific numeric value.

The `Hand` sends an array of its five cards to the first *evaluator* in the chain. Of course, we would likely build this chain in an object factory, and so the hand would not "see" anything more than a single service object.

The `Royal Flush Eval` object looks at these five cards and then determines yes or no, if they qualify as a royal flush. If the cards do qualify, the `Royal Flush Eval` object returns the numeric value we have assigned to `Royal Flushes`. If the cards do not qualify, the `Royal Flush Eval` delegates to the next object in the chain and waits for a result. It then returns that result to the `Hand`.

This delegation continues until one of the `Eval` objects self-elects, and then the value returns up the chain and back to the `Hand`. Note that every possible poker hand has some card that is highest, and so we have a default condition we can use to end the chain, the `High Card Eval`.

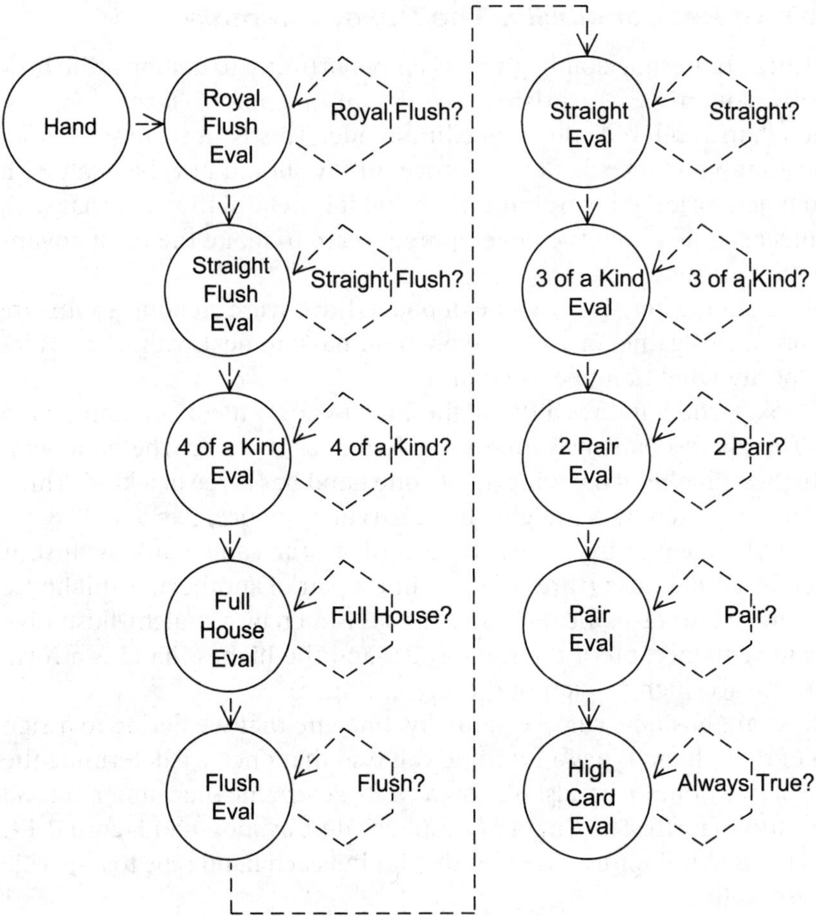

Figure B.14 The Chain of Responsibility

The key point here is this: A Royal Flush is also a Flush. It is also a Straight. If we hand five cards, which were in fact a Royal Flush, to the `Straight Eval` class, it responds in the positive: "Yes, that is a Straight." So, 3 of a Kind is also a pair, a Full House is also 3 of a Kind, and so forth.

There is a business rule about this: If you have a Royal Flush, no one can call your hand a Straight even though this is technically true. There is an ordering dependency about these rules: After you determine that a hand is a Full House, you do not ask if it is a Pair.

This design captures this set of dependencies, but not in conditional code. It is captured simply in the order of the evaluators in the chain, and can therefore be maintained simply by changing that order (there are many variations on Poker, as you may know).

The point is not to say that all procedural logic should be converted to object structures. This would create overly complex designs, would tend to degrade performance, and would challenge many developers who tried to understand the design. However, it is important to know that object structures are a possible solution to issues that we would normally think of procedurally, to enable us to make informed decisions.

The advantages to using an object structure include testability, encapsulation, and open-closed-ness.

The Composite Pattern

Contextual Forces

Motivation

Model simple and complex components in such a way as to allow client entities to consume their behavior in the same way. The Composite pattern captures hierarchical relationships of varying complexity and structure.

Terms:

- *Simple component.* A single class, also called a *leaf.*
- *Complex component.* A class that contains pointers to subordinate or "child" instances, and may delegate some or all of its responsibilities to them. These child instances may be simple or complex themselves. Also called a *node.*

Encapsulation

The difference between a simple (Leaf) and a complex (Node) component.

The structure of the composite relationship: a tree, ring, web, and so on (see the upcoming section, "Options in Implementation," for a discussion).

Customer Records

CustID	Fname	Lname	Address	MaxPurchase
XYZ123	Fred	Scerbo	1122 4th ave	$2100
ABC456	Brad	Konapick	8989 D st.	$800

Sales Records

CustID	Item SKU	Quantity	Price
ABC456	382733	1	$10.95
ABC456	354433	1	$101.55
ABC456	534321	10	$1.25

Inventory

ItemSKU	Qty On Hand	VendorID	Price
382733	45	HH63633	$10.95
543554	0	DRV445	$15.95
677553	1244	UA2332	$.99

Figure B.15 Procedural analog

The behavior of the complex components: aggregating, best/worse case, investigatory, and so on (see the upcoming section, "Questions, Concerns, Credibility Checks," for a discussion).

Procedural Analog

In procedural systems, process and data are usually represented separately. In data structures, there is a clear analog to a Composite pattern in the way tables can contain foreign keys to other tables, allowing for variation in the depth of the data being represented. As with most procedural analogs, encapsulation is missing in Figure B.15.

Non-Software Analog

In the military, responsibilities flow from the top of a hierarchy down to the bottom in various ways. Let us assume that a Captain is assigning responsibilities for a number of tasks.

- She orders a Lieutenant to write up a set of reports for the Pentagon. This Lieutenant writes the reports himself with no further delegation.
- She orders another Lieutenant to create a training program for the upcoming maneuvers. This Lieutenant actually delegates the specifics to a set of Drill Sergeants and then assembles their work into a plan. He then reports back to the Captain.
- She orders a third Lieutenant to take hill 403. This Lieutenant delegates this responsibility to a set of Sergeants who delegate further to Corporals, Privates, and other resources (medics, an armor squad), each of whom may delegate further, in a very complex arrangement.

In each case, the Captain "orders" a single Lieutenant. Figure B.16 illustrates the variations in how these orders are accomplished are encapsulated.

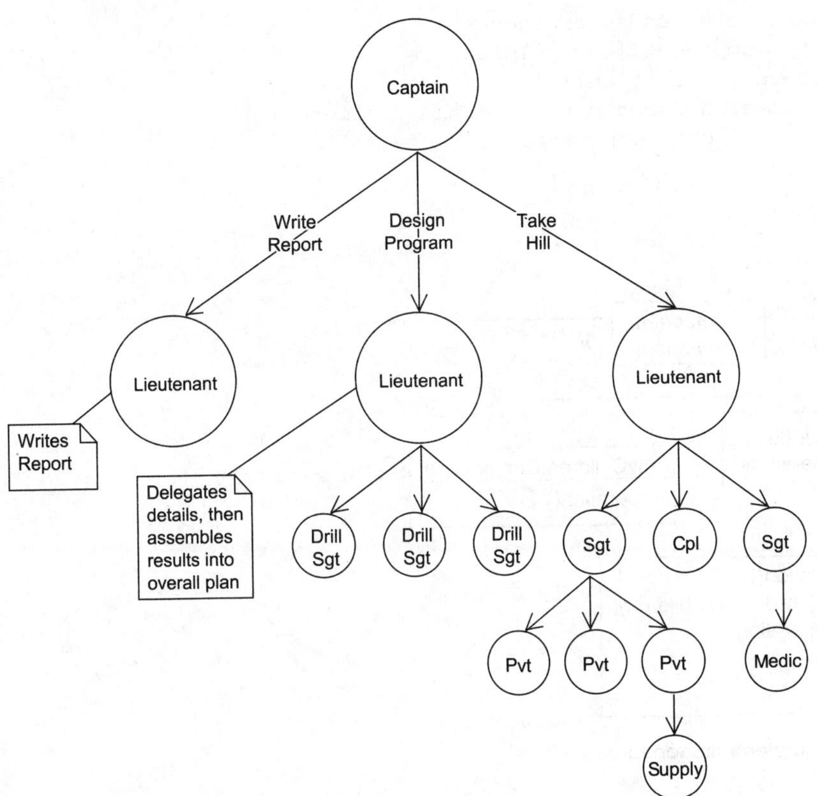

Figure B.16 Non-software analog

Implementation Forces

Example

See Figure B.17.

Code

```
public abstract class Component{
      public abstract void operation();
}

public class Leaf extends Component{
      public void operation() {
            // leaf operation goes here
      }
}

public class Node extends Component{
      private Component[] myChildren;
      public void operation() {
            foreach(Component Child in myChildren) {
                  child.operation();
            }
      }
}
```

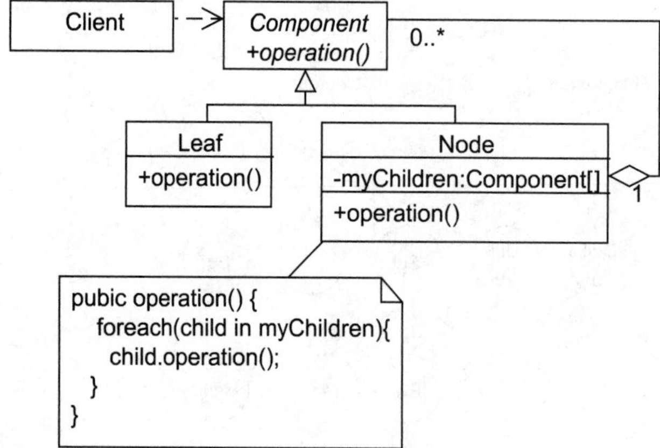

Figure B.17 Implementation forces

Questions, Concerns, Credibility Checks

There are many different forms of the Composite pattern, but at a high level they can generally be grouped into one of two categories: Bill of Material and Taxonomy.

A Bill of Material Composite captures the relationship that exists when a complex object is composed of many smaller objects, each of which may be further composed of other, yet smaller objects. For example, your car could be said to be composed of a body and a chassis. The body is further made up of fenders, doors, panels, a trunk, a hood, and so on. The chassis is further composed of a drive train and suspension. The drive train is still further composed of an engine, transmission, differential, wheels, and so on.

A Taxonomical Composite captures the logical relationships that exist between more and less general types. The biological phylum works this way. Living things are divided into Mammals, Amphibians, Fish, and Birds. Mammals are further subdivided into oviparous (egg-laying) and viviparous (live birth), and so forth.

This distinction is important because it gives us clues into the decisions we have to make when implementing the pattern (see "Options in Implementation").

If we are implementing a Taxonomical Composite, our motivation is almost certainly to allow a client entity to traverse the structure, to find information or classify an entity within the context of the existing structure.

If we are implementing a Bill of Material Composite, however, we have many options when implementing its behavior, each of which has different implications for encapsulation.

- *Aggregating behavior*. If we need to determine the weight of the car, for example, we need to aggregate the weights of all the subparts (which in turn need to aggregate their subparts and such). Often, this behavior can be hidden from consuming client entities in the way the Node component is implemented.
- *Best/worst case behavior*. If we need to determine the overall "health" of the car, the rule might be that the car is healthy if and only if all its parts are healthy. If any one part is in error, perhaps, we might say the entire car is in error. Thus, we would say the car is the worst case of all its parts. Again, this behavior can often be hidden from the consuming class in the way the Node component is implemented.
- *Investigatory*. If we need to determine something specific about a part or about a set of parts that meet a criteria (all the parts of the car that

> come in contact with oil, for example), we might need to allow the client entity to "walk the tree of parts," looking for those that qualify. In this case, we may not be able to hide the specifics of the composite, much as we generally cannot in a Taxonomical Composite.

In any case, there is a key decision to make when creating a Composite: whether to put methods into the target abstraction that allow for the client entity to traverse the Composite. These *traversal methods* create coupling between the client and the components and should not be included unless they are needed.

In Taxonomy, traversal methods are almost always needed, since the purpose of the Composite is for the client to traverse it.

In a Bill of Material, traversal methods may or may not be needed, depending on the behavior desired.

Options in Implementation

The nature of traversal methods, if they are needed, reflects the nature of the Composite. The standard Composite, shown in Figure B.18, is the tree hierarchy.

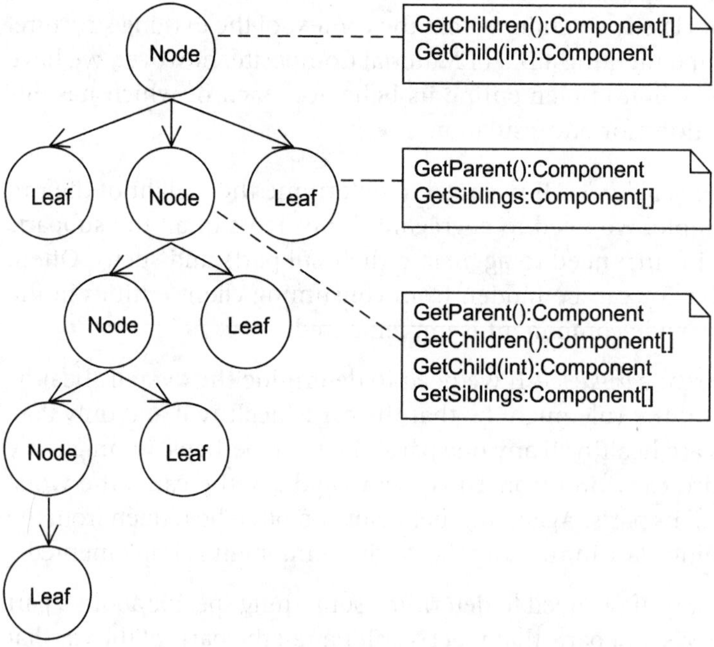

Figure B.18 The tree Composite

However, there are many other Composite structures possible. For example, Figure B.19 is also a Composite.

This is a ring and, as you can see, the traversal methods are different. Similar to this form of Composite is also the bi-directional ring, which allows for "next" and "previous" traversal (not shown).

Yet another Composite is a web, as shown in Figure B.20, which has yet again different traversal methods implied by its structure.

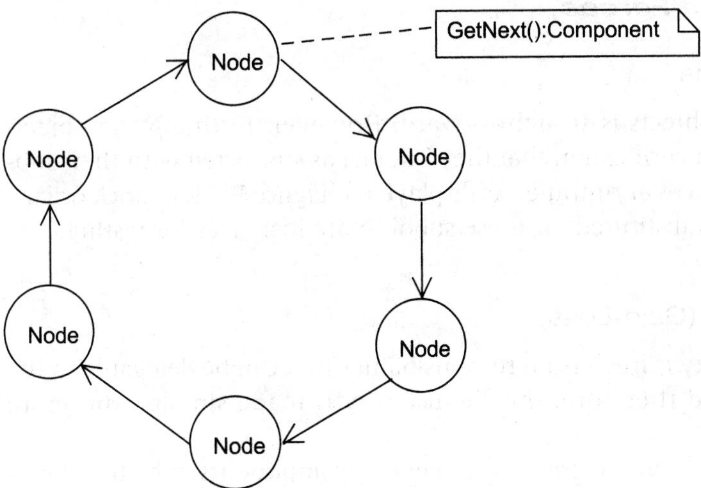

Figure B.19 A ring Composite

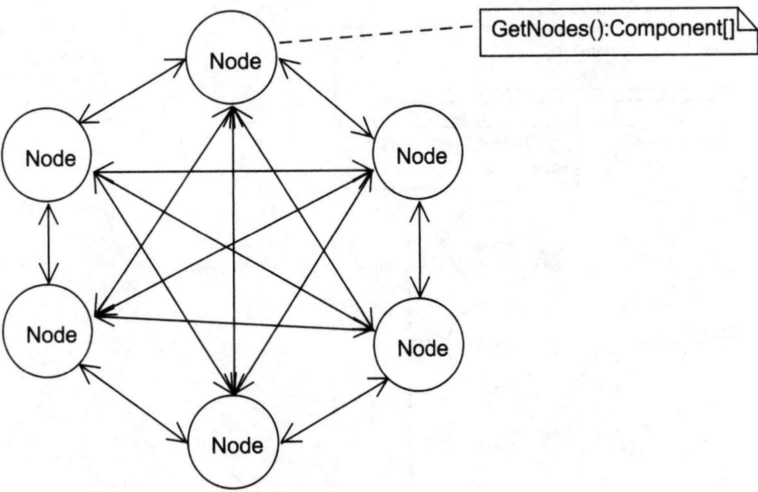

Figure B.20 A web Composite

The point is that the nature of the Composite structure is reflected in the traversal methods provided. Therefore, if traversal methods are provided, the fact that a Composite is a tree, ring, web, or any other structure is not encapsulated from entities that consume it. If a Composite were to begin as a tree, then later be changed to a ring, the client entities that interacted with it via these traversal methods would all have to be maintained.

Consequent Forces

Testing Issues

Testing Leaf objects is straightforward. However, testing Node objects should include verification that they interact as suspected with their subordinate instances at runtime. As displayed in Figure B.21, a mock or fake object can be substituted for these subordinate instances for testing.

Cost Benefit (Gain-Loss)

The client entity is freed from responsibilities that can be delegated to the Composite and therefore, the client entity is made simpler and more cohesive.

However, we tend to create very generic components, which can create difficulties when attempting to model very complex behavior.

The Composite is always a trade-off between these forces.

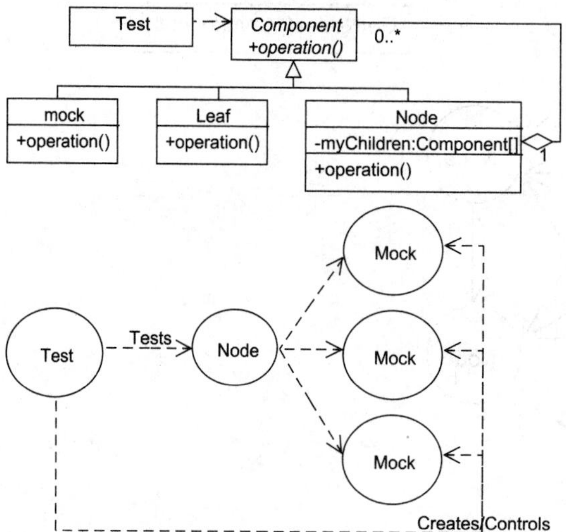

Figure B.21 Testing Node objects

The Decorator Pattern

Contextual Forces

Motivation

Add optional, additional behaviors to an entity dynamically. Ideally, the design should allow for a wide variety of combinations of these additional behaviors without altering the clients that consume the results.

Encapsulation

The number (cardinality) and order (sequence) of the optional behaviors. Ideally, the fact that a Decorator is being used can also be hidden from the client. In all the runtime variations shown in Figure B.22, the client takes the same action.

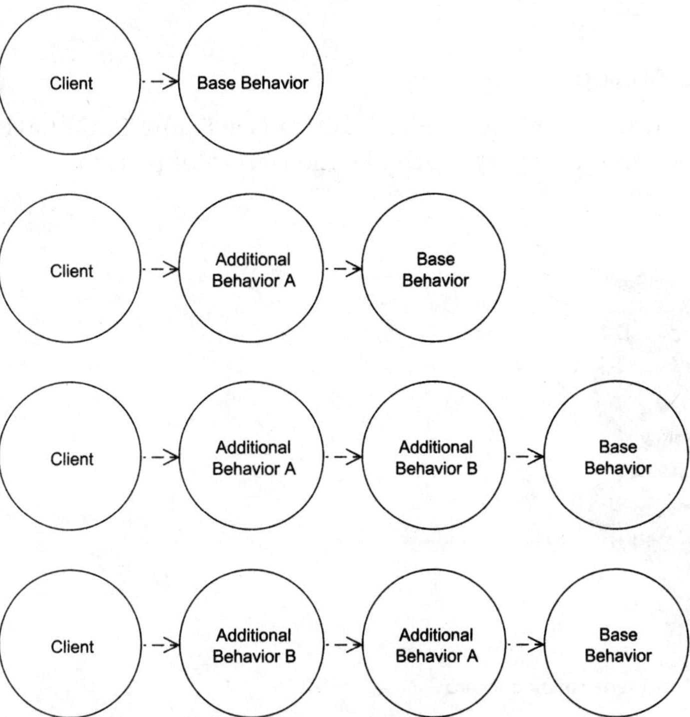

Figure B.22 Case 1: Base behavior only. Case 2: Base behavior and a single additional behavior. Case 3: Base behavior and multiple additional behaviors. Case 4: Base behavior and the same additional behaviors in a different sequence.

Procedural Analog

A "stack" of simple conditionals is analogous to one main aspect of the Decorator—that is, the capability to add one, many, all, or none of a set of optional behaviors.

```
//Non-optional behavior here

if(conditionA) {
      // Optional Behavior A
}

if(conditionB) {
      // Optional Behavior B
}

//Non-optional behavior here
```

This procedural approach does not allow for variations in the order of the behaviors, however. It is, therefore, only a partial analog.

Non-Software Analog

Those who have used a single-lens reflex camera (see Figure B.23) have experienced a design that is very much like the Decorator pattern.

Figure B.23 Single lens reflex camera

Such a camera has a basic behavior set that is required for it to fulfill its function in photography.

- It allows light to enter the camera through a lens.
- It focuses the light at a fixed point called the backplane where the film is held rigid.
- It opens the shutter for a controllable and reliable period of time.
- It advances the film.

The first step of this process can be altered without changing anything about the camera itself by using a filter, or any number of filters, that change the light before it enters the camera. The resulting photograph will be different, but the camera (and the outside world) remains unchanged.

The filters are designed to attach to the front of the camera lens. They have male threads on their trailing edges that mate to the female threads on the leading edge of the lens housing. However, they also have these female threads on their leading edges as well, so a filter can be attached to a lens or to another filter, allowing them to be stacked up. The overall effect on the resulting photograph is the accumulated effect of all the filters currently included in the stack.

A camera can take a photograph without any filters at all; it is sufficient by itself.

A filter cannot accomplish any kind of photograph alone. It must always be attached to something—either another filter or the camera lens. This is enforced in its design.

Implementation Forces

Example

See Figure B.24.

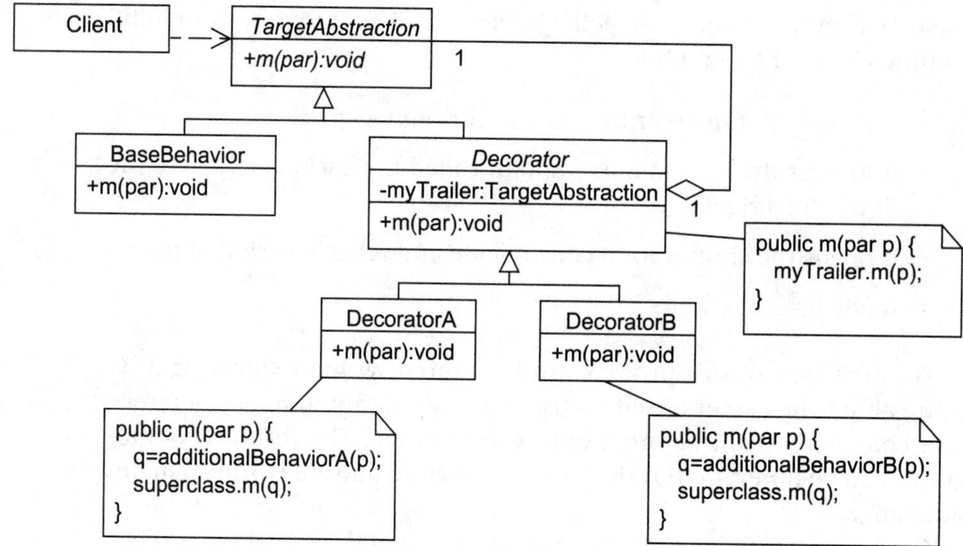

Figure B.24 Implementation forces

Code

```
public class TargetAbstraction {
      public abstract void m(par p);
}

public class BaseBehavior extends TargetAbstraction {
      public void m(par p) {
            // Base behavior
      }
}

public abstract Decorator extends TargetAbstraction {
      private TargetAbstration myTrailer;
      public Decorator(TargetAbstraction aTrailer) {
            myTrailer = aTrailer;
      }
      public void m(par p) {
            myTrailer.m(p);
      }
}
```

```
public class DecoratorA extends Decorator {
      public DecoratorA(TargetAbstraction aTrailer) {
            superclassConstructor(aTrailer);
      }
      public void m(par p) {
      // Decorator A behavior here
            superclass.m(p);
      }
}

public class DecoratorB extends Decorator {
      public DecoratorB TargetAbstraction aTrailer) {
            superclassConstructor(aTrailer);
      }
      public void m(par p) {
            // Decorator B behavior here
            superclass.m(p);
      }
}
```

Questions, Concerns, Credibility Checks

- Can the various Decorators and the base behavior share a common interface? If there are differences between them, how can this be resolved without sacrificing any key capabilities?
- What is the structure of the collection for the Decorators and the base behavior? The classic implementation uses a linked list (see preceding), but a Decorator can also be implemented using an array, a vector, or any suitable collection.
- Do the methods being decorated have a void return (aggregating behaviors in a pass-down the chain), or is there a return from them? If there is a return, each Decorator has two opportunities to add behavior, as the calls propagate down the chain, and as the returns propagate back up. (See the next section, "Options in Implementation," for more on this issue.)
- Can the Decorator be totally encapsulated? That is, can the client be designed to use any combination of decorators, and/or the base behavior, in precisely the same way? (See the next section, "Options in Implementation," for more on this issue.)

- Are there particular combinations of Decorators and/or particular sequences that should be prevented? If so, an object factory to build only the legitimate decorator chains is advised. In this case, if the restriction is highly critical, all concrete classes (everything apart from the `Client` and the `TargetAbstraction` in the preceding code) can be private inner classes of the factory.

Options in Implementation

An alternate form of the Decorator, shown in Figure B.25, uses a method or methods that have a return. This creates three different types of Decorators: those that act "on the way down," those that act "one the way back up," and those that do both.

These three types can then be implemented for different behaviors by subclassing. Also, a void return Decorator can be implemented with similar behavior, by coding some Decorators to simply wait until the next call returns before they take action. This behavior is simply easier to see and understand when we discuss it in terms of a nonvoid return.

Sometimes, one of the Decorators is used to add methods to the interface of the target abstraction. When this is done, the client is exposed to the presence of the Decorator, the specific decorating type, and the fact that this particular Decorator must be first in the chain.

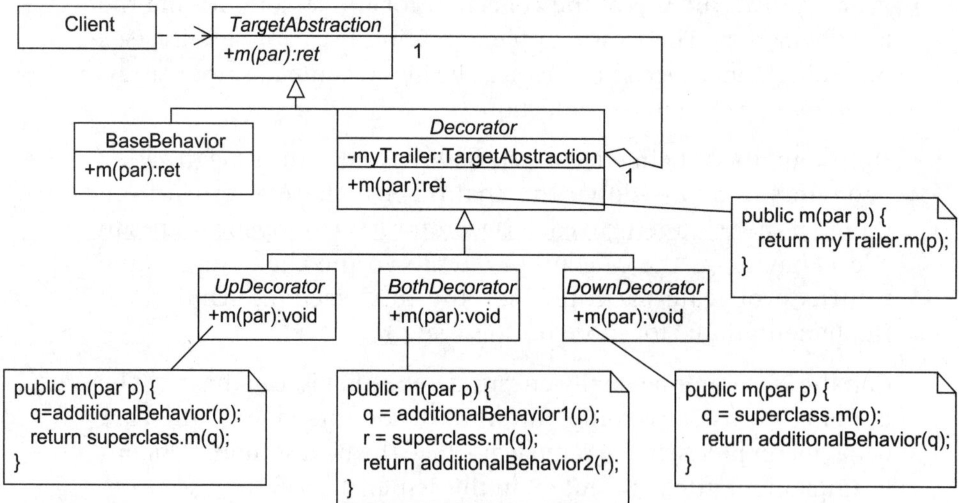

Figure B.25 The Bucket Brigade form of the Decorator pattern

An example of this is the way streaming I/O is done in Java. Figure B.26 is not literally accurate, but shows the general design of the I/O API in Java and similar languages.

A similar approach is taken to the `OutputStream` type. This creates an important bit of functionality in that it allows developers to use this API without requiring them to compose and decompose their data into bytes before using the IO capabilities of the framework. The Data version of the Decorator does this for them.

The downside is that the client must hold this Decorator in a downcast to its specific type, and therefore it cannot be encapsulated. Furthermore, the client must hold this reference directly (see Figure B.27).

The first case works, but the second does not, because the client has no reference to the `DataInputStream` instance, and therefore cannot use the expanded interface (it consequently provides no value).

In other words, the `DataInputStream` must be the first object in the chain. The design of the specific Decorator being used and the presence of the pattern are all visible to the client, and are therefore not encapsulated. This was considered a worthwhile trade-off given the importance of the Data interface.

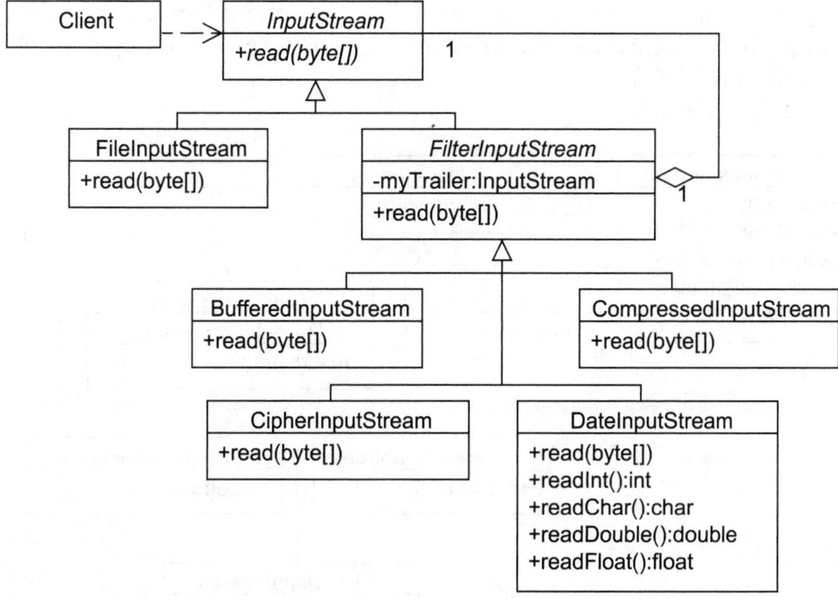

Figure B.26 Streaming I/O with Java

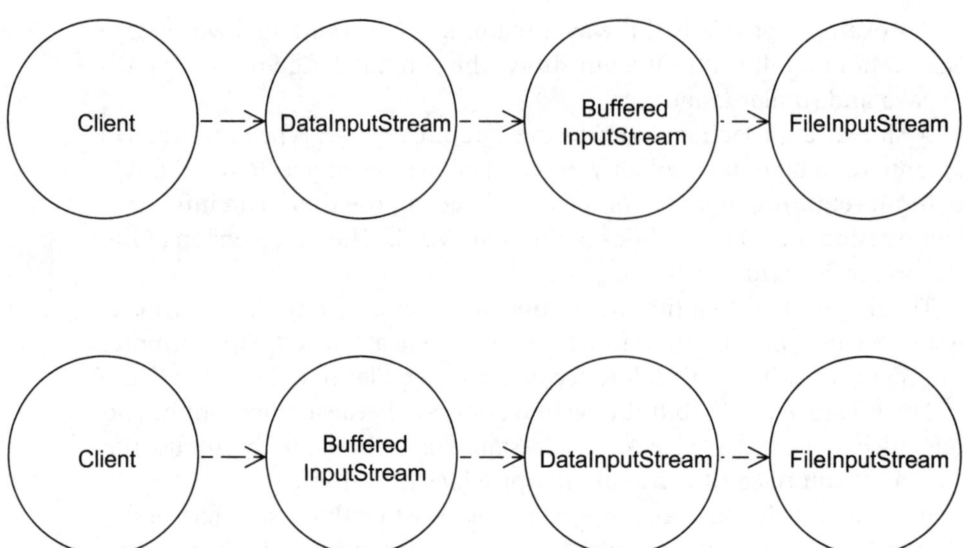

Figure B.27 Case 1 and Case 2 (with error)

However, if, we consider the patterns as *collections of forces* as we are suggesting here, there is another alternative. Reusing behavior with a changed interface is a contextual force of the Adapter pattern. If we think of our problem in this way, the following design, as shown in Figure B.28, comes to mind.

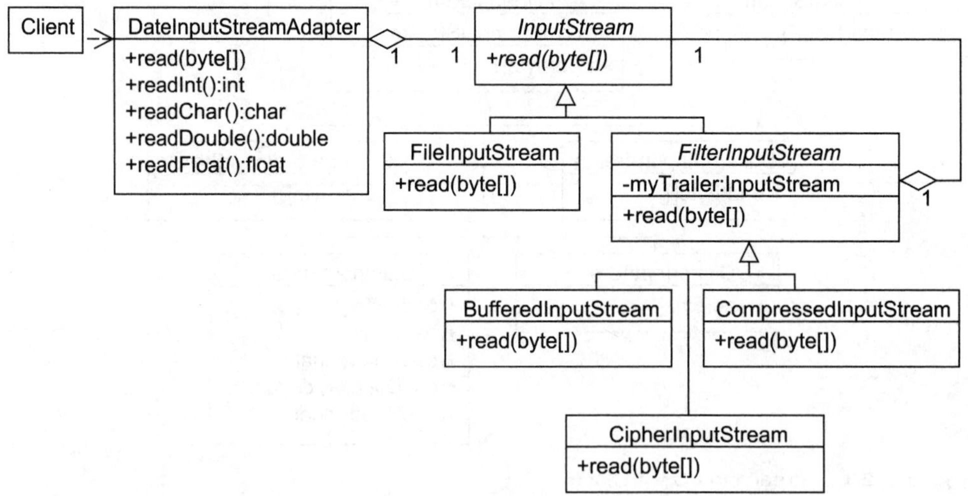

Figure B.28 Decorator with Adapter

This keeps the Decorator design encapsulated, and only exposes the Adapter, which of course the client would have to have visibility to (this is a force in the Adapter, after all).

Consequent Forces

Testing Issues

The base behavior can be tested in a normal way, but the Decorators impose a bit of a challenge in that they are designed to *decorate something*. If we want to test them in isolation from one another, we can use a mock or fake object to stand in place of the next object in the chain. Figure B.29 is an example of this. This allows us to inspect the effect of the decorator being tested by examining the state of the mock or fake object after the decorator behaves.

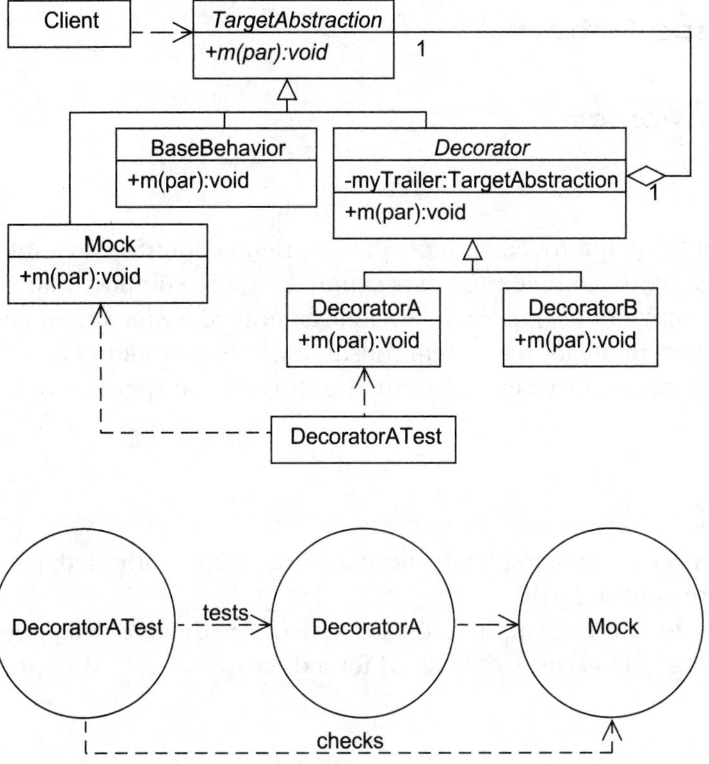

Figure B.29 Testing base behavior with mock objects

Cost-Benefit (Gain-Loss)

- The design is extremely flexible, allowing for different combinations of additional behavior, different numbers of behaviors, and different sequences to put them in.
- Avoids creating a feature-laden class. Features can be easily added with decorators.
- Promotes strong cohesion.
- New Decorators can be derived later, leaving the design very open-closed.
- The design can confuse developers who are not familiar with it.
- Some combinations of Decorators may be unwise, buggy, or violate business rules.

The Façade Pattern

Contextual Forces

Motivation

Provide a simplified, improved, or more object-oriented interface to a subsystem that is overly complex (or may simply be more complex than is needed for the current use), poorly designed, a decayed legacy system, or otherwise inappropriate for the system consuming it. Façade allows for the reuse of a valuable subsystem without coupling to the specifics of its nature.

Encapsulation

The subsystem's nature (complexity, design, decay, object-oriented, procedural nature, and so forth).

Optionally, the presence of the subsystem itself. See the upcoming section, "Questions, Concerns, Credibility," for a discussion.

Procedural Analog

Often, when creating large procedural systems, we create a *gateway routine* as a sort of API that allows the aggregation of many different parts of the system into a single called routine. This gateway routine makes the system easier to use and is essentially the precursor to a Façade in an object-oriented system. It is not strictly an analog; it is in fact an early version of the pattern.

Non-Software Analog

A hotel concierge (at an upscale hotel) stands between the hotel guest and all the various services that are needed to make for a successful, satisfying stay at the hotel.

The guest has goals, which are expressed from the guest's point of view. The concierge translates these goals into needed interactions with the concrete services needed to achieve them.

For example, the guest may say, "We would like to go out to an evening dinner, and a show, and then return to the hotel for an intimate dessert in our room."

The concierge, as shown in Figure B.30, handles all the nitty-gritty details. She arranges for a taxi, restaurant reservations, theatre tickets, housekeeping prep of the room, the kitchen preparing the dessert, and room-service delivery, among other responsibilities.

The concierge here in Figure B.30 is the Façade analog.

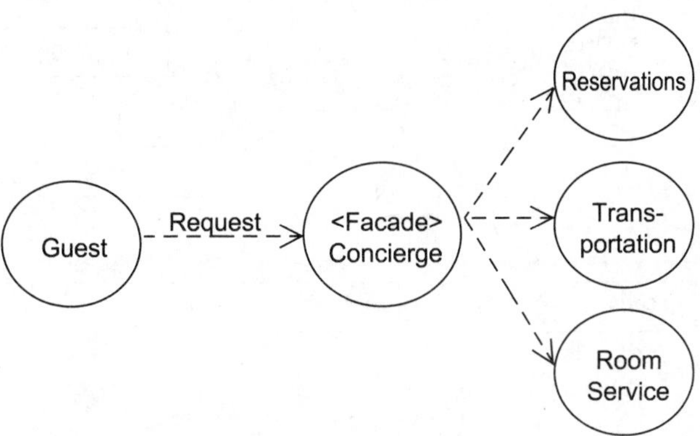

Figure B.30 The concierge as a Façade analog

Implementation Forces

Example

See Figure B.31.

Code

```
public class Facade {
      public void m1() {
           // make all calls into the existing system,
           // hiding the complexity
      }
      public string m2() {
           // make all calls into the existing system,
           // converting the return
           return rval;
      }
}
```

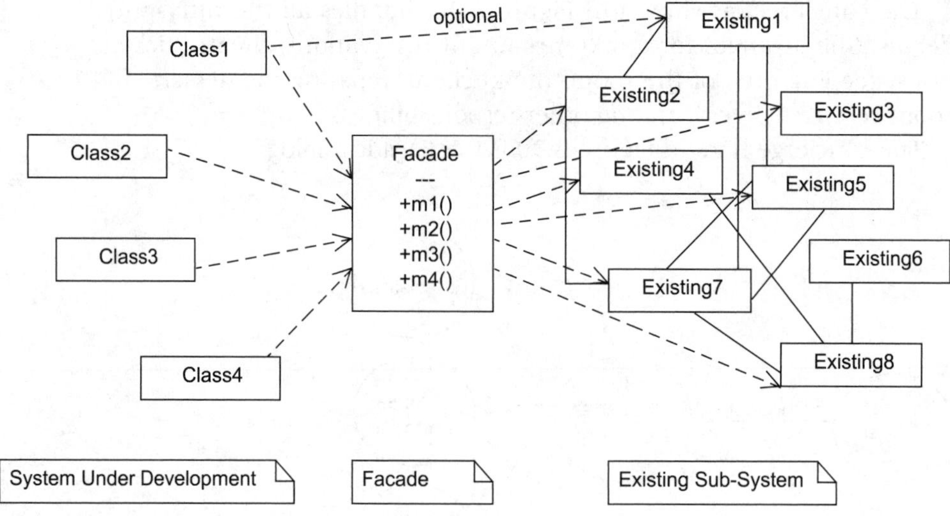

Figure B.31 Implementation forces

Questions, Concerns, Credibility Checks

Can we totally encapsulate the subsystem? The Façade can be a convenience service or a constraining service.

- *Convenience.* The system under development can "go around" and use the existing subsystem directly for infrequent, unusual, or orthogonal needs. This keeps the interface of the Façade relatively small and cohesive but couples the system under development to the subsystem. The call marked "optional" in the diagram shown in Figure B.31 shows this behavior.
- *Constraining.* The system under development must use the Façade for all accesses to the existing subsystem. This may broaden the interface of the Façade and weaken its cohesion, but it makes the subsystem itself completely swappable. Because the subsystem is hereby encapsulated, we often refer to such a Façade as an *Encapsulating Façade*.

Can we make the Façade stateless? Façades are often fairly heavyweight and instantiating them can impact performance. Therefore, if they can be made stateless, they can be implemented as Singletons, which alleviates the performance and resource impact of the Façade.

Options in Implementation

Façade is often implemented using other patterns

In fact, the Façade is not really a specific design but rather a role that is implemented in whatever way is considered most appropriate given the forces in the problem.

For example, Figure B.32 shows a Façade implemented using a Chain of Responsibility.

To keep a Façade stateless, often it is advisable to externalize the state into a lightweight object (see Figure B.33).

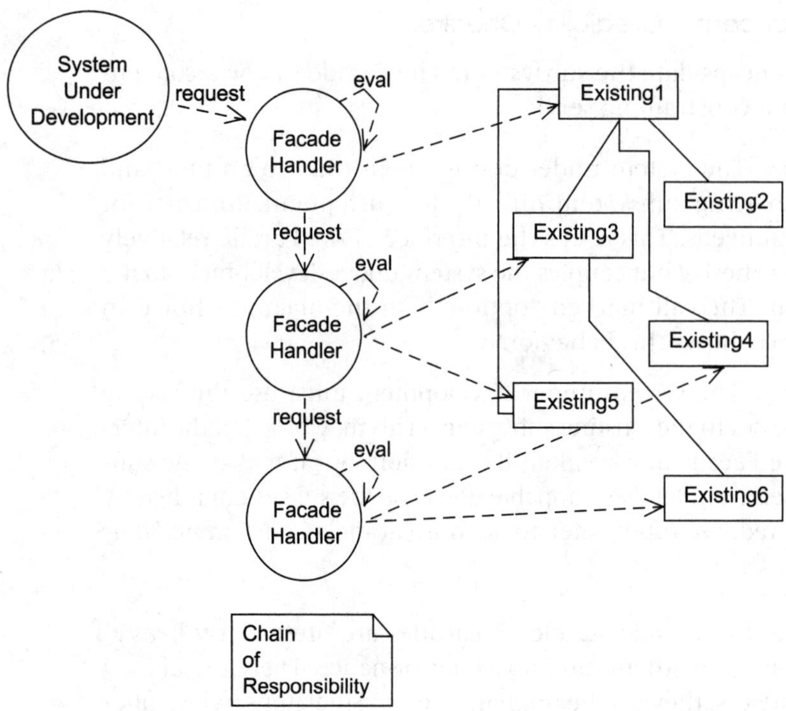

Figure B.32 A Façade implemented using a Chain of Responsibility

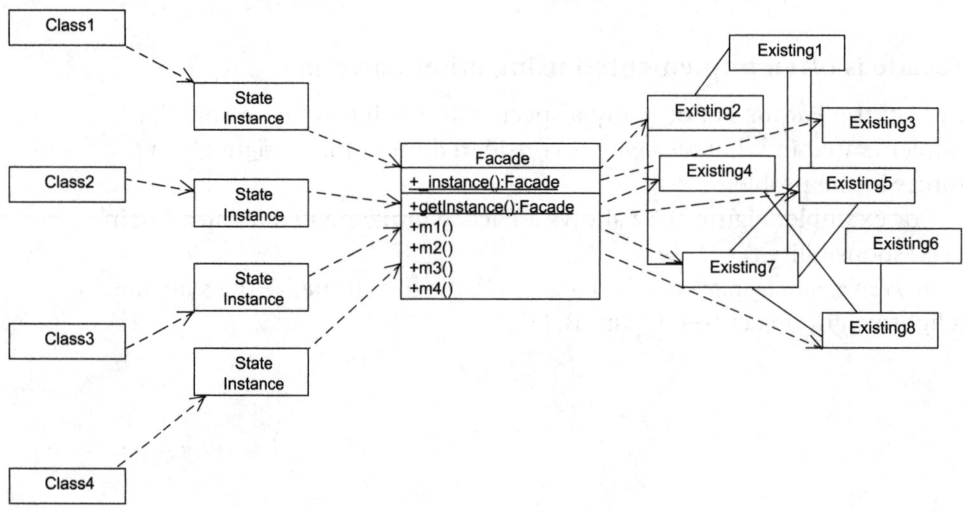

Figure B.33 Externalizing the state into a lightweight object

Legacy conversion

Façades can also have a strong role in converting legacy systems incrementally to more modern software.[2]

"Strangling" a Legacy System

Imagine an old, decayed, and poorly implemented legacy system. You have probably had to work with one or more of these in your practice. We often think of them as shown in Figure B.34, a "big ball of mud," because they are incomprehensible, brittle, and dense.

Job one is to stop using the system in the old way when writing new code that has to interact with it. If we could, we would stop here and refactor or rewrite the system entirely, but often that is simply not an option: We have to live with it, at least for now.

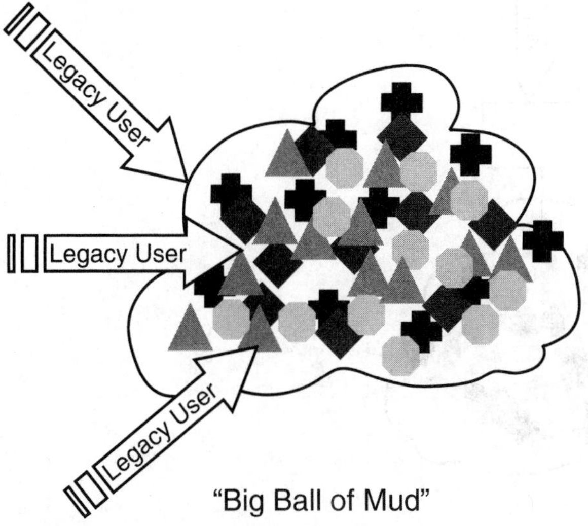

Figure B.34 Poor legacy system

---

2. This example is drawn from the work of Martin Fowler. I came across it while reading Brian Marick's work on testing, reflected in his blog, "Exploration Through Example" (http://www.testing.com/cgi-bin/blog/2005/05/11).

However, using the old system directly (as the legacy users do) means writing code that is similar in nature to the code in the system. At the very least, we want our new code to be clean, tested, and object-oriented. So, we create a Façade with the interface that we wish we had (see Figure B.35) and then delegate from there into the various routines in the legacy system.

Now that we have this in place, the new users can be developed more cleanly and with higher quality. Figures B.36, B.37, B.38, and B.39 all show that now, over time, and without significant time pressure on the project, we can incrementally pull out behaviors from the legacy system into more clean, tested, object-oriented code, and delegate from the old routines into the new ones.

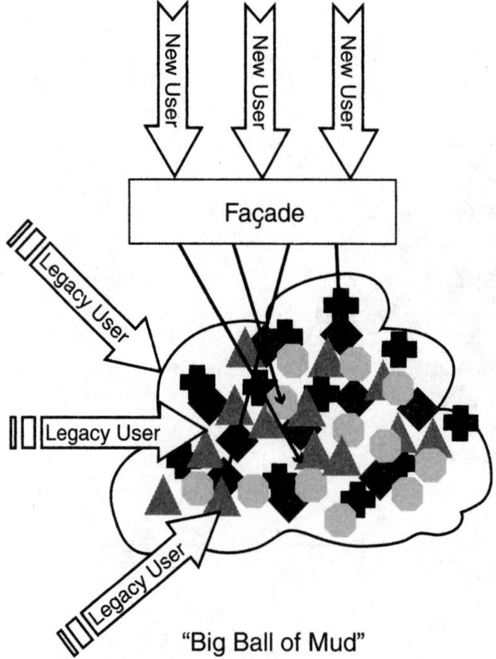

Figure B.35 Interface we wish we had

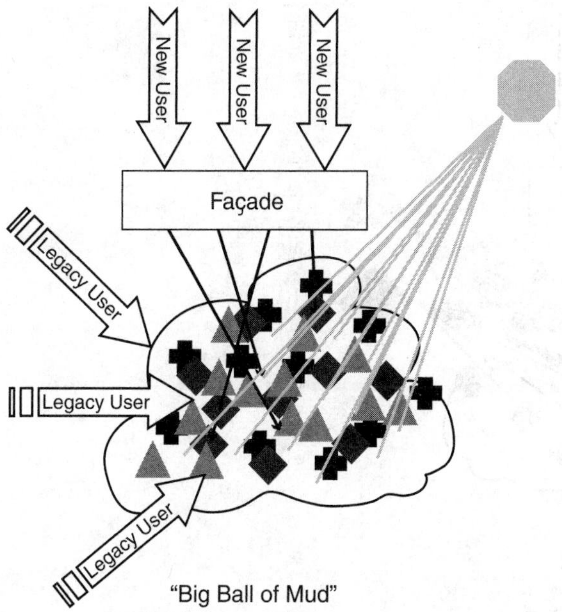

Figure B.36 New users developed cleanly with high quality

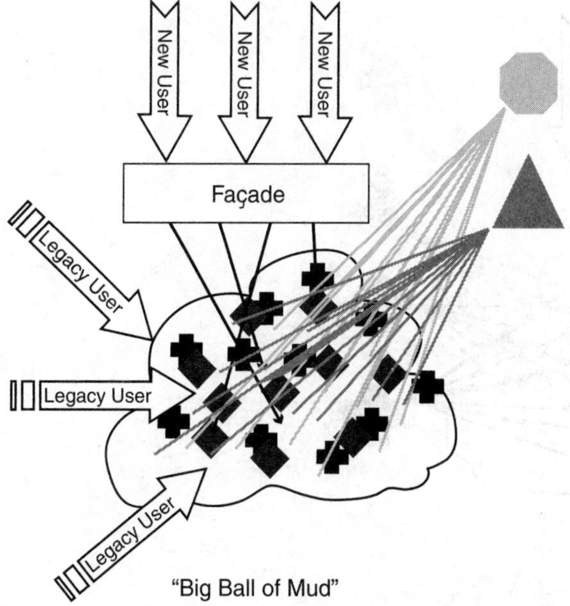

Figure B.37 Another new user developed cleanly with high quality

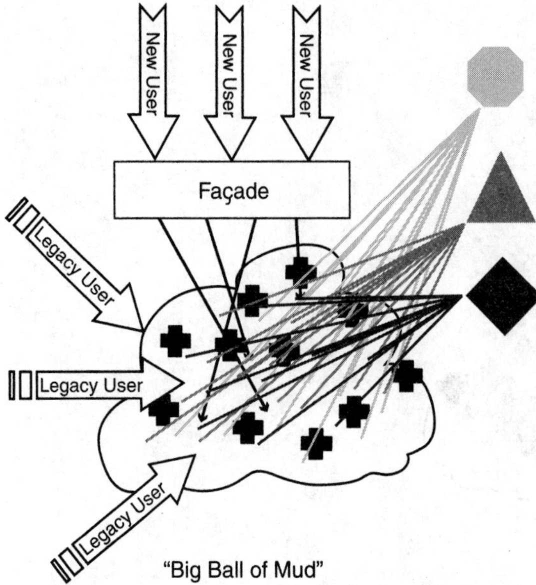

Figure B.38 A further increment in new development

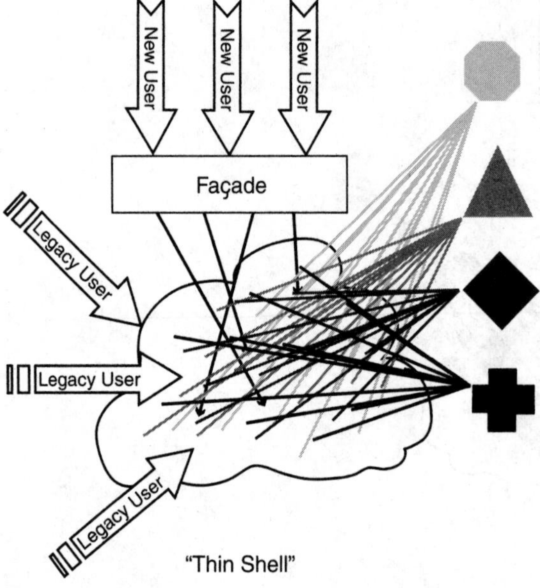

Figure B.39 A thin shell

After we reach the point that the legacy system remains only as a series of delegation points and nothing but a thin shell, as shown in Figure B.39, around the new behaviors, we can begin to refactor the legacy users to use the Façade instead of the delegating routines in the older system. As Figure B.40 shows, the Façade itself can also be refactored to use the new code directly. Again, this can be done incrementally, as time permits, without a lot of pressure. Naturally, after all of the legacy users and the Façade no longer use the thin-shell legacy system, as shown in Figure B.41, it can be retired.

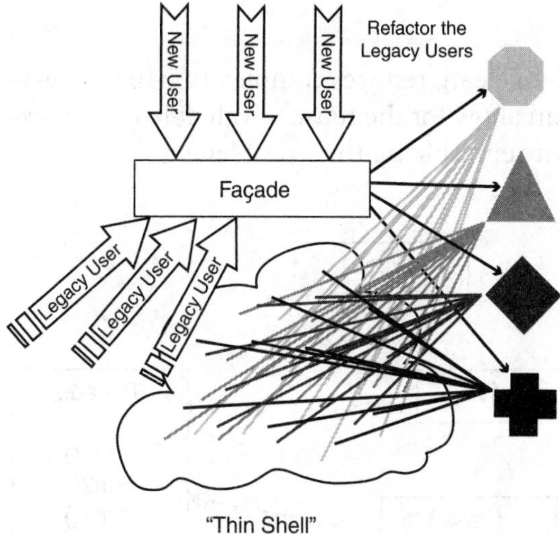

Figure B.40 Refactoring the legacy users and a thin shell

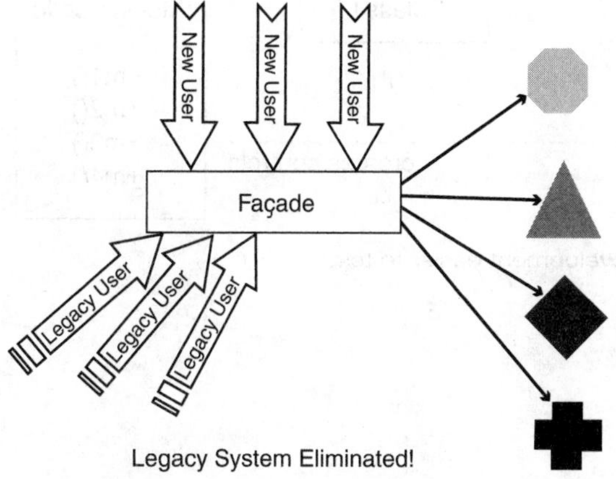

Figure B.41 Legacy system eliminated

Consequent Forces

Testing Issues

Façades are inherently difficult to test if (as is common) the subsystems that they cover are hard to test. However, the presence of the Façade makes the system under development fundamentally easier to test, as shown in Figure B.42, because the Façade, once in place, can be mocked or faked to eliminate unpredictable dependencies.

Cost-Benefit (Gain-Loss)

A Façade keeps the client system clean, reduces complexity when accessing existing subsystems, and can allow for the reuse of valuable legacy systems in a new context without reproducing their problems.

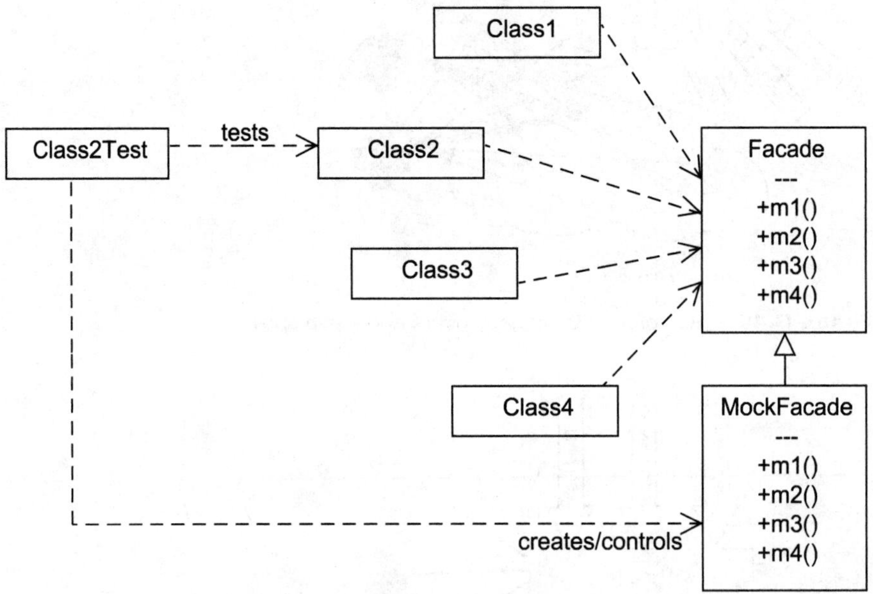

Figure B.42 System under development easier to test

An Encapsulating Façade decouples the client system entirely from the subsystem. This means that the subsystems can be swapped, eliminated, crippled, and so on. This allows for easy creation of

- *Demonstration versions of software.* A demo version of the Façade can create stubbed-out behavior for the subsystem, and stand in its place, allowing the frontend system to be demonstrated without the back-end software/hardware present.
- *Crippled versions of software.* A crippling Façade can create a limited-functionality version of a system, which can easily be upgraded to the full version by replacing the crippling Façade with the full Façade.
- *Testing.* The Façade can be mocked or faked (see the preceding section, "Testing Issues") making the client system testable, which would otherwise be much more difficult.
- *Training versions of software.* Similar to Demos, a training Façade can be used to create predictable scenarios for training while allowing the students to interact with the "real" frontend of the overall system.

Façade and N-Tier Architecture

Imagine that we are working on an application with a three-tiered architecture (UI, Middle, Data), and we want to work in a test-driven way. Unfortunately, our teams are all blocked.

- *UI Tier.* I cannot start until the middle tier is done; they provide the interface for the services I will consume.
- *Middle Tier.* I cannot start until the data layer is done, because I need to access it in order to provide services to the UI.
- *Data Layer.* I cannot start until I know what the data needs are. Also, I am involved in day-to-day business, which must always take priority over new development. I will get to it when I get to it.

We can use Façades to separate these layers. The Façades present the interface of the consuming layer, and later can be coded to the implementation of the service layer in each case, when this becomes available (it can be stubbed out, initially). Also, each Façade is a mockable entity, and so, as in Figure B.43, the layers can be test-driven.

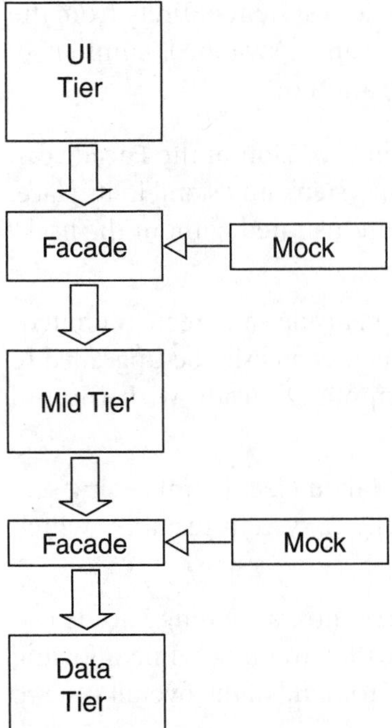

Figure B.43 Each Façade as a mockable entity

The Proxy Pattern

Contextual Forces

Motivation

We want to add an optional behavior to an existing class. This new behavior may protect the class, log access to it, or delay its behavior or instantiation, or any other single additional behavior. We also need to be able to use the existing class at times without this additional behavior.

Encapsulation

It is hidden from the client whether the additional behavior is in place at any given point at runtime. We may also want to hide the fact that an optional behavior exists at all.

Procedural Analog

A simple condition to include or exclude an optional behavior in the midst of non-optional behavior:

```
//Non-optional behavior here

if(condition) {
      // Optional Behavior here
}

//Non-optional behavior here
```

Non-Software Analog

I use a handheld hose to water my garden. A few times a year, I add a container between the hose fitting and the watering head that puts plant food into the water as it passes through (see Figure B.44).

I take no different action when watering in this way, and yet there is additional behavior, like feeding the plants. Also, various different plant foods could be introduced in this way, and again I would take no different action at watering time.

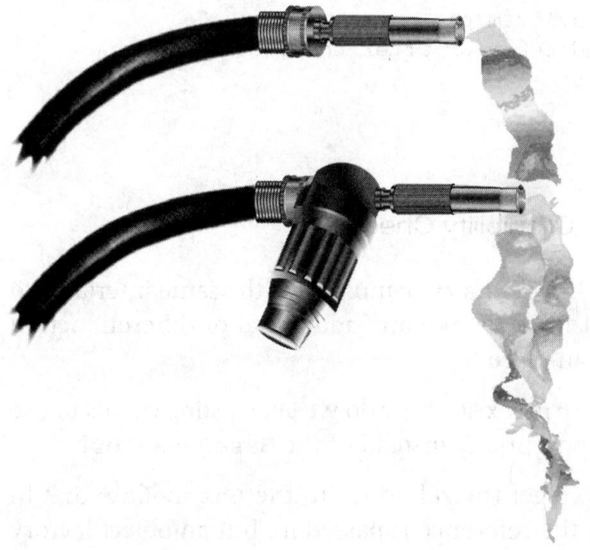

Figure B.44 Handheld hose with container for plant food

Implementation Forces

Example

See Figure B.45.

Code

```
public abstract class TargetAbstraction {
      public abstract ret m(par p);
{

public class BaseBehavior extends TargetAbstraction {
      public ret m(par p) {
            // unproxied, or base behavior
      }
}

public class Proxy extends TargetAbstraction {
      private BaseBehavior myBaseBehavior;
      public Proxy(BaseBehavior aBaseBehavior) {
            myBaseBehavior = aBaseBehavior;
      }
      public ret m(par p) {
            // Can add behavior before the base behavior
            myBaseBehavior.m(p);
            // Can add behavior after the base behavior
            return ret;
      }
}
```

Questions, Concerns, Credibility Checks

- The proxy and the `BaseBehavior` must have the same interface, so the client does not have to take any additional or different action when the proxy is in place.
- If the `BaseBehavior` preexists, how do we get existing clients to use the proxy, when appropriate, instead of the `BaseBehavior`?
- How does the proxy get the reference to the `BaseBehavior`? In the code example, the reference is passed in, but an object factory or other encapsulating entity can be used as well.

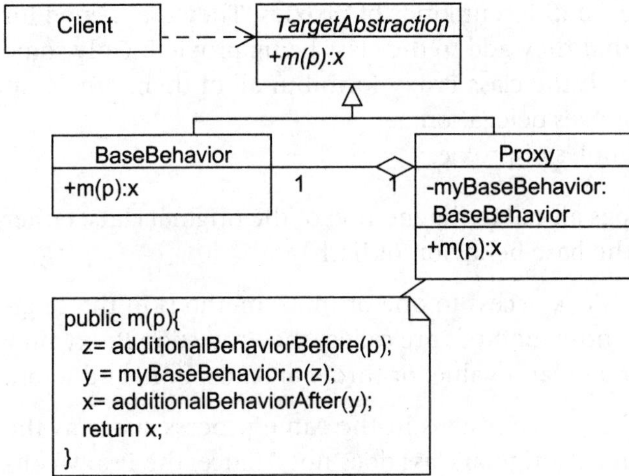

Figure B.45 Implementation forces

Options in Implementation

The preceding form uses delegation from the proxy to the `BaseBehavior` class to reuse the preexisting behavior. Another form of the proxy, as shown in Figure B.46 (called the *class Proxy*), uses inheritance instead.

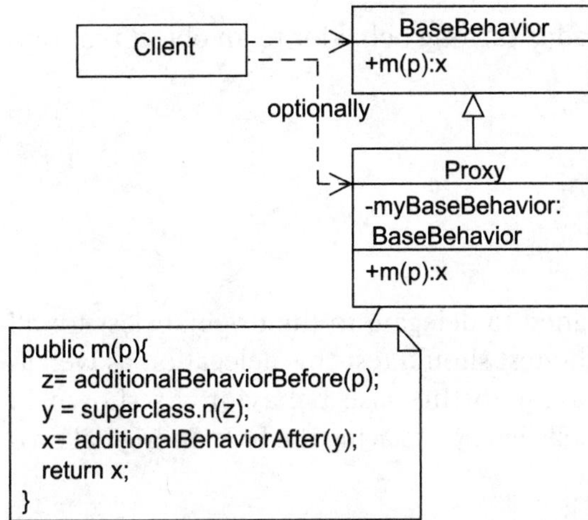

Figure B.46 The class Proxy that uses inheritance instead

There are a number of different kinds of proxies. They are named for the type of behavior that they add to the class being proxied. Only some proxies are possible with the class Proxy form but all of them are possible with the form that uses delegation.

Here are some examples of proxies:

- *Logging Proxy*: Logs all call to the method of the original class, either before or after the base behavior, or both.
- *Protection Proxy*: Block access to one or more methods in the original class. When those methods are called, the Protection Proxy may return a null, or a default value, or throw an exception, and so on.
- *Remote Proxy*: The proxy resides in the same process space as the client object, but the original class does not. Hence, the Proxy contains the networking, piping, or other logic required to access the original object across the barrier. This cannot be accomplished with a class Proxy.
- *Virtual Proxy*: The proxy delays the instantiation of the original object until its behavior is called for. If its behavior is never called for, the original class is never instantiated. This is useful when the original class is heavyweight and/or there are a large number of instances needed. The Virtual Proxy is very lightweight. This cannot be accomplished with a class Proxy.
- *Cache Proxy*: The proxy adds caching behavior to an object that represents a data source.

Consequent Forces

Testing Issues

The proxy is specifically designed to delegate to the original class for all the base behavior, and thus the test should test this delegation as well as the correct addition of behavior to the base behavior. As shown in Figure B.47, this can be accomplished by replacing the base or original class with a mock or fake object.

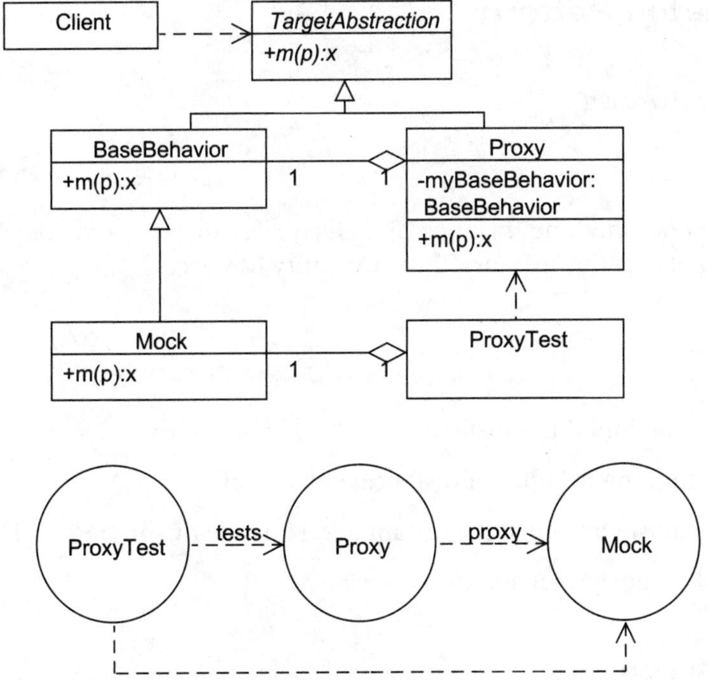

Figure B.47 Proxy designed to delegate to original class for all base behavior

Cost-Benefit (Gain-Loss)

- Proxies promote strong cohesion.
- Proxies simplify the client object and the object being proxied (by hiding complex issues like remoting and caching, and so on).
- If the instantiation of all classes is encapsulated by policy, inserting a proxy at a later time is significantly easier.
- Proxies often evolve into Decorators when multiple additional behaviors are needed. Knowing this, you do not have to introduce the Decorator until it is needed; this helps you to avoid over-design and analysis paralysis.

The Singleton Pattern

Contextual Forces

Motivation

Allow for one and only one instance of a given class to exist. Provide a mechanism to obtain this instance that any entity can access.

Encapsulation

- The construction of the instance
- The fact that the number of instances is constrained
- The mechanism by which the instantiation is made threadsafe, if it is
- Optionally, the destruction of the instance

Procedural Analog

Since the Singleton is concerned with instantiation, which is not an issue in procedural software, a direct analog is difficult to determine. However, the Singleton serves as a similar role to a global variable or function, and in fact can be used to eliminate the need for globals. Therefore, wherever you might consider the need for a global, you might consider the possibility of using a Singleton.

Non-Software Analog

A radio station broadcasts at a specific frequency and within a given context (a market). No other station can broadcast at this same frequency.

Any radio in the same context can receive the program currently being broadcast by tuning to the frequency assigned to the station in question. No matter how many radios are tuned to this station, there is and can be only one broadcast at a given point in time on it.

The number of radios tuned to the station is unconstrained, and thus the station is not designed for any particular number of listeners. The radios in the market can tune in the station by themselves, without any interaction with a controlling entity.

Radio stations and radios interact through an established protocol, which is part of their design.

Implementation Forces

Example

See Figure B.48.

Code

```
public class Singleton{
      private static Singleton _instance;
      private Singleton(){}
      public static Singleton getInstance(){
            if(_instance == null) {
                  _instance = new Singleton();
            }
            return _instance;
      }
}
```

Questions, Concerns, Credibility Checks

The example as shown is not threadsafe. If `Singleton` is not reentrant and is deployed in a multithreaded environment, a threadsafety option must be chosen. See "Options in Implementation" for various ways of accomplishing this.

Does `Singleton` have read-write state? This should be avoided if possible as this is essentially the creation of a global variable in the system. Global variables are to be avoided because they make coupling very difficult to control.

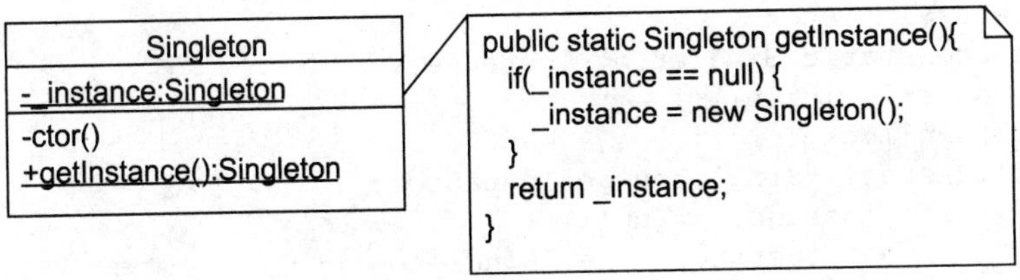

```
Singleton
-------------------------
- _instance:Singleton
-------------------------
-ctor()
+getInstance():Singleton
```

```
public static Singleton getInstance(){
  if(_instance == null) {
    _instance = new Singleton();
  }
  return _instance;
}
```

Figure B.48 Implementation forces

Options in Implementation

The Singleton is typically instantiated lazily—that is, the instance is not created until it is needed, and perhaps never (if no other entity ever calls `getInstance()`). However, this introduces a threadsafety problem if it is possible for one thread to be engaged in the creation of the instance while another is checking for null. In this worst-case scenario, it would be possible for two instances to be created. The first thread would have its own private instance; the second thread would have the instance that all other entities will now get. If this is a critical issue, there are other implementations that should be considered.

Deterministic instantiation

If the "lazy" aspect of the Singleton is not important in a given circumstance, the instance can be created as the class loads. This is threadsafe, as it uses the class loader, which must be threadsafe.

```
public class Singleton {
      private static Singleton _instance = new Singleton();
      private Singleton(){}
      public static Singleton getInstance() {
            return _instance;
      }
}
```

This is possibly the simplest solution, and is preferred where lazy instantiation is not necessary. An alternative implementation of this same solution is to use a static constructor, if the language/platform provides one. In either case, the load is atomic and deterministic.

Using a synchronization semaphore

Most languages have a way of locking access to a method while a thread is running it. If you require lazy instantiation, you can use a lock, synchronize, or similar mechanism to ensure threadsafety.

```
public class Singleton {
      private static Singleton _instance;
      private Singleton(){}
      //obtain lock
      public static Singleton getInstance() {
            if(_instance == null) {
                  _instance = new Singleton();
            }
```

```
            return _instance;
        }
        //release lock
}
```

The problem, potentially, is performance. Obtaining the lock is typically a fairly costly action, in terms of speed, and yet the lock is really only needed on the first call. Once the instance is created, the check for null never passes. We pay the locking price on every call, however.

If performance is not critical, this is a simple way to achieve threadsafety and lazy instantiation.

Double-Checked, Locking Singleton

A common suggestion for obtaining both high-performance and laziness in a threadsafe Singleton is to use the following implementation, typically called a Double-Checked, Locking Singleton.

```
public class Singleton {
        private static Singleton _instance;
        private Singleton(){}
        public static Singleton getInstance() {
                if(_instance == null) {  // once the instance is
                                         // created, we bypass
                                         // the lock

                        //obtain lock here
                        if(_instance == null) { // a thread which
                                                // waited for the
                                                // lock now checks
                                                // to see if the
                                                // instance is
                                                // still null.

                                _instance = new Singleton();
                        }
                        //release lock
                }
                return _instance;
        }
}
```

This double-check ensures that a thread, which was waiting for the lock, checks again after the thread obtains the lock, in the off chance (worst-case scenario) that the previous thread created the instance while it was waiting. When the instance is created, the first check never passes and so the lock is never taken, improving performance.

The potential problem has to do with compiler optimization and memory management, and the issues are complex and contentious. One example, however, is this: The compiler may notice that there are two identical null checks on instance, and that there is no code between them that could potentially change the state of the variable. Therefore, a compiler may "feel free" to optimize out one of the two calls, which destroys our threadsafety without our knowledge (unless we analyze the generated bytecode or machine language).

In some languages/platforms, this may or may not be a concern, but it is certainly controversial at this point:

- Java discussion: http://www.cs.umd.edu/~pugh/java/memoryModel/DoubleCheckedLocking.html
- .Net discussion: http://blogs.msdn.com/cbrumme/archive/2003/05/B/51445.aspx

Nested class

Another option for high-performance, lazy threadsafety is to use a nested class. Again, we are simply leaning on the threadsafety of the class loader, but the nested class (if it loads only when referenced) makes the `Singleton` lazy as well.

```
public class Singleton {
     private Singleton(){}
     public static Singleton getInstance() {
          return Nested.instance; // causes the nested
                                  // class to load, on
                                  // first reference
     }
     private class Nested { // does not load until a
                            // member is referenced
          public static Singleton instance;
          static       {
               instance = new Singleton();
          }
     }
}
```

There are specific implementations in different languages and on different platforms (in .Net, for instance, the nested class must be marked `BeforeFieldInit` to make sure it does not load when Singleton loads), but the concept is the same.

Refactoring Issue

The Singleton is easily refactored from a simple encapsulated constructor.

```
public class User {
      private user(){}
      public static User getInstance() {
            return new User();
      }
}
```

This is a recommended general practice, making it easy to refactor a simple class into a Singleton without changing the entities that consume its services.

Encapsulated Destruction

In systems that do not manage memory for you (a.k.a. unmanaged code), you may want to encapsulate the potential destruction of the instance as well.

```
public class Singleton {
      private static Singleton _instance;
      private Singleton(){}
      public static Singleton getInstance() {
            if(_instance == null) {
                  _instance = new Singleton();
            }
            return _instance;
      }
      public static void returnInstance(Singleton anInstance){
            //Take whatever action is needed
      }
}
```

All client entities are coded to call `getInstance()` to obtain the instance, and `returnInstance()` when they are done with it.

In a typical Singleton, no action is needed in `returnInstance()`, but this allows for instance counting and the cleanup of memory, if this is desired. Essentially, this introduces a simple form of memory management to an unmanaged environment.

As mentioned in the preceding "Refactoring Issue," this is also a best-practice for encapsulating the destruction of entities in general.

Consequent Forces

Testing Issues

The unit test for the `Singleton` primarily is concerned with its functional aspects, which are not covered here as they vary from case to case. However, the test can assert that two or more calls to the `getInstance()` method returns the same instance, using `AssertSame` or a similar call (depending on the testing framework used).

```
public void TestGetInstance() {
      Singleton 1stInstance = Singleton getInstance();
      Singleton 2ndInstance = Singleton getInstance();
      AssertSame(1stInstance, 2ndInstance);
}
```

Whether this is necessary to test varies from project to project. If this test is in place, it can be used to test-drive a change in `Singleton` for load-balancing (see the next section, "Cost-Benefit (Gain-Loss)").

Cost-Benefit (Gain-Loss)

- A limited-use resource can be protected from erroneous multiple use without complicating the consuming client entities.
- Singleton can easily scale to two, three, or more instances for load-balancing. Since the cardinality issue is encapsulated, this can be freely changed if this is deemed appropriate.
- If the Singleton gains statefullness, care must be taken to avoid creating a global.

The Strategy Pattern

Contextual Forces

Motivation

A single behavior with varying implementation exists and we want to decouple consumers of this behavior from any particular implementation. We may also want to decouple them from the fact that the implementation is varying at all.

Encapsulation

The various versions of the behavior, how many variations there are, which variation will be used under a given circumstance, and the design of each varying implementation are all hidden from the client. We may also encapsulate the fact that the behavior is varying at all, depending on implementation.

Procedural Analog

A simple switch or other branching logic: where the condition that drives the branch is a concern of the client or system, but not the algorithm itself (see the Chain of Responsibility pattern).

```
if (condition) {
      // Algorithm 1
} else {
      // Algorithm 2
}
```

Non-Software Analog

When I was a young boy, I used to have a Mattel Superstar airplane that had a little plastic disk inside (see Figure B.49). The grooves and notches on the disk made the airplane fly in a given pattern.

Figure B.49 Mattel Superstar airplane

By changing the disk the plane held, as shown in Figure B.50, I would get a different flight path. Each disk had a different shape, and as it was rotated on a cam, a feeler rod was moved back and forth, turning the rudder as the plane flew.

I did not need to change anything about the plane to get a different flight path; I just gave it a different-shaped disk.

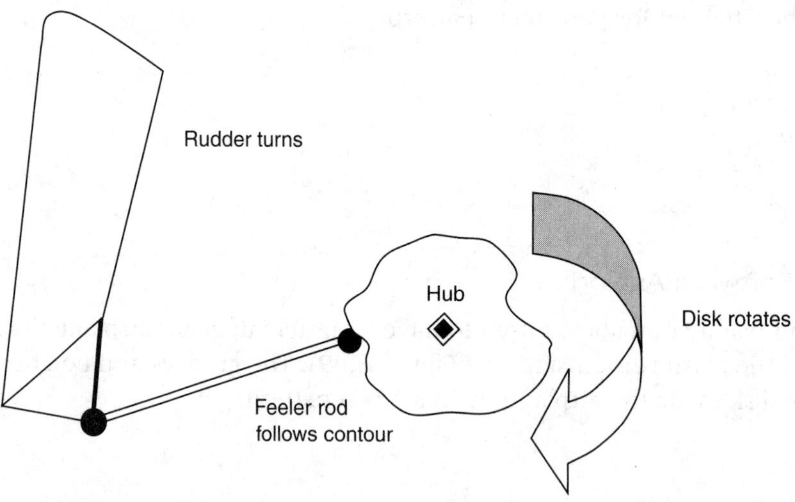

Figure B.50 Different flight paths when different disks are inserted before flight

All the disks fit in the plane because they were under the maximum size and had a particular little diamond-shaped hole in their hub that allowed them to mount on the rotating cam. This was the disk's interface, which the plane was designed to accept. So long as the disk conformed to this, I could make new disks that did not even exist when the plane was created, and they would work, creating new flight behaviors. Only one disk could be mounted at a time, of course.

In this analogy, the plane is the context object and the disks are the implementation of the Strategy Object. The size of the disks and the shape/size of the hole at their center is the interface of the Strategy.

Implementation Forces

Example

See Figure B.51.

Code

```
public class Context {
      public void request(Strategy s) {
            s.operation();
      }
}

public abstract class Strategy {
      public abstract operation();
}

public class Strategy_V1 extends Strategy{
      public void operation() {
            // Implementation V1
      }
}

public class Strategy_V2 extends Strategy{
      public void operation() {
            // Implementation V2
      }
}
```

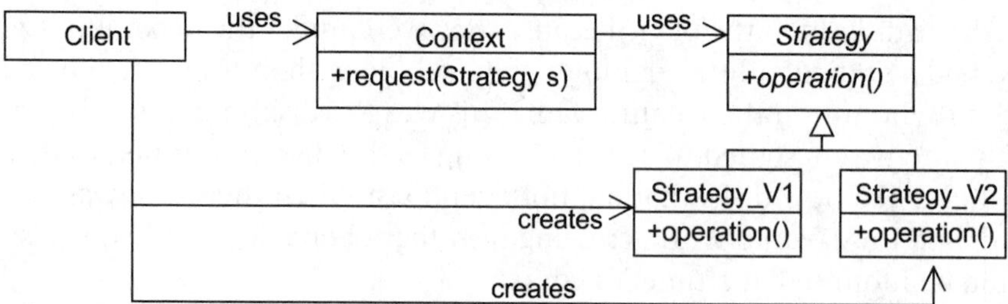

Figure B.51 Implementation forces

Questions, Concerns, Credibility Checks

- Can all the versions of the algorithm (`Strategy`) really share the same interface? What are the differences between them, and how can I resolve them in such a way that they all can be used in the same way?
- How does the `Context` object obtain an instance of a Strategy implementation to delegate to?
- How often and under what circumstances does the particular Strategy implementation the client is using change?
  - Each time the request is called?
  - Each time the `Context` is instantiated?
  - Each time the application is loaded?
  - Each time the application is installed?

Options in Implementation

- Does the `Client` hand in a `Strategy` implementation each time it interacts with the `Context`?
- Is an object factory used?
- If an object factory is used, does the `Client` or the `Context` interact with the factory?
- Is there a factory that builds the `Context` and hands the `Strategy` in via its constructor?

These are illustrated in Figures B.52, B.53, and B.54.

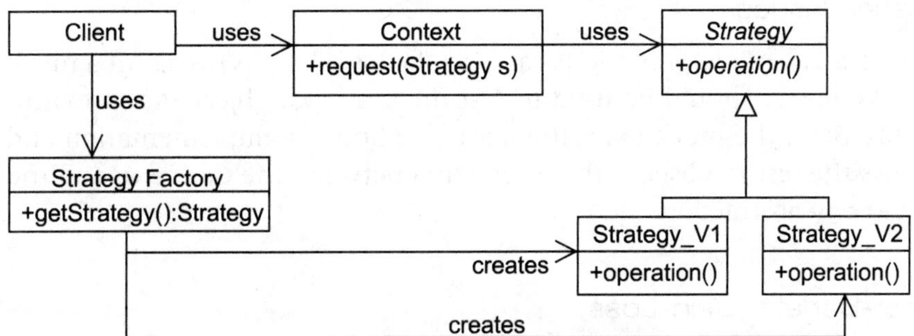

Figure B.52 Strategy with factory, Client uses the factory

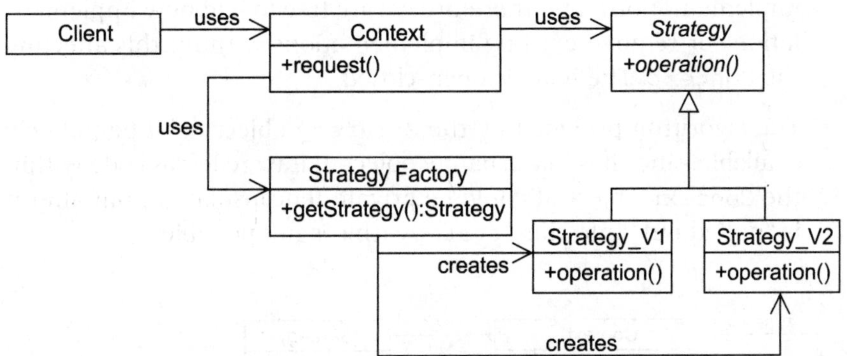

Figure B.53 Strategy with factory, Context uses the factory

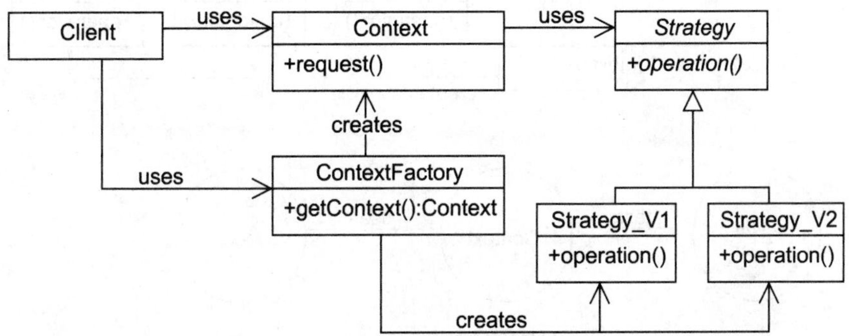

Figure B.54 Strategy with factory, built by a factory

Consequent Forces

Testing Issues

The Strategy implementations can each be tested on its own, but a mock or fake object should be used to test the `Context` object. As shown in Figure B.55, the mock takes the place of a Strategy implementation and allows the test to observe the interaction between the `Context` and the `Strategy` abstraction.

Cost-Benefit (Gain-Loss)

- The `Context` and the `Strategy` objects tend toward strong cohesion.
- The `Context` object is decoupled from the particular `Strategy` implementations, and therefore we are free to add new implementations or remove existing implementations without this affecting the `Context`. The issue is open-closed.
- The algorithm provided by the `Strategy` object must be publicly available, since it is in a separate object. If it were left as code within the `Context` object, it could be private (encapsulated), but after it is "pulled out" into the `Strategy`, this is not possible.

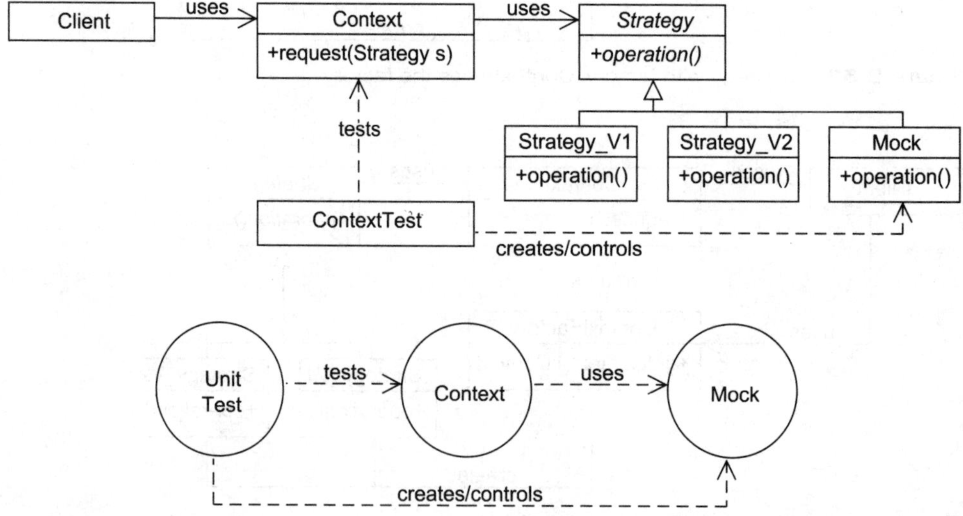

Figure B.55 The mock takes the place of a Strategy implementation

- The algorithm cannot directly access the state of the `Context` object. Any state needed by the algorithm must be "passed in" via parameters. Any effect that should propagate back to the `Context` must be returned. This decouples them and makes testing easier, but it can lead to a very broad interface on the `Strategy` abstraction. This can reduce its reusability.
- More classes are needed when compared to a simple procedural solution within `Context` (branching logic).
- The delegation from the context to the `Strategy` object introduces a small degradation in performance.

The Template Method

Contextual Forces

Motivation

Abstract out the skeletal steps of an algorithm, allowing subclasses to override the specific implementations of each step.

Encapsulation

- The steps of the algorithm
- The implementation of each step
- The variation of the implementations (how many and the fact that they are varying)

Procedural Analog

When a series of steps varies and they all transition from one variation to another at the same time, as a set, you can accomplish this procedurally with a series of logical branches or switch/case statements. These are all based on the state of a common value.

```
int var = //state set here

//Step one
switch var {
      case 1:
      // first step, variation 1

      case 2:
      // first step, variation 2

      case 3:
      // first step, variation 3
}

//Step two
switch var {
      case 1:
      // second step, variation 1

      case 2:
      // second step, variation 2

      case 3:
      // second step, variation 3
}

//Step three
switch var {
      case 1:
      // third step, variation 1

      case 2:
      // third step, variation 2

      case 3:
      // third step, variation 3
}
```

Non-Software Analog

Recipes are sometimes expressed as a series of steps for preparation, combination, processing (cooking), and finishing for consumption. Sometimes, however, the same recipe can be used to feed a varying number of people. When this is the case, the amounts are sometimes omitted to be filled in based on the number of people to be fed. In these cases, the recipe is the same, but the amounts all vary together, based on the state "number to be fed." The recipe (the non-changing part) is the template method, and the amounts are the delegated methods that are overridden.

Implementation Forces

Example

See Figure B.56.

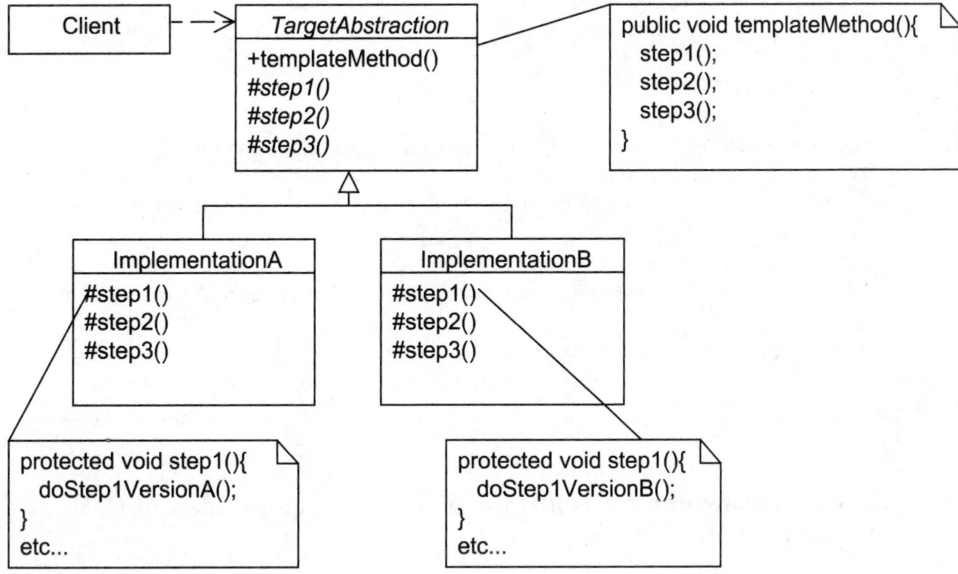

Figure B.56 Implementation forces

Code

```
public abstract class TargetAbstraction {
      public void templateMethod() {
            step1();
            step2();
            step3();
      }

      protected abstract void step1();
      protected abstract void step2();
      protected abstract void step3();
}

public class implementationA extends TargetAbstraction {
      protected void step1() {
            // Implementation of Step1, version A here
      }
      protected void step2() {
            // Implementation of Step2, version A here
      }
      protected void step3() {
            // Implementation of Step3, version A here
      }
}

public class implementationB extends TargetAbstraction {
      protected void step1() {
            // Implementation of Step1, version B here
      }
      protected void step2() {
            // Implementation of Step2, version B here
      }
      protected void step3() {
            // Implementation of Step3, version B here
      }
}
```

Or, to show our non-software analog (see Figure B.57) in UML, see Figure B.57.

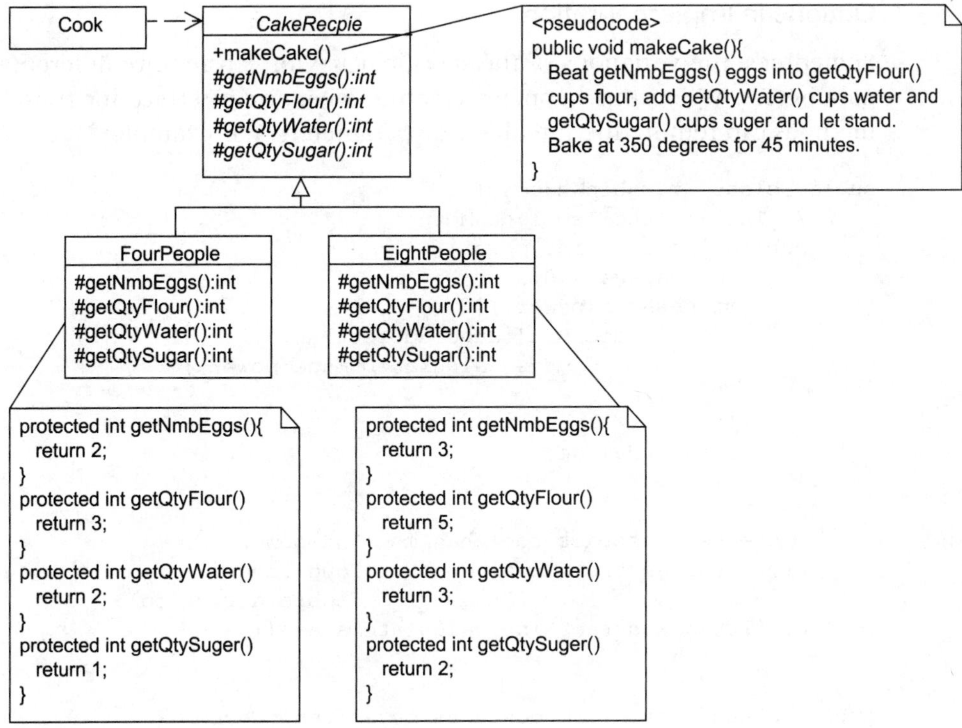

Figure B.57 Non-software analog in UML

Questions, Concerns, Credibility Checks

Can all of the variations of this behavior be resolved to the same set of steps without making them overly generic or without forcing any one of them to give up critical behavior?

Do some subclasses require different/more parameters or returns from the delegated methods? See the discussion of "ignore parameters" in the following "Options in Implementation" section.

The delegated methods, which are overridden in the subclasses, should not be made public to avoid any possibility that other entities will become coupled to them. If the implementation language does not allow abstract methods to be protected (some languages force all abstract methods to be public), you should implement the methods in the base class with default or stubbed-out behavior.

Options in Implementation

Sometimes, the variations of the specific behavior can require different parameters. When this happens, creating a generic interface for these methods can require the use of ignore parameters. For example:

```
public class StarshipWeapon {
     // This is the Template Method
     public int fire(int power){
          int damage = 0;
          if(hasAmmo(power)){
               if(doesHit(range, direction)){
                    damage=calculateDamage(power);
               }
          }
          return damage;
     }

     protected abstract bool hasAmmo(int power);
     protected abstract bool doesHit(long range,
                                     double direction);
     protected abstract int calculateDamage();
}

public class PhotonTorpedos extends StarshipWeapon {
     protected bool hasAmmo(int ignorePower){
          // return true if there are torpedos remaining,
          // else return false
     }
     protected bool doesHit(long range, double direction){
          // Calculation based on range and bearing to the
          // target return true if hit, false if miss
     }
     protected int calculateDamage(){
          // Torpedoes always do full damage if they hit
          return 500;
     }
}

public class Phasers extends StarshipWeapon {
     protected bool hasAmmo(int Power){
          // Store power for later use in calculating damage
          // return true if there is enough energy to fire
          // phasers at this power
     }
```

```
    protected bool doesHit(long range, double ignoreDirection){
          // Store range for later use in calculating damage
          // Phasers always hit
          // Direction is irrelevant for Phasers, so name
          // the parameter accordingly
          return true;

    }
    protected int calculateDamage(){
          // Take power, attenuate for range, and return the
          // reduced amount as the damage to be applied
    }
}
```

The use of the term `ignoreXXX` as the parameter names in subclasses that do not use the parameter makes it clearer during maintenance that this is being done. This allows all subclasses to operate using the same template method.

Consequent Forces

Testing Issues

As shown in Figure B.58, the base class algorithm can be tested by deriving a Fake object just for testing.

Cost-Benefit (Gain-Loss)

The use of a Template Method pushes redundant aspects (skeletal algorithm or template method) to the base class, leaving nonredundant aspects (variation) in derived classes. This separates what changes from what does not and it improves cohesion. In addition, it does the following:

- It can create overly generic designs.
- Implementing new subclasses is simpler because they do not have to implement the skeletal algorithm.
- It improves readability.

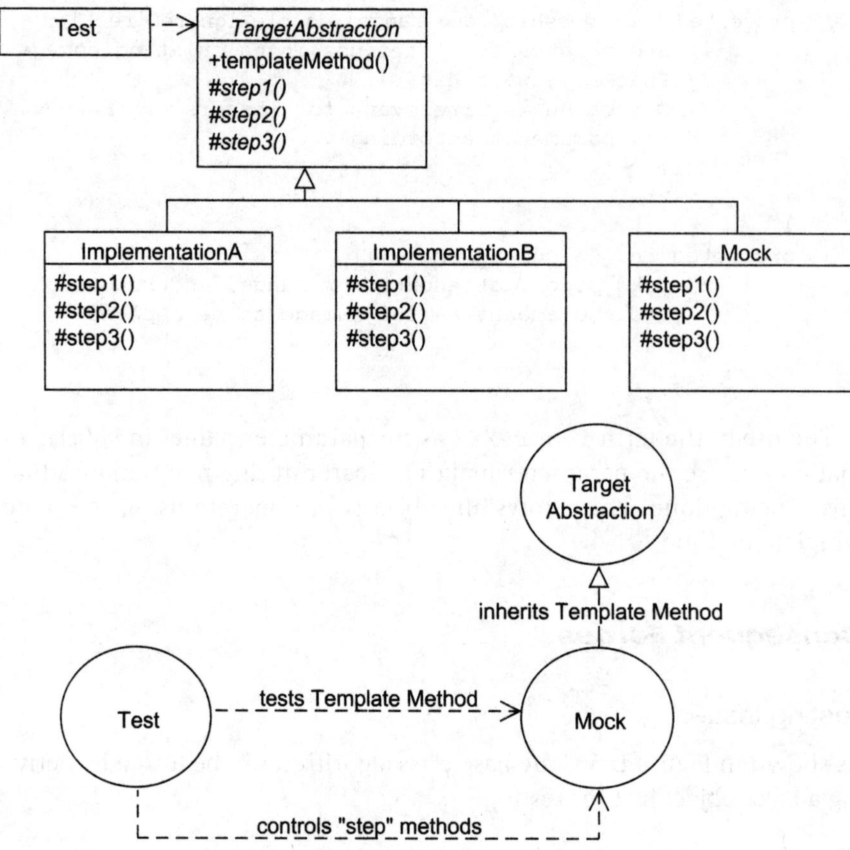

Figure B.58 Testing of a base class algorithm

Appendix C

The Principle of the Useful Illusion

My View

Scott Bain

Computers cannot add.

This is not a flippant or cleverly misleading statement. It is a plain fact. Computers, regardless of all outward appearances, cannot add two numbers together and determine their sum. Computers do not know what numbers are, or what adding is, or anything else for that matter. They certainly cannot add.

Clearly they appear to do so—routinely and constantly and without fail. That computers appear to add numbers together, and yet they do not, is an example of what I call *the principle of the useful illusion*.

To understand the importance of this, we must first come to agree that computers cannot, in fact, add.

Computers cannot add in the same sense that hammers cannot build houses. Hammers can *be used* to build houses, but we can easily understand that it is the carpenter who wields the hammer that is doing the building, not the hammer itself.

Hammers and computers are the same in this sense. In fact, it is interesting to note that a computer and a hammer operate, ultimately, in the same way. They obey the laws of physics, as they must, and when they are placed in a given situation they will affect their surroundings in a predictable way.

Raise the hammer up high and propel it downward, providing it energy through the use of your muscles and with the assistance of gravity, and, given the Newtonian principle of inertia when the hammer encounters an object along its path of motion (hopefully a nail, and not a thumbnail), then the effect will be to impart kinetic energy to the object, and thus affect it in some way. The design of the hammer is such that it reliably causes nails (which were also designed with an understanding of physics in mind) to penetrate wood and other porous materials.

Computers are designed to operate in consideration of the laws of magnetism, electricity, thermodynamics, and so forth. Press the key on your keyboard that is inscribed with the A symbol and you will set into motion a series of events within the device, each a practical application of a principle of physics which will ultimately cause a particular pattern of phosphors on your monitor or LCD panel to change color. To you, the human operator, the letter A will have "been entered" into the computer, but this is only your interpretation.

In fact, a series of electromagnetic interactions will have taken place, and nothing more. The humans who designed the computer and the software it is running arranged for this illusion. Therefore, it tends to be consistent with our expectations since we are more or less like-minded with those designers.

This is an off-putting notion at first, considering the enormously complex ways in which we make use of our computers. But it is easier to accept when we consider other, equally complex interactions that we engage in with technology.

Television is a good example. When I watched *The West Wing* on my television, I understood that Martin Sheen was not actually in the television set. I knew that I was actually watching a pattern of colored light that appeared to be him. And I did not ascribe the entertainment that I had experienced to the television itself: I would never exclaim, "My television sure was dramatic this week!" I understand that it is the people behind the recorded presentation who are actually creating the story.

We tend to forget this concept when we interact with computers, however. We think of the computer "doing" things all the time: calculating payroll, showing us monsters and letting us shoot them, recording our emails and letters and printing them, and so on. But this is no more real than the seemingly six-inch-high actor inside your television is real. The interaction with the computer is more complex than the interaction with the television, and it is far more complex than the interaction with the hammer, yet it is essentially the same: We are affected in a given way by the activity of the device, and we find this effect entertaining, constructive, enlightening, or otherwise useful.

Alan Turing, one of the pioneers of computing technologies, proposed a test that could be used to determine when and if a computing machine had actually become intelligent, in the human sense. In essence, he said that if a human was allowed to communicate with the machine via a membrane that did not allow the human to know that it was a machine being communicated with, and if the *human could not distinguish this* from a communication with another human, then the machine would be said to have achieved intelligence.

In proposing his *Turing Test*, Turing was essentially positing the notion that what computers do is an illusion and that the only question is how convincing that illusion is. The more convincing it is (from the users' perspective), the more useful the computer will be. Where I am diverging from Turing (if I understand him properly) is that I do not believe such a computer will "have become intelligent," but rather that it will *appear* to have become intelligent; but that is all that is important in my view anyway. Maybe that is what he meant.

This leads me, however, to reconsider what we are doing when we create software.

At the very least, we have to acknowledge that software, like the computer, does not do anything. People do things and can use software as a tool to help them. Perhaps it is easier to keep this logically in mind if we say it this way: Computers (and software) cannot *accomplish* anything. Accomplishments are relegated solely to people.

Why is this important? For some developers, I think it will make it more natural to become validation-centric rather than function-centric in the way they design and develop software. In other words, it moves us away from "does it work?" as the primary concern, and toward "is it what the users need to accomplish things?"

As an industry, we tend to write a lot of clever, well-functioning code that nobody uses.

According to the Standish Group,[1] in a 10-year-survey of more than 35,000 software development projects, fully 45% of the features created had *never* been used. We might, from the functional-centric point of view, tend to believe that this unused software had value anyway since it was "capable." However, if we believe software cannot accomplish anything, that only people can accomplish things, then software that is unused by people has no value whatsoever. The useful illusion is never created, and so in a sense the software does not exist.

1. www.thestandishgroup.com

If *The West Wing* plays on the airwaves but no television is tuned to the signal with a person watching it, is there a show? I think not. Not in any way that is sensible to me.

This point of view can change what we create, but it can also change how we create it. If I hold as a fundamental truth the notion that software is only real when it is used, then naturally part of creating it will be getting a user to use it. Agile development processes mandate this: I must get my software validated as early and as frequently as possible along the way, to allow me to adjust what I am doing without excessive waste.

Agility proponents have many good reasons for this, but here we have discovered another, supportive point of view: I have not *actually made anything* until a user has tried out my software, because it does not actually *exist* until it is in use. Part of making software is getting a user to use it, and thus to validate that it is what they actually need.

I also think that considering the use of software to be its only value will tend to make me consider the *usability* of the software earlier in my design. I know that there is a lot of software that *I* use, every day, that could be much easier to use, in terms of where things are on menus, how options are arranged, how functions interact with each other, and so forth. If the designers of those products had asked me, as the user, where to put things and how they should work, I guarantee the applications would be significantly different.

I also submit that the applications would be better, if we believe that the use of software is the only point of software. As the user, my perspective would therefore be considered paramount. In his terribly interesting and useful book *The Design of Everyday Things*, Donald Norman explored this notion: If things are hard to use properly, the fault is in the design, not in the user, because the design has failed to match the expectations and the natural use that the user will try to put the device to. The value of the device lies purely in the use it can be put to; therefore, a design that cannot be used, or used well, has failed to some degree.

As I write this, I am using a computer. I am striking keys and watching as "characters" "appear" on the "page." None of this is actually happening, of course. It is all in my mind, in the expectations I have and how the things I see match those expectations.

You, when you read this, will be separated in time and in space from me. We will likely never meet, and so the notion that "I will communicate to you" is fiction. The truth is that I am causing an arrangement of magnets to line up in a certain way. Hopefully, as you later view this arrangement, you will think about something that is similar to what I am thinking about now. The communication is purely an illusion.

Hopefully it will be a useful one.

An Alternate View[2]

Alan Shalloway
CEO, Net Objectives

Several years ago, I attended a course that dealt with language and how communication is transferred. Or rather, how information is transferred from one person to another—the process we call *communication*. One of the distinctions we had made early in the morning was that when two people talk to each other, the *words* are different from the *communication*. The words, we decided, were essentially "tokens" of the communication. Put another way, the words represent the meaning of the communication, but are not the communication.

Actually, in any form of communication, there are always tokens. In this article, the words being read are the tokens of the communication between me and whoever is reading this. These words themselves are not the communication. They are the means by which I pass the communication. If I am a good writer, readers can use these words to get valuable insights.

Anyway, this course I was attending was not your normal course. It was run by an organization where most of the people in it were very open to pretty much any type of discussion. It was, actually, pretty neat. They expected us to adhere strictly to the guidelines of the course. If someone diverged from a guideline, it was not unusual for a discussion to occur to see why this had happened.

For example, someone came back late after lunch. The instructor casually asked what happened. The woman who was late said that it was her mother's birthday and she'd had to get her a gift, and that lunch was the only time for her to do that. The instructor asked her why the gift was so important. She said because she wanted to let her mother know that she loved her.

---

2. These two concepts are synergistic. The second gives you a different way to think about the first. In other words, imagine you have a person responding only to the typed information of another person at a keyboard. What set of rules could you write to help out the person? This is different than saying, "I have this program that the person using the computer needs to learn how to use."

The instructor told her the gift would not let her mom know she loved her. At this, the woman got a little agitated and said that it certainly would. He held his ground and said, unequivocally, that it would not. This went back and forth a little bit, and each time she got a little more agitated, and each time he stayed just as firmly insistent that the *gift* would not let her mom know she loved her.

Finally, the instructor asked if *he* had sent the gift to her mom would her mom think *he* loved her. She sort of laughed and said of course not, that the gift just showed her mom that *she* loved her. This was his point. The gift was just a token of her love for her mom.

While I was listening to this, I will admit to being a little bored with the conversation. I was half listening and half just looking at the front of the room. The real purpose of this course was to investigate some new communication software. Because of this, there was a computer at the front of the room (this was in the mid-1980s before that was a commonplace thing). I happened to be looking at the computer while the instructor was making his point about the gift just being a token of love.

I realized that the computer was just the same. That it was not "the computer running the software" that was important. The software was just a token of the programmer's intentions.

At this time, I was developing software for PCs. I realized that the ideal situation would actually be for me to come up with a way to have "Alan in a box." Buy your PC and software and I would be in there doing just what you needed. Of course, this would work only once and given these were PCs and not mainframes I would be pretty uncomfortable.

Realizing this, I thought the next best thing would be to write software that would respond the way I would if I *were* in the box. In other words, it would communicate with the user as a normal person would (assuming I am normal). The computer software would be a set of tokens that would replace my presence. Now, I was not thinking that I could write a Turing machine that would appear to the user to be a normal person, but being even a little oriented toward a person-to-person interaction would be a big improvement over most computers. In other words, take the input from the user the way a person would.

For example, what is the order you would put these numbers into?

- 10
- 9

Or how about this: are these two numbers equal?

- 9
- 09

How about these words, are they the same?

- happy
- Happy

Virtually every computer program would tend to answer these questions differently than a person would. Truly, find me a person who would answer them the way a computer would. That would be an unusual person indeed.

The problem is that most computer software is written based on the rules of the computer—not on the rules or expectations of the user. It turns out that this is not really that hard. For example, if you are using some software and there is a name field filled in with Alan and you press the spacebar (replacing the A with a space) and then move on to the next field, which is more likely?

- You meant that the person's name was really lan.
- You accidentally pressed the space bar without realizing it.

Or how about this: You are editing a document, using word-processing software. Most people when they first learned about PCs assumed that word processing was the equivalent of writing on paper.

Without a computer, when you write on a simple piece of paper, you do not have to tell the ink to stay there. I mean, it never happens that if you pick up the paper and shake it (without having said, "Ink, save yourself!") that it falls off or disappears, as it can from your computer screen.

Clearly, someone who wrote the computer software decided to make the user understand the computer and not have the computer understand people. For example, software written from a person's point of view would just save the document. But what if they did not mean to save it? Well, so what? Isn't it more likely they did? In any case, you could have the computer keep the original if you wanted to go back to it. That would be more natural to a human user.

Unfortunately, most people think that what they see is something that is real, not that what they see is just a token for reality.

Bibliography

Adams, Douglas. *The Hitchhiker's Guide to the Galaxy.* Del Rey, 1995.

Alexander, Christopher. *The Timeless Way of Building.* New York: Oxford University Press, 1979.

Beck, Kent. *Extreme Programming Explained: Embrace Change.* Reading, MA: Addison-Wesley, 1999.

Beck, Kent. *Test-Driven Development: By Example.* Boston: Addison-Wesley, 2003.

Bloch, Joshua. *Effective Java Programming Language Guide.* Boston: Addison-Wesley, 2001.

Cook, Steve and John Daniels. *Designing Object Systems,* 1st ed. Englewood Cliffs, NJ: Prentice Hall, 1994.

Coplien, James. *Multi-Paradigm Design for C++,* 1st ed. Reading, MA: Addison-Wesley, 1998.

Feathers, Michael. *Working Effectively with Legacy Code.* Upper Saddle River, N.J.: Prentice Hall, 2005.

Fowler, Martin et al. *Refactoring: Improving the Design of Existing Code.* Reading, MA: Addison-Wesley, 1999.

Fowler, Martin. *UML Distilled: A Brief Guide to the Standard Object Modeling Language,* 2nd ed. Reading, MA: Addison-Wesley, 1999.

Freeman, Elisabeth et al. *Head-First Design Patterns.* Sebastopol, CA: O'Reilly Media, 2004.

Gamma, Erich et al. *Design Patterns: Elements of Reusable Object-Oriented Software.* Reading, MA: Addison-Wesley, 1995.

Hunt, Andrew and David Thomas. *The Pragmatic Programmer: From Journeyman to Master.* Boston: Addison-Wesley, 2000.

Kerievsky, Joshua. *Refactoring to Patterns.* Boston: Addison-Wesley, 2005.

Martin, Robert C. *Agile Software Development, Principles, Patterns, and Practices.* Upper Saddle River, N.J.: Prentice Hall, 2003.

McConnell, Steve. *Code Complete,* 2nd ed. Microsoft Press, 2004.

Norman, Donald A. *The Design of Everyday Things.* New York: Basic Books, 1988.

Shalloway, Alan and James R. Trott. *Design Patterns Explained: A New Perspective on Object-Oriented Design.* Boston: Addison-Wesley, 2002.

Index

A

B

C

F

G

H

M

S

T

U

V

W

Y-Z

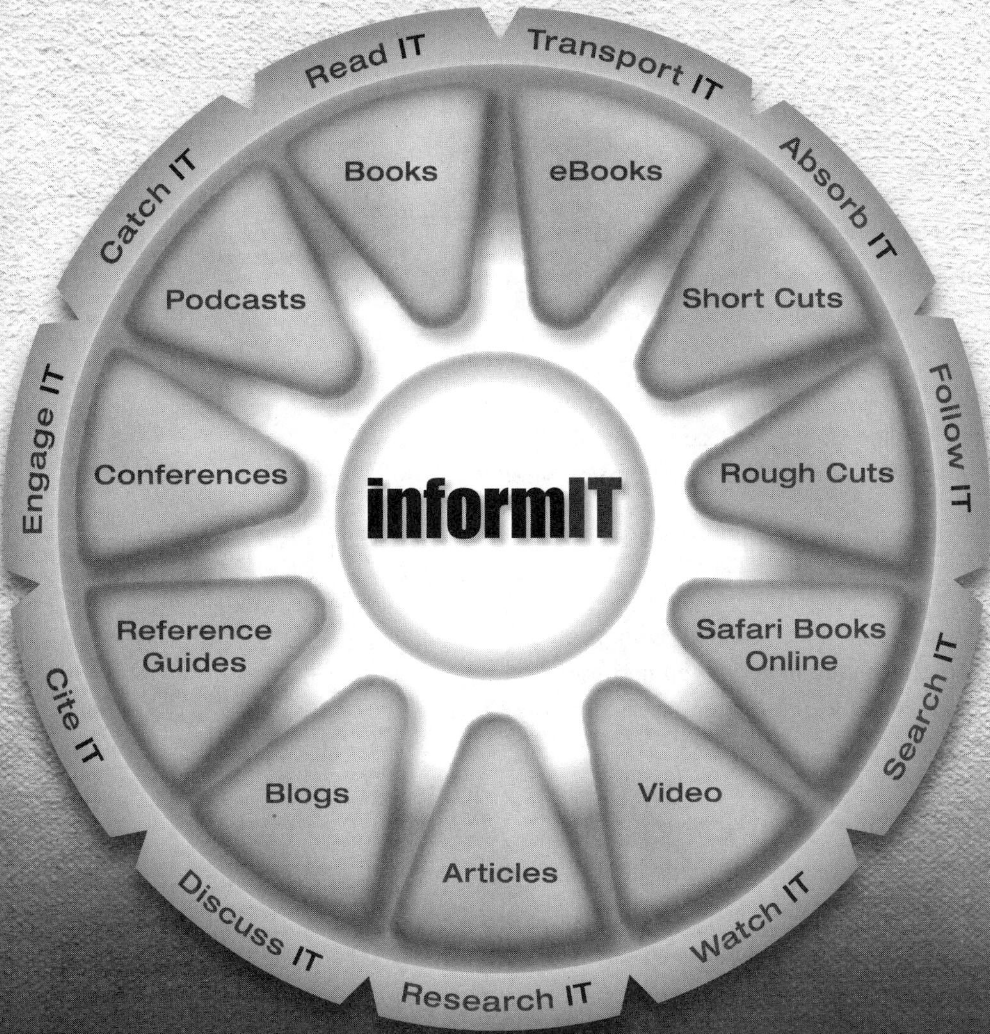